GOVERNING DISASTERS

With growing awareness of the devastation caused by major natural disasters – alongside integration of governance and technology networks – the parameters of humanitarian aid are becoming more global. At the same time, humanitarian instruments are increasingly recognizing the centrality of local participation. Drawing on six case studies and a survey of sixty-nine members of the relief sector, this book suggests that the key to the efficacy of post-disaster recovery is the primacy given to local actors in the management, direction and design of relief programs. Where local partnership and knowledge generation and application is ongoing, cohesive, meaningful and inclusive, disaster relief efforts are more targeted, cost-effective, efficient and timely. *Governing Disasters: Engaging Local Populations in Humanitarian Relief* examines the interplay between law, governance and collaborative decision making with international, state, private-sector and community actors, in order to understand the dynamics of a global decentralized yet coordinated process of post-disaster humanitarian assistance.

DR. SHAHLA F. ALI is Associate Professor and Deputy Head of the Department of Law and Deputy Director of the LLM in Arbitration and Dispute Resolution at the Faculty of Law at the University of Hong Kong.

GOVERNING DISASTERS

Engaging Local Populations in Humanitarian Relief

SHAHLA F. ALI
University of Hong Kong

CAMBRIDGE
UNIVERSITY PRESS

CAMBRIDGE
UNIVERSITY PRESS

32 Avenue of the Americas, New York NY 10013

Cambridge University Press is part of the University of Cambridge.

It furthers the University's mission by disseminating knowledge in the pursuit of education, learning and research at the highest international levels of excellence.

www.cambridge.org
Information on this title: www.cambridge.org/9781107106390

First published 2016

A catalog record for this publication is available from the British Library.

Library of Congress Cataloging in Publication Data
Names: Ali, Shahla F., author.
Title: Governing disasters : engaging local populations in humanitarian relief / Shahla F. Ali.
Description: New York NY: Cambridge University Press, 2016. | Includes bibliographical references.
Identifiers: LCCN 2015040747 | ISBN 9781107106390 (hardback)
Subjects: LCSH: Disaster relief – Law and legislation. | Disaster relief.
Classification: LCC K1980.A95 2016 | DDC 363.34/8–dc23
LC record available at http://lccn.loc.gov/2015040747

ISBN 978-1-107-10639-0 Hardback

Justice is dependent upon universal participation and action by all members and agencies of society.

(*Institute for Studies in Global Prosperity*, Nov. 2008)

CONTENTS

FIGURES AND TABLES

Figures

Tables

ACKNOWLEDGMENTS

The research for this book has been made possible by funds from the Government of Hong Kong's Research Grants Council (HKU 757412H). Without the valuable input and views from humanitarian aid workers, members of local, national and international relief agencies, the practical insights in this book would not be possible. Specifically, special thanks go to members of humanitarian agencies and professional associations including the Asia Foundation in Beijing; Oxfam in Boston, MA; USAID in Washington, DC; RedR in India; the UN Office for the Coordination of Humanitarian Affairs in Geneva; UN Women in NY; UNDP in Bangkok, Thailand; the World Health Organization in Geneva; Mercy in Malaysia; the Cash Learning Partnership in Oxford; the Bill & Melinda Gates Foundation in Seattle, WA; the CDC in Atlanta, GA; the DOJ Community Relations Service in Chicago; the World Bank Legal Office in Washington, DC; Fundacion in Macau; the International Committee for the Red Cross and Humanitarian and Disaster Aid research centers at Tufts University, Harvard University and UC Berkeley; and individuals working at Red Cross centers in Yangoon, Myanmar; Lijiang, Hainan and Shenzhen, People's Republic of China; Hong Kong; Houston, Texas; Macau SAR; Istanbul, Turkey; Haifa, Israel and Kuala Lumpur, Malaysia.

Many people have helped with this book. John Berger, editor at Cambridge University Press, expertly oversaw the review and publication of this project. Anonymous reviewers provided extremely valuable input at the early stages. Finola O'Sullivan provided initial comments and suggestions. Special thanks go to an outstanding team of research assistants; they include Tom Kabau, Vickie Yau, Viviana Wu, Linus Hug, Gabriel Lee, Cynthianna Yau, Odysseas Repousis, Perry J. H. Sea, William Yang, Holly Hoi Ching Cheng, He Li, Candice Li, Helena Wing Sum Wong, Jack Li and Emily Jo Yee Chan.

Many colleagues have provided valuable insights that have improved this book. I am grateful for fruitful exchanges with Professor Daniel Farber of UC Berkeley, Dean David Caron of Kings College London, Professor Lawrence Susskind of MIT and Ken Feinberg for their helpful insights in the area of disaster law. I am also thankful to our deans Johannes Chan and Michael Hor and department heads Douglas Arner and Lusina Ho for providing a supportive research environment at the University of Hong Kong Law Faculty. I am also grateful to participants who shared valuable feedback at the following conferences: the Law and Society Association Annual Conference (Seattle, WA), the ABA Section on Dispute Resolution – Spring Conference (Seattle, WA), the ABA Asia Pacific Mediation Summit (New Delhi, India), the Transnational Governance Workshop Kings College London, (London, UK), the Myanmar Public Law Workshop HKU (Hong Kong), the UNCITRAL Asia Pacific Conference (Macau), the International Association of Conflict Management Conference (Leiden, The Netherlands), the Law and Society Association Annual Conference (Minneapolis, MN), the Shantou University Mediation and the Rule of Law Conference (Shantou, PR China), the ICC Roundtable (Paris, France), the ILA-ASIL Asia Pacific Research Forum (Taipei, Taiwan), the Human Security: Humanitarian Perspectives and Responses Conference (Istanbul, Turkey), the Law and Society Association Annual Conference (Boston, MA), the International Humanitarian Conference (Kuala Lumpur, Malaysia), the Law and Society Association in East Asia Conference (Shanghai, PR China), the ABA Section on Dispute Resolution Spring Conference (Chicago, IL) and the University of Haifa Regulating Disasters through Private and Public Law: Compensation and Policy (Haifa, Israel).

This book is dedicated to the millions of individuals who have been affected by natural disasters, their families and their communities. All that is positive in this book reflects the generosity and support of colleagues, research participants, friends and associates. All errors and omissions are my own.

TREATIES

African Union Convention for the Protection and Assistance of Internally Displaced Persons in Africa, adopted October 22, 2009 (entered into force December 6, 2012). Retrieved from www.refworld.org/docid/4ae572d82.html.

Convention Governing the Specific Aspects of Refugee Problems in Africa, adopted September 10, 1969, 1001 UNTS 45 (entered into force June 20, 1974).

Convention Relating to the Status of Refugees, adopted July 28, 1951, 189 UNTS 150 (entered into force April 22, 1954).

Food Assistance Convention, adopted April 25, 2012 (entered into force January 1, 2013). Retrieved from www.foodassistanceconvention.org/convention/FoodAssistance.pdf.

Geneva Convention for the Amelioration of the Condition of the Wounded and Sick in Armed Forces in the Field (First Geneva Convention), adopted August 12, 1949, 75 UNTS 31 (entered into force October 21, 1950).

Geneva Convention for the Amelioration of the Condition of Wounded, Sick and Shipwrecked Members of Armed Forces at Sea (Second Geneva Convention), adopted August 12, 1949, 75 UNTS 85 (entered into force October 21, 1950).

Geneva Convention Relative to the Protection of Civilian Persons in Time of War (Fourth Geneva Convention), adopted August 12, 1949, 75 UNTS 287 (entered into force October 21, 1950).

Geneva Convention Relative to the Treatment of Prisoners of War (Third Geneva Convention), adopted August 12, 1949, 75 UNTS 135 (entered into force October 21, 1950).

International Covenant on Economic, Social and Cultural Rights, adopted December 16, 1966, 993 UNTS 3 (entered into force January 3, 1976).

Protocol Additional to the Geneva Conventions of 12 August 1949, and Relating to the Protection of Victims of International Armed Conflicts (Protocol I), adopted June 8, 1977, 1125 UNTS 3 (entered into force December 7, 1979).

Protocol Additional to the Geneva Conventions of 12 August 1949, and Relating to the Protection of Victims of Non-international Armed Conflicts (Protocol II), adopted June 8, 1977, 1125 UNTS 609 (entered into force December 7, 1978).

Protocol to the Convention Relating to the Status of Refugees, adopted January 31, 1967, 606 UNTS 267.

Treaty of Lisbon Amending the Treaty on European Union and the Treaty Establishing the European Community, adopted December 13, 2007, *Official Journal of the European Union*, C 306, Volume 50, December 17, 2007.

OTHER INTERNATIONAL INSTRUMENTS

Committee on Economic, Social and Cultural Rights, *Substantive Issues Arising in the Implementation of the International Covenant on Economic, Social and Cultural Rights: General Comment 12; the Right to Adequate Food*, E/C.12/1999/5 (Geneva: April 26–May 14, 1999).

Declaration on Principles of International Law Concerning Friendly Relations and Co-operation among States in Accordance with the Charter of the United Nations, UNGA Res 2625 (XXV) (New York: October 24, 1970).

Declaration on the Inadmissibility of Intervention in the Domestic Affairs of States and the Protection of Their Independence and Sovereignty, UNGA Res 2131 (XX) (New York: December 21, 1965).

Definition of Aggression, UNGA Res 3314 (XXIX) (December 14, 1974).

Good Humanitarian Donorship, *Principles and Good Practice of Humanitarian Donorship* (Stockholm, June 17, 2003).

High-Level Panel on Threats, Challenges and Change, *A More Secure World: Our Shared Responsibility*, UN Doc A/59/565 (December 2, 2004).

Joint Statement by the Council and the Representatives of the Governments of the Member States Meeting within the Council, European Parliament and the European Commission, "The European Consensus on Humanitarian Aid." *Official Journal of the European Union*, C 25/1 (January 30, 2008).

Sphere Project. (2011) *Humanitarian Charter and Minimum Standards in Humanitarian Response* (3rd edn.). Retrieved from www.sphereproject.org/resources/download-publications/?search=1&keywords=&language=English&category=22 (April 3, 2015).

Strengthening of the Coordination of Emergency Humanitarian Assistance of the United Nations, UN Doc A/RES/58/114 (February 5, 2004).

Strengthening of the Coordination of Emergency Humanitarian Assistance of the United Nations, UN Doc A/RES/63/139 (December 11, 2008).

Strengthening of the Coordination of Humanitarian Emergency Assistance of the United Nations, UN Doc A/RES/46/182 (December 19, 1991).

United Nations General Assembly, *Guiding Principles on Internal Displacement*, UN Doc E/CN.4/1998/53/Add.2 (February 11, 1998).

United Nations Office for Disaster Risk Reduction, *World Conference on Disaster Reduction (Hyogo Declaration)*, UN Doc A/CONF.206/6 (January 22, 2005).

UNSC Res 794 (December 3, 1992) UN Doc S/RES/794.

UNSC Res 1674 (April 28, 2006) UN Doc S/RES/1674.

UNSC Res 1894 (November 11, 2009) UN Doc S/RES/1894.

World Summit Outcome Document, UN Doc A/RES/60/1 (October 24, 2005).

CASES

Military and Paramilitary Activities in and against Nicaragua (*Nicaragua v United States of America*) (Merits) [1986] ICJ Rep 14.

North Sea Continental Shelf (*Federal Republic of Germany v Denmark; Federal Republic of Germany v Netherlands*) (Judgment) [1969] ICJ Rep 3.

Introduction

Countries throughout the world have been devastated by major disasters, including most recently the 2014 floods in Thailand, the 2011 Tohoku Earthquake and Tsunami in Japan, the 2010 Haiti earthquake, the 2005 Hurricane Katrina in the United States and the 2004 Indian Ocean Tsunami. Scholarship[1] in disaster relief governance is growing as more natural and man-made disasters occur with increasing frequency and intensity throughout the world.[2] Therefore, research in this area is timely

[1] See, for example, David D. Caron, Michael J. Jelly and Anastasia Telesetsky. (2014, August). *The International Law of Disaster Relief*. Cambridge: Cambridge University Press; Andrea Guttry, Marco Gestri and Gabriella Venturini. (2012). *International Disaster Response Law*. Hague, Netherlands: T.M.C. Asser Press; Herman B. Leonard. (2009). *Managing Crises: Responses to Large-Scale Emergencies* (coeditor and coauthor with Arnold M. Howitt) Washington, DC: CQ Press; C. Raj Kumar and D. K. Srivastava. (2006). *Tsunami and Disaster Management: Law and Governance*. Hong Kong: Sweet and Maxwell Asia; Charles Gould. (2009). The Right to Housing Recovery after Natural Disasters. *Harvard Human Rights Journal*. 22(1), 169. (Focus on the less vigorous upholding of human rights after disasters, particularly on the right to housing.) Daniel Farber. (2007). Disaster Law and Inequality. *Law and Inequality*. 25, 297; Daniel Farber, Jim Chen, Robert Verchick and Lisa Sun. (2009). *Disaster Law and Policy* (2nd edn.). Philadelphia, PA: Wolters Kluwer Law & Business and Aspen Publication; Daniel Farber and Michael Faure. (2010). *Disaster Law*. Cheltenham: Edward Elgar Publishing; Jonathan Hooks and Trisha Miller. (2006–2007). The Continuing Storm: How Disaster Recovery Excludes Those Most in Need. *California Western Law Review*. 43, 21; Robert Verchick. (2012–2013). Disaster Justice: The Geography of Human Capability. *Duke Environmental Law and Policy Forum*. 23, 23; Sharona Hoffmann. (2008–2009). Preparing for Disaster: Protecting the Most Vulnerable in Emergencies. *U.C. Davis Law Review*. 42, 1491; Shibo Jiang. (2013). International Disaster Response Law and Policy in China: Evolution, Problem and Resolution. *Chinese Journal of International Law*. 12(3), 455 (considers the development of disaster response law in the context of China); Ruth Miller. (2009). *Law in Crisis – The Ecstatic Subject of Natural Disaster*. Stanford, CA: Stanford University Press; Simon Butt, Hitoshi Nasu and Luke Nottage. (2014). *Asia-Pacific Disaster Management – Comparative and Socio-legal Perspectives*. Heidelberg: Springer.

[2] See, for example, Debby Guha-Sapir, Femke Vos, Regina Below and Sylvain Ponserre. (2011). *Annual Disaster Statistical Review 2010 – The Number and Trends*. Brussels: Centre for Research on the Epidemiology of Disasters (CRED) and Université Catholique de Louvain. Retrieved from http://crmi-undp.org/documents/documentos/98.pdf. See p. 3 (table 1);

not only in relation to its contribution to further discourses in disaster law, humanitarian assistance, multi-stakeholder collaboration and new governance scholarship, but also from a humanitarian perspective given the scale of suffering involved.

This book presents empirical research about the perceptions, observations and experiences of sixty-nine humanitarian aid practitioners working in post-disaster response from more than eighteen countries and regions including those most recently affected by major disasters in Thailand, Myanmar, Japan, Haiti, the United States and Indonesia. Through the use of surveys and case studies, an effort is made to glean insights into the governance dynamics, challenges and lessons learned in local engagement from the perspective of those directly engaged in the work of post-disaster relief.

Specifically, this book aims to contribute empirical research to a growing body of disaster law scholarship on the impact of local coordination and planning in disaster response and the role of institutions in post-disaster humanitarian aid. It will do this by examining lessons learned and best practices in local post-disaster collaborative governance processes through comparison of three instances of post-disaster response: first state led, the second multilateral and the third a hybrid of state–civil society collaboration. Examples of such interventions at the state level include Thailand's response to recent flooding, Japan's response to the Tohoku Earthquake and Tsunami and the United States' response to Hurricane Katrina. At the multilateral level, the intervention programs of the UN Office for the Coordination of Humanitarian Affairs (OCHA) in Haiti will be examined, as well as international response programs in Indonesia following the Indian Ocean Tsunami. At the public–private-sector level, examples

Jose Barredo. (2007). Major Food Disasters in Europe: 1950–2005. *Nat Hazards*. 42, 125, see p. 126 (1st paragraph) and p. 143 (table 2); Les Coleman. (2006). Frequency of Man-made Disasters in the 20th Century. *Journal of Contingencies and Crisis Management*. 14(1), 3. See p. 6, noting an "exponential increase" in the number of recorded man-made disasters during the twentieth century; Nick Brooks and W. Neil Adger. (2003). Country-level risk measures of climate-related natural disasters and implications for adaption to climate change. Tyndall Centre Working Paper No. 26. Tyndall Centre for Climate Change Research and Centre for Social and Economic Research on the Global Environment. Retrieved from www.researchgate.net/publication/228647518_Country_level_risk_measures_of_climate-related_natural_disasters_and_implications_for_adaptation_to_climate_ change/file/9fcfd50ac160b4645e.pdf. See p. 7 (paragraph 3.2) and p. 8 (figure 1); Stephan Baas, Selvaraju Ramasamy, Jennie Dey de Pryck and Federica Battista. (2008). *Disaster Risk Management Systems Analysis – A Guide Book*. Rome: Food and Agriculture Organization of the United Nations. Retrieved from ftp://ftp.fao.org/docrep/fao/011/i0304e/i0304e.pdf. See p. 1 for a brief account.

of community-driven response in Myanmar following Cyclone Nargis and SecondMuse's coordination of public–private collaboration between members of civil society, local actors and multilateral organizations to design humanitarian post-disaster open source mobile applications will be studied. This book examines these responses alongside surveys and empirical data with a view to offering insights into how governments, civil society and international organizations may navigate complex emergencies to achieve a decentralized yet coordinated process of humanitarian assistance.

This research builds on insights from Caron and Leben's work on *The International Aspects of Natural and Industrial Catastrophes* (2001), which highlights aspects of the as yet undeveloped international legal order giving rise to an "incoherence of legal and institutional … responses"[3] that "leaves many holes in the collective effort"[4] to respond to catastrophes, beset by tensions "between governance and sovereignty, between solidarity and self-interest, between the asserted obligation to assist in the provision of basic human rights and the reluctance of States to recognize a 'hard' duty to do so."[5] What emerges is the outline of a set of principles of "humanitarian assistance, solidarity and good governance."[6] From this perspective, states are seen "as the agents of humanity" with an "emerging obligation … to provide humanitarian assistance"[7] while recognizing that at present, "there are few means whereby a norm of assistance or solidarity may be enforced."[8]

Building local institutional capacity for coordination with international bodies remains an important area for continued scholarship. In the constellation of international, state and local institutions, Caron highlights the need for the "development of the capacity of a community in cooperation with others to respond in a timely and effective manner to a catastrophic event thereby mitigating the resultant harm."[9] "Even though individuals in solidarity often become more cooperative and humane amidst a catastrophe, the ability of institutions to cooperate and be more humane requires

[3] David D. Caron and Charles Leben. (2001). *The International Aspects of Natural and Industrial Catastrophes*. Hague: The Hague Academy of International Law: Martinus Nijhoff Publishers, pp. 3–4.

[4] Ibid., p. 4.

[5] Ibid., p. 5.

[6] Ibid., p. 13.

[7] Ibid., p. 13.

[8] Ibid., p. 15.

[9] Ibid., p. 21.

preplanning and the institutionalization of such values."[10] This impetus to move beyond "crisis-driven law-making"[11] to a more conscious understanding of the dynamics of effective community engagement and collaboration is a key objective of this project.

In relation to the term "disaster" as understood in this book, useful insights were drawn from the work of Smith,[12] Farber and Faure, and Caron and Leben, notably the importance of understanding the role of human agency, sociolegal dynamics and governance in how we understand and define "disasters." In particular, ongoing catastrophes "such as poverty, malnutrition, post-conflict turmoil, and environmental degradation ... can exert a strong destabilizing influence on the social and physical infrastructure of a given community" and when "a sudden natural ... catastrophic event occurs, this infrastructural instability worsens ... and the community doubly experiences the impact of the immediate catastrophe."[13] As Caron and Leben note, "omissions are as much a part of human agency as actions."[14] "Increased vulnerability stems largely from ... demographic pressures and political and institutional gaps."[15]

At the community level, the capacity to participate in "the creation of knowledge" and the ability "to act upon such knowledge" are central.[16] For example, in land planning decisions, soil overutilization and clear cutting often resulting from disparate access to resources increase "the likelihood that a natural fluctuation in weather will cascade into a catastrophic event."[17] Such conditions not only highlight the notion that "access to knowledge ... and participation in its generation, application and diffusion [is] a responsibility that all must shoulder,"[18] but it also extends responsibility at the state and regional levels to examining gaps in existing regulations that give rise to excessive wealth in some areas and extreme blight in others.

[10] Ibid., p. 21, citing Martin Wachs and Nabil Kamel. (Spring 1996). Decision-Making after Disasters: Responding to the Northridge Earthquake. *Access*. 8, 24–29.

[11] Ibid., p. 27.

[12] Neil Smith. (June 11, 2006). There's No Such Thing as a Natural Disaster, *Understanding Katrina: Perspectives from the Social Sciences*. available at http://understandingkatrina.ssrc.org/Smith.

[13] Farber and Faure (2010), *supra* note 1.

[14] Caron and Leben (2001), *supra* note 3, p. 7.

[15] Ibid., citing Philippe Masure. (1994). A Disaster in Waiting. *New Scientist*. 11.

[16] Ibid., pp. 8–9.

[17] Ibid., p. 9.

[18] Universal House of Justice, Ridvan Message 2010.

Summary of Findings

The principal finding of the sixty-nine-person survey and seven case studies is that there is a statistically significant correlation among the level of engagement with a local community, existing capacity for consultation and coordination and perceived effectiveness of response.[19] Case studies supplement this finding showing that in post-disaster contexts such as in Indonesia where individuals were involved in a long-term process of decision making regarding redevelopment goals, resource use, materials and design through a "community-driven development strategy," projects achieved higher satisfaction and usage rates because they were developed on the basis of local knowledge of needs, resources and preferences. Local participation enabled quick response to the most urgent needs[20] and reduced the problem of marginalization.[21] In addition, projects adopting a community-driven development (CDD) model were completed eighteen months ahead of schedule, they produced more output than any other program, and they cost 56 percent less than those adopting a conventional approach.[22] In addition, the occupancy rate for housing built by such programs was 97 percent, whereas that of similar houses built by other programs was more than 10 percent lower. Where local institutions were engaged directly in the rebuilding process, capacity was built, which was key to the true and sustainable recovery of the affected communities.[23]

At the same time, the findings show that international aid without community input can lead to significant complications. In areas that did not directly and systematically draw on community input, many rebuilt homes had to be demolished and replaced by a new road.[24] Such

[19] See Chapter 11.

[20] B. Dercon and M. Kusumawijaya (2007). Two Years of Settlement Recovery in Aceh and Nias: What Should the Planners Have Learned? Paper submitted to the 43rd ISOCARP Congress, Antwerp, Belgium, p. 3.

[21] T. Ophiyandri, D. Amaratunga and C. Pathirage. (2010). *Community Based Post Disaster Housing Reconstruction: Indonesian Perspective.* CIB 2010 World Congress, Conference Proceedings May 10–13, 2010. University of Salford, Salford Quays, United Kingdom, p.13.

[22] World Bank Group. (2009). *Five Years after the Tsunami: Continuing the Commitment to Reconstruction*, December, p. 23.

[23] Aceh Community Assistance Research Project. (2007). The Acehnese Gampong Three Years On: Assessing Local Capacity and Reconstruction Assistance in Post-tsunami Aceh. Report of the Aceh Community Assistance Research Project (ACARP), December.

[24] I. MacKinnon. (2008, August 15). Indonesia: Aceh Villagers Face Homelessness Again – In Name of Tsunami Aid from US Government. *The Guardian*. Retrieved from www.guardian.co.uk/world/2008/aug/15/tsunami2004.naturaldisasters.

incidents reflected poor levels of understanding regarding the needs of the community and also led to a waste of funds.[25] Conversely, community cohesion and consultation are essential to successful recovery program implementation,[26] as demonstrated by a small community in Myanmar where preexisting capacity for consultation enabled careful planning and systematic and coordinated follow-up with only modest targeted loans.[27]

These findings therefore engage with insights from collaborative governance and multi-stakeholder dispute resolution literature.[28] Recent findings have documented the relevance[29] of collaborative governance processes in facilitating intersociety engagement[30] in postcrisis situations, the utility of such processes in sustaining collaboration[31] and the importance of harnessing private expertise to bolster productivity, capture information and augment resources through mechanisms that simultaneously motivate and empower partners to create public value.[32] Key variables that will influence successful outcomes include the prior history of conflict or cooperation, the incentives for stakeholders to participate and the degree of resource access, leadership and institutional design.[33] A virtuous cycle of collaboration tends to develop when collaborative forums focus on "small wins" that deepen trust, commitment and shared understanding.[34]

[25] J. Levs. (2012, April 11). Tsunami Scare Tests New Life-Saving Procedures. *CNN*. Retrieved from http://edition.cnn.com/2012/04/11/world/asia/indonesia-earthquake-differences/index.html.

[26] Aceh Community Assistance Research Project, (2007), *supra* note 23.

[27] See Chapter 9.

[28] See, for example, L. Susskind et al. (1999). *The Consensus Building Handbook*. Thousand Oaks, CA: Sage Publications.

[29] John Donahue. (2004, March). On Collaborative Governance. *Corporate Social Responsibility Initiative – Working Paper No.2*. Retrieved from www.hks.harvard.edu/m-rcbg/CSRI/publications/workingpaper_2_donahue.pdf

[30] Andrew Wear. (2012). Collaborative Approaches to Regional Governance – Lessons from Victoria. *Australian Journal of Public Administration*. 71(4), 469.

[31] Johari Efendi. (2013, June). Civic engagement and collaborative governance in post-conflict societies. Case study, Ambon, Indonesia. Digital dissertation consortium. Thesis (M.A.), the University of Oregon. Retrieved from https://scholarsbank.uoregon.edu/xmlui/bitstream/handle/1794/13274/Efendi_oregon_0171N_10705.pdf?sequence=1

[32] John D. Donahue. (2011). *Collaborative Governance: Private Roles for Public Goals in Turbulent Times*. Princeton, NJ: Princeton University Press.

[33] Chris Ansell and Alison Gash. (2007). Collaborative Governance in Theory and Practice. *Journal of Public Administration Research and Theory*. 18(4), 543; Stephen Page. (2010). Integrative Leadership for Collaborative Governance: Civic Engagement in Seattle. *The Leadership Quarterly*. 21(2), 246.

[34] Ibid.

The findings also show that international institutions face the greatest challenge in effective engagement with local communities, while state agencies are in a somewhat better position to collaborate and coordinate in response planning. For example, despite the approximately 3.5 billion dollars international aid inflow into Haiti[35] following the 2010 earthquake, due to a combination of limited understanding of the local context, limited situation analysis, inequitable distribution of resources, insufficient coverage of affected areas, nonalignment of resources with actual needs and harm to the local private sector including Haitian construction companies, medical staff, pharmacists, rice farmers and food vendors who were driven out due to the availability of free international aid–supported alternatives, communities in Haiti continue to suffer from the effects of the disaster more than five years after the earthquake struck in 2010.

These findings echo recent insights from sociolegal scholars of disaster studies that "factors of inequality contribute to producing higher rates of vulnerability" in disaster contexts and usually reflect "the profound asymmetry that divides those who decide from those who will be affected by such decisions."[36] The origins and effects of disasters are "global and local at the same time."[37] To a limited extent, the findings also engage with the debate surrounding the role of institutions in social and economic development[38] including the importance of building community capacity for participation and engagement in the evolution of strong institutions.

[35] Source: http://fts.unocha.org/reports/daily/OCHA_R24_E15939.XLS and source: http://fts.unocha.org/reports/daily/OCHA_R24_E15797.XLS

[36] Valerio Nitrato Izzo. (2013). Law, State and the Politics of Catastrophes: A Critical Perspective on Epiphanies of Injustice and the Need for Protection. In Susan Sterett (Ed.), *Disaster and Sociolegal Studies*. Onati Socio-legal Series. New Orleans, LA: Quid Pro Books, p. 71.

[37] Ibid., p. 73.

[38] See: D. Acemoglu and J. Robinson. (2012). *Why Nations Fail*. New York: Crown and subsequent debate: William Easterly. (2012, March 24). The Roots of Hardship: Despite Massive Amounts of Aid, Poor Countries Tend to Stay Poor. Maybe Their Institutions Are the Problem. *Wall Street Journal*, available at: wsj.com/articles/SB10001424052702304724404577293714016708378; Jared Diamond. (2012, July 06). What Makes Countries Rich or Poor? *New York Review of Books*; Jeffrey Sachs. (2012, September/October issue). Government, Geography, and Growth: The True Drivers of Economic Development. *Foreign Affairs;* David Henderson. (2013, April 4). Acemoglu and Robinson on the Wealth of Nations. *EconLog*, available at: http://econlog.econlib.org/archives/2013/04/acemoglu_and_ro_1.html; Bryan Caplan. (2013, November 13). *Why Nations Fail*: A Contrarian Take. *EconLog*, available at: http://econlog.econlib.org/archives/2013/11/why_nations_fai.html

Data Collection Method

Survey data and case studies were collected in order to gain insight into the dynamics of local involvement, if any, in the planning, implementation and distribution of humanitarian post–natural disaster aid and resulting challenges and lessons learned. While it must be noted that "the random nature of disasters and multiplicity of players makes comprehensive analysis difficult,"[39] and given the small sample size (N=69), the purpose of the survey and case studies is not to provide generalizable findings, but rather to offer insights into how institutional capacities for community participation and engagement might be built.

The study was conducted between April 2013 and April 2015. A total of seventy-one surveys were distributed in person and initiated via a web link portal and sixty-nine surveys were completed. The sample pool consisted of humanitarian aid practitioners working in post-disaster response from more than eighteen countries and regions. The sample group was selected from contacts made with members of international humanitarian agencies and professional associations.[40] Of the respondents, fifty-five worked for an international organization, nine worked for a private entity, three worked for a state agency, and seven worked for a public–private partnership organization. The majority of respondents (thirty-six) had more than ten years of experience.

Emerging Global Policy Support for Local Participation in Humanitarian Relief

In recent years, the participation of beneficiaries in post-disaster reconstruction has become one of the core issues in the development of

[39] T. E. Drabek and D. A. McEntire. (2002). Emergent Phenomena and Multiorganizational Coordination in Disasters: Lessons from the Research Literature. *International Journal of Emergencies and Disasters* [online]. 20(2), 197–224. Available from: http://ijmed.org/articles/574/download/ (accessed on October 29, 2012).

[40] These included the Asia Foundation in Beijing; Oxfam in Boston, MA; USAID in Washington, DC; RedR in India; the UN Office for the Coordination of Humanitarian Affairs in Geneva; UN Women in NY; UNDP in Bangkok, Thailand; the World Health Organization; Mercy Malaysia; the Cash Learning Partnership in Oxford; the Bill & Melinda Gates Foundation in Seattle, WA; the CDC in Atlanta, GA; Fundacion Macau; and individuals working at Red Cross centers in Yangoon, Myanmar; Lijiang, Hainan and Shenzhen, PRC, Hong Kong; Houston, Texas; Macau SAR; Istanbul, Turkey; Haifa, Israel; Kuala Lumpur, Malaysia; the International Committee for the Red Cross; and humanitarian and disaster aid research centers at Tufts University, Harvard University and UC Berkeley.

contemporary humanitarian relief standards.[41] This represents, as some have suggested, the development of an emerging norm of international law to require local participation in relief efforts.[42] Legal instruments adopted by states, and self-regulatory mechanisms of NGOs, such as the Sphere Charter, are evidence of the progressive codification of an obligation to ensure local participation in relief activities.[43] The 1991 Declaration on Strengthening of the Coordination of Humanitarian Emergency Assistance of the United Nations states that country-level coordination should include the use of locally available relief capacities.[44] The 2005 Hyogo Declaration, adopted by states under the auspices of the United Nations Office for Disaster Risk Reduction, affirms the necessity of community-level capacities as a mechanism of diminishing disaster risk.[45] The 2008 European Consensus on Humanitarian Aid provides that humanitarian activities by the European Union have the objective of supporting "local responses to humanitarian crises through a partnership approach with the affected communities."[46] The Good Humanitarian Donorship consortium of states emphasizes the need to involve "beneficiaries in the design, implementation, monitoring and evaluation" of relief activities.[47] Article 2(c) (ii) of the 2012 Food Assistance Convention stipulates one of the governing principles in the provision of food assistance as being the involvement of the "beneficiaries in the assessment of their needs" of relief activities.[48] Additional support for an emerging standard

41 Béatrice Pouligny. Supporting Local Ownership in Humanitarian Action. *Humanitarian Policy Paper Series* 6–7. www.gppi.net/fileadmin/gppi/GPPiPPR_local_ownership_2009.pdf (accessed on April 20, 2014).

42 For complete discussion, see T. Kabau and S. Ali. (2015). A Human Rights Based Approach to the Regulation of Humanitarian Relief: The Emerging Obligation to Incorporate Local Participation. *Brooklyn Journal of International Law*. 40(3), 791.

43 Ibid.

44 United Nations General Assembly. (1991, December 19). *Strengthening of the Coordination of Humanitarian Emergency Assistance of the United Nations*. UN Doc A/RES/46/182.

45 United Nations Office for Disaster Risk Reduction. (2005, January 22). *World Conference on Disaster Reduction (Hyogo Declaration)*. UN Doc A/CONF.206/6 paragraph 4.

46 Joint Statement by the Council and the Representatives of the Governments of the Member States Meeting within the Council, European Parliament and the European Commission, "The European Consensus on Humanitarian Aid." Official Journal of the European Union. C 25/1 (2008, January 30) paragraph 4.

47 Good Humanitarian Donorship, "Principles and Good Practice of Humanitarian Donorship" (endorsed in Stockholm, June 17, 2003) paragraph 7. Available at: www.goodhumanitariandonorship.org/gns/principles-good-practice-ghd/overview.aspx (accessed on May 19, 2014).

48 Food Assistance Convention (adopted April 25, 2012, entered into force January 1, 2013). Available at: www.foodassistanceconvention.org/convention/FoodAssistance.pdf (accessed on May 11, 2013).

of local participation can be found in the 2008 Civil-Military Guidelines and Reference for Complex Emergencies by the United Nations and the Inter-Agency Standing Committee (IASC), which states that local personnel should be involved, to the extent possible, "in the design, management and implementation of assistance, including in civil-military coordination."[49] The Sphere Humanitarian Charter, drafted by a consortium of NGOs, expressly states that its principles and standards are based on a "rights-based and people-centred approach" to the provision of humanitarian relief.[50]

Such emerging principles supporting an obligation to ensure effective local participation can best be appreciated within the context of emerging scholarship in the transnational law and world community fields outlining new regulatory "spaces" within which pluralist approaches to global regulation are developing[51] as well as expanding notions of community reflecting the development of collective interest over "egoistic interests of individual states."[52] The concept of community is increasingly understood as a descriptive term to designate interactions in which "participants in pursuit of their own objectives must regularly take account of the activities and demands of others."[53] Research underscores the link between perception and action through the observation that "it is the perception of interdependence in community process that leads participants to appreciate the relevance of pursuing common interests and motivates them to clarify it."[54] It also provides a lens through which to "assess the regulatory challenges arising in an increasingly interdependent, globalizing world."[55] For example, Scott posits that because effective regulation

[49] United Nations and the Inter-Agency Standing Committee. (2008). *Civil-Military Guidelines and Reference for Complex Emergencies*, 19. Available at: https://docs.unocha.org/sites/dms/Documents/ENGLISH%20VERSION%20Guidelines%20for%20Complex%20Emergencies.pdf (accessed on May 5, 2014).

[50] Sphere Project. (2011). *Humanitarian Charter and Minimum Standards in Humanitarian Response* (3rd edn.), Bourton on Dunsmore, Rugby, UK: Practical Action Publishing, Schumacher Centre for Technology and Development, 6.

[51] C. Scott. (2010). Analysing Regulatory Space: Fragmented Resources and Institutional Design. *Public Law*. (Summer), 329–353.

[52] Bruno Simma and Andreas L. Paulus. (1998). The "International Community": Facing the Challenge of Globalization. *European Journal of International Law*. 9, 266.

[53] Myres S. McDougal, Michael W. Reisman and Andrew R. Willard. (1988). The World Community: A Planetary Social Process. *Faculty Scholarship Series*, Paper 753.

[54] Ibid.

[55] Peer C. Zumbansen. (2006). Transnational Law. In Jan Smits (Ed.), *Elgar Encyclopedia of Comparative Law* (1st edn.). Cheltenham: Edward Elgar, pp. 738–754; updated version titled "Transnational Law, Evolving," in Jan Smits (Ed.), *Elgar Encyclopedia of Comparative*

of an area is "the product of the resources, perspectives and relationships of… various actors in the sphere,"[56] institutional design or reform ought to be "sensitive" to resource allocation to effect compliance with regulatory objectives.[57] Zumbansen (2013)[58] offers insights into a "transnational legal pluralist" model of global regulation entailing a shift in focus from state-based government to a focus on the fragmented coexistence of state and non-state actors, hard and soft norms and processes within regulatory spaces.[59] Sassen (2008)[60] similarly observes the incipient proliferation of highly specialized normative orders in the global arena, termed "assemblages"[61] (akin to the regulatory spaces), which signifies a new multipolar order unsettling existing state-oriented institutional arrangements.[62] Such work provides a helpful perspective to examine the operation and dynamics of international, national and local humanitarian aid response within the context of expanding notions of community and offers a useful analytic framework recognizing the multiplicity of governance-related resources and information (e.g., formal and informal authority, local knowledge, organizational capacities) among concerned actors in the context of disaster relief.

Organization of Book

This book is divided into five parts, each of which successively analyzes the interplay among law, governance and new forms of decision making to address post-disaster relief efforts.

Law (2nd edn.). (2012). Cheltenham: Edward Elgar, pp. 898–925. Preprint: Osgoode CLPE Research Paper No. 27/2011 http://ssrn.com/abstract=1975403 [Refereed]. Review: Larry Catá Backer, January 1, 2012: http://lcbackerblog.blogspot.com/2012/01/transnational-law-as-field-or-method.html (accessed on April 15, 2015).

56 Scott (2010), *supra* note 51, p. 347.

57 Ibid., p. 354.

58 P. Zumbansen (2013). Law and Legal Pluralism: Hybridity in Transnational Governance. In P. Jurcys, P. F. Kjaer and R. Yatsunami (Eds.), *Regulatory Hybridization in the Transnational Sphere*. Leiden, Boston, MA: Martimus Nijhoff Publishers, pp. 49–70. *See also*: P. Zumbansen. (2011). Defining the Space of Transnational Law: Legal Theory, Global Governance & Legal Pluralism. *Osgoode CLPE Research Paper 21/2011 Vol. 7 No. 05*. Available at SSRN: http://ssrn.com/abstract=1934044.

59 Zumbansen (2013), *supra* note 58, p. 57.

60 S. Sassen. (2008). Neither Global nor National: Novel Assemblages of Territory, Authority and Rights. *Ethics & Global Politics*. 1(1–2), 61–79. Jarfalla, Sweden: Co-Action Publication. *See also*: S. Sassen. (2006). *Territory, Authority, Rights from Medieval to Global Assemblages*. Princeton, NJ: Princeton University Press.

61 Sassen (2008), *supra* note 60, p. 61.

62 Ibid., p. 62.

Part I examines the contribution of collaborative and new governance scholarship to providing insights into the emergence and dynamics of post-disaster governance mechanisms. In exploring the coordination of decision-making efforts among state and non-state actors in addressing humanitarian aid efforts, the concepts of new governance and international community networks provide a helpful lens through which to observe the dynamic nature of international cooperation in the context of globalization. This includes analysis of the contribution of collaborative governance to expanded participation and partnership on the part of governments and non-state actors in solving public problems;[63] the questioning of doctrinal divides between legal fields;[64] a learning-focused orientation;[65] the use of public–private partnership in regulatory reform;[66] the role of the state as a convener, catalyst and coordinator;[67] and the relationship between new governance and problem-solving capacity building.[68]

Following an outline of the theoretical foundations of humanitarian aid, Part I goes on to examine emerging international law and policy supporting local participation in humanitarian assistance such as provisions contained within the 1991 Declaration on Strengthening of the Coordination of Humanitarian Emergency Assistance of the United Nations,[69] the 2005 Hyogo Declaration,[70] the 2008 European Consensus

[63] Jason M. Solomon. (2008). Law and Governance in the 21st Century Regulatory State. *Texas Law Review*. 86, 819–856.

[64] Orly Lobel. (2004b). The Renew Deal: The Fall of Regulation and the Rise of Governance. *Minnesota Law Review*. 89, 342.

[65] Solomon (2008), *supra* note 63; Amy J. Cohen. (2008). Negotiation, Meet New Governance: Interests, Skills, and Selves. *Law & Society Inquiry*. 33, 503; see also T. Heikkila and A. K. Gerlak. (2013). Building a Conceptual Approach to Collective Learning: Lessons for Public Policy Scholars. *Policy Studies Journal*. 41, 484–512.

[66] Lisa T. Alexander. (2009). Stakeholder Participation in New Governance: Lessons from Chicago's Public Housing Reform Experiment. *Georgetown Journal of Poverty Law & Policy*. 16, 117.

[67] Michael C. Dorf and Charles E. Sabel. (1998). A Constitution of Democratic Experimentalism. *Columbia Law Review*. 98, 267; Solomon (2008), *supra* note 63; Cohen (2008), *supra* note 65.

[68] Cohen (2008), *supra* note 65.

[69] United Nations General Assembly. (1991, December 19). *Strengthening of the Coordination of Humanitarian Emergency Assistance of the United Nations*. G.A. Res. 46/182, Annex, 34, 36, U.N. Doc. A/RES/46/182, which states that country-level coordination should include the use of locally available relief capacities.

[70] United Nations Office for Disaster Risk Reduction. (2005, January 22). "World Conference on Disaster Reduction (Hyogo Declaration)," UN Doc A/CONF.206/6 paragraph 4, which affirms the necessity of community-level capacities as a mechanism of diminishing disaster risk.

on Humanitarian Aid,[71] the Good Humanitarian Donorship consortium of states[72] and Article 2(c) (ii) of the 2012 Food Assistance Convention,[73] alongside global efforts to develop a growing body of disaster response principles.[74]

Following Part I, each of the case studies presented in Parts II, III and IV systematically examine the disaster incident, international, state and local response, private-sector collaboration, outcomes and lessons learned within each region in order to better understand the dynamics of local involvement in global relief efforts.

Part II explores the workings of multilateral response to disaster aid in Indonesia and Haiti. In examining case studies of these international-led relief efforts, the distinctions between post-disaster approaches in Indonesia and Haiti provide useful insights. While a variety of factors in Haiti, including high levels of social and economic inequality, poverty, malnutrition, unemployment and mortality,[75] contributed to the

[71] Joint Statement by the Council and the Representatives of the Governments of the Member States Meeting within the Council, European Parliament and the European Commission, "The European Consensus on Humanitarian Aid," Official Journal of the European Union, C 25/1 (2008, January 30) paragraph 4, which provides that humanitarian activities by the European Union have the objective of supporting local responses to humanitarian crises through a partnership approach with the affected communities.

[72] Good Humanitarian Donorship, "Principles and Good Practice of Humanitarian Donorship" (endorsed in Stockholm, 2003, June 17) paragraph 7. Available at: www.goodhumanitariandonorship.org/gns/principles-good-practice-ghd/overview.aspx (accessed on May 19, 2014), which emphasizes the need to involve the "beneficiaries in the design, implementation, monitoring and evaluation" of relief activities.

[73] Food Assistance Convention (adopted April 25, 2012, entered into force January 1, 2013). Available at: www.foodassistanceconvention.org/convention/FoodAssistance.pdf (accessed on May 11, 2013), which stipulates one of the governing principles in the provision of food assistance as being the involvement of the "beneficiaries in the assessment of their needs and in the design, implementation, monitoring and evaluation" of relief activities.

[74] Hans-Joachim Heintze and Andrej Zwitter (Eds.). (2011). *International Law and Humanitarian Assistance: A Crosscut through Legal Issues Pertaining to Humanitarianism*. New York: Springer. Efforts have been made in recent years by the United Nations ("UN"), the European Union ("EU") and the International Law Commission ("ILC") to develop a growing body of disaster response principles. Two major General Assembly resolutions have been passed: (1) An Agenda for Peace (A/RES/47/120[B]) and (2) Strengthening of the Coordination of Humanitarian Emergency Assistance of the United Nations (A/RES/46/182). The latter resolution created the position of the Emergency Relief Coordinator and the Inter-Agency Standing Committee, which has provided a foundation for international coordination of humanitarian response by multiple actors.

[75] Haiti Equality Collective. (2010). Ensuring Haitian Women's Participation and Leadership in All Stages of National Relief and Reconstruction – A Gender Shadow Report of the 2010 Haiti PDNA, 1, available at www.genderaction.org/publications/2010/gsr.pdf (accessed on May 8, 2013).

challenges surrounding post-disaster relief efforts, these challenges were compounded by limited understanding of the local context, limited situation analysis, inequitable distribution of resources to earthquake-affected areas, nonalignment of resources with actual needs and harm to the local private sector. On the other hand, in Indonesia, following the 2004 tsunami where international institutions engaged individuals in a long-term process of decision making regarding redevelopment goals, resource use, materials and design through a "community-driven development strategy," projects achieved higher satisfaction and usage rates because they were developed on the basis of local knowledge of needs, resources and preferences. Local participation enabled quick response to the most urgent needs[76] and reduced the problem of marginalization.[77]

Part III then goes on to examine state-led models in three regions: Thailand, Japan and the United States. Through examination of state-driven relief efforts, in particular comparing the response of Japan and the United States to recent disasters, the differences between a centralized state policy as in the case of Japan[78] and a factionalized, divergent response at times clouded by prejudice in the case of the United States demonstrate the important role of state institutions in coordinating with local actors.

Part IV examines public–private partnerships by exploring post-disaster collaboration in selected villages in Myanmar and the work of emerging crowd-sourced organizations in facilitating the development of collaborative solutions to disaster challenges. Among the lessons learned from the village response to Cyclone Nargis in Myanmar was the importance of community-based partnerships building on existing structures of collaboration and consultation. This section also examines a growing number of public–private partnerships including those involved in the development of crowd source technology for humanitarian relief fueled by local participation and knowledge. The growing use of crowd source technology such as crowd mapping and resource tracking being universally accessible, collaboratively designed, subject to ongoing improvement and responsive to on-the-ground needs reflects in many respects the emerging

[76] Dercon and Kusumawijaya (2007), *supra* note 20, pp. 19–23.

[77] Ophiyandri, Amaratunga and Pathirage (2010), *supra* note 21, p.13.

[78] Scholars have also highlighted significant shortcomings and challenges in relation to Japan's compensation policy. See, for example, Eric A. Feldman. (2013). Fukushima: Catastrophe, Compensation, and Justice in Japan. *DePaul Law Review*. 62, 335; Daniel Farber. (2012). Introduction: Legal Scholarship, the Disaster Cycle, and the Fukushima Accident. *Duke Environmental Law and Policy Forum*. 23, 1; Joel Rheuben. (2014). Government Liability for Regulatory Failure in the Fukushima Disaster: A Common Law Comparison. *Pacific Rim Law and Policy Journal*. 23, 113; Harold S. Yun. (2015). Fukushima and New Zealand v. France

UN governance mechanisms developed to support the creation of such technology.[79] These tools can harness the power of mass collaboration to quickly aggregate, gather, translate, geolocate, publish and distribute information about urgent needs, using crowd-based technologies.[80]

Part V, building on the results of a comparative cross-jurisdictional analysis of disaster recovery case studies in six jurisdictions, presents statistical analysis of survey findings of sixty-nine humanitarian aid practitioners regarding their insights into the dynamics, challenges and lessons learned in post-disaster local engagement. Specifically, the principal finding of the survey and follow up questions is that there is a statistically significant correlation between the level of engagement with a local community and perceived effectiveness of response.[81] Building on this key finding, policy recommendations are presented concerning the role of the state, the private sector and local actors in disaster response. The policy recommendations include suggestions regarding local capacity building and training, logistical support at the local level, improvement in networking and coordination, initiating planning at the community level, accountability and information sharing and greater attention to cultural sensitivity and language.

While the case studies and surveys in this book indicate that the success of humanitarian aid efforts is ultimately measured by the extent to which local actors are effectively involved in decision-making processes concerning relief efforts, much remains to be examined in the area of capacity building including measures for training individuals and institutions in post-disaster coordination. In-depth knowledge about developing effective components of post-disaster humanitarian aid coordination is essential to advancing the role of states, transnational governance and legal networks and global non-state actors in contributing to humanitarian post-disaster response. Such insights will be useful globally as states and organizations increasingly implement and coordinate relief efforts with civil society participants.

Nuclear Tests: Can Japan Be Brought to the International Court of Justice for Damages Caused by the Fukushima Plants? *Minnesota Journal of International Law*. 24, 387.

79 For complete discussion, see: S. Ali (2014). *Crowd Sourced Governance in a Post-disaster Context*, International and Comparative Law Quarterly, Cambridge University Press.

80 UN Foundation. *Disaster Relief 2.0*. (2011). Available at: www.unfoundation.org/assets/pdf/disaster-relief-20-report.pdf (accessed on March 19, 2014).

81 For additional discussion, see S. Ali Toward Peer Presence in Post-disaster Governance: An Empirical Study. *Hastings Journal of International and Comparative Law* (2015).

PART I

Overview

1

New Governance and Humanitarian Aid

Overview

This chapter provides a theoretical overview of multi-stakeholder governance principles as they relate to humanitarian response. This literature is important in helping to situate the role of the state, international institutions and local community members in responding to natural disasters while examining the opportunities, limitations and challenges of each. In examining new governance scholarship including new and old forms of governance, principles, attitudes and applications, standardization versus diversification and accountability, the focus is on how such insights can help us understand the dynamics of the post-disaster response case studies presented in the chapters that follow.

New Governance Scholarship

New governance scholars have provided extensive insight into the development and dynamics of emerging governance mechanisms. This has included thoughtful analysis of the contribution of new governance to expanded participation and partnership on the part of governments and non-state actors in solving public problems;[1] the questioning of doctrinal divides between legal fields;[2] a learning-focused orientation;[3] the use of public–private partnership in regulatory reform;[4] the role of the state as

[1] Jason M. Solomon. (2008). Law and Governance in the 21st Century Regulatory State. *Texas Law Review*. 86, 819–856.

[2] Orly Lobel. (2004b). The Renew Deal: The Fall of Regulation and the Rise of Governance. *Minnesota Law Review*. 89, 342.

[3] Solomon (2008), *supra* note 1; Amy J. Cohen. (2008). Negotiation, Meet New Governance: Interests, Skills, and Selves. *Law & Society Inquiry*. 33, 503.

[4] Lisa T. Alexander. (2009). Stakeholder Participation in New Governance: Lessons from Chicago's Public Housing Reform Experiment. *Georgetown Journal on Poverty Law and Policy*. 16, 117.

a convener, catalyst and coordinator;[5] and the relationship between new governance and development of problem-solving capabilities.[6] This form of decision making has largely responded to a growing dissatisfaction with the inefficiencies of rigid "top-down" decision-making styles. In addition, recent scholarship has examined the challenges facing new governance; including ensuring participants have the necessary skills for participation,[7] the development of managerial and procedural safeguards,[8] the difficulties of achieving stakeholder participation under conditions of social conflict[9] and distributional inequalities.[10]

Yet, while both the opportunities and challenges of new governance mechanisms have been examined extensively, little attention has been given to the role of new governance mechanisms in global transnational decision-making processes in the context of humanitarian disaster response. This chapter aims to fill this gap by examining the applications of new governance insights to the dynamics of post-disaster humanitarian aid practice.

New and Old Forms of Governance

In examining insights from new governance scholarship, it is important to first understand its relationship to "old forms of governance," particularly in the context of long-standing debates regarding the role of economics in governance theory.[11] New governance has typically been understood as involving multi-stakeholder decision making and rule making. However, such

[5] Michael C. Dorf and Charles E. Sabel. (1998). A Constitution of Democratic Experimentalism. *Columbia Law Review*. 98, 267; Solomon (2008), *supra* note 1; Cohen (2008), *supra* note 3.

[6] Cohen (2008), *supra* note 3.

[7] Ibid.

[8] Lester M. Salamon. (2001). The New Governance and the Tools of Public Action: An Introduction. *Fordham Urban Law Journal*. 28, 1611.

[9] Alexander (2009), *supra* note 4.

[10] Ibid.

[11] See, for example, Grzegorz Ekiert and Stephen E. Hanson. (2003). *Capitalism and Democracy in Central and Eastern Europe: Assessing the Legacy of Communist Rule*. Cambridge: Cambridge University Press. (The book is a collection of articles analyzing the change of post-communist countries from a historical and theoretical perspective.); Herman Willem Hoen. (2001). *Good Governance in Central and Eastern Europe: The Puzzle of Capitalism by Design*. Cheltenham: Edward Elgar Publication. (The book examines the fall of communism and the transformation to a market economy of Central and Eastern Europe.); Jamie Peck and Jun Zhang. (2013). A Variety of Capitalism … with Chinese Characteristics? *Journal of Economic Geography*. 13(3), 357. (The article recognizes the "varieties of capitalism" framework and applies it to the Chinese context. It analyzes the transformation of China from a communist state to a capitalist economy.); John Galbraith and Stanislav Menshikov. (1988). *Capitalism, Communism, and Coexistence: From the*

decision-making approaches have tended to face limits when applied in the context of wide-scale humanitarian suffering. One example of this interplay between new and old governance has been examined in the context of setting appropriate humanitarian standards in global resource distribution[12] through which a mix of centralized legislation ("old governance") and multi-stakeholder involvement ("new governance") has been considered preferable to reliance on new governance approaches alone.

In particular, new governance approaches have been found to be relevant when the insights and shared learnings of a broad range of stakeholders are required to address a complex or newly identified social problem because new governance tends to foster dialogue.[13] The 1990s saw the proliferation of new governance approaches to decision making.[14] This has been particularly true when rules are needed to address a novel or rapidly evolving situation that demands an ability to alter the rules if necessary.[15]

Bitter Past to a Better Prospect. Boston, MA: Houghton Mifflin. (The book records the transcript of meetings of the two authors. It identifies the history and future of capitalism and communism and suggests that they can coexist.); Mark Sandle. (2006). *Communism*. Oxon: Routledge. (The book provides a full account of the history of communism and how it revolutionized the twentieth century, as well as an account of how far communism impacts the development of capitalism.); Nina Bandelj. (2007). *From Communists to Foreign Capitalists: The Social Foundations of Foreign Direct Investment in Postsocialist Europe*. Princeton, NJ: Princeton University Press. (The book identifies the shift of several post-socialist European countries from communism to capitalism. As a result of globalization, they actively engage in institutionalizing and legitimizing foreign direct investments to undergo economic transformation.); Niaz Murtaza. (2011). Pursuing Self-Interest or Self-Actualization? From Capitalism to a Steady-State, Wisdom Economy. *Ecological Economics*. 70, 577. (The article compares communism and capitalism and argues the role of self-actualization as the ultimate driving force for a steady state.); Stephen A. Resnick and Richard D. Wolff. (2002). *Class Theory and History: Capitalism and Communism in the USSR*. Oxon: Routledge. (The book provides a detailed description as to the theories of communism and capitalism. Through reviewing communism's history and development in the Soviet Union during the twentieth century, the authors question whether a communist class structure ever existed in the Soviet Union. The book further notes the route of economic transformation to capitalism in the USSR.); Veronica Anghel. (2012). The Challenges of Liberal Democracy: A Study of the Reconversion of Romanian Communist Elites in Transition to Democracy. *Revista de Stiinte Politice*. 35, 12. (The article examines how democracy affected the transformation of Romania away from communism and its recent tendency to return to communism.)

12 Amy Lehr. (2010). Old and New Governance Approaches to Conflict Minerals: All Are Better than One. *Harvard International Law Journal*. 58, 148–151.

13 Ibid., p. 153, and Jason M. Solomon. (2010). New Governance, Preemptive Self-Regulation, and the Blurring of Boundaries in Regulatory Theory and Practice. *Wisconsin Law Review*. 2010(2), 591–598.

14 Lehr (2010), *supra* note 12, p. 152.

15 Ibid., pp. 152–153.

In such circumstances, the command-and-control mechanisms in old governance is arguably limited because regulators may not have the expertise to devise appropriate rules, nor the resources needed to enforce them in multiple jurisdictions.[16]

Principles of New Governance

In relation to new governance generally, scholarship places primacy on (1) collaborative process, (2) stakeholder participation, (3) local experimentation, (4) public–private partnership, and (5) flexible policy formation, implementation and monitoring.[17]

New governance places stakeholder participation as a central tenet.[18] Participatory process recognizes diverse stakeholders in public problems and attempts to give those stakeholders a voice in policy formation.[19] In participatory governance, stakeholders, including organizations (institutions, public agencies, private firms and NGOs), interact, share responsibility and together generate policy.[20]

New governance scholarship eschews centralized federal regulation in favor of decentralized local authority. Indeed, the focus on stakeholder participation relates to new governance's emphasis on localism. States and localities are expected to be better situated to facilitate participatory processes, and once solutions are found, they are best suited to monitor implementation.[21]

New governance stresses public–private partnerships. Public problems are not entrusted merely to public agencies, but instead private interests affected by public action involve themselves in policy formation. In this sense, new governance places the focus on "the relationships among private and public actors rather than on the substantive prescription of state legislation, rules, and judicial decisions."[22] This public–private rethinking attempts to harness the late twentieth-century turn toward private firms and markets to provide what had otherwise been public services.[23] The

[16] Ibid., p. 153.
[17] Ibid., p. 332.
[18] Ibid., p. 333.
[19] Ibid.
[20] Ibid.
[21] Lobel (2004b), *supra* note 2 at pp. 381–382.
[22] Orly Lobel. (2004a). Setting the Agenda for New Governance Research. *Minnesota Law Review*. 89, 498, 505.
[23] See Lobel (2004) *infra* note 46, at pp. 373–374.

increased interdependence between public and private actors blurs previously stable boundaries between them.[24]

In terms of domains, new governance principles are wide reaching. Rooted in administrative and regulatory projects, these principles have been applied by scholars in an array of substantive domains – including occupational safety, environmental regulation, corporate governance, community lawyering, constitutionalism, education and health care.[25]

While the applications of new governance theory are wide ranging, scholars have suggested[26] that much more analysis on an "on the ground" basis must be conducted – and this necessarily includes examples of both success and failure.[27] This would include the need for greater on-the-ground analysis of post-disaster response dynamics.

New Governance as an "Attitude"

In recent times, scholars of new governance have suggested that beyond a mere regulatory approach, new governance can be considered as an "attitude," or a "regulatory state of mind."[28] Scholars writing from this vantage suggest that new governance's strength is in its capability to blur boundaries and thus adapt to new circumstances.[29]

The idea of blurred boundaries in new governance theory consists of (1) blurring of the *roles* of regulatory actors; (2) blurring of the *stages* of regulation; (3) blurring of the *modes* of regulation; (4) blurring of the *functions* of a regulatory regime; and (5) blurring of the *structure* of the regulatory regime.[30] In sum, new governance blurs the boundaries between law and enforcement, and policy and implementation.

Perhaps most important to us in examining new governance theory in the context of post-disaster humanitarian aid are (1) the *roles* of regulatory actors, and (5) the *structure* of the regulatory regime. With respect to roles, new governance blurs the roles of state actors, the private sector and

[24] See ibid., at p. 374.

[25] See NeJaime (2009) *infra* note 97, pp. 338–341.

[26] Susan Sturm. (2006). Gender Equity Regimes and the Architecture of Learning. In Grainne de Burca and Joanne Scott (Eds.) *Law and New Governance in the EU and the US*. Oxford; Portland, OR: Hart Publishing, p. 323.

[27] See NeJaime (2009) *infra* note 97, pp. 346–347.

[28] Jason M. Solomon. (2010). New Governance, Preemptive Self-Regulation, and the Blurring of Boundaries in Regulatory Theory and Practice. *College of William and Mary Law School Faculty Publications. Paper* 680, 592–593.

[29] Ibid., p. 593.

[30] Ibid., p. 594.

third parties.[31] This may be through regulated entities' involvement in setting their own standards,[32] third parties may be involved in monitoring and enforcement, and state actors may serve as facilitators who oversee mechanisms for information pooling, rather than experts in administrative agencies as first envisaged.[33] The "private role in public governance" may even be second-order agreements implementing regulatory standards that in turn operate to change the actual standard required or expected in the future.[34]

With respect to structure, regulatory approaches are commonly characterized as either centralized or decentralized; new governance blurs the lines between these two.[35] Whereas new governance is commonly characterized as decentralized, the center plays an important role in pooling information and providing a backstop enforcement mechanism.[36]

Applications of New Governance

Recent studies of new governance have sought to track its potential application to diverse contexts including climate change.[37] By first understanding the key features of new governance: (1) collaboration, (2) deliberation, (3) experimentalism, (4) localism, (5) flexibility and adaptability, and (6) noncoerciveness[38] its prospects for wider application can be examined.

Collaboration and deliberation involve the active participation of multiple stakeholders and are often seen as the "core" principles of new governance.[39] The process is also characterized as experimentalist, "a recursive process of provisional goal-setting and revision based on learning from the comparison of alternative approaches to advancing them in different contexts."[40] Large-scale public problems such as climate change, in particular, benefit from local decision making.[41] This is because

[31] Ibid.

[32] Colin Scott. (2010). Standard-Setting in Regulatory Regimes. *The Oxford Handbook of Regulation* (R. Baldwin et al. (Eds.)), available at http://ssm.com/abstract = 1393647

[33] See Solomon (2010), *supra* note 28, p. 595.

[34] Michael P. Vandenbergh. (2005). The Private Life of Public Law. *Columbia Law Review*. 105, 2029.

[35] Solomon (2010), *supra* note 28, p. 597.

[36] Ibid.

[37] Jerome Van der Heijden. (2013). Looking Forwards and Sideways: Trajectories of New Governance Theory. *Amsterdam Law School Legal Studies*. Research Paper No. 2013-04, 3.

[38] Ibid., p. 4.

[39] Ibid., pp. 4–5.

[40] C. Sabel and J. Zeitlin. (2011). Experimentalist Governance. In D. Levi-Faur (Ed.), *The Oxford Handbook of Governance*. Oxford: Oxford University Press, pp. 169–185.

[41] See Van der Heijden (2013), *supra* note 37, p. 6.

experimentation, inclusion of local knowledge, and collaboration between stakeholders can take place more readily in the community context.[42]

Scholars working in political science, public administration and law have found useful insights from examining new governance mechanisms in practice. For political science scholars, new governance "pulls" non-state experience in the governing process and "establishes robust ongoing communication mechanisms" between state and non-state actors.[43] For public administration scholars, new governance offers distinctive "tools or instruments through which public purposes are served."[44] For law scholars, new governance offers the potential for a new form of decision making to supplement law and regulation.[45]

Regulatory Applications

Considering ways in which new governance may contribute to state regulation through public–private partnerships is an ongoing area of inquiry.[46] The challenge is to promote legitimate, effective and active participation in the work of regulation by the private parties themselves without devolving into deregulation.[47] New governance as a regulatory approach seems to be effective in various areas, for example, in environmental law, occupational safety and financial regulation.[48] Such regulatory areas can benefit from increased participation of non-state actors; public–private collaboration; diversity and competition within the market; decentralization; integration of policy domains; noncoerciveness ("soft law"); adaptability and constant learning; and coordination.[49]

Whether regulatory approaches work must be the focus of continual examination as many argue, since the answers are fundamentally empirical and change over time.[50] Increasingly, empirical evidence indicates that

[42] Ibid.

[43] C. Ford. (2008). New Governance, Compliance, and Principles-Based Securities Regulation. *American Business Law Journal.* 45(1), 1–60.

[44] See Salamon (2001), *supra* note 8, p. 1624.

[45] D. Trubek and L. Trubek. (2010). The World Turned Upside Down. *Wisconsin Law Review.* 719, 719–726.

[46] Orly Lobel. (2012). New Governance as Regulatory Governance. *University of San Diego Legal Studies Research Paper Series.* Research Paper No. 12–101 (November), 3.

[47] Ibid.

[48] Ibid., pp. 3–4.

[49] Orly Lobel. (2004). The Renew Deal: The Fall of Regulation and the Rise in Governance in Contemporary Legal Thought. *Minnesota Law Review* 89, 342–470.

[50] See Lobel (2012), *supra* note 46, p. 6.

in most contexts, institutional culture and design have a significant impact on action.[51] Enforcement and monitoring alongside initial standard setting and rule revision are necessary in order to set the stage for private participation in regulatory governance.[52]

Scholars have found that in a cooperative regime, the role of the government changes from regulator and controller to facilitator, and law becomes a problem-solving process rather than an ordering activity.[53] Instead of focusing on substantive prohibitions and adversarial enforcement, new governance approaches attempt to involve private parties in the legal process – the government largely facilitates self-regulation and programs of collaborative, semi-voluntary compliance.[54] Fruitful scholarship is emerging in the related area of examining the reach of a decision maker's jurisdiction in the context of overlapping regimes.[55]

The mechanism of new governance is that government agencies foster a culture of compliance by offering practical and reputational rewards (such as safe havens, variance accommodation and public certification for responsible practices), as well as consultation and assistance, in exchange for effective self-regulation from the private actors in the regulated industries.[56] These regulations are established as norms rather than rigid rules, and may require actors to give reasons or set their own reflexive processes, and preventative measures such as training, data collection and continuing education.[57] As a result, rather than a rigid top-down regime, new governance creates a relational contract between government and industry that in turn supports the generation of private norms.[58]

Applications of New Governance Approaches in the Humanitarian Context

Looking specifically at the applications of new governance approaches to the post-disaster humanitarian aid context, scholars have begun to

[51] Ibid.

[52] Ibid., p. 7.

[53] See Lobel (2004), *supra* note 49.

[54] See Lobel (2012), *supra* note 46, p. 10.

[55] See Robert B. Ahdieh. (2007). From Federalism to Intersystemic Governance: The Changing Nature of Modern Jurisdiction. *Emory Law Journal*. 57(1); Emory Law and Economics Research Paper No. 08-30. Available at SSRN: http://ssrn.com/abstract=1121417.

[56] Lobel (2012), *supra* note 46, pp. 10–11.

[57] Ibid., p. 11.

[58] R. McMaster and J. W. Sawkins. (1996). The Contract State, Trust Distortion, and Efficiency. *Review of Social Economy*. 54, 145, 149–156.

examine the "Cluster Approach," which is the UN's latest effort to impose order on the increasingly unwieldy environment of large-scale humanitarian catastrophes, especially since the 2004 Indian Ocean Tsunami and the crisis in Darfur.[59] The key innovation of the Cluster Approach was the assignment of a "lead agency" for each sector, which "is responsible for mapping needs, planning, monitoring, coordination and reporting. It acts as the first port of call and provider of last resort."[60] The Cluster Approach works at two levels: global and national.[61] Global-level clusters are standing bodies where lead agencies coordinate standard setting, dissemination of best practices and capacity building among responders.[62] Country-level clusters are assembled as needed when disaster strikes, and lead agencies are tasked with ensuring "adequate coordination mechanisms . . . adequate preparedness, as well as adequate strategic planning."[63] Country clusters are often subdivided by geographic scale, establishing national-level clusters in the capital and subnational clusters at the provincial or local level.[64]

The "lead agency" of a local cluster is determined by the UN official overseeing operations (the "Humanitarian Coordinator"), and it is not necessarily, though preferably, the same as lead agencies at the global level.[65] Clusters are activated in all "major emergencies" and should be chosen on the basis of "existing operations and capacities" within forty-eight hours.[66] Clusters are responsible for coordinating with key partners and ensuring that "cross-cutting issues," such as gender, are properly taken into account.[67]

59 Jan Egeland. (2005). Towards a Stronger Humanitarian Response System. *Forced Migration Review*. 24 (IDP Supplement), 4.

60 Ibid.

61 Inter-Agency Standing Committee (IASC). (2006, November 24). *Guidance Note on Using the Cluster Approach to Strengthen Humanitarian Response*, 2.

62 Ibid., pp. 2–4.

63 Ibid., p. 10.

64 IASC. (2010). *Handbook for RCS and HCS on Emergency Preparedness and Response*. Geneva: IASC. 35. Available at: http://eird.org/publicaciones/Handbook.pdf

65 See IASC (2006), *supra* note 61, pp. 11–13.

66 IASC provides for a six-step standard operating procedure for designating cluster leads: (1) consultations with local government, UN agencies, NGOs and other IOs to determine capacities, leaders, cross-cutting issues and needed OCHA support; (2) proposal is drafted by the humanitarian coordinator and forwarded to New York; (3) the OCHA head reviews the proposal with the members of IASC; (4) the OCHA head ensures that IASC agrees at the global level; (5) OCHA informs the in-country coordinator of its decision; (6) the coordinator informs local government and country-level partners. IASC Task Team. (2007, May). *Operational Guidance on Designating Sector/Cluster Leads in Major New Emergencies*, 2, Geneva.

67 Ibid., p. 8.

Standardizing versus Diversification

The framework for accountability established by the Cluster Approach, scholars have suggested, has led in some cases to a breakdown in the relationship with the central leadership (UN Office for the Coordination of Humanitarian Affairs (OCHA)), resulting in actors feeling less accountable to the Humanitarian Coordinator.[68] This delegation of power by the UN to certain cluster leaders is said to give rise to two potential problems. First, given the significant influence of cluster leaders over decisions regarding policy and funding, there is a greater tendency for policy to move toward uniformity rather than allowing for experimentation and competition.[69] This standardization in the cluster system is criticized for giving too much power to certain groups that are backed by powerful donors, thereby possibly channeling resources and funds to further the political goals of such donors, thus potentially risking the neutrality of humanitarian actors and frustrating access.[70]

Similarly, by selecting a "lead agency" to manage the response in each sector, the Cluster Approach exercises a form of institutional choice that magnifies the power of a particular agency and brings its unique practices and principles to bear on an affected population.[71] The lead agency has considerable power in choosing which actors will be involved in the humanitarian efforts (and hence how funds should be distributed and which affected groups to attend to), and this clearly gives rise to questions of accountability and legitimacy.[72]

Accountability and Supervision in UN Humanitarian Assistance

In response to questions regarding accountability and legitimacy, actors within the cluster system have begun to emphasize "peer review" and "horizontal accountability" as alternatives to a formal supervisory structure.[73] On paper, under the formal structure, the in-country Humanitarian Coordinator, a UN official, appoints and has the power to fire the cluster "lead agencies"; this Humanitarian Coordinator is in turn supervised by the head of OCHA in New York, who may hire and fire the in-country

[68] Ibid., p. 9.
[69] Ibid., p. 10.
[70] Ibid., pp. 11–12.
[71] Ibid., p. 13.
[72] Ibid., pp. 14–16.
[73] Ibid., p. 18.

coordinator.[74] While such a system may be effective in certain areas such as service delivery, additional thought must be given to maintaining experimentation and oversight of operations.[75]

Given that an ongoing challenge of the cluster system has been accountability to the Humanitarian Coordinator,[76] increasingly the oversight structure is moving toward a system of "peer review." This peer review system has been adopted to differing extents – ranging from informal "lessons learned" and review of funding proposals, to more structured standards for assessment and submission of recommendations to the next higher level in the structure.[77] Scholars have suggested that "peer review" provides the seeds for an alternative model of accountability in the cluster system, one based on the concept of "experimentalist" governance.[78]

By experimentalism, scholars refer to a range of regulatory techniques that seek alternatives both to command-and-control regulation and to the "minimalism" of deregulatory approaches.[79] Experimentalism is often considered as part of an array of "new governance" techniques.[80] These strategies grant broad discretion to local-level actors to pursue certain goals, with very little steering from the top down.[81] Some form of "peer review" is necessary to get this process going. The price of broad delegation and discretion to innovate is ongoing reporting and monitoring.[82]

As a result, in certain areas, such as the Democratic Republic of Congo and Myanmar, where direct accountability is often difficult given limited access to local contacts, a peer review approach has been recommended.[83] In turn, scholars have outlined some of the factors that have contributed

[74] Ibid., p. 20.

[75] Ibid., p. 21.

[76] Julie Steets et al. (2010). *Cluster Approach Evaluation 2:* Synthesis Report 24.

[77] See Heath (2012). Accountability in the United Nations Humanitarian System: The Consequences of Institutional Choice in Disaster Response, 24. Paper presented at ASIL 2012 Midyear Meeting (2012, October 20–21).

[78] Ibid.

[79] For the origins of the concept, see Michael C. Dorf and Charles F. Sabel. (1998). A Constitution of Democratic Experimentalism. *Columbia Law Review*. 98, 267.

[80] See Heath (2012), *supra* note 77, p. 25. See also Charles F. Sabel and William H. Simon. (2011). Minimalism and Experimentalism in the Administrative State. *Georgetown Law Journal*. 100, 53; Gráinne de Búrca. (2010). New Governance and Experimentalism: An Introduction. *Wisconsin Law Review*. 227.

[81] See Dorf and Sabel (1998), *supra* note 79, p. 322.

[82] Ibid., p. 288.

[83] See Heath (2012), *supra* note 77, p. 26.

to effective monitoring and inclusion. They include: active and clear rule making and reflexivity of policy making.[84]

A careful balance between experimental locally directed action and centralized monitoring and oversight is desirable.[85] Originally, the "cluster lead" was given a wide-ranging portfolio of responsibilities, including ensuring adherence to global norms and standards and participation of key actors, and addressing "cross-cutting issues."[86] In turn, the Humanitarian Coordinator was to ensure the lead agency's fulfillment of these responsibilities, a task then overseen by OCHA.[87] In effect, the Cluster Approach advocates for the balance of having a "supervisory authority in a decentralized system"; however, scholars note that this ideal is probably far more attainable in some sectors than others.[88] There is a need to find a better balance to overcome the tension between coordination and autonomy – and experimentalism, some suggest, may provide us with guidance.[89] Scholars suggest that the system of peer review and experimentalism does not represent a transfer of power from states to international and nongovernmental organizations, but a technical improvement that incorporates, rather than solves, the tension between coordination and autonomy.[90]

Strengths and Shortcomings of New Governance

In the ideal context, new governance[91] gives rise to ownership, responsibility and follow-through by stakeholders given that solutions are derived from community input.[92] Deliberation on the part of diverse participants, some argue, yields wiser results;[93] and collaboration in many cases may give rise to higher levels of transparency and accountability.[94]

On the other hand, potential shortcomings of new governance include inequality arising from power imbalance,[95] and limited accountability and

[84] Ibid., pp. 27–30.
[85] Ibid., p. 35.
[86] Ibid.
[87] Ibid.
[88] Ibid., p. 36.
[89] Ibid.
[90] Ibid., p. 37.
[91] For example, see Sabel and Zeitlin (2011), *supra* note 40.
[92] See Van der Heijden (2013), *supra* note 37, p. 9.
[93] B. S. Noveck. (2011). The Single Point of Failure. In S. Van der Hof and M. Groothuis (Eds.), *Innovating Government*. The Hague: Asserr Press, pp. 77–99.
[94] See Van der Heijden (2013), *supra* note 37, p. 10.
[95] See Noveck (2011), *supra* note 93.

legitimacy absent state oversight.[96] Some have suggested that the voices of stakeholders with limited access to resources are unlikely to be heard, resulting in a potentially elitist rather than democratic process.[97] Some have suggested that in order to benefit from privatization, devolution, decentralization, public–private partnerships, potential for distributive justice and stakeholder collaboration,[98] the necessary conditions include (1) the broadest possible degree of stakeholder participation compatible with effective decision making, and (2) effective and informed monitoring.[99]

New governance approaches aim to bring together insights from various interdisciplinary research in light of rapidly changing demands in a new global economy.[100] Additional research must be conducted in order to achieve a sophisticated analysis and a deep understanding of the comparative advantages of private and public action in solving social problems.[101] Challenging traditional regulatory regimes with top-down legal rules at one end of the spectrum, with market-based approaches at the other end, new governance aims to strike a balance between the two.[102] In this process, multiple governance possibilities can be continually explored; including standard setting, implementation, enforcement and governmental interaction with regulated parties to bring about more effective and legitimate governance.[103] Many scholars believe that in order to arrive at a clearer understanding of the strengths and limitations of new governance approaches, more rigorous empirical work examining the successes and failures of new governance and, the interaction between the individual, state, law and policy must be conducted.[104]

Recent work has begun to call for specific examination of the applications of new governance approaches in the context of post-disaster

[96] Solomon (2008) supra note 1.

[97] For example, G. De Burca. (2010). New Governance and Experimentalism: An Introduction. *Wisconsin Law Review*. 227, 227–238; and D. NeJaime (2009). When New Governance Fails. *Ohio State Law Journal*. 70(2), 323–399.

[98] Lisa T. Alexander. (2010). Reflections on Success and Failure in New Governance and the Role of the Lawyer. *Wisconsin Law Review Symposium Afterword*. 737, 738.

[99] Ibid., pp. 740–741; see also S. Ali. 2010. Measuring Success in Devolved Collaboration. *Journal of Land Use and Environmental Law*. 26 (Fall), 93–112.

[100] See Ali (2010), *supra* note 99, 93–112.

[101] Ibid.

[102] Ibid.

[103] Ibid.

[104] See Van der Heijden (2013), *supra* note 37, pp. 20–22.

humanitarian aid. Specifically, recent work has examined how institutions and policies affect environmentally induced migration, and gaps in current governance frameworks for rapid- and slow-onset environmental change.[105] Existing strategies of humanitarian relief will help some people fleeing from rapid-onset disasters. However, the analysis suggests that new governance modes are needed to bridge gaps in protection and assistance for climate change migrants who cannot return after disasters, and people made mobile because of longer-term environmental change.[106] These new modes of governance must take into account dynamic social and migrant networks, and enhance resilience in flexible rather than control-based ways.[107]

Assessment in Light of the Research Objectives

New governance principles are wide reaching. Rooted in administrative and regulatory projects, scholars have applied such insights in an array of substantive domains – including occupational safety, environmental regulation, corporate governance, community lawyering, constitutionalism, education and health care.[108]

In particular, insights from new governance literature will assist in assessing the strengths and challenges of the three typologies of humanitarian assistance to be examined in the chapters that follow. The literature described earlier provides useful insights into the contribution of new governance to expanded participation and partnership on the part of governments and non-state actors in solving public problems;[109] a learning-focused orientation;[110] the use of public–private partnership in regulatory reform;[111] the role of the state as a convener, catalyst and coordinator;[112] and the relationship between new governance and development of problem-solving capabilities.[113] This form of decision making has largely responded to a growing dissatisfaction with the inefficiencies of

[105] Koko Warner. (2013). Assessing Institutional and Governance Needs Related to Environmental Change and Human Migration (Funded by the German Marshall Fund, United States). Available at: www.ehs.unu.edu/file/get/5301.

[106] Ibid.

[107] Ibid.

[108] See NeJaime (2009), *supra* note 97, pp. 338–341.

[109] See Lobel (2004) and Solomon (2008), *supra* note 1.

[110] See Solomon (2008) and Cohen (2008), *supra* note 3.

[111] See Alexander (2009), *supra* note 4, p. 117.

[112] See Dorf and Sabel (1998), Solomon (2008) and Cohen (2008), *supra* note 5.

[113] Cohen (2008), *supra* note 5.

rigid "top-down" decision-making styles. In addition, recent scholarship has examined the challenges facing new governance, including ensuring participants have the necessary skills,[114] the development of managerial and procedural safeguards,[115] the difficulties of achieving stakeholder participation under conditions of social conflict[116] and distributional inequalities.[117]

While the applications of new governance theory are wide ranging, scholars have argued[118] that much more analysis on an "on the ground" basis must be conducted – and this necessarily includes examples of both success and failure.[119] This would include the need for greater on-the-ground examination of local global post-disaster response mechanisms as will be discussed in the chapters that follow.

[114] Ibid.
[115] See Salamon (2001), *supra* note 8, p. 1611.
[116] See Alexander (2009), *supra* note 4.
[117] Ibid.
[118] See Sturm (2006), *supra* note 26.
[119] See NeJaime (2009), *supra* note 97, pp. 346–347.

2

Legal Background: Post-disaster Humanitarian Aid Law and Policy

Introduction

Building on an assessment of new governance literature, this chapter provides background on the legal and policy foundations of post-disaster humanitarian aid. It examines challenges regarding the implementation of humanitarian legal obligations, principles regulating humanitarian aid, new humanitarianism, collaboration with local stakeholders and how globalization impacts the practice of humanitarian policy. This chapter also touches on the delicate interface between humanitarian aid and the theory of humanitarian intervention. This legal background provides a regulatory basis for the examination of the three typologies of networked post-disaster humanitarian assistance programs that will be examined in the chapters that follow.

Meaning of Humanitarian Aid

The term "humanitarian" is used in relation to a variety of actions that are humane and positive in nature.[1] According to the Austrian Development Cooperation, the objective of humanitarian assistance is "to protect life, reduce suffering and safeguard the human dignity of the persons affected during and after a humanitarian crisis" and is premised on the "principles of humanity, impartiality, neutrality and independence."[2] Consisting of both short-term and long-term measures, it includes disaster prevention, rehabilitation and reconstruction relief efforts.[3] The concept of humanitarian assistance during war was conceived through the experiences and

[1] B. S. Chimni. (2000). Globalization, Humanitarianism and the Erosion of Refugee Protection. *Journal of Refugee Studies*. 13(3), 243–263, 244.

[2] Austrian Development Cooperation. (2009). International Humanitarian Aid Policy Document. (Vienna). 8 www.entwicklung.at/uploads/media/PD_International_humanitarian_aid_03.pdf (accessed on April 18, 2013).

[3] Ibid.

actions of Jean Henri Dunant during the battle of Solferino in 1859.[4] After witnessing thousands of injured soldiers suffering in agony and dying due to lack of care, "the wealthy Genevan sent for medical supplies, enlisted local women and set about tending to the wounded."[5] Dunant and his associates would, some years later, institutionalize the concept of humanitarian assistance through the International Committee of the Red Cross (ICRC).[6]

Legal and Policy Issues in Humanitarian Aid

This chapter will examine the legal and policy issues surrounding the provision of humanitarian aid. Traditionally, the concept of "humanitarian aid" in the legal context has referred to short-term assistance by relief organizations during or following armed conflict. However, in recent years, within the international community and among intergovernmental and nongovernmental organizations, the term has broadened to include support for human welfare including disaster prevention, rehabilitation and reconstruction. According to the Financial Tracking Service (FTS), which is managed by the United Nations Office for Coordination of Humanitarian Affairs (OCHA), "humanitarian aid" is broadly defined as "an intervention to help people who are victims of a natural disaster or conflict meet their basic needs and rights."[7] Beyond this, the phrases "humanitarian aid," "humanitarian relief" and "humanitarian assistance" are often used interchangeably. As the Joint Inspection Unit of the United Nations noted, while "life-saving" is a central concept of humanitarian operations, an operational definition of humanitarian assistance or humanitarian operations is lacking.[8]

The ICRC defines "humanitarian" as including everything from emergency relief to disaster preparedness, early recovery, capacity building, judicial action, restoring the rule of law and institutional reconstruction. It also acknowledges that humanitarian action has moved beyond

[4] Fiona Fox. (2001). New Humanitarianism: Does It Provide a Moral Banner for the 21st Century? *Disasters*. 25(4), 275–289, 276.

[5] Ibid.

[6] Ibid.

[7] www.un.org/partnerships/Docs/FTS_Haiti.doc (accessed on April 23, 2014).

[8] Tdanori Inomata. (2012). *Financing for Humanitarian Operations in the United Nations System*. Geneva: United Nations, JIU/REP/2012/11, 133. www.unjiu.org/en/reports-notes/JIU%20Products/JIU_REP_2012_11_English.pdf (accessed on April 23, 2014).

immediate response and has now placed more emphasis on the causes and consequences of crises.[9]

In the sections that follow, this chapter will examine the legal basis for regulation of humanitarian aid, challenges in implementation of aid policy, principles of humanitarian aid provision, the interrelationship between humanitarian aid and humanitarian intervention and public participation in humanitarian response.

Legal Basis and Regulation of Humanitarian Aid

Various legal regimes, such as norms and laws established under international human rights law and refugee law, are part of the legal framework that regulate humanitarian aid.[10] Consequently, one can identify the legal regime that governs humanitarian aid only by examining "the norms and practice under various branches of international law" as there is no such thing as an international law of humanitarian assistance."[11] First, with regard to the relevant international human rights framework, it imposes responsibilities on state parties to the relevant instruments "to respect, protect and fulfill the rights of those within their territory or subject to their jurisdiction."[12]

While the right to life (as articulated in relevant international human rights instruments) creates minimal rights for individuals to access humanitarian assistance, "economic and social rights create the legal space for individuals to demand the full range of humanitarian aid."[13] For

[9] "Strengthening of the coordination of humanitarian and disaster relief assistance of the United Nations, including special economic assistance," United Nations, General Assembly, 67th session, Plenary, Iteam70(a) of the agenda, statement by the ICRC, New York, December 13, 2012. www.icrc.org/eng/resources/documents/statement/2012/12-13-united-nations-humanitarian-coordination.htm (accessed on April 23, 2014). Similar to the United Nations, while the phrases "humanitarian aid," "humanitarian relief" and "humanitarian assistance" are used by the ICRC, it appears that the terms are not defined.

[10] Guglielmo Verdirame. (2001). Testing the Effectiveness of International Norms: UN Humanitarian Assistance and Sexual Apartheid in Afghanistan. *Human Rights Quarterly*. 23(3), 733–768, 741. See also Rebecca Barber. (2009). Facilitating Humanitarian Assistance in International Humanitarian and Human Rights Law. *International Review of the Red Cross*. 91(874), 371–397, 381; for additional discussion, please see also S. Ali and T. Kabau. (2014). Self Governance by Humanitarian Non-state Actors in Health and Nutrition Relief. *DePaul Journal of Health Law*. 16(2), 141–164.

[11] Verdirame (2001), *supra* note 10.

[12] Barber (2009), *supra* note 10.

[13] J. Benton Heath. (2011). Disasters, Relief, and Neglect: The Duty to Accept Humanitarian Assistance and the Work of the International Law Commission. *International Law and Politics*. 43, 419–477, 439.

instance, Article 11(1) of the 1966 International Covenant on Economic, Social and Cultural Rights recognizes the rights of individuals "to an adequate standard of living ... including adequate food, clothing and housing, and to the continuous improvement of living conditions."[14] Article 11(1) of the Covenant also obligates state parties to adopt appropriate measures to facilitate realization of the right, while appreciating "the essential importance of international cooperation based on free consent."[15] Further, Article 11(2) provides that state parties, "recognizing the fundamental right of everyone to be free from hunger, shall take, individually and through international co-operation, the measures, including specific programmes, which are needed."[16] In addition, Article 12 of the Covenant provides that the state parties "recognize the right of everyone to the enjoyment of the highest attainable standard of physical and mental health."[17]

According to Paragraph 19 of the General Comment 12 on the Right to Adequate Food under Article 11 of the International Covenant on Economic, Social and Cultural Rights, violation of the right to food by states can occur through activities that amount to "the prevention of access to humanitarian food aid in internal conflicts or other emergency situations."[18] "Therefore, there is an obligation upon a state to consent to the provision of food aid to its citizens."[19] Paragraph 38 of General Comment 12 also emphasizes that "[s]tates have a joint and individual responsibility, in accordance with the Charter of the United Nations, to cooperate in providing disaster relief and humanitarian assistance in times of emergency, including assistance to refugees and internally displaced persons depending on their ability."[20]

Important sources of international humanitarian law include the "1949 Geneva Conventions and their 1977 and 2005 Additional Protocols."[21] In

14 International Covenant on Economic, Social and Cultural Rights (adopted December 16, 1966, entered into force January 3, 1976) 993 UNTS 3.

15 Ibid.

16 Ibid.

17 Ibid.

18 Committee on Economic, Social and Cultural Rights. (1999, April 26–May 14). Substantive Issues Arising in the Implementation of the International Covenant on Economic, Social and Cultural Rights: General Comment 12; the Right to Adequate Food. E/C.12/1999/5 (Geneva).

19 Heath (2011), *supra* note 13.

20 Committee on Economic, Social and Cultural Rights (1999), *supra* note 18.

21 Leonard Blazeby and David Fisher. (2010). Promoting International Humanitarian Law and International Disaster Response Laws, Rules and Principles within the Commonwealth, *Commonwealth Law Bulletin*. 36(4), 709–715, 709. See Geneva Convention for the Amelioration of the Condition of the Wounded and Sick in Armed Forces in the Field (First

addition, failure to consent to humanitarian assistance where it could lead to "starvation or otherwise threaten the survival of a civilian population" could amount to a violation of customary international law as opined in a 2005 study on customary rules by the International Committee of the Red Cross.[22] In addition, novel work has begun to examine principles of humanitarian intervention from the perspective of fundamental ethical principles in international law and world religions.[23]

Third, there is also a specific convention that regulates the implementation of humanitarian relief efforts with respect to food aid in the form of the Food Assistance Convention of 2012.[24] The Convention entered into force on January 1, 2013, after ratifications by the United States, Austria, Canada, Switzerland, Denmark, the European Union, Japan and Finland.[25] The Convention generally:

> expands the traditional focus of previous Food Aid Conventions and now includes all forms of food assistance that will protect and improve access to food for those most in need. The new Convention includes a new commitment structure, a broader toolbox of eligible activities and food assistance products, as well as a commitment to improved transparency and accountability.[26]

Article 1 of the Food Assistance Convention outlines the objectives of the Convention "addressing the food and nutritional needs of the most vulnerable populations through . . . food assistance" and "ensuring that food

Geneva Convention) (adopted August 12,1949) 75 UNTS 31; Geneva Convention for the Amelioration of the Condition of Wounded, Sick and Shipwrecked Members of Armed Forces at Sea (Second Geneva Convention) (adopted August 12, 1949) 75 UNTS 85; Geneva Convention Relative to the Treatment of Prisoners of War (Third Geneva Convention) (adopted August 12, 1949) 75 UNTS 135; Geneva Convention Relative to the Protection of Civilian Persons in Time of War (Fourth Geneva Convention) (adopted August 12, 1949) 75 UNTS 287; Protocol Additional to the Geneva Conventions of August 12, 1949, and Relating to the Protection of Victims of International Armed Conflicts (Protocol I) (adopted June 8, 1977) 1125 UNTS 3; Protocol Additional to the Geneva Conventions of August 12, 1949, and relating to the Protection of Victims of Non-international Armed Conflicts (Protocol II) (adopted June 8, 1977) 1125 UNTS 609.

22 Barber (2009), *supra* note 10.

23 See Brian D. Lepard. (2003). *Rethinking Humanitarian Intervention: A Fresh Legal Approach Based on Fundamental Ethical Principles in International Law and World Religions.* University Park: Penn sylvania State University Press.

24 Food Assistance Convention. "About FAC." www.foodassistanceconvention.org/en/about_fac/about.aspx (accessed on May 10, 2013).

25 Ibid.

26 Ibid.

assistance provided to the most vulnerable populations is appropriate, timely, effective, efficient, and based on needs and shared principles."[27]

Fourth, based on its powers and mandate under Articles 24 and 25, and Chapter VII of the United Nations Charter, the Security Council of the United Nations can authorize both forceful and nonforceful intervention within a state, which may include the provision of humanitarian assistance. For instance, in Resolution 794 of 1992, the Security Council determined that the humanitarian catastrophe in Somalia constituted a threat to international peace and security, partly due to the obstruction of the delivery of humanitarian aid.[28] The Security Council, therefore, proceeded to cite its powers under Chapter VII of the UN Charter while authorizing member states to use "all necessary means" to establish a safe environment for the delivery of humanitarian aid.[29]

Fifth, United Nations General Assembly Resolutions and activities provide "soft" law with respect to the provision of humanitarian aid, which may eventually evolve into proper customary international law. As the International Court of Justice (ICJ) has previously observed, rules of customary international law are formed through state practice and *opinio juris*.[30] Some have noted that General Assembly resolutions are an important component of state practice.[31] In 1998, the General Assembly adopted the Guiding Principles on Internal Displacement,[32] which, although not explicitly binding upon states, are a significant source of "soft" law on the issue of internally displaced persons and may contribute to the evolution of customary international law on the matter. Principle 25(1) emphasizes that the "primary duty and responsibility for providing humanitarian assistance to internally displaced persons lies with national authorities."

[27] Food Assistance Convention (adopted April 25, 2012, entered into force January 1, 2013). www.foodassistanceconvention.org/convention/FoodAssistance.pdf (accessed on May 11, 2013).

[28] UNSC Res 794 (December 3,1992) UN Doc S/RES/794.

[29] Ibid.

[30] See *Military and Paramilitary Activities in and against Nicaragua* (*Nicaragua v United States of America*) (Merits) [1986] ICJ Rep 14 paragraph 207; *North Sea Continental Shelf* (*Federal Republic of Germany v Denmark; Federal Republic of Germany v Netherlands*) (Judgment) [1969] ICJ Rep 3 paragraph 77.

[31] Rosalyn Higgins. (1986). The Attitude of Western States towards Legal Aspects of the Use of Force. In A. Cassese (Ed.), *The Current Legal Regulation of the Use of Force*. Dordrecht: Martinus Nijhoff Publishers, p. 435.

[32] United Nations General Assembly. "Guiding Principles on Internal Displacement." UN Doc E/CN.4/1998/53/Add.2 (1998).

Establishing a basis for humanitarian action by external actors, Principle 25(2) states that:

> International humanitarian organizations and other appropriate actors have the right to offer their services in support of the internally displaced. Such an offer shall not be regarded as an unfriendly act or an interference in a State's internal affairs and shall be considered in good faith. Consent thereto shall not be arbitrarily withheld, particularly when authorities concerned are unable or unwilling to provide the required humanitarian assistance.[33]

In addition, Principle 25(3) requires states to "grant and facilitate the free passage of humanitarian assistance and grant persons engaged in the provision of such assistance rapid and unimpeded access to the internally displaced."[34] Further, Principle 26 proscribes attacks or acts of violence aimed at persons involved in the provision of humanitarian aid, and specifically obligates states to respect and protect them, including their means of transport and supplies.[35]

In order to ensure effective implementations of its legal and policy mandate on humanitarian assistance, the UN has established specialized agencies and institutions within its Secretariat. For instance, the United Nations Office for Disaster Risk Reduction (UNISDR) is an important institution within the United Nations Secretariat.[36] It was established in December 1999 in order to facilitate effective implementation of the International Strategy for Disaster Reduction.[37]

Even the International Court of Justice in the 1986 *Nicaragua* case stated that the provision of humanitarian aid to address and curb humanitarian suffering, and if done without discrimination, cannot be deemed to constitute an intervention in the domestic affairs of a state.[38] In the judgment, the Court essentially balanced the necessity of protecting the sovereignty of states with that of safeguarding the interests of victims of humanitarian catastrophes to receive assistance.[39] The ICJ specifically stated that:

> An essential feature of truly humanitarian aid is that it is given "without discrimination" of any kind. In the view of the Court, if the provision of

[33] Ibid.

[34] Ibid.

[35] Ibid.

[36] United Nations Office for Disaster Risk Reduction. "UNISDR in the UN System." www.unisdr.org/who-we-are/unisdr-in-un (accessed on April 10, 2013).

[37] United Nations Office for Disaster Risk Reduction. "Who We Are." www.unisdr.org/who-we-are (accessed on April 10, 2013).

[38] *Military and Paramilitary Activities in and against Nicaragua* (1986), *supra* note 30, paragraph 243.

[39] Verdirame (2001), *supra* note 10, p. 743.

> "humanitarian assistance" is to escape condemnation as an intervention in the internal affairs of Nicaragua, not only must it be limited to the purposes hallowed in the practice of the Red Cross, namely "to prevent and alleviate human suffering," and "to protect life and health and to ensure respect for the human being"; it must also, and above all, be given without discrimination to all in need.[40]

Seventh, there is an obligation incumbent upon states to cooperate in order to achieve social and economic progress. Under Article 56 of the United Nations Charter, member states "pledge themselves to take joint and separate action in cooperation" with the UN in order to facilitate the achievement of economic and social concerns as outlined in Article 54, which include solutions to post-disaster issues. International cooperation, as articulated in the UN Charter, seems to require that the principles of sovereignty and nonintervention be interpreted in the context of the duty to cooperate for purposes of human rights[41] and the achievement of solutions to economic and social predicaments.

Eighth, various participants and actors in the humanitarian assistance domain have created important standards and guidelines, which, although not legally binding, have moral and ethical significance. For instance, the Humanitarian Charter and Minimum Standards in Humanitarian Response, adopted under the auspices of the Sphere Project, is an important guide for qualitative and effective administration of humanitarian assistance by the relevant agencies.[42] The Sphere Project:

> was initiated in 1997 by a group of humanitarian non-governmental organisations (NGOs) and the International Red Cross and Red Crescent Movement. Their aim was to improve the quality of their actions during disaster response and to be held accountable for them. They based Sphere's philosophy on two core beliefs: first, that those affected by disaster or conflict have a right to life with dignity and, therefore, a right to assistance; and second, that all possible steps should be taken to alleviate human suffering arising out of disaster or conflict.[43]

40 *Military and Paramilitary Activities in and against Nicaragua* (1986), *supra* note 30.

41 Heath (2011), *supra* note 13, p. 441.

42 See, Sphere Project, *Humanitarian Charter and Minimum Standards in Humanitarian Response* (3rd edn. Sphere Project 2011) 4 www.sphereproject.org/resources/download-publications/?search=1&keywords=&language=English&category=22 (accessed on May 10, 2013).

43 Ibid.; for additional discussion, please see S. Ali and T. Kabau. (2014). Non-state Actors and the Evolution of Humanitarian Norms: Implications of the Sphere Charter in Health and Nutrition Relief. *Journal of International Humanitarian Legal Studies*. 5(1), 70–104. Brill/Nijhoff.

The Sphere Project reflects an attempt by various actors in the humanitarian aid domain to "establish universal minimum standards, key criteria and benchmarks for the purpose of ensuring quality and accountability" in humanitarian assistance activities.[44] The Sphere Project's Humanitarian Charter is premised on "the principle of humanity" and the existing legal framework on humanitarian assistance such as "the rights to protection and assistance reflected in the provisions of international humanitarian law, human rights and refugee law."[45] However, one of the challenges to the effective implementation of the Humanitarian Charter is the attempt to "apply a uniform set of standards" even in radically different situations and circumstances.[46] In some cases, some of the guidelines negotiated under the auspices of international NGOs and civil societies may be adopted by the General Assembly and, therefore, acquire the beneficial authority of a "soft" law, and the capacity to be taken into account as part of state practice in the analysis of emerging international customary law. For instance, in Resolutions 63/139, 63/141 and 63/137 of 2008, the General Assembly adopted the Guidelines for the Domestic Facilitation and Regulation of International Disaster Relief and Initial Recovery Assistance (the "IDRL Guidelines"), which were negotiated under the auspices of the International Federation of Red Cross and Red Crescent Societies (IFRC).[47] The IDRL Guidelines are aimed at assisting governments to provide timely and quality humanitarian aid in addition to addressing common legal challenges in international relief efforts.[48]

Ninth, some regions have local legal mechanisms that clarify or enhance the obligation to either provide or consent to humanitarian assistance, including regulations for such action. One of the most advanced mechanisms is the European regional mechanism for humanitarian assistance. The most important legal framework within the European Union is the 2007 Treaty of Lisbon, which amended the Treaty on the European Union and the Treaty Establishing the European Community.[49] Article

[44] Max R. O'Donnell, Dimitri Bacos and Michael L. Bennish. (2002). Nutritional Response to the 1998 Bangladesh Flood Disaster: Sphere Minimum Standards in Disaster Response. *Disasters*. 26(3), 229–241, 231–232.

[45] Sphere Project (2011), *supra* note 42, 21.

[46] O'Donnell, Bacos and Bennish (2002), *supra* note 44, pp. 238–239.

[47] International Federation of Red Cross and Red Crescent Societies (IFRC). "IDRL Guidelines." www.ifrc.org/en/what-we-do/idrl/idrl-guidelines/ (accessed on May 10, 2013).

[48] Ibid.

[49] Treaty of Lisbon amending the Treaty on European Union and the Treaty Establishing the European Community (adopted December 13, 2007). *Official Journal of the European Union*, C 306. 50, December 17, 2007.

214(1) of the Lisbon Treaty provides that the EU's humanitarian assistance especially to third states "shall be conducted within the framework of the principles and objectives of the external action of the Union."[50] Article 214(2) of the Treaty reaffirms the traditional principles governing the provision of humanitarian assistance.[51] It states that humanitarian relief by the Union "shall be conducted in compliance with the principles of international law and with the principles of impartiality, neutrality and non-discrimination."[52] Under Article 214(3), the European Parliament and the Council are granted the mandate to develop regulations through which the EU's humanitarian assistance operations may be implemented.[53] Article 214(5) envisages the establishment of the European Voluntary Humanitarian Aid Corps in order to enhance the participation of young Europeans in the EU's humanitarian operations.[54] Another significant provision is Article 214(7), which obligates the EU to "ensure that its humanitarian aid operations are coordinated and consistent with those of international organisations and bodies, in particular those forming part of the United Nations system."[55] An elaborate regional mechanism is important due to the fact that as of 2012 the EU together with its member states was the world's leading provider of humanitarian assistance, providing an approximated 45 percent of global humanitarian aid.[56]

From the foregoing discussion on the international legal and policy basis for humanitarian assistance, it is clear that a unified and coherent legal regime is lacking to define the rules and principles of humanitarian aid including in the post-disaster context. As Guglielmo Verdirame concisely observes:

> The vast majority of humanitarian emergencies are, in contrast, characterized by elements that could warrant at least a partial recourse to more than one of these regimes. In addition, there is a degree of conceptual fluidity with notions, categories, and principles moving across these legal regimes, often accompanied by a process of partial re-definition and contextual adaptation.[57]

[50] Ibid.
[51] Ibid.
[52] Ibid.
[53] Ibid.
[54] Ibid.
[55] Ibid.
[56] European Commission. "The Union's Humanitarian Aid: Fit for Purpose? Stakeholder Consultation Document." http://ec.europa.eu/echo/files/policies/consultations/20121210_Fit-for-purpose.pdf (accessed on April 18, 2013).
[57] Verdirame (2001), *supra* note 10, p. 746.

Challenges in Implementing Humanitarian Legal Obligations

Despite the existence of an international legal and policy framework that highlights the obligation to both grant and consent to humanitarian assistance by states, and the right to assistance for the victims, there have been serious challenges in the implementation of states' obligations. In particular, it is not always possible to hold states that refuse to consent to humanitarian assistance accountable, despite their violations of rules and principles of international human rights law and international humanitarian law. While economic and military sanctions and intervention may provide an opportunity for enforcement of the obligations for states that violate the obligation to alleviate humanitarian suffering of their citizens, there are also legal and political restrictions to such actions. In addition, they may contribute to an even greater humanitarian catastrophe and third states may be unwilling to undertake either economic or military action due to the implications of such action.

Consequently, states often refuse to consent to external humanitarian assistance, or create internal impediments for such action, without being held to account. Agencies providing life-saving and humanitarian aid that alleviates suffering have been obstructed from carrying out their activities or even expelled from states. For instance, sometime around March 2009, approximately thirteen international NGOs were expelled from the Darfur region of Sudan (where there was a civil conflict) in addition to the revocation of licenses of three domestic NGOs.[58] In the case of the catastrophic Cyclone Nargis in Myanmar in 2008, the government refused to consent to humanitarian assistance, an action that aggravated the damage, with at least 85,000 people losing their lives and an approximated one million people in dire need of help more than a month later.[59] Even when international humanitarian agencies were granted entry into the state, they were largely restricted to Yangon City for weeks after the cyclone.[60]

There is often a lack of domestic legislation and policy in some states to facilitate external humanitarian assistance,[61] in addition to complementing international legal norms and principles. The concepts of state sovereignty and nonintervention in the domestic affairs of a state continue

[58] Barber (2009), *supra* note 10, p. 377.
[59] Heath (2011), *supra* note 13, p. 420.
[60] Ibid.
[61] Blazeby and Fisher (2010), *supra* note 21, p. 712.

to have a significant influence despite the continued progression of the international human rights protection legal regime and the importance of humanitarian action to alleviate human suffering. The principles of sovereignty and nonintervention are protected under the UN Charter. For instance, Article 2(1) of the Charter safeguards "the principle of the sovereign equality" of all states while under Article 2(7) even the UN is proscribed from intervening "in matters which are essentially within the domestic jurisdiction of any state" except where it involves "enforcement measures" as provided for under Chapter VII of the UN Charter. In addition, under Article 39 of the UN Charter, the Security Council authorizes enforcement measures only where it determines that a situation within a state constitutes a threat or breach of international peace and security. Nevertheless, there is opportunity for intervention on that basis to alleviate humanitarian suffering. For instance, the UN Charter does not restrict the Security Council in its interpretation of which events within a state amount to a threat to international peace and security. Some humanitarian catastrophes within a state have a direct implication on neighboring states, such as through the flow of refugees and may, therefore, disrupt "peace" within other states.

Various General Assembly resolutions have also endorsed and reaffirmed the principles of state sovereignty and nonintervention, in addition to their protection under the UN Charter. These resolutions include the 1965 Declaration on the Inadmissibility of Intervention in the Domestic Affairs of States and the Protection of Their Independence and Sovereignty,[62] the 1970 Declaration on Principles of International Law[63] and the 1974 Resolution on Definition of Aggression.[64] Further, even in circumstances where the General Assembly has adopted resolutions to strengthen humanitarian assistance among states, it has also at times affirmed the sovereignty and territorial integrity of states, including the necessity for the prior consent of the affected state.[65] For instance, in 1991, while adopting the Resolution on Strengthening of the Coordination of

[62] Declaration on the Inadmissibility of Intervention in the Domestic Affairs of States and the Protection of Their Independence and Sovereignty, UNGA Res 2131 (XX) (December 21, 1965).

[63] Declaration on Principles of International Law Concerning Friendly Relations and Co-operation among States in Accordance with the Charter of the United Nations, UNGA Res 2625 (XXV) (October 24, 1970).

[64] Definition of Aggression, UNGA Res 3314 (XXIX) (December 14,1974).

[65] Verdirame (2001), *supra* note 10, p. 743.

Humanitarian Emergency Assistance of the United Nations, the General Assembly explicitly stated that:

> The sovereignty, territorial integrity and national unity of States must be fully respected in accordance with the Charter of the United Nations. In this context, humanitarian assistance should be provided with the consent of the affected country and in principle on the basis of an appeal by the affected country.[66]

It has convincingly been argued that the "cautious position of the General Assembly" in some of the resolutions indicates "the reluctance of states to give express recognition to a limitation of state sovereignty on humanitarian grounds."[67] However, in recent years, the concept of "responsibility to protect" has emerged, and it progressively conceptualizes sovereignty as responsibility to protect populations from humanitarian catastrophes.[68] Having been endorsed by both the Security Council and the General Assembly,[69] the concept of responsibility to protect may eventually crystallize into a proper legal norm. That way, the concept may eventually contribute to a fundamental shift in the interpretation of the principle of state sovereignty and nonintervention, including the obligation to accept or provide humanitarian assistance. However, to an extent, the responsibility to protect concept at present has a close connection with military intervention and "raises serious humanitarian concerns that make it inappropriate for disaster relief."[70] There have also been calculated political reasons for some states opposing the development and implementation of the concept of responsibility to protect.[71]

Principles Regulating Humanitarian Aid

There are core principles regulating the administration of humanitarian assistance that contribute to the existing legal and policy framework.

[66] United Nations General Assembly. (1991, December 19). *Strengthening of the Coordination of Humanitarian Emergency Assistance of the United Nations.* G.A. Res. 46/182, Annex, 34, 36, UN Doc. A/RES/46/182.

[67] Verdirame (2001), *supra* note 10, pp. 743–744.

[68] See International Commission on Intervention and State Sovereignty. "The Responsibility to Protect." (December 2001), paragraphs 2.1–2.15. http://idl-bnc.idrc.ca/dspace/bitstream/10625/18432/6/116998.pdf (accessed on May 13, 2013).

[69] See, for instance, High-Level Panel on Threats, Challenges and Change. "A More Secure World: Our Shared Responsibility." UN Doc A/59/565 (December 2, 2004), paragraph 203; World Summit Outcome Document, UN Doc A/RES/60/1 (October 24, 2005), paragraphs 138 and 139; UNSC Res 1674 (April 28, 2006), UN Doc S/RES/1674; UNSC Res 1894 (November 11, 2009), UN Doc S/RES/1894.

[70] Heath (2011), *supra* note 13, p. 433.

[71] Ibid.

In the 1991 Resolution on the Strengthening of the Coordination of Humanitarian Emergency Assistance of the UN, the General Assembly stated that "[h]umanitarian assistance must be provided in accordance with the principles of humanity, neutrality and impartiality."[72] The General Assembly emphasized the principles of impartiality and humanity in the provision of humanitarian assistance in the 1998 Guiding Principles on Internal Displacement.[73] In 2004, the General Assembly added the principle of independence in its Resolution on Strengthening of the Coordination of Emergency Humanitarian Assistance of the United Nations.[74] The principle of humanity implies that no discrimination should take place while providing assistance to alleviate human suffering.[75] It requires that human suffering "be addressed wherever it is found."[76] The principle of neutrality implies that humanitarian actors should not favor any party while providing assistance.[77] The principle also implies that humanitarian agencies should avoid getting involved in political, ideological, racial and religious disputes wherever they operate.[78] This reflects a broad pattern, as outlined by Sarooshi, of agency relationships, delegation and transfer of powers between member states and international organizations.[79]

The principle of impartiality states that humanitarian assistance should be provided "on the basis of need alone, giving priority to the most urgent cases of distress and making no distinctions on the basis of nationality, race, gender, religious belief, class or political opinions."[80] According to the General Assembly, the principle of independence implies "the autonomy of humanitarian objectives from the political, economic, military or other

[72] United Nations General Assembly (1991), *supra* note 66.

[73] United Nations General Assembly. "Guiding Principles on Internal Displacement." UN Doc E/CN.4/1998/53/Add.2 (1998).

[74] Strengthening of the Coordination of Emergency Humanitarian Assistance of the United Nations. UN Doc A/RES/58/114 (February 5, 2004).

[75] Neil Greet. (2008). ADF Experience on Humanitarian Operations: A New Idea? *Security Challenges*. 4(2), 45–61, 46.

[76] Office for the Coordination of Humanitarian Affairs. "OCHA on Message: Humanitarian Principles." https://ochanet.unocha.org/p/Documents/OOM-humanitarianprinciples_eng_June12.pdf (accessed on May 14, 2013).

[77] Greet (2008), *supra* note 75; Office for the Coordination of Humanitarian Affairs, *supra* note 76.

[78] Fox (2001), *supra* note 4, p. 277; Office for the Coordination of Humanitarian Affairs, *supra* note 76.

[79] Dan Sarooshi. (2005). *International Organizations and Their Exercise of Sovereign Powers*. Oxford: Oxford University Press.

[80] Office for the Coordination of Humanitarian Affairs, *supra* note 76.

objectives that any actor may hold with regard to areas where humanitarian action is being implemented."[81]

While it has been easier for humanitarian actors to observe the principle of impartiality, opposition to the principle of neutrality has increased in recent years.[82] This is largely due to the fact that "[w]hile the principle of 'impartiality' allows aid agencies to speak out publicly during a conflict as long as they apply equal terms to all warring sides, neutrality actually demands that agencies remain silent and abstain completely from the politics of a crisis."[83] The concept of new humanitarianism is emerging, challenging the principle of neutrality in the context of evolving moral and human rights considerations in international politics.[84] In that context, even the ICRC has been criticized for its continued failure "to speak out against human rights abuses" and its policy to "remain neutral in every conflict," which differs from "the more political approach adopted by newer agencies like Oxfam, ActionAid and Médecins Sans Frontières ('MSF')."[85]

The Interrelationship between Humanitarian Intervention and Humanitarian Assistance: Legal and Policy Perspectives

In some instances, the concept of humanitarian intervention has ambiguously been used to broadly refer to all forms of humanitarian assistance, whether involving the use of military force or not. However, as the 2001 International Commission on Intervention and State Sovereignty (ICISS) pointed out, humanitarian agencies are often avidly opposed to the militarization of the term "humanitarian."[86] ICISS observed that "it is anathema for the humanitarian relief and assistance sector" for the term to be "appropriated to describe any kind of military action."[87] The ordinary and strict use of the phrases "humanitarian intervention" and "humanitarian assistance" refers to distinct activities, with differing legal and policy implications.

81 *Strengthening of the Coordination of Emergency Humanitarian Assistance of the United Nations*. UN Doc A/RES/58/114 (February 5, 2004).

82 Fox (2001), *supra* note 4, p. 277.

83 Ibid.

84 Ibid.

85 Ibid.

86 International Commission on Intervention and State Sovereignty, "The Responsibility to Protect." (Report). (December 2001), paragraph 1.40 http://idl-bnc.idrc.ca/dspace/bitstream/10625/18432/6/IDL-18432.pdf (accessed on April 20, 2014).

87 Ibid.

As defined by the Austrian Development Cooperation, humanitarian assistance (also referred to as humanitarian aid or relief) has the objective of alleviating the suffering, safeguarding the dignity and protecting the lives of populations affected by humanitarian crises.[88] In 1991, the UN General Assembly emphasized that humanitarian assistance should be provided "in accordance with the principles of humanity, neutrality and impartiality."[89] Humanitarian assistance does not connote the use of military force. On the other hand, humanitarian intervention, in a legal sense, "is one form of foreign forcible intervention."[90] As Reisman observes, the phrase "humanitarian intervention" is often used in reference to "military intervention conducted in order to provide urgent relief from serious and persistent human rights violations."[91]

Note that Article 2(4) of the UN Charter proscribes the "use of force against the territorial integrity or political independence of any state, or in any other manner inconsistent with the Purposes of the United Nations." However, use of force is legally permissible if authorized by the Security Council on the basis of its powers under Articles 24 and 25, and Chapter VII of the Charter. The UN Charter does not expressly recognize "humanitarian intervention" as an exception to the prohibition of use of force in interstate relations.

However, the right of humanitarian intervention is still often advocated by some states and scholars as a justification for intervention for human rights purposes in the absence of authorization by the UN Security Council.[92] As Kolb points out, if the subject state consents to an

[88] Austrian Development Cooperation (2009), *supra* note 2.

[89] United Nations General Assembly (1991), *supra* note 66.

[90] Robert Kolb. (2003). Note on Humanitarian Intervention. *International Review of the Red Cross*. 85(849), 119–134, 119.

[91] W. Michael Reisman. (1997). Hollow Victory: Humanitarian Intervention and Protection of Minorities. *American Society of International Law Proceedings*. 91, 431–435, 431. For similar definitions, see also Allen Buchanan. (2003). Reforming the International Law of Humanitarian Intervention. In J. L. Holzgrefe and Robert O. Keohane (Eds.), *Humanitarian Intervention: Ethical, Legal and Political Dilemmas*. Cambridge: Cambridge University Press, pp. 130–173, 130; Fernando R. Tesón. (1988). *Humanitarian Intervention: An Inquiry into Law and Morality*. New York: Transnational Publishers, p. 5.

[92] For instance, the United Kingdom at one point justified its 1992 military interventions in northern and southern Iraq, alongside the United States and France for purposes of protecting Kurds and Shiites, on "the customary international law principle of humanitarian intervention." Statement by Aust, Legal Counsellor, before the House of Commons Foreign Affairs Committee on December 2, 1992, quoted in Ian Brownlie and C. J. Apperley. (2000). Kosovo Crisis Inquiry: Memorandum on the International Law Aspects. *International and Comparative Law Quarterly*. 49(4), 878–905, 882–883; United Kingdom Materials on

intervention, then there is no need "to invoke the concept of humanitarian intervention" as such action amounts to consensual intervention which is legally permissible.[93] In addition, if the Security Council provides authorization for forceful intervention to a state, it will have a proper legal basis for its actions and there is no need to raise the controversial issue of humanitarian intervention.[94]

In order to counter allegations of the existence of the "right" of humanitarian intervention, Brownlie and Apperley have carried out a comprehensive analysis of state practice and scholarly views and have reached an accurate conclusion that such intervention is legally unjustifiable on the basis of the UN Charter or customary international law.[95] Due to its lack of a proper basis in international law, proponents of humanitarian intervention have often advocated ethical and political considerations for its justification. For instance, Greenwood has argued that "[t]o accept a permanent dichotomy between law and morality on something as important as the right to prevent genocide or other humanitarian catastrophes is to undermine law and morality and, indeed, international society itself."[96] He therefore asserts that "[i]f it is morally right to use force to prevent a humanitarian emergency, then it should be legally permissible as well."[97] However, note that the international legal system does not proscribe all forms of forceful intervention for humanitarian purposes. It only requires that any forceful intervention be undertaken within the United Nations system, through authorization by the Security Council. It takes away the freedom of any state or regional organization to act as its own judge on forceful intervention matters, which may be necessary for the maintenance of the international rule of law.

Therefore, besides humanitarian intervention being distinct from humanitarian assistance, it has no proper legal basis in international law. With regard to humanitarian assistance, the International Court of Justice clarified, in the *Nicaragua* case, that "the provision of strictly humanitarian aid to persons or forces in another country, whatever their political

International Law (1992) *British Yearbook of International Law* 616, 824. The UK interventions were not authorized by the Security Council. On use of the concept of humanitarian intervention to justify military actions not authorized by the Security Council, see Kolb (2003), *supra* note 90.

93 Kolb (2003), *supra* note 90.

94 Ibid., p. 120.

95 Brownlie and Apperley (2000), *supra* note 92, p. 904.

96 Christopher Greenwood. (2002). Humanitarian Intervention: The Case of Kosovo. *Finnish Yearbook of International Law*. 141–175, 145.

97 Ibid., p. 144.

affiliations or objectives, cannot be regarded as unlawful intervention, or as in any other way contrary to international law."[98]

It is instructive to note that the United Nations Charter can be a basis for forceful intervention for human rights or humanitarian purposes, on the basis of Security Council powers under Articles 24 and 25, and Chapter VII of the Charter, where the crisis within a state is deemed to constitute a breach or threat to international peace and security. However, the Security Council has never referred to any military action authorized for human rights or humanitarian purposes as "humanitarian intervention."

Humanitarian catastrophes such as the obstruction of humanitarian assistance have been the basis of authorization of forceful intervention by the Security Council. For instance, in Resolution 794 of 1992, the Security Council established that the obstruction of supply of humanitarian assistance in Somalia contributed to a serious humanitarian tragedy and was a threat to international peace and security.[99] It therefore authorized states to use all means necessary to establish a secure environment for the delivery of humanitarian relief in Somalia, on the basis of its Chapter VII powers under the United Nations Charter.[100] In addition, in Resolution 1973 of 2011, the Security Council relied on Chapter VII of the UN Charter while authorizing member states and regional organizations to use all measures, including the enforcement of a no-fly zone, to protect civilians in Libya.[101]

A state or regional organization intending to undertake forceful intervention in order to ensure delivery of humanitarian assistance and alleviate gross violations of human rights requires authorization by the Security Council in accordance with Articles 24 and 25, and Chapter VII of the UN Charter. Even the emerging norm of "responsibility to protect" has not resulted in a paradigm shift with regard to forceful intervention, as it has the objective of maintaining such action within the United Nations system.[102] As Peters observes, even under the concept of responsibility to protect, United Nations authorization for intervention for humanitarian purposes is still required.[103]

98 *Military and Paramilitary Activities in and against Nicaragua*, *supra* note 38, paragraph 242.

99 UNSC Res 794 (December 3, 1992) UN Doc S/RES/794.

100 Ibid.

101 UNSC Res 1973 (March 17, 2011) UN Doc S/RES/1973.

102 See High-Level Panel on Threats, Challenges and Change. "A More Secure World: Our Shared Responsibility." UN Doc A/59/565 (December 2, 2004) paragraph 203; World Summit Outcome Document, UN Doc A/RES/60/1 (October 24, 2005) paragraph 139.

103 Anne Peters. (2009). Humanity as the A and Ω of Sovereignty. *European Journal of International Law*. 20(3), 513–544, 537.

New Humanitarianism

The emerging "new humanitarianism" has been defined as a "principled," "human rights based," "politically sensitive" form of humanitarian action that has the objective of "peace and stability" within the developing world.[104] In a sense, it exemplifies the rejection of the principle of neutrality and the merging of human rights protection and peace building with humanitarian assistance.[105] It provides an important framework through which humanitarian actors can articulate their moral concerns.[106] It establishes a basis on which humanitarian assistance activities and approaches that have been blamed for the undesirable effect of "fuelling conflicts, prolonging wars and standing neutral in the face of genocide" can be addressed and rectified.[107]

Despite the opportunities of promoting human rights and development under new humanitarianism, there are also some demerits. First, some NGOs and humanitarian actors are opposed to what they interpret as external regulation by donor states.[108] Second, some argue that the approach could contribute to humanitarian assistance emerging as the primary mode of political engagement in states affected by conflicts.[109] Besides the relegation of humanitarian imperatives, humanitarian workers may not be competent to address technical and complex issues that require access to privileged intelligence.[110] Third, claims of neutrality and impartiality of humanitarian agencies may not be accepted by the parties to a conflict.[111] Humanitarian actors may be deemed agents of Western and donor governments' policies and interests, which may not be purely humanitarian.[112] Fourth, there is the risk that moral perspectives and lack of neutrality (which may imply siding with those deemed victims) could contribute to a hierarchy of victims between those who deserve humanitarian assistance and those perceived as undeserving of aid.[113]

104 Fox (2001), *supra* note 4, p. 275.
105 Ibid., p. 276.
106 Ibid., p. 275.
107 Ibid.
108 Mark Duffield, Joanna Macrae and Devon Curtis. (2001). Politics and Humanitarian Aid. *Disasters*. 25(4), 269–274, 271.
109 Ibid., p. 272.
110 Ibid.
111 Fox (2001), *supra* note 4, p. 282.
112 Ibid.
113 Ibid.

New Forms of Decision Making: Participants and Stakeholders

Local Participation

Despite the necessity of incorporating local expertise, many humanitarian agencies sent to respond to humanitarian emergencies continue to rely only on their own assessment teams to the exclusion of the local community.[114] Often, it is the local authorities and the locally affected people who are able to respond immediately if a humanitarian catastrophe occurs.[115] This implies that the local community is an important and indispensable stakeholder in emergency operations.[116]

In some cases, decision making in emergency response is determined by the internal objectives of humanitarian agencies rather than the actual needs of the beneficiaries on the basis of objective assessment criteria.[117] Often, important policy and implementation issues are assigned only to powerful outsiders without incorporation of local perspectives.[118] When the structures for the implementation of humanitarian assistance are established, and the needs, roles and views of the local community fail to be put into consideration at the initial stage, it becomes more difficult to uncover its perspectives at a later stage.[119] In its 2007 Report, the Tsunami Evaluation Coalition (TEC), which evaluated the Indian Ocean earthquake and tsunamis of December 26, 2004, emphasized the "profound need to put people's priorities at the heart of any future disaster response."[120] It pointed out that:

> The international community time and again descends into crisis situations in large numbers and often leaves the communities it aims to assist undermined. There is a tremendous need to do better and actually support

[114] Marcia Perry. (2007). Natural Disaster Management Planning: A Study of Logistics Managers Responding to the Tsunami. *International Journal of Physical Distribution and Logistics Management*. 37(5), 409–433, 412.

[115] Ibid., p. 411.

[116] Ibid.

[117] Helen Young. (1999). Public Nutrition in Emergencies: An Overview of Debates, Dilemmas and Decision-Making. *Disasters*. 23(4), 277–291, 281.

[118] Oliver Bakewell. (2000). Uncovering Local Perspectives on Humanitarian Assistance and Its Outcomes. *Disasters*. 24(2), 103–116, 104.

[119] Ibid.

[120] Tsunami Evaluation Coalition. (2007). *Synthesis Report: Expanded Summary – Joint Evaluation of the International Response to the Indian Ocean Tsunami*. London: Tsunami Evaluation Coalition. Preface. www.alnap.org/ourwork/tec.aspx (accessed May on 12, 2013).

> and facilitate communities' own relief and recovery efforts, and work alongside national counterparts and structures.[121]

It is increasingly understood that local participation is likely to improve effectiveness of humanitarian aid.[122] In addition, good ethical practices require that the rights and capacity of the local people be given sufficient consideration.[123] In addition, involving local populations in relief work is part of a larger orientation toward building capacity to address the long-term aspects of disasters and prepare them to respond to similar emergencies in the future. In its 2007 report on the Indian Ocean Tsunami, TEC emphasized the need "to invest much more in disaster risk reduction and preparedness" through local community initiatives since such people "were the first to assist in saving lives."[124] Some have similarly argued that there should have been a "government-led integrated master plan and management approach involving the vulnerable Communities" before the tsunami in Thailand.[125] Following recent earthquakes, initiatives to train and create awareness among local populations of Southeast Asian states on the perils of a tsunami have taken place.[126] The Thai government, for instance, organized tsunami warning and response drills involving thousands of people along the Andaman coast in December 2005.[127] However, the impediments to developing an effective mechanism for local participation in humanitarian activities include national and international disaster management bureaucracies, especially if they are "slow moving."[128]

One of the benefits of local community participation, especially in post-disaster relief, is that it can create a framework for addressing long-term solutions and development concerns that may prevent future crises. Programs such as the community-based therapeutic care initiative (CTC)[129] have been helpful in addressing the underlying problems of food insecurity and nutrition concerns since it provides a framework for "high levels of community involvement and mobilization."[130] The CTC

[121] Ibid.
[122] Bakewell (2000), *supra* note 118, p. 104.
[123] Ibid.
[124] Tsunami Evaluation Coalition (2007), *supra* note 120.
[125] Perry (2007), *supra* note 114, p. 415.
[126] Ibid.
[127] Ibid., p. 416.
[128] Ibid.
[129] Miriam S. Chaiken, Hedwig Deconinck and Tedbabe Degefie. (2006). The Promise of a Community-Based Approach to Managing Severe Malnutrition: A Case Study from Ethiopia. *Food and Nutrition Bulletin*. 27(2), 95.
[130] Ibid.

concept in humanitarian assistance has successfully been implemented by some NGOs as part of humanitarian relief efforts for food aid in situations where severe malnutrition is widespread and the concerned organization is seeking to minimize dependence while achieving the highest possible coverage under the relief program.[131] For instance, Save the Children USA has implemented the CTC program in southern Ethiopia.[132]

In nutrition relief, the CTC concept views the local community as a partner, including in the management of severe emergencies, and local participants are recruited to be the primary actors in nutrition surveillance activities that are often an integral part of such relief activities.[133] Under the CTC concept:

> severely malnourished children are monitored and treated at home, with trained community volunteers helping to ensure that parents have the knowledge and resources to successfully rehabilitate their children. The effectiveness of CTC programs is a consequence of local capacity building, timely and sufficient delivery of supplies, and coordinated efforts between nongovernmental organizations and local and national governments.[134]

Further, as recommended in the Final Report on the "Review of Existing Practices to Ensure Participation of Disaster Affected Communities in Humanitarian Aid Operations"[135] to the Directorate-General for Humanitarian Aid (DG ECHO) it was recommended that "needs [be] increasingly addressed in ways that prove more connected and involve further local participation and ownership."[136]

Likewise the United States Agency for International Development (USAID) "Field Operations Guide for Disaster Assessment and Response"[137] stresses the need for greater local participation: "Shelter needs should not be derived or assumed based on damage assessments alone, but also through interaction with affected populations."[138]

In many countries governments routinely affected by disasters have become proficient in response and prevention. However, international

[131] Ibid.

[132] Ibid.

[133] Chaiken, Deconinck and Degefie (2006), *supra* note 129, pp. 95–96.

[134] Ibid., p. 96.

[135] Neil Barry and Jane Barham. (2012). Review of Existing Practices to Ensure Participation of Disaster Affected Communities in Humanitarian Aid Operations.

[136] Barry and Barham (2012), *supra* note 135, p. 29.

[137] United States Agency for International Development (USAID). (2005). "Field Work Operations Guide for Disaster Assessment and Response," 4.

[138] Ibid., III-93.

response often arrives as though this were not the case, sweeping aside local responders and adding to the chaos rather than alleviating it.[139] The Humanitarian Emergency Response Review identifies four categories of governments in responding to disaster:[140]

- Strong and capable governments who take the lead (e.g., India)
- Capable but under-resourced governments who need help to lead (e.g., Mozambique)
- Governments who are unable to lead, and need the international community to do this on their behalf for a time (e.g., Haiti)
- Governments who are unable or unwilling to lead and are obstructive (e.g., Niger in 2009)

Each of the four categories requires different international community responses. However, reality has not often reflected the different needs of the local community. For example, in Haiti, the rural hinterland was not much affected by the earthquake and markets were able to resume quickly. Nevertheless large-scale food aid was imported, potentially harming the agricultural economy as a result.[141]

Moreover the Uganda experience reflects that domestic response has a significant role to play in a number of different situations: particularly in the period between the onset of disaster and the arrival of international agencies, in areas of remote access, and for the implementation of DRR activities during nondisaster times.[142] Local participants also have the advantage of being able to understand the language, culture and context as compared to international agencies.[143]

Plan International's mobilization of children and youth in El Salvador, Central America, is another example of how local participation can play a significant role in environmental resources management and disaster risk reduction.[144] The El Salvador experience has shown that providing

139 Humanitarian Emergency Response Review. (2011), 13. www.gov.uk/government/uploads/system/uploads/attachment_data/file/67579/HERR.pdf (accessed on April 21, 2014).

140 Ibid.

141 Ibid., 37.

142 Global Humanitarian Assistance. *Domestic Response in Uganda*, 33. www.globalhumanitarianassistance.org/report/domestic-response-in-uganda. (accessed on April 22, 2014).

143 Ibid.

144 United Nations. (2007). *Building Disaster Resilient Communities: Good Practices and Lessons Learned – A Publication of the "Global Network of NGOs" for Disaster Risk Reduction.* Geneva, June, 12. www.unisdr.org/files/596_10307.pdf (accessed on April 22, 2014).

youth the opportunity to be directly involved in DRR activities enables them to develop skills to be prepared for future challenges.[145] This project emphasized the need for inclusion of youths' voice and agency in ensuring a holistic approach to disaster management.[146] Key lessons learned from this practice include:[147]

- Not only do children and youth have unique needs in disasters, they also offer a potential role as a resource or receiver of information.
- Young people can act as informants within unofficial communication networks, which evolve within a community setting as the need arises and therefore play an important role in disseminating information.
- In communities with high poverty indices, children and youth already play a major role as interpreters and relays of messages to their households and communities.

The Role of Nongovernmental Organizations and Civil Society Bodies

Beyond the active participation of NGOs and civil society organizations in humanitarian assistance, it is now acknowledged that such entities significantly influence the making and implementation of international law,[148] including legal norms that regulate humanitarian activities. As the Austrian Development Cooperation acknowledges, NGOs, civil society organizations and multilateral organizations are the primary actors in humanitarian aid activities.[149] With respect to the significant role of non-state actors in humanitarian aid, the International Federation of Red Cross and Red Crescent Societies (IFRC), for instance, "is the world's largest humanitarian organization," and it includes "187 member

145 Ibid.

146 Ibid., 14.

147 Ibid.

148 On the role of NGOs in the making of international law, see Eric Suy. (2002). New Players in International Relations. In Gerard Kreijen, Marcel Brus, Jorri Duursma, Elisabeth de Vos and John Dugard (Eds.), *State, Sovereignty, and International Governance*. Oxford: Oxford University Press, pp. 373, 376. Christine Chinkin. (1998). The Role of Non governmental Organizations in Standard Setting, Monitoring and Implementation of Human Rights. In Joseph J. Norton, Mads Andenas and Mary Footer (Eds.), *The Changing World of International Law in the Twenty-First Century: A Tribute to the Late Kenneth R Simmonds*. The Hague: Kluwer Law International, pp. 45–52.

149 Austrian Development Cooperation (2009), *supra* note 2. See also Philippe Biberson and François Jean. (1999). The Challenges of Globalization of International Relief and Development. *Nonprofit and Voluntary Sector Quarterly*. 28, 104–108, 106.

Nations."[150] The IFRC is part of the International Red Cross and Red Crescent Movement,[151] which comprises the ICRC also. The IFRC helps build the capacity of the national societies that it works with, and whose roles include "disaster response and preparedness, community health and care, and promotion of humanitarian principles and values."[152]

An Emerging Obligation to Ensure Local Participation in Humanitarian Assistance

The participation of beneficiaries has become one of the core issues in contemporary humanitarian relief standards.[153] The 1991 Declaration on Strengthening of the Coordination of Humanitarian Emergency Assistance of the United Nations states that country-level coordination should include the use of locally available relief capacities.[154] The 2005 Hyogo Declaration, adopted by states under the auspices of the United Nations Office for Disaster Risk Reduction, affirms the necessity of community-level capacities as a mechanism of diminishing disaster risk.[155] The 2008 European Consensus on Humanitarian Aid provides that humanitarian activities by the European Union have the objective of supporting "local responses to humanitarian crises through a partnership approach with the affected communities."[156] The Good Humanitarian Donorship consortium of states emphasizes the need to involve the "beneficiaries in the design, implementation, monitoring and evaluation" of relief

150 International Federation of Red Cross and Red Crescent Societies. "The International Federation of Red Cross and Red Crescent Societies (IFRC)." www.ifrc.org/en/who-we-are/the-movement/ifrc/ (accessed on May 9, 2013).

151 Ibid.

152 David Fisher. (2009). The International Federation of Red Cross and Red Crescent Societies and the IDRL Guidelines. *Commonwealth Law Bulletin*. 35(4), 743–754, 743.

153 Béatrice Pouligny. "Supporting Local Ownership in Humanitarian Action." *Humanitarian Policy Paper Series*, 6–7. www.gppi.net/fileadmin/gppi/GPPiPPR_local_ownership_2009.pdf (accessed on April 20, 2014); for complete discussion, see T. Kabau and S. Ali. (2015). A Human Rights Based Approach to the Global Regulation of Humanitarian Relief: The Emerging Obligation to Incorporate Local Participation. *Brooklyn Journal of International Law*. 40(3), 791–826.

154 United Nations General Assembly (1991), *supra* note 66.

155 United Nations Office for Disaster Risk Reduction. "World Conference on Disaster Reduction (Hyogo Declaration)." UN Doc A/CONF.206/6 (January 22, 2005), paragraph 4.

156 Joint Statement by the Council and the Representatives of the Governments of the Member States Meeting within the Council, European Parliament and the European Commission. "The European Consensus on Humanitarian Aid." *Official Journal of the European Union*. C 25/1 (January 30, 2008), paragraph 4.

activities.[157] Article 2(c) (ii) of the 2012 Food Assistance Convention stipulates one of the governing principles in the provision of food assistance as being the involvement of the "beneficiaries in the assessment of their needs and in the design, implementation, monitoring and evaluation" of relief activities.[158]

The 2008 Civil-Military Guidelines and Reference for Complex Emergencies by the United Nations and the Inter-Agency Standing Committee (IASC) states that the beneficiaries of relief and local personnel should be involved, to the extent possible, "in the design, management and implementation of assistance, including in civil-military coordination."[159] The Sphere Humanitarian Charter, drafted by a consortium of NGOs, expressly states that its principles and standards are based on a "rights-based and people-centered approach" to the provision of humanitarian relief.[160] The Sphere Charter specifically affirms that its standards and principles are based on the need of involving the beneficiaries of assistance and local authorities.[161] It has been argued that the Sphere Charter may, in the future, contribute to the formation of international customary law with respect to "the rights of beneficiaries to a specific quality of response" by the states and nongovernmental organizations in situations of humanitarian disaster.[162] Legal instruments adopted by states, and self-regulatory mechanisms of NGOs, such as the Sphere Charter, reflect the adoption of a human rights approach to humanitarian assistance, and are evidence of the progressive codification of an obligation to ensure local participation in relief activities.

The Code of Good Practice of the People in Aid, a network of NGOs, requires that policies give consideration to local legal and cultural issues, through the notion of thinking globally but acting locally.[163] The HAP

157 Good Humanitarian Donorship. "Principles and Good Practice of Humanitarian Donorship." (endorsed in Stockholm, June 17, 2003), paragraph 7. www.goodhumanitariandonorship.org/gns/principles-good-practice-ghd/overview.aspx (accessed on May 19, 2014).

158 Food Assistance Convention, *supra* note 27.

159 United Nations and the Inter-Agency Standing Committee. (2008). "Civil-Military Guidelines and Reference for Complex Emergencies," 19. https://docs.unocha.org/sites/dms/Documents/ENGLISH%20VERSION%20Guidelines%20for%20Complex%20Emergencies.pdf (accessed on May 5, 2014).

160 Sphere Project, *supra* note 42, p. 6.

161 Ibid.

162 Max R. O'Donnell, Dimitri Bacos and Michael L. Bennish. (2002). Nutritional Response to the 1998 Bangladesh Flood Disaster: Sphere Minimum Standards in Disaster Response. *Disasters*. 26(3), 229–241, 238–239.

163 Principle Two on staff policies and practices, People in Aid, "Code of Good Practice in the Management and Support of Aid Personnel," 10. www.peopleinaid.org/pool/files/code/code-en.pdf (accessed on May 19, 2014).

Project aims at stimulating accountability of humanitarian agencies to the beneficiaries through standards on quality and accountability, and it includes certification mechanisms.[164] In addition, HAP provides a forum through which relief beneficiaries can articulate their grievances against humanitarian agencies.[165] The ECB Project formulates tools and mechanisms for ensuring the participation of the local people during the project assessment, design, implementation and monitoring.[166] The 2001 "Responsibility to Protect" Report of the International Commission on Intervention and State Sovereignty cautioned that:

> [A] reconstruction and rehabilitation programme which does not take sufficient account of local priorities and excludes local personnel could create an unhealthy dependency on the intervening authority, stultify the regrowth of local institutions and the economy, and infinitely delay the population's desire or ability to resume responsibility for its own government.[167]

Globalization and Aid

Increasing globalization is influencing the conduct of international humanitarian assistance and its resulting interface with local communities, with both positive and negative implications. Globalization may be defined as "a set of economic, political, social and cultural processes that increase the degree of interconnectedness and interdependence between societies across the globe."[168] Indeed, as the president of ICRC observed:

> Today's world has indeed become a global village. This is illustrated by three phenomena: the tendency for the traditional institutions of national sovereignty to lose their supremacy in favour of supranational, regional and local mechanisms; the growing interdependence between the centres of political, military and economic power; and the rapid expansion

164 Humanitarian Accountability Partnership. "About Us." www.hapinternational.org/who-we-are/about-us.aspx (accessed on October 30, 2013).

165 Jacqui Tong. (2004). Questionable Accountability: MSF and Sphere in 2003. *Disasters*. 28(2), 176–189, 176.

166 Emergency Capacity Building Project. (2007). "Impact Measurement and Accountability in Emergencies: The Good Enough Guide," 34–35. www.ecbproject.org/inside-the-guide/view-the-good-enough-guide (accessed on May 19, 2014).

167 International Commission on Intervention and State Sovereignty. "The Responsibility to Protect." (Report). (December 2001), paragraph 5.27. http://idl-bnc.idrc.ca/dspace/bitstream/10625/18432/6/IDL-18432.pdf (accessed on April 20, 2014).

168 Peter Viggo Jakobsen. (2002). The Transformation of United Nations Peace Operations in the 1990s: Adding Globalization to the Conventional "End of the Cold War Explanation." *Cooperation and Conflict*. 37, 267–282, 268.

> of transnational networks of influence, such as the media, religious circles and organized groups in society.[169]

According to Robert Keohane and Joseph Nye, globalization involves networks of interdependence and linkages across the world that develop from flows and influences of people, information, capital and goods, in addition to the influence and flows of biologically and environmentally relevant substances, for instance, disease pathogens.[170] Problems that were traditionally regional or local have been put on the world stage by the recent enormous progress in worldwide telecommunications and travel.[171]

There are various positive implications of globalization with regard to humanitarian assistance. The globalization of the media, for instance, the global reach of the Cable News Network (CNN) makes millions of people across the world aware of humanitarian emergencies, and therefore contributes to a rise in donor and public support for humanitarian responses.[172] For instance, despite the difficulties and bureaucratic breakdowns in the initial response to the 2005 Hurricane Katrina in the United States, "what appeared on television screens all over the world evoked a need by many to 'do something'."[173] During "the first hurricane to hit the United States amid continuous television coverage," the extensive media exposure helped the rest of the world appreciate that humanitarian disasters and emergencies are global in nature, and can affect any state.[174]

Globalization has also meant an increased diversity of state and regulatory actors in humanitarian assistance. For example, countries in Asia are seeking to strengthen and develop a well-articulated legal and policy

[169] International Committee of the Red Cross. (1998). "International Solidarity and the Globalization of Responsibility in Meeting Today's Humanitarian Challenges." *Address by Mr. Cornelio Sommaruga, President of the International Committee of the Red Cross, at the Opening Meeting of UNHCR 49th Executive Committee.* Geneva, October 5. www.icrc.org/eng/resources/documents/misc/57jpef.htm (accessed on April 18, 2013).

[170] Robert O. Keohane and Joseph S. Nye Jr. (2000). Globalization: What's New? What's Not? (And So What?). *Foreign Policy.* 118, 104–119, 105.

[171] David Alexander. (2006). Globalization of Disaster: Trends, Problems and Dilemmas. *Journal of International Affairs.* 59(2), 1–22, 1.

[172] Egbert Sondorp, Tania Kaiser and Anthony Zwi. (2001). Beyond Emergency Care: Challenges to Health Planning in Complex Emergencies. *Tropical Medicine and International Health.* 6(12), 965–970, 965.

[173] Angela M. Eikenberry, Verónica Arroyave and Tracy Cooper. (2007). Administrative Failure and the International NGO Response to Hurricane Katrina. *Public Administration Review.* 160–170, 164.

[174] Ibid.

framework to address humanitarian assistance. With the 1997 inclusion of China, Japan and South Korea into the Association of Southeast Asian Nations (ASEAN's) activities through what is referred to as "ASEAN+3," there are opportunities for greater funding in humanitarian activities.[175] North Korea and Afghanistan have generally benefited from significant food aid from South Korea, India and China.[176] The government of Japan is also a significant provider of humanitarian assistance as it seeks to uphold the principles of "humanity, impartiality, neutrality and independence" in its activities.[177] Japan has provided humanitarian assistance in the form of food, shelter and water to internally displaced persons and refugees through international organizations.[178]

Globalization has also partly contributed to the increasing role of non-state actors such as NGOs and civil society organizations in international relations,[179] including in humanitarian activities. The positive implication of a weaker role of the nation-state in international humanitarian activities is that the traditional notions of state sovereignty and a rigid interpretation of the principle of nonintervention are increasingly being rendered less relevant. It has been noted that in recent years, "leading governments, UN agencies, NGOs and private companies have gained unprecedented access and varying degrees of influence over the internal affairs of many weaker or contested states in the unstable zones of the world."[180]

Globalization has also contributed to the capacity of humanitarian agencies to raise funds for their activities. For instance, the continued "proliferation and globalization of media communication" has helped Médecins Sans Frontières (MSF) raise funds for its missions through publicization of humanitarian crises, in addition to its overall expansion.[181] Further, globalization has promoted the ideology of global humanitarianism, which has

[175] Adele Harmer and Lin Cotterrell. (2005, September 20). Diversity in Donorship: The Changing Landscape of Official Humanitarian Aid. *Humanitarian Policy Group Research Report*, 14. http://dspace.cigilibrary.org/jspui/bitstream/123456789/22633/1/Diversity%20in%20Donorship%20The%20changing%20landscape%20of%20official%20humanitarian%20aid%20fe1.pdf?1 (accessed on May 10, 2013).

[176] Ibid, 22.

[177] Ministry of Foreign Affairs. (2011). "Humanitarian Aid Policy of Japan." www.mofa.go.jp/policy/emergency/pdfs/aid_policy_japan.pdf (accessed on April 18, 2013).

[178] Ibid.

[179] Mark Duffield. (2001). Governing the Borderlands: Decoding the Power of Aid. *Disasters*. 25(4), 308–320, 308.

[180] Ibid, p. 309.

[181] D. Robert Dechaine. (2002). Rhetoric of Global Community Humanitarian Space and the Social Imaginary: Médecins Sans Frontières/Doctors Without Borders and the Rhetoric of Global Community. *Journal of Communication Inquiry*. 26, 354–369, 356.

been promoted by various international humanitarian agencies.[182] It has been noted that humanitarian actors such as CARE, Save the Children, Red Cross, World Vision, Médecins Sans Frontières and Oxfam have historically promoted and institutionalized the concept of global humanitarianism.[183] It is from such foundations that humanitarian NGOs currently collectively advocate "an ethic of global compassion and promote the normative discourse of universal human rights" in humanitarian activities.[184]

However, despite the positive consequences of globalization, negative implications include restrictions on access to important health supporting supplements such as generic medicines. For instance, the concept of a global unrestricted market for pharmaceutical drugs advocates that the medications dispensed in Mozambique and India be identical to those used in treatment in North America and Europe.[185] The production of generic medicines is restricted while significant profits accrue from dissemination of new medicines that are protected through patents and legal monopolies.[186] States such as India and Mozambique have been forced to adopt patent protection laws for pharmaceutical products in order to gain or maintain their membership in the World Trade Organization (WTO).[187] The absence of cheaper generic medicines, including the legal proscription of such drugs, threatens the survival and health of millions of people in the developing and least developed states, in addition to severely restricting the capacity of humanitarian agencies to provide medical assistance. In particular, Gorik Ooms and Rachel Hammonds lament that:

> As globalization rendered many poor Mozambicans poorer, and health workers and medicines more expensive, one might expect the heralds of globalization to promote corrective or protective global solutions to Mozambique's health crises. The opposite is true. When it comes to healthcare – and other social services – the heralds of globalization suddenly plead national self-reliance or the importance of local solutions. Global interdependence is good when it comes to trade, but when it comes to healthcare it is undesirable aid-dependency.[188]

[182] Simon Cottle and David Nolan. (2007). Global Humanitarianism and the Changing Aid-Media Field. *Journalism Studies*. 8(6), 862–878, 862.

[183] Ibid.

[184] Ibid.

[185] Gorik Ooms and Rachel Hammonds. (2008). Correcting Globalisation in Health: Transnational Entitlements versus the Ethical Imperative of Reducing Aid-Dependency. *Public Health Ethics*. 1(2), 154–170, 156.

[186] Ibid.

[187] Ibid.

[188] Ibid.

The transmission of economic sovereignty from states to international organizations under current international law has also meant that critical decision making has shifted to supranational institutions without as yet fully formed mechanisms to draw on local input.[189] Thus, in many instances, the development of aid policy absent input from local populations has led to detrimental consequences such as imposition of aid conditionalities and lack of accountability by the relevant supranational institutions to the people whose economic, social and political matters they determine.[190] These issues will be examined more fully in the chapters that follow.

Summary and Conclusion

A review of the legal and policy foundations of humanitarian aid, including the challenges of implementing humanitarian legal obligations, principles regulating humanitarian aid, new humanitarianism, collaboration with local stakeholders and the impact of globalization on humanitarian aid policy, provides a basis for the examination of the three typologies of networked humanitarian assistance programs that will be examined in the chapters that follow.

[189] Chimni (2000), *supra* note 1, p. 247.
[190] Ibid.

PART II

International-Led Response

3

Theory and Practice of International Response

Introduction

In examining case studies of international-led engagement with local populations in relation to relief efforts, this part will begin by reviewing existing insights into effective international-local engagement in pre- and post-disaster relief planning. These insights include the importance of (1) contingency planning, (2) access to accurate and reliable information, (3) effective communication and cultural awareness and (4) an engaged community-based process of identifying priority needs and resources.

Contingency Planning

Many studies have highlighted the importance of contingency planning as the prerequisite for rapid and effective emergency response.[1] It is argued that without prior contingency planning much time will be lost in the first days of an emergency. Contingency planning builds organizational capacity and provides a helpful foundation for operations planning and emergency response.[2] Moreover, the capacity of local actors to respond in an emergency will be enhanced by their previous involvement in the contingency planning process.

Contingency planning and operations planning are different concepts. Both contingency planning and operations planning set strategic and sectoral objectives and develop an action plan to achieve these objectives. The major difference between the two is that contingency planning involves making assumptions and developing the scenarios on which planning is based, whereas in the case of operations planning, the starting point is known, and the planning will build on needs and resources assessments.[3]

[1] Office of the United Nations High Commissioner for Refugees. *Handbook for Emergencies.* 2nd edn., 2000. Retrieved from www.disaster-info.net/watermitigation/i/publications/Handbook/index_en.HTML.

[2] Ibid.

[3] Ibid.

Studies have found that many pitfalls in contingency planning can be avoided by planning collectively, marshaling the widest range of local skills, and complementing these by external inputs. Contingency planning is best achieved through a cooperative and coordinated effort wherein all concerned work together with shared objectives over a period of time. A single meeting that produces a plan is usually insufficient. The contingency planning process therefore revolves around regular meetings and follow-up.[4]

Coordination at the Site Level

At the site level,[5] community members should play a major role in planning activities. A clear understanding of the aims and objectives of the emergency operation and proper coordination are even more important at the site level than centrally, for it is here that failures and misunderstandings will directly affect the community.[6]

Community Involvement in Planning

Research has found that community involvement in planning measures involves careful organization. Efforts to establish systems of representation can be helpful at the outset to reflect the communities' concerns.[7] Drawing on existing community skills and resources is essential. Special emphasis on capacity building among women and adolescents has been identified as key to unlocking capacities among this population.[8] Finally

[4] Ibid.

[5] Ibid., p. 60.

[6] Ibid., p. 60.

[7] Ibid., p. 61; this study has suggested that the system of representation should:

(1) be truly representative of the different interests and sectors of the community and of both men and women;
(2) include various level of representatives and elders to ensure adequate representation and access for individuals;
(3) avoid unconscious bias, for example, on the basis of language. Bear in mind that there is no reason why an individual should be representative of the community simply because he or she has a common language with those providing outside assistance;
(4) be based on traditional leadership systems as much as possible but provided these allow proper representation (for example, if the traditional leadership system excludes women, there should nevertheless be women representatives);
(5) be consistent with the physical divisions in the layout of the site.

[8] Ibid., p. 61; to ensure women's participation, the following practices are suggested:

(1) Include women in leadership functions and give them responsible roles in the community including participation in decision-making bodies;

education and information dissemination on key recovery approaches will require coordinated action.

In addition to planning, engaging community members in the implementation of relief efforts is critical.[9] Volunteer collaboration[10] within a community enables participatory mapping of priorities and needs, facilitates collaboration with elders and leaders for advocacy and support, identifies volunteers who can help in organizing the community to address problems and enables reporting information to the coordination body or local district.[11]

Access to Accurate and Reliable Information

An important element in disaster response is ensuring the reliability of information regarding post-disaster conditions.[12] Accurate and reliable information about local conditions, both pre- and post-disaster, is important in empowering local communities to take action on recovery plans and fill in necessary gaps in recovery efforts. If information is unreliable, this will create unnecessary confusion and chaos, potentially paralyzing local efforts, as was the case in the aftermath of Hurricane Katrina.[13]

One of the methods used by international bodies to ensure reliability of information regarding post-disaster situations is the United Nations' Cluster Approach. In response to a "growing number of stakeholders [calling for] accountability in the disaster response environment, the UN has proposed humanitarian reform and the use of a cluster approach, which

(2) Ensure that women have equal access to services and facilities, particularly health and reproductive health care services, and inform persons concerned about these resources;
(3) Encourage activities such as adult literacy classes which will help empower women and bring them together for mutual support;
(4) Provide community support to women by organizing recreational and educational activities for children;
(5) Develop preventive protection mechanisms with the community to ensure protection of women against all forms of abuse;
(6) Work with the elders and other influential groups to gain their support for the participation of women in management.

9 M. A. Connolly. (2005). *Communicable Disease Control in Emergencies: A Field Manual.* WHO, p. 88.

10 Ibid., p. 89.

11 Ibid., p. 89.

12 G. Bobby Kapur and Jeffrey Smith. (2011). *Emergency Public Health: Preparedness and Response.* Sudbury: Jones & Bartlett.

13 Ibid.

aims to coordinate key disaster responders."[14] In 2005, the UN's Office of Coordination of Humanitarian Affairs (OCHA) redesigned its response plan into a cluster-based approach to disaster relief. The cluster strategy was first employed in the wake of the Kashmir earthquake. The plan designated ten clusters of need,[15] each with its own command center, to streamline the system, provide a structure to organize the myriad of NGOs and governmental aid entities, and ensure response efforts were more nimble. The clusters consist of shelter, nutrition, health, water and sanitation, camp management, logistics, protection, education, telecommunications and early reconstruction planning. The leadership of each cluster is allocated to a particular UN agency.[16] While these approaches have helped to generate increasingly reliable information, the challenges of this approach were demonstrated in the aftermath of the Kashmir earthquake.[17] The OCHA's "cluster approach did spread out jurisdiction over the operations as designed, but the clusters were found to overlap to a large degree. For example, camp management intrinsically incorporates elements of shelter, sanitation, nutrition and numerous other clusters. This overlap decreased clarity in the lines of authority."[18]

Information gathering and response through interdisciplinary team efforts has been found particularly effective in the post-disaster context.[19] Research focusing on the Pan-American Health Organization (PAHO), which established a Regional Disaster Response Team at the request of the Ministers of Health in the Region of the Americas, found that the "multidisciplinary team" approach with "health and disaster specialists with the necessary experience and training to collaborate in emergency and disaster response" was a particularly effective model. The team included individuals "from a variety of technical areas, including epidemiology, mental health, water and sanitation, health services, environmental health, administration, and logistics, as well as communication specialists."[20] The main functions of the Regional Disaster Response Team are to "support the health sector of the affected country, conduct damage and needs

[14] Ibid., p. 89.

[15] World Health Organization. (2007). "The Cluster Approach." Retrieved from www.who.int/hac/techguidance/tools/manuals/who_field_handbook/annex_7/en/index.html.

[16] Kapur and Smith (2011), *supra* note 12, p. 391.

[17] Ibid.

[18] Ibid., pp. 394–395.

[19] Susan Arroyo, Martha Rodriguez and Ricardo Prex. (2009). *Information Management and Communication in Emergencies and Disasters Manual for Disaster Response Teams.* Washington, DC : Pan American Health Organization.

[20] Ibid., pp. 15–16.

assessments, provide technical advice to PAHO/WHO offices and local and international counterparts, and support, when necessary, in the activation of the health cluster and other specialized working groups in the framework of the United Nations Humanitarian Reform."[21]

The objectives of the Regional Disaster Response Team are to "quickly mobilize specialists who can support the emergency operations led by the health sector in the country or countries affected by disaster.[22] In cooperation with national authorities and other actors, the team calculates the potential risk to the public health of affected populations, carries out rapid assessment of damages to and needs of the health sector and shares results of assessments with humanitarian stakeholders involved in disaster response.[23] An important function of the team is to gather, produce and distribute necessary information so that local authorities, PAHO/WHO, donors, agencies in the United Nations system, and other actors can take decisions and set life-saving operations into motion."[24]

Among the contributions of such multidisciplinary teams is the preparation of "situation reports (SITREPs) and other technical documents" drawing on local community input.[25] The teams also assist in "preparing project proposals, coordinate the timely and effective distribution of information, organize the exchange of information with major national and international health sector agencies, collect, organize, and preserve reports and other technical or scientific information relating to the emergency or disaster."[26]

In comparing the PAHO's Regional Disaster Response Team with the UN's Cluster Approach, it appears that the PAHO's approach tends to support existing systems in place in a particular country by providing technical expertise, assessing damage and identifying urgent needs. The UN's Cluster Approach, in contrast, takes on a greater leadership role, which requires efforts in coordinating with local, regional and national governments.

Crisis-Mapping Communications

New information and communication technologies, new information providers and new international communities of interest are increasingly

21 Ibid., pp. 15–16.
22 Ibid., p. 16.
23 Ibid., p. 16.
24 Ibid., p. 16.
25 Ibid., p. 16.
26 Ibid., pp. 17–18.

changing the way information is collected, shared and managed.[27] This was particularly apparent during the Haiti earthquake response. Social networking media, mobile phone text messaging, open source software applications and commercial satellite imagery are being used more than ever before. Studies have found that beyond the established international humanitarian community, volunteers and participatory reporters from the affected population have become new sources of data and information.[28] Humanitarian organizations, host governments and the donor community will have to adapt to this new information environment.[29]

In the case of the Haitian earthquake of 2010,[30] within hours after the report of the earthquake, a new community of virtually connected volunteers affiliated with ICT consulting companies, private corporations, open source software proponents, academic/research institutions, NGOs and even the Haitian diaspora community began applying new ICT applications to the earthquake response. These ICT volunteers were affiliated with organizations such as Google, InSTEDD, Fortius One/GeoCommons, OpenStreet Map, Tufts/Harvard Universities, Frontline SMS, ICT4Peace, Sahana, Thompson Reuters Foundation, MicroSoft and others.[31] They utilized portals/platforms such as CrisisMappers.net, SMS 4636, Ushahidi, STAR-TIDES, Haiti Voices, ICT4Peace Inventorization Wiki, CrisisCamp Haiti, CrisisCommons Wiki, crisescomm.ning.com and blogs.[32]

Studies have found that "Web 2.0" social network media were used as a new means for crowd-sourced data collection, information sharing and collaboration. Within days, individuals from this community, with support from the US State Department, worked with ICT companies to establish an SMS 4636 code for the free transmission of text message information to and from Haiti.[33] Google adapted its suite of tools for applications to support the Haiti earthquake response and helped develop a Person Finder application to help find and connect persons in Haiti who could not be contacted.[34]

[27] Available at: https://hiu.state.gov/Products/Haiti_EarthquakeHumanitarianInformation_2010Jul_HIU.pdf.

[28] Ibid.

[29] Ibid.

[30] Dennis King. (2010). The Haiti Earthquake: Breaking New Ground in the Humanitarian Information Landscape, *Humanitarian Exchange Magazine*, p. 4. Retrieved from https://hiu.state.gov/Products/Haiti_EarthquakeHumanitarianInformation_2010Jul_HIU.pdf.

[31] Ibid.

[32] Ibid.

[33] Ibid.

[34] Ibid.

Moreover, a nascent, virtual CrisisMappers network began utilizing an open source interactive mapping platform, known as Ushahidi (Swahili for "witness"), to gather, extract and plot geo-referenced data on a public domain Web site.[35] Over the course of the disaster, Ushahidi and volunteer diaspora translators received more than 80,000 text messages; approximately 3,000 of these were used in some way during response activities.[36] Other geo-referenced data were gleaned from Twitter, blogs, the news media and humanitarian situation reports to provide fast turnaround situational awareness products, including imagery-based maps.[37]

Research has found that this virtual humanitarian response network must be recognized as a new player in the humanitarian information environment, and in order to be most effective, it also needs to work with the established international humanitarian actors and follow their humanitarian codes of conduct and information management best practices and principles.[38]

However, one potential problem is that SMS crowdsourcing may be subject to misinformation, and could overwhelm the system and divert responses from identified emergency needs of affected populations that have been objectively assessed by national and international response teams. This nascent ICT community is also dependent on volunteerism and pro bono resourcing, which faces the challenges of ensuring sustainability and integration with the host country and international humanitarian system, particularly as response activities transition into the recovery phase.[39]

Effective Communication, Participation and Cultural Awareness

Many studies have identified the importance of facilitating effective communication among diverse communities in contributing to effective disaster response.[40] Understanding community perspectives and the sociocultural factors that influence the behavior of communities is an important first step in emergency response. Guiding principles for effective community participation in complex emergencies include ensuring

[35] Ibid.

[36] Ibid.

[37] Ibid.

[38] Ibid.

[39] Ibid., pp. 4–5.

[40] World Health Organization. (2005). *Malaria Control in Complex Emergencies: An Inter-agency Field Handbook*. Retrieved from http://whqlibdoc.who.int/publications/2005/924159389X_eng.pdf.

that the community is involved in collecting information and in planning and implementation and ensuring that communications are culturally appropriate.

Importantly, effective community participation involves working with the community to identify priority needs and activities.[41] Priorities should be based on community needs and perspectives, but will also depend on the resources that are available and on what can be achieved in the local context. This may involve the following: (1) define together the problems, their causes and the possible solutions; (2) involve community representatives in planning and implementing qualitative research to gather information and in analyzing the data collected; and (3) be sensitive to gender and ethnicity, understanding that community leaders may not represent the views of women or minority groups.[42] Regular community meetings are also important to keep the members informed and to provide an opportunity to raise concerns and to find joint solutions to problems.[43]

Challenges in International-Led Response

Among the challenges faced in international-led disaster response efforts is lack of clarity with relation to who is in charge of leading the relief efforts. For example, in the case of the 2005 Kashmir earthquake, the Pakistani government established the Federal Relief Commission (FRC) in response.[44] The FRC worked in conjunction with the UN's OCHA, as the disaster response was coordinated by both bodies. "Although the OCHA health cluster was placed in charge of designating sites for temporary hospitals, the FRC actually chose the sites, often poorly. Weakness of OCHA leadership combined with operating within a sovereign nation led to decreased OCHA effectiveness in coordinating a humanitarian response. Relief workers often operate in the absence of a recognizable state structure, such as in Darfur or Bosnia, and may be unprepared to operate under the auspices of a functioning military regime such as exists in Pakistan."[45] The groups that were able to lend help most effectively in the aftermath of the Kashmir earthquake were the outlawed Islamic militia groups. "Within the first 24 hours after the earthquake, these militias had mobilized to provide assistance by extricating trapped

[41] Ibid., p. 148.
[42] Ibid., p. 148.
[43] Ibid., p. 151.
[44] Kapur and Smith (2011), *supra* note 12.
[45] Ibid., p. 395.

individuals; providing temporary shelter, food, and blankets; and clearing roads. One group in particular, Lashkar-e-Taiba, played a large role in coordinating attacks across the border in India; this group arrived in force to provide a large degree of humanitarian relief long before any federal response could be organized, likely saving many lives of those trapped and garnering much credit among local populations for being present in their time of need. Militia groups such as these represented the first – and in more remote regions, the only – form of de facto emergency public health response, even though it was not organized by any official agency; in fact, the existence of such groups was outlawed."[46]

[46] Ibid., pp. 395–396.

4

Indonesia's Tsunami of 2004

In the following chapters, we will explore the dynamics of international-led response to post-disaster planning in Indonesia and Haiti. In addition to the existing complex and challenging conditions pre-disaster, the presence in some cases of long-term international entities in the region and limited local resources available to respond to mass-scale natural disasters gave rise to a relatively greater reliance on international support. These chapters will pay particular attention to the challenges and lessons learned in the response process with the aim of gleaning insights that might shed light on how effective local engagement might be facilitated.

Introduction

One of the world's deadliest earthquakes struck the west coast of Northern Sumatra in the early hours of the morning on Boxing Day in 2004. With magnitude measuring greater than 9.0 on the Richter scale, it was recorded as the fourth largest earthquake since 1900, and the largest in fifty years.[1] The megathrust earthquake triggered a catastrophic tsunami striking various coastal countries in the region, as a result of which more than 150,000 people were killed and 25,000 bodies were missing.[2] While Indonesia had the highest death toll of at least 110,229, Sri Lanka, India, Thailand and Somalia also reported a high number of fatalities as the impact of the disaster stretched through the Indian Ocean.[3] This chapter will review the incident and focus on how international bodies such as the United Nations coordinated with local communities in relief planning and coordination.

[1] World Bank Group. (2005). *World Bank Response to the Tsunami Disaster*, Washington, DC: World Bank. Available at http://documents.worldbank.org/curated/en/2005/02/5774146/world-bank-response-tsunami-disaster.

[2] Geology.com. (2004). Indonesia Tsunami Maps, 2005. Retrieved from http://geology.com/articles/tsunami-map.shtml.

[3] Ibid.

Following the earthquake, countless homes, roads, bridges, schools, health facilities, government offices and business equipment, along with other private assets, were damaged.[4] It is estimated that up to 5 million lives were adversely affected by the destructive event based on studies in surrounding villages of Aceh.[5] It is also estimated that Indonesia alone would account for US$ 4.45 billion in losses and damage out of the US$ 7 billion suffered by the affected region as a whole.[6] The private sector,[7] which included family businesses and micro-enterprises, the agricultural sector[8] and the fishery sector,[9] was hit most severely.

The impact on gross domestic product (GDP) at the national level was relatively small, estimated to be about 2.7 percent. However, in the most badly hit provinces such as Aceh, the total loss and damage was 97 percent of provincial GDP. The per capita income for the people of Aceh declined by as much as 32 percent in 2005.[10]

As will be seen in this chapter, the rebuilding projects in Indonesia that more directly engaged local communities achieved higher satisfaction than other programs because they were developed on the basis of local knowledge of needs and preferences. Given the close ties within the communities, the gathering and dissemination of such information was quicker and more effective. Local participation could therefore enable quick response to the most urgent needs[11] and reduce the problem of

[4] World Bank Group (2005), *supra* note 1; E. Scheper. (2006). *Impact of the Tsunami Response on Local and National Capacities*. Tsunami Evaluation Coalition.

[5] L. Marulanda and S. Rizal. (2006). *Tsunami Evaluation Coalition: The International Community's Funding of the Tsunami Emergency and Relief – Local Response Study*. Tsunami Evaluation Coalition.

[6] World Bank Group (2005), *supra* note 1.

[7] "The private sector, including family businesses, suffered 77 per cent of the total damage and loss. An estimated 80,000 small enterprises, which had provided income to some 140,000 people, were destroyed. The number of micro-enterprises lost is not known." See Scheper (2006), *supra* note 4.

[8] The agricultural sector faces additional challenges with flooded land and years of soil degradation. For further information, see Scheper (2006), *supra* note 4.

[9] The fishery sector was already suffering from over fishing and heavy indebtedness to local moneylenders. For further information, see Scheper (2006), *supra* note 4.

[10] BAPPENAS. (2005). *Indonesia: Preliminary Damage and Loss Assessment: The December 26, 2004 Natural Disaster*. BAPPENAS and the International Donor Community, p II:1; for a summary of the casualties and destruction done to the affected villages, see Aceh Community Assistance Research Project. (2007, December). *The Acehnese Gampong Three Years On: Assessing Local Capacity and Reconstruction Assistance in Post-tsunami Aceh.*

[11] B. Dercon and M. Kusumawijaya. (2007). *Two Years of Settlement Recovery in Aceh and Nias: What Should the Planners Have Earned?* 43rd ISOCARP Congress: Antwerp, Belgium, September 19–23.

marginalization.[12] In addition, projects adopting a community-driven development (CDD) model were completed eighteen months ahead of schedule, they produced more output than any other program, and they cost 56 percent less than those adopting a conventional approach.[13] In addition, the occupancy rate for housing built by such programs was 97 percent, whereas that of similar houses built by other programs was more than 10 percent lower. Where local institutions were engaged directly in the rebuilding process, capacity was built, which was key to the true and sustainable recovery of the affected communities.[14]

Policy Background

The Disaster Management Structure

At the time of the tsunami, the governmental body responsible for disaster management was the National Coordinating Agency for Natural Disaster and Refugees Relief (BAKORNAS PBP). It is an ad hoc structure activated only in times of disaster. It has no contingency budgets for emergencies.[15] It operates through a three-level structure:

The first level consists of the National Coordinating Board (BAKORNAS). It is chaired by the vice-president of Indonesia and consists of the relevant ministers (including the ministers of home affairs, social affairs, health, public works, finance and Transportation), the chief commander of the Indonesian national army and the head of the National police.[16] Its main duties include formulating policies in disaster management and providing guidelines and directives on disaster management activities such as prevention, mitigation, rescue, rehabilitation and reconstruction.[17]

12 T. Ophiyandri, D. Amaratunga and C. Pathirage. (2010). *Community Based Post Disaster Housing Reconstruction: Indonesian Perspective.* CIB 2010 World Congress, May 10–13, 2010, Salford Quays, United Kingdom, p. 13.

13 World Bank Group. (2009). *Five Years after the Tsunami: Continuing the Commitment to Reconstruction*. December, p. 23. Available at: http://documents.worldbank.org/curated/en/2009/12/11528668/five-years-after-tsunami-continuing-commitment-reconstruction.

14 Aceh Community Assistance Research Project (2007), *supra* note 10.

15 Scheper (2006), *supra* note 4.

16 Ibid.

17 Office for the Coordination of Humanitarian Affairs and World Health Organization. (2002, July–October). Annex 6 – Information Sheet BAKORNAS of *Assessment on Emergency Preparedness in Disaster Situations: Integrated Approach on Nationwide Preparedness Capacities and Capabilities within the Republic of Indonesia*. Retrieved from www.who.int/disasters/repo/8449_Attachements/Annex6-InformationSheetBAKORNAS.doc.

The second level consists of the provincial coordinating units (SATKORLAK). These are groups chaired by the governor and their main role is to coordinate the execution of disaster management policies within the catchment areas as directed by BAKORNAS.[18]

Finally, the local-level body consists of the district implementing units (SATLAK). It is chaired by the mayors or the bupati (i.e., the elected head of the district).[19] Similar to the provincial coordinating units, it is also a non-structural group. It is responsible for executing and implementing disaster management activities within the catchments as directed by the governor.[20]

The Government's Responses

On the first day after the tsunami, the government declared a national disaster.[21] In the afternoon of December 26, 2004, the vice-president of BAKORNAS PBP brought with him US$ 5 million from private funds and visited Aceh to assist the local district implementing units in assessing the damage.[22]

On December 27, 2004, the government requested international assistance and permitted foreign military teams to begin search and rescue operations.[23]

On December 29, 2004, BAKORNAS PBP formed a special coordination unit to specifically deal with the situation in Aceh.[24] It was cochaired by Indonesia's vice-president, the coordinating minister for people's welfare and the deputy governor of Aceh. The Ministry of Home Affairs sent some of its staff members to the affected areas to set up *posko* (i.e., command post) systems to coordinate the relief operations at the district level.[25]

The Ministry of Environment also sent its staff to the affected area within the first few days after the event. They set up an emergency group, which consisted of both their staff and volunteers to carry out preliminary assessments, collect data and samples so as to facilitate the planning process,

18 Ibid.

19 Scheper (2006), *supra* note 4.

20 Office for the Coordination of Humanitarian Affairs and World Health Organization (2002), *supra* note 17.

21 J. Telford, J. Cosgrave and R. Houghton. (2006). *Joint Evaluation of the International Response to the Indian Ocean Tsunami: Synthesis Report.* Tsunami Evaluation Coalition, p. 44.

22 Scheper (2006), *supra* note 4.

23 Ibid.

24 Ibid.

25 Ibid.

including both emergency planning at the initial stage and subsequent rehabilitation planning. It sought technical assistance from the United Nations Environment Programme (UNEP) to help identify environmental impacts, risks and recovery needs.[26] The Indonesian military played a critical role in the rescue by providing initial logistic support, delivering emergency aid and relief, and arranging access for humanitarian agencies.[27]

The Indonesian Marines also provided invaluable assistance in the emergency relief operations. They helped deliver humanitarian assistance to the remote areas such as the Aceh Jaya district, which had become inaccessible as the tsunami washed away all the roads.[28]

Coordination of Responses

The scale and magnitude of the disaster attracted the attention of a large number of actors at the local, national and international levels, all of which were trying to make some contribution. The BAKORNAS therefore took ad hoc measures to deal with multiagency responses at the national and provincial levels.[29]

However, while the authorities did try to collaborate with organizations both local[30] and foreign, such as the Red Crescent, to provide basic needs for displaced victims,[31] it became evident that the government was not in a position to provide greater assistance to international relief responses.[32]

At the central level, the government had challenges leading, coordinating and guiding the relief operations in the affected regions. On one hand, in Aceh for example, the international rescue teams noticed little of the national coordination and guidance from Jakarta. But on the other hand, the teams observed that the international agencies simply did not follow BAKORNAS response procedures. Although there were talks between international agencies and high-ministers, those ministers were not well

[26] Ibid

[27] Ibid.

[28] R. Cohen. (2006, January 12). *Measuring Indonesia's Response to the Tsunami at Workshop on "One Year after the Tsunami: Public Perceptions and Policy."* Washington DC: Woodrow Wilson Center.

[29] Scheper (2006), *supra* note 4.

[30] For an example of local efforts, see www.directrelief.org/emergency/2004-indian-ocean-earthquake-tsunami/.

[31] Médecins Sans Frontières. (2006, July 20). *Indonesia: Quick Local Response to Tsunami.* Retrieved from: www.msf.org.hk/index.php?option=com_content&view=article&id=365:indonesia-quick-local-response-to-tsunami&lang=en.

[32] Scheper (2006), *supra* note 4.

informed about the operations and situations on the ground. There were also bureaucratic challenges resulting in slow disbursement of funds to the affected areas and delay in reconstruction.[33]

At the local level, the governments were unprepared and had insufficient contingency plans. This was further exacerbated by the breakdown of the "ad hoc disaster management structures," as the tsunami caused a loss of personnel and the collapse of district disaster management units and government offices.[34] In Nias, for example, the "poor to non-existent road system and minimally functioning internal administrative systems" significantly hindered the delivery of humanitarian assistance.[35]

Despite the relatively prompt emergency responses immediately after the tsunami, the pace of reconstruction remained slow. Up until May 2005, "[t]here were no roads being built, ... no bridges being built ... no harbors being built."[36]

Around late April 2005, as an attempt to centralize the disaster response decision-making process, the Indonesian president issued a decree replacing the provincial coordinating units with the Rehabilitation and Reconstruction Agency (BRR). The BRR would operate for a period of four years. It was directly accountable to the president and funded through international donations.[37]

While the centralization and disparity in terms of resources allocation created tension between the provincial administration and the centrally coordinated BRR,[38] it was generally agreed that the BRR had improved the coordination of response and had contributed to the progress of recovery and reconstruction.

Nevertheless, the government's top-down approach was criticized for including little if any input from the affected communities and hence failing to meet the needs of the ultimate beneficiaries of their projects.[39] For example, housing was set up too far away from the livelihoods of the survivors and from transport.[40]

[33] Cohen (2006), *supra* note 28.
[34] Scheper (2006), *supra* note 4.
[35] Ibid.
[36] By Kuntoro Mangkusubroto, the head of the BRR, as quoted in Cohen (2006), *supra* note 28.
[37] Ibid.
[38] Scheper (2006), *supra* note 4.
[39] Cohen (2006), *supra* note 28.
[40] Norma Susanti Manalu. (2005, April 14). Oral Statement to UN Commission on Human Rights at International Non-government Organization Forum on Indonesian Development, Geneva.

International Response

Despite local obstacles and challenges, the international community was keen to contribute support and aid. The total donations offered from all over the world[41] was impressive with the United States alone pledging US$ 350 million in addition to military support and the European Union donating at least US$ 40.5 million.[42] Private firms around the world also channeled their contributions through nongovernmental organizations.[43] Additionally, staff members of firms such as IBM were encouraged to volunteer their efforts to help victims and to donate.[44] Moreover, nongovernmental organizations promoted various ways for firms to allow employees to participate.[45] The magnitude of the disaster inspired an outpouring of support.[46]

Effectiveness of the International Response

With the large amount of donations, the major concern was no longer resource mobilization but the effective deployment of funds.[47] Generally speaking, international donations supported the initial recovery. Children were back in school, health facilities and services were restored or even improved, shelters and housing were built. By the end of a six-month period in Aceh, some 500,000 people had a solid roof over their heads (albeit mostly in host families, homes while some 70,000 were still living in tents).[48]

Yet a number of factors limited the effectiveness of the responses: Due to the Free Aceh Movement (Gerakan Aceh Merdeka, or simply GAM), of which the primary goal was to seek independence of the Aceh region from Indonesia, the region had suffered many years of conflict.[49] As a result, only a handful of international nongovernmental organizations had a local

41 For a list of tsunami aid by country, see http://news.bbc.co.uk/2/hi/asia-pacific/4145259.stm.

42 R. H. Williams. (2005). Response to the 2004 Tsunami: An International Perspective. In *Raising the Bar*. Berlin, Germany: Global Public Policy Institute.

43 Marulanda and Rizal (2005), *supra* note 5.

44 IBM Corporation. (2005). *2005 Tsunami Relief Efforts WHO Conference Panel 2.17*. Retrieved from www.who.int/hac/events/tsunamiconf/presentations/2_17_private_sector_brent_ppt.pdf.

45 Médecins Sans Frontières (2006), *supra* note 31.

46 Williams (2005), *supra* note 42.

47 IBM Corporation (2005), *supra* note 44.

48 Telford, Cosgrave and Houghton (2006), *supra* note 21.

49 The conflict was ended by a Memorandum of Understanding entered into by the Indonesian government and GAM on August 15, 2005.

presence in the region prior to the tsunami. Save the Children and the International Organization for Migration were among them. Immediately after the tsunami, they mobilized their resources to assist in the distribution of goods and supplies using trucks and helicopters.[50]

A number of other international nongovernmental organizations arrived in Indonesia shortly after the tsunami to take part in the relief operations. For instance, the United States Agency for International Development (USAID) collaborated with the US Navy to distribute medicines, food and tents in Aceh; Oxfam International provided water and sanitation infrastructure; Médecins Sans Frontières (MSF) contributed medical assistance.[51]

However, their long absence during the years of conflict had rendered them unfamiliar with the local environment, which in turn slowed down their response. The result of the lack of knowledge and experience was that while the initial response of foreign agencies was generally considered timely and helpful, some of the relief efforts were considered "ad hoc, unfocussed and slowed down by too many coordination meetings."[52]

During the first few months, the government had been giving confusing signals about whether or which international agencies would be able to stay in Indonesia after the three-month emergency period. Some have observed that these coordination challenges (including international and local, official and nongovernmental agencies) paralyzed the rehabilitation and reconstruction planning,[53] and interrupted the implementation of the recovery programs.

The United Nations High Commissioner for Refugees (UNHCR) was one of the first agencies that set up coordinating offices in the affected areas.[54] It worked closely with the Ministry of Public Works to provide shelter for displaced survivors. However, as political pressure mounted, UNHCR was asked to withdraw from the region by the end of the emergency phase, even though it was engaged in a pilot permanent shelter project to build up to 25,000 permanent houses in Aceh.[55] The project was left untouched for a period of four months. It was only after the establishment of the BRR that the situation continued to improve. UNHCR was invited back to continue with the project and

[50] Scheper (2006), *supra* note 4.
[51] Ibid.
[52] Ibid, quoting an interview with USAID staff.
[53] Telford, Cosgrave and Houghton (2006), *supra* note 21.
[54] Scheper (2006), *supra* note 4.
[55] Ibid., quoting an interview with USAID staff.

a large number of international agencies and organizations were able to establish local presence.[56]

The proliferation of international organizations in Indonesia created another challenge due to limited background, knowledge or experience in rehabilitation and reconstruction.[57] The inability to plan and to execute restoration projects had led to the abandonment of projects, or worse, the demolition of what they had constructed, which wasted a significant portion of the resources.

The large number of international organizations and their insistence on distinct programs also resulted in a fragmented approach, which diverted valuable resources from reconstruction to coordination, caused unnecessary duplication and confusion of efforts and was counterproductive.[58] The situation improved slightly after the establishment of the local Interagency Standing Committee (IASC) in Banda Aceh, as it promoted the principles, standards and policy in recovery projects such as the construction of temporary living centers.[59] On the other hand, the United Nations special envoy, former US president Bill Clinton, also played a part in promoting interagency coordination and improving the effectiveness of the responses.[60]

Community-Driven Development (CDD) Strategy

An example of an effective international–local coordination approach was the CDD strategy adopted by the World Bank. Fifteen international donor partners established a multi-donor fund (MDF) of US$ 700 million to be centrally managed by the World Bank.[61] In search for a sustainable reconstruction plan that local communities would accept, the World Bank adopted the CDD strategy that involved local communities directly in the planning and implementation of the reconstruction projects. Unlike the traditional top-down approach, the CDD strategy is community driven. It engages the local communities and it builds on existing networks. It is a democratic and participatory process by which affected persons can determine who receives funds, in what accounts, and for which projects.

[56] Cohen (2006), *supra* note 28.

[57] Dercon and Kusumawijaya (2007), *supra* note 11.

[58] Telford, Cosgrave and Houghton (2006), *supra* note 21.

[59] Marulanda and Rizal (2005), *supra* note 5.

[60] Telford, Cosgrave and Houghton (2006), *supra* note 21.

[61] World Bank Group. (n.d.). *The World Bank at Aceh, Indonesia: A Model for Community-Driven Development.*

While the process of building trust and effective engagement with local communities was time-consuming at the outset, such investment of time was proven worthwhile and the strategy a success: projects adopting a CDD strategy were completed eighteen months ahead of schedule, they produced more output than any other program, and they cost 56 percent less than those adopting a conventional approach.

The World Bank CDD projects have rebuilt 140,000 houses, constructed 2,500 miles of road and supported 200,000 small and medium businesses.[62] It was observed that the beneficiaries of the CDD projects were highly satisfied.[63] The occupancy rate for housing built by the World Bank CDD project was 97 percent, whereas that of similar houses built by the United Nations Human Settlements Programme (UN-HABITAT) was only about 82 percent.

Local community engagement was the key to the CDD's successful outcomes. Engagement was achieved through an initial investment in time and resources to build capacity for group decision making.[64] According to the World Bank, "while the upfront investment required to engage with communities may seem time-consuming, it has proven to pay massive dividends once projects commence."[65]

The first step was building institutional and social infrastructure. According to the World Bank report, "the creation of the community councils or committees can be one of the most rigorous and difficult steps. It involves educating the community about moral leadership and having the council elected on the basis of merit and trustworthiness, which usually results in the local government elites (who have typically exploited community funds in the past) being generally excluded from the councils."[66] The result is that community members come to see themselves more as partners as opposed to customers or recipients in a development process.[67]

The community councils facilitate transparency and resource efficiency through comparing a number of proposals submitted by village members. Each village can submit "up to two proposals to the Kecamatan council. This always leads to more proposals than there are funds, so the villagers must negotiate among themselves which proposals are the most worthy.

62 Ibid., quoting an online statement by Joachim von Amsberg, country director for Indonesia of the World Bank Group.

63 World Bank Group (2009), *supra* note 13, p. 23.

64 World Bank Group (n.d.), *supra* note 61.

65 Ibid.

66 World Bank Group (n.d.), *supra* note 61, citing Hancock's personal communications.

67 Ibid.

KDP rules require that any village group submitting a proposal must send a delegation of at least two women and one man to the Kecamatan decision meeting where villagers present and decide on which proposals will be funded."[68] This process is followed by oversight by a technical facilitator who "explains the project's rules, monitors participation, and trains the village facilitators; the technical facilitator helps the villagers assess the quality of their infrastructure and trains them in maintenance."[69]

Transparency and accountability is another key element of the success of the CDD process. Independent NGOs and journalists have a role in continuous oversight of the projects by being supported with funding to visit the project sites and publish stories on how the projects are performing.[70] There is no prior review of what the journalists publish, and no prior notice is given before a site visit.[71]

Compared to the traditional approach, the CDD approach was able to yield higher satisfaction and reduce costs for the following reasons:

First, it empowered and supported local communities, which were more capable of gathering and disseminating information to assist the planning, prioritizing and implementation of the projects.[72] With better information flow and better communication, there was less duplication of efforts.

Second, CDD projects procured building materials and other resources locally rather than internationally or through national bidding processes. Moreover, the local communities contracted labor and supervised the works themselves. They incurred fewer management costs[73] and were less likely to be abandoned halfway owing to the cessation of flows of funds.[74]

Third, the transparent CDD projects were less prone to corruption. International auditors found that corruption rates were less than 3 percent of CDD programs, which was much lower than most other government projects.[75] This enabled a more effective use of the funds.[76]

[68] Ibid.

[69] Ibid.

[70] Ibid.

[71] Ibid.

[72] Ibid.

[73] Ibid.

[74] Florian Steinberg and P. Smid. (2010). *Rebuilding Lives and Homes in Aceh and Nias, Indonesia*. Mandaluyong City, Philippines: Asian Development Bank.

[75] L. Campeau. (2007, May). Aceh and Nias, Indonesia: Results Achieved Using Community Reconstruction Following the Tsunami Disaster in December 2004. *Sourcebook on Emerging Good Practice*. 2nd edn. Retrieved from www.mfdr.org/sourcebook/2ndEdition/5-4Indonesia-Aceh&Nias.pdf.

[76] World Bank Group (n.d.), *supra* note 61.

Nevertheless, as the World Bank itself had noted, its success was largely attributable to the fact that it was able to leverage its existing resources in the Aceh region by partnering with the Kecamatan Development Program (KDP), a well-established local organization that had substantial on-the-ground expertise and experience in using the CDD strategy.[77] Without such a partner, the initial trust- and rapport-building exercise and the introduction of the CDD initiative to the local communities might have taken a longer period of time and might have been fraught with further complications.

Local Participation

Apart from foreign aid pouring into the local community, there was solidarity observed by those from villages and town residents who decided to initiate their own rescue efforts.[78] With a delay in communication and cooperation between local governments and overseas assistance, the local culture known as "gotong royong" (i.e., voluntary mutual assistance)[79] allowed for the most immediate possible solution to the situation provided by its own people.

Apart from initial emergency support, local communities were engaged in the subsequent restoration and reconstruction process. As discussed earlier, the World Bank partnered with the local KDP to engage local communities in the recovery and reconstruction work using CDD. Moreover, the BRR was tasked with restoring the livelihoods and infrastructure and strengthening communities in Aceh and Nias using a coordinated, community-driven reconstruction and development program.[80]

There were doubts as to the feasibility and efficiency of the decentralized approach, especially if it was done on a large scale. For example, there was fear that the implementation would be chaotic. The concern was also raised that it would too time-consuming in a post-disaster situation.[81]

However, studies show that disaster responses were the most effective when they empowered, supported and were accountable to local communities.[82] This is exemplified in the housing projects. The following table summarizes the results of a survey that compared the quality,

[77] Ibid.
[78] Marulanda and Rizal (2005), *supra* note 5.
[79] Ibid.
[80] BRR, Cohen (2006), *supra* note 28.
[81] Dercon and Kusumawijaya (2007), *supra* note 11.
[82] Telford, Cosgrave and Houghton (2006), *supra* note 21.

Table 4.1. *Results of housing reconstruction aceh*

Organizations	Construction quality[a] (0–4)	Satisfaction score (–9–9)	Accountability score (0–10)
All organizations in 2006	2.58	1.2	6.0
All contractor-built programs	2.55	0.8	5.9
**All community organizations programs	2.67	2.1	6.7

[a] Ibid. According to Dercon and Kusumawijaya, a house that conforms to the Indonesian Building Code should have a score of 3. It is considered unsafe if the score is lower than 2.5. From the results of the survey, the houses built in Aceh are mainly in the gray area.

satisfaction and accountability of housing reconstruction projects in Aceh undertaken by different types of organizations (Table 4.1).[83]

Projects that engaged local communities achieved higher satisfaction because the community members themselves had the most relevant information and knowledge as to their needs and preferences. Given the close ties within the communities, the gathering and dissemination of such information and knowledge were quicker and more effective. Local participation could therefore meet the specific needs of a particular community, enable quick response to the most urgent needs,[84] and reduce the problem of marginalization.[85]

Furthermore, studies show that the tsunami had brought as much, if not more, devastation to the social institutions as to the physical infrastructures and facilities. By encouraging local participation in the rehabilitation and reconstruction projects, it helped create social capital, strengthen local institutions and increase local confidence and capacities, which was key to the true and sustainable recovery of the affected communities.[86]

Private-Sector Collaboration

The outcome from international responses was undeniably significant in the recovery of the affected zones. The development of local health clinics

83 Dercon and Kusumawijaya (2007), *supra* note 11.
84 Ibid.
85 Ophiyandri, Amaratunga and Pathirage (2010), *supra* note 12, p. 13.
86 Aceh Community Assistance Research Project (2007), *supra* note 10.

provided an improvement to preexisting health care.[87] Other signs of development have been seen in areas like Aceh with ongoing infrastructure construction and large amounts of coffee beans exported by multinational corporations.[88] These improvements are not limited to Indonesia. Thailand, Sri Lanka and Maldives also received many benefits from relief programs aimed at reconstructing the damaged zones.[89]

Outcome

It appears that, overall, in spite of the tragedy, collective efforts brought aid and healing to those in need. Today the impact of the devastation can barely be seen and the livelihoods in the affected communities have resumed if not improved.

However, international aid without community input can lead to significant complications. In areas that did not utilize CDD, many rebuilt homes had to be demolished and replaced by a new road.[90] Such incidents reflected poor levels of understanding regarding the needs of the community and also led to waste of funds.[91] In addition, with more foreign organizations present, local organizations became lost amidst the power play between big agencies, leaving many wondering what is actually best for the community.[92]

There were also concerns in relation to the "cash for work" programs, which were initially introduced in Banda Aceh within the first two weeks after the tsunami, and later spread to other areas. A concern was raised that the "cash for work" programs would weaken unity in the communities and lead to the decline of the gotong royong mutual assistance tradition.[93]

87 Direct Relief International. (2004). Indian Ocean Earthquake and Tsunami, 2005. Retrieved from www.directrelief.org/emergency/2004-indian-ocean-earthquake-tsunami.

88 USAID. (2005, January). *Tsunami Relief and Reconstruction*. Retrieved from http://indonesia.usaid.gov/en/USAID/Activity/340/Tsunami_Relief_and_Reconstruction.

89 Australian Red Cross. (2009). Five Years On. Retrieved from www.redcross.org.au/asia-quake-and-tsunamis-disaster.aspx.

90 I. MacKinnon. (2008, August 15). Indonesia: Aceh Villagers Face Homelessness Again – in Name of Tsunami Aid from US government. *The Guardian*. Retrieved from www.guardian.co.uk/world/2008/aug/15/tsunami2004.naturaldisasters.

91 J. Levs. (2012, April 11). Tsunami Scare Tests New Life-Saving Procedures. *CNN*. Retrieved from http://edition.cnn.com/2012/04/11/world/asia/indonesia-earthquake-differences/index.html.

92 B. A. Sipayung. (2007, July). Local versus International Response: Call for Humility. In *Enhancing Southern Capacity: Rhetoric and Reality* (Forced Migration Review). Issue 28. Oxford: Refugees Studies Centre, University of Oxford.

93 Aceh Community Assistance Research Project (2007), *supra* note 10, pp. 153–154.

It was also observed that as long as there were casual employment opportunities, the local communities would have little interest in resuming fishing or agriculture.[94]

Lessons Learned Regarding Local Participation in Humanitarian Aid

Designing the Local Participation Mechanism

While local participation has been regarded as an effective way to reconstruct a disaster-stricken region, its execution can be difficult. As noted by Professor Bobby Setiawan of Gajah Mada University: "[n]ot all communities are as romantically communal as we thought."[95] Hence, prior to engaging local communities, a sound analysis of the social environment should be conducted. The design of any community-driven project should be based on consideration of the following questions:[96]

(1) What social units are suitable for the community-driven process?
(2) What are the capacities of the communities to work together and make decisions?
(3) How do the local communities manage money?
(4) To what extent have the local administrations been affected?
(5) Who are the trusted and capable leaders in the communities?

Research shows that there is a strong correlation between frequent village meetings and successful recovery program implementation.[97] In addition, an effective community-driven strategy should possess the following qualities:[98]

(1) Form an operational team that possesses the necessary skills for community-driven approaches such as technical expertise and knowledge of the government systems;

[94] Ibid., p. 116.

[95] Concluding remark during the seminar in Yogyakarta, August 29, 2006 – Mendampingi Masyarakat Korban Bencana untuk Membangun Kembali Rumah yang Lebih Baik. Belajar dari Aceh dan Nias. (Facilitating Communities Affected by Disaster to Rebuild Better Housing. Learning from Aceh and Nias.)

[96] MDF – JRF Secretariat. (2012, October). *Lessons Learned from Post-disaster Reconstruction in Indonesia*. World Bank Group, p. 5.

[97] Aceh Community Assistance Research Project (2007), *supra* note 10.

[98] MDF – JRF Secretariat (2012), *supra* note 97, p. 5.

(2) Empower local communities to carry out planning and decision-making processes for their own recovery;
(3) Invest in good facilitators and support their work;
(4) Involve the local authorities;
(5) Develop clear and simple systems, procedures and guidelines to ensure that the communities understand how the participatory process works;
(6) Make clear arrangement for ownership of newly built infrastructure and if necessary, hand such ownership over to local authorities after completion;
(7) Develop good communication systems;
(8) Ensure timely distribution of funds;
(9) Establish systems for ensuring transparency and accountability (particularly in relation to both funds and results);
(10) Develop a highly visible and robust complaint-handling mechanism;
(11) Include prescriptive measures to ensure broad-base participation, with a view to increase participation of women and marginalized groups.

As can be seen from the World Bank's experience, it would be even more beneficial to partner with a local agency that already has the expertise and experience in organizing community-driven projects. After all, "no matter how smart you are, this is all about finding a great local person and investing the time and the small amount of money it takes for him or her to become effective in working with communities in a particular region."[99]

Planning and Designing Post-disaster Reconstruction and Development via Local Participation

A comprehensive understanding of the extent and distribution of impact in terms of loss of life, property, infrastructure, livelihood and economy is essential to the planning of post-disaster reconstruction and development. In this regard, participatory assessments can help ensure appropriate humanitarian response as it allows those who are affected to articulate their needs and aspirations.[100]

[99] Ibid., p. 7, quoting from a personal interview of Christopher M. Johnson, field director of Choice Humanitarian, in 2011.

[100] Jo Da Silva. (2010). *Lessons from Aceh: Key Considerations in Post-disaster Reconstruction.* Practical Action Publishing. Retrieved from www.alnap.org/pool/files/lessonsfromaceh.pdf, p. 13; MDF – JRF Secretariat (2012), *supra* note 97, pp. 2 and 4.

In relation to the housing projects, engaging local communities in the planning process "prevent[ed] houses being left unoccupied after completion and create[d] sustainable communities in the longer term."[101]

Post-disaster reconstruction presents an opportunity for improving building practices, materials and technologies, which could in turn reduce the affected populations' future vulnerability to disasters. In this regard, technical support should be sought so that the relevant national and international standards will be met. Nevertheless, while improvement can be made, it should be balanced against various factors including cultural acceptability, requirements for skilled labor, future adaptability and the timescale of the response in order to maximize satisfaction.[102]

To enable successful implementation, some have suggested that a detailed project plan should be made. It should define the scope of the project clearly and include a cost plan, how resources are to be procured and an activity schedule. It should also highlight major risks that might negatively impact the delivery process so that they can be proactively managed. A project plan can be used as a tool to monitor the quality, budget and progress of the projects.[103]

Execution of Reconstruction and Development Plans and Projects via Local Participation

The common methods of implementation are: self- or community-build, contractor-build or direct implementation by international agencies. The choice of implementation methods is in fact very flexible. Each method can be used in isolation or in combination. In one project, the international agency initially provided completely finished housing but, upon review, shifted to the provision of "core houses" that were structurally complete, leaving the finishes, such as painting and fixing tiles, to the owners of the house.[104]

In order to ensure the effectiveness of self- or community-build programs, the following factors should be considered:

(1) *The skills and capacity of the affected population*: It is advisable, if not essential, to conduct an assessment at the outset to determine whether

[101] Ibid., p. 12.
[102] Ibid., p. 17.
[103] Ibid., p. 16.
[104] MDF – JRF Secretariat (2012), *supra* note 97, p. 4.

the local populations have the necessary construction skills. If not, resources should be dedicated to training and recruitment.[105]

(2) *The type and complexity of construction*: In the reconstruction of a village, for example, the affected villagers might prefer building their own houses themselves so that they can customize their houses according to their own desires, but the settlementwide infrastructure might more suitably be built by contractors as they possess relevant skills, expertise and equipment.[106]

(3) *The availability of construction materials*: It goes without saying that building work cannot be done without building materials. The availability of quality building materials at reasonable costs is therefore crucial to the successful implementation of reconstruction projects. It is not uncommon that during post-disaster times the costs of building materials will increase due to high inflation. The quality may also deteriorate as a result of the large demand. Hence strategic assessment of local resources and sufficient planning should be carried out so as to identify any shortage and possible alternatives where necessary.[107]

(4) *Quality control*: Mechanisms to ensure quality should also be in place. The purpose is to identify substandard construction at the earliest opportunity so that remedial measures can be taken and otherwise unnecessary demolition avoided.[108]

(5) *The transition of ownership*: In order to facilitate the transition of completed construction projects to new owners, the agency involved in the construction should stay for an agreed period after the handover to assist with the curing of defects should there be any.[109] The length of the period will depend on the type of construction, and it should be longer if it is a school or hospital so as to ensure that the equipment and facilities are fully functional.[110]

Policy Recommendations

The following policy recommendations in relation to local engagement arise from reviewing the experiences of the CDD and related recovery efforts in post-tsunami Indonesia:

[105] Da Silva (2010), *supra* note 101, p. 18.
[106] Ibid., p. 16.
[107] Ibid., p. 17.
[108] Ibid., p. 18.
[109] Ibid.
[110] Ibid.

Recognize the Importance of Local Knowledge and Institutions

Local populations and communities are the ultimate beneficiaries and end users of the reconstruction and development programs. Although some communities are more communal than others, they are inherently more familiar with the local environment and have stronger ties and networks in the local community. Therefore, local populations and communities are in a better position to assess loss and damage, identify needs, prioritize projects, gather local resources and supervise progress. In recognizing the importance of local knowledge and institutions, the reconstruction and development programs can be customized to fit local norms, conditions, constraints and capacities.

Develop and Sustain Engagement with Local Governments

In engaging with local governments, a forum for the exchange and transfer of information, knowledge and know-how is useful. Where local governments have undeveloped capabilities in organizing or coordinating responses, engagement in the reconstruction and development processes can serve as a means to develop skills and capabilities through training, technical assistance and mentoring.[111] On the other hand, international agencies that lack contextual knowledge and local language skills may benefit from the involvement of the local governments.[112]

Capacity Building

Research has found that it is more sustainable to help national and local governments build their disaster management capacities than to simply deliver resources as requested. Disaster preparedness should be developed at both national and local levels.[113] Moreover, the 2004 tsunami experience has suggested that the local governments required expanded opportunities to develop their capacities in the areas of planning, procurement, meeting facilitation, mediation and conflict resolution, accounting and reporting, auditing, monitoring and evaluation.[114]

[111] Aceh Community Assistance Research Project (2007), *supra* note 10, p. 168.
[112] Scheper (2006), *supra* note 4, p. 50.
[113] Ibid., p. 53.
[114] Aceh Community Assistance Research Project (2007), *supra* note 10, p. 169.

Capacity building should also be carried out at the community level. For instance, grants for small-scale infrastructure projects, combined with appropriate mentoring and technical assistance, have proven an effective way to strengthen the communities' capacity to plan and carry out future self-help projects.[115] This will not only facilitate disaster recovery but also result in improvement in terms of physical assets and social capital beyond the pre-disaster level.

Foster an Enabling Environment

The advocacy for freedom of expression, the rights of women and vulnerable groups also contributes to a more enabling environment that encourages local participation.[116]

In addition, the provision of meeting facilities and village government offices enables better planning and coordination, which eventually results in better execution and implementation of reconstruction and development programs.[117]

Improve Transparency and Accountability

Transparency and accountability play a very important role in the success of reconstruction and development projects. It is necessary in every aspect of project implementation including decision making, financial and information management and evaluation and reporting.[118]

Participatory processes are the means of achieving greater transparency and accountability as they allow participation of affected people and empower them to make a difference at different stages of the processes. But at the same time, participatory processes also create the need and call for greater transparency and accountability, which in turn strengthen people's confidence in the processes, encourage further participation, develop a stronger sense of responsibility and ownership, and eventually lead to better governance, higher quality of construction and greater levels of satisfaction.[119]

115 Ibid., p. 172.
116 Scheper (2006), *supra* note 4, p. 52.
117 Aceh Community Assistance Research Project (2007), *supra* note 10, p. 169.
118 Ibid., p. 169.
119 Ibid.

5

The Haitian Earthquake of 2010

Introduction

A second example of international-led response to post-disaster aid was the activities of the United Nations (UN) Office for the Coordination of Humanitarian Affairs (OCHA) following the earthquake in Haiti on January 12, 2010. In particular, this chapter will examine the challenges and lessons learned in OCHA's engagement with local populations in providing relief. Unlike the Indonesian case, the absence of a program akin to the community-driven development model led to a number of ongoing challenges, including limited understanding of the local context, limited situation analysis, inequitable distribution of resources, insufficient coverage of affected areas, nonalignment of resources with actual needs and harm to the local private sector, including Haitian construction companies, medical staff, pharmacists, rice farmers and food vendors who were driven out due to the availability of free aid-supported alternatives.

OCHA: History and Structure

The key agency leading the recovery efforts in Haiti was OCHA. OCHA was established by the General Assembly in 1991 as the Department of Humanitarian Affairs to strengthen the Coordination of Humanitarian Emergency Assistance[1] and reorganized into OCHA with an expanded mandate in 1998 by the secretary-general.[2] OCHA is responsible for "coordinating effective and principled humanitarian action in partnership with national and international actors in order to alleviate human suffering in disasters and emergencies."[3] To fulfill this task, OCHA employs

[1] United Nations General Assembly. (1991, December 19). *Strengthening of the Coordination of Humanitarian Emergency Assistance of the United Nations.* G.A. Res. 46/182, Annex, 34, 36, U.N. Doc. A/RES/46/182.

[2] OCHA. History of OCHA. www.unocha.org/about-us/who-we-are/history (accessed on April 16, 2013).

[3] OCHA.Who We Are. www.unocha.org/about-us/who-we-are (accessed on April 16, 2013).

in-country humanitarian leaders, known as Humanitarian Coordinators (HCs) or Resident Coordinators (RCs), who lead Humanitarian Country Teams (HCTs) and work together with the Emergency Relief Coordinators (ERCs).[4]

Besides overseeing humanitarian actions, OCHA's two other core pillars are the coordination of humanitarian advocacy and policy.[5] Policy setting and best practices for humanitarian coordination are developed by the Inter-Agency Standing Committee (IASC), whose members consist of all the United Nations operational agencies.[6] In addition, "standing invitations" are extended to the International Committee of the Red Cross, the International Federation of Red Cross and Red Crescent Societies and the International Organization for Migration, as well as relevant nongovernmental organizations (NGOs) on an ad hoc basis.[7]

In order to ensure that there is predictable leadership and accountability in all areas of humanitarian response, the cluster system was introduced in 2005.[8] Each sector of humanitarian response was assigned a lead agency with matching technical capacity to respond to the tasks of that sector.[9] The lead agency acts as "first port of call and provider of last resort"[10] and is "accountable for adequate and appropriate assistance."[11]

[4] OCHA. Leadership. www.unocha.org/what-we-do/coordination/leadership/overview (accessed on April 15, 2013); OCHA. Coordination. www.unocha.org/what-we-do/coordination/overview (accessed on April 15, 2013).

[5] OCHA. *supra* note 2.

[6] Current members of the IASC are OCHA, the Food and Agriculture Organization (FAO), the Development Programme (UNDP), the Population Fund (UNFPA), the Human Settlements Programme (UNHABITAT), High Commissioner for Refugees (UNHCR), the Children's Fund (UNICEF), the World Food Programme (WFP) and the World Health Organization (WHO) (IASC, *About the Inter-Agency Standing Committee*. www.humanitarianinfo.org/iasc/pageloader.aspx?page=content-about-default (accessed on April 16, 2013)).

[7] United Nations General Assembly (1991), *supra* note 1.

[8] OCHA, *supra* notes 3 and 4.

[9] Ibid.: "Global cluster leads are designated in the following sectors: Agriculture/FAO; Camp Coordination and Camp Management/UNHCR for conflict IDPs and IOM for disaster situations; Early Recovery/UNDP; Education/UNICEF and Save the Children; Emergency Shelter/UNHCR and IFRC; Emergency Telecommunications/WFP; Logistics/WFP; Nutrition/UNICEF; Protection/UNHCR for conflict IDPs and UNHCR/OHCHR/UNICEF for disasters and civilians affected by conflict other than IDPs."

[10] Jan Egeland. (2005). Towards a Stronger Humanitarian Response System. *Forced Migration Review*. 24(IDP Supplement) 4, available at www.fmreview.org/FMRpdfs/FMR24/IDP%20Supplement/01.pdf (accessed on May 10, 2013).

[11] OCHA. *Cluster Coordination*. www.unocha.org/what-we-do/coordination-tools/cluster-coordination (accessed on April 16, 2013).

The lead agency's role also includes "overall strengthening of capacity in its sector, i.e. through building strong stand-by partnerships with other international organizations, NGOs and regional and local authorities."[12] Considering the institutional boundaries of UN agencies, the interests of powerful donors and diversity in relief policies, the task of coalescing around a single strategic objective has been found quite challenging.[13]

Haiti: Vulnerabilities and Aid Dependence

Prior to the earthquake in 2010, Haiti faced a number of serious challenges, including high levels of social and economic inequality. "While post-disaster reconstruction is complex in any society, fragile and impoverished states with systemic weaknesses face even more daunting challenges. Nearly 80 percent of Haitians live in extreme poverty, and more than half suffer from malnutrition. Unemployment is a staggering 70 percent, and tens of thousands of people die each year from preventable illnesses related to a lack of clean water."[14] Causal factors in this inequality can be attributed to trade policies that have permitted Western nations to subsidize rice crops that drive local rice farmers from relatively stable mountain terrain to the highly vulnerable low-lying shanty towns in Port-au-Prince. This population migration into unsafe living environments resulted in increased casualties during the earthquake in 2010.[15]

The highly privatized Haitian economy lacks many basic services, making life a daily struggle for the vast majority of both the rural and urban populations.[16] Even before the earthquake, most schools and hospitals

[12] Egeland (2005), *supra* note 10, p. 5.

[13] Sarah Longford. (1999). OCHA One Year On: Is Humanitarian Coordination any Better? *Humanitarian Exchange Magazine.* 13(10), 10, available at www.odihpn.org/humanitarian-exchange-magazine/issue-13/ocha-one-year-on-is-humanitarian-coordination-any-better.

[14] Haiti Equality Collective. (2010). Ensuring Haitian Women's Participation and Leadership in All Stages of National Relief and Reconstruction. *A Gender Shadow Report of the 2010 Haiti PDNA*, 1, available at www.genderaction.org/publications/2010/gsr.pdf (accessed on May 8, 2013).

[15] See Dr. Paul Kadetz, Problematizing the Inevitability of the Epidemiological Transition: Trade, Transnational Food Corporations and the Rapid Rise of Non-communicable Disease in Low Income Countries, Speech at the University of Hong Kong, April 30, 2013.

[16] Andrea Binder, Francoise Grunewald and Yvio Georges. (2010, August 31). Inter-agency Real-Time Evaluation in Haiti: 3 Months after the Earthquake, Final Report, 20. www.alnap.org/pool/files/haiti-ia-rte-1-final-report-en.pdf (accessed on May 5, 2013).

were run by international NGOs in an uncoordinated way. NGOs have been criticized by some as creating a parallel state-like structure leading to a marginalization of the state.[17] In contrast to democratically elected governments, NGOs are accountable only to their donors[18] and as a result have not achieved adequate progress in provision of basic services for everyone, leaving impoverished Haitians in an extremely vulnerable state.[19] While many Haitians depend on remittances from Haiti's particularly engaged diaspora,[20] foreign aid flows into Haiti from the United States and the UN.[21] In addition, due to Haiti's troubled recent past,[22] the Integrated UN Stabilization Mission for Haiti (MINUSTAH) was established in 2004 to strengthen security, governance and the rule of law.[23] OCHA, in contrast, had a weak presence in Haiti. Thus, MINUSTAH largely acted as a focal point for local authorities and NGOs in coordinating humanitarian issues.[24]

17 See Darlye Elise Innocent. (2010). *Untying the Hands to Tie the Feet: A Qualitative Look at the Vulnerabilities of Post-earthquake Haiti and the Transformative Process Necessary for National Refoundation* (Dissertation, Arizona State University), 27.

18 Paul Collier. (2010, March 3). The Crisis in Haiti Shows We Need a New Approach to NGOs: A Hybrid Agency Run by Government and Donors Could Better Direct Aid. *The Independent*. www.independent.co.uk/voices/commentators/paul-collier-the-crisis-in-haiti-shows-we-need-a-new-approach-to-ngos-1917822.html (accessed on May 15, 2013). See also Vijaya Ramachandran and Julie Walz. *Haiti: Where Has All the Money Gone?* CGD Policy Paper 004. Washington, DC: Center for Global Development. www.cgdev.org/content/publications/detail/1426185 (accessed on May 10, 2013), concluding that "[t]he dominance of international NGOs and private contractors in Haiti has created a parallel state structure more powerful than the government itself. These entities have built an alternative infrastructure for the provision of social services, but do not have much accountability to the Haitian government or people."

19 Paul Farmer. (2010, July 27). *Testimony to the Congressional Black Caucus: Focus on Haiti*. 2 www.pih.org/blog/focus-on-haiti-the-road-to-recovery-a-six-month-review (accessed on May 12, 2013).

20 Innocent (2010), *supra* note 17, p. 25.

21 Justin Shore. (2010, March 20). Haitian NGOs Call for Inclusion on Reconstruction Plan. *The Human Rights Brief*. Center for Human Rights and Humanitarian Law. http://hrbrief.org/2010/03/haitian-ngos-call-for-inclusion-on-reconstruction-plans/ (accessed on April 15, 2013).

22 See, for example, Frantz Douyon and Daniel Holly. (2004). *Haïti de l'indépendance à la dépendance*. Editions L'Harmattan.

23 See Binder, Grunewald and Georges (2010), *supra* note 16, pp. 20–21, noting that while the Haitian state is persistently recognized as weak, governance has particularly improved through increased decentralization.

24 Abhijit Bhattacharjee and Roberta Lossio. (2011, January). Evaluation of OCHA Response to the Haiti Earthquake, Final Report, 64, https://ochanet.unocha.org/p/Documents/Evaluation%20of%20OCHA%20Response%20to%20the%20Haiti%20Earthquake.pdf (accessed on April 30, 2013).

While Haiti suffered from strong underlying vulnerabilities even before the earthquake, the aid system was already complex, involving different stakeholders with overlapping and uncoordinated mandates.[25]

The Disaster: The Earthquake of January 12, 2010

An earthquake registering 7.0 on the Richter scale struck Haiti on January 12, 2010. In Leogane, the closest city to the epicenter, located less than 25 kilometers from Port-au-Prince, 80 to 90 percent of buildings were damaged or destroyed. The earthquake left more than 230,000 dead and 300,000-plus injured. Two million people were suddenly left homeless and about 1,300,000 of these relocated to spontaneous settlements.[26]

These devastating figures can mainly be explained in two ways. First, the earthquake occurred in a highly populated urban area. Second, even though there was a continual threat[27] of natural disasters in Haiti,[28] the country was underprepared for disasters due to systemic poverty and fragile governance.[29] Also, modern houses were built with heavy roofs to resist hurricanes, which transformed many concrete blocks into deadly traps.[30]

[25] An overview is given by Binder, Grunewald and Georges (2010), *supra* note 16, p. 21, footnote 20: "The Group of 11 (G11), bringing together key donors, facilitates dialogue with the government. The Groupe d'Appui de la Coopération Internationale (GACI) includes UN agencies, MINUSTAH, international development agencies, donors and international NGOs; facilitates the coordination of international efforts regarding disaster preparedness and response, to coordinate fundraising and technical cooperation. The *Comité Permanent Inter-organisations* (CPIO) is the equivalent to a Humanitarian Country Team (HCT) and has been the coordination structure between international humanitarian organizations. UN coordination took place via MINUSTAH and the UN Country Team (UNCT), which were both complementary and competitive. Finally, international NGOs with long time in Haiti created the *Comité de Liaison des ONG* (CLIO) bringing together national and international NGOs. Several national civil society platforms were also in place, often with a sector-specific focus (e.g. human rights) or a corporate approach (e.g. farmer unions). Dialogue between the civil society groups and the different coordination forums was often problematic but progress had been made by the time of the earthquake."

[26] Ibid., p. 7.

[27] Jonathan Patrick. (2001, June). Haiti Earthquake Response: Emerging Evaluation Lessons. *Evaluation Insights*. 1, 2, available at www.oecd.org/countries/haiti/50313700.pdf (accessed on April 15, 2013).

[28] Haiti had suffered nine serious storms over the previous twenty years affecting 3.5 million people and killing more than 7,000.

[29] Patrick (2001), *supra* note 27, p. 2. For a detailed account of the reasons for Haiti's underlying vulnerabilities, see F. Pierre-Louis. (2011). Earthquakes, Nongovernmental Organizations, and Governance in Haiti. *Journal of Black Studies*. 42(2), 186.

[30] By contrast, traditional wooden houses and light constructions in slums resisted better (Binder, Grunewald and Georges (2010), *supra* note 16, p. 22).

The vulnerabilities of weak urban planning were worsened by the fact that rural dwellers who migrated to the capital for decades settled in poor-quality buildings that rarely conformed to the lax building codes.[31]

Furthermore, the very institutions that would normally be at the center of a disaster response were devastated: more than half the hospitals in the affected area were destroyed or damaged,[32] while twenty-eight of twenty-nine government ministries were physically leveled,[33] leaving the government paralyzed for several days after the earthquake. The UN was severely affected as it lost some of its most senior officials on the day of the earthquake. OCHA had only a small office with a team of seven including the head of office (HoO), who lost his entire family in the quake. Office premises of OCHA and most of the UN were destroyed or severely damaged. To the extent that the in-country capacity of critical players was severely affected, Haiti was an exceptional disaster, unlike any other disaster in recent humanitarian history.[34]

The UN's Response and Challenges

Overall Positive Early Response

The UN, the Red Cross Movement, international and national NGOs, the government of Haiti and bilateral and multilateral donors launched a major humanitarian operation. OCHA, for its part, declared Haiti's earthquake a "corporate emergency"[35] and deployed significant resources to support the response.[36] Despite immense logistical obstacles due to the

[31] William O'Neill. (2010, January 14). *Haiti: Can Catastrophe Spur Progress?* www.ssrc.org/features/view/haiti-can-catastrophe-spur-progress/ (accessed on May 3, 2013); see also Innocent (2010), *supra* note 17, p. 20.

[32] Stephanie Julmy. (2011, February). Coordinating the Earthquake Response: Lessons from Leogane, Western Haiti. *Humanitarian Exchange Magazine.* 49, 26, 27, available at www.odihpn.org/humanitarian-exchange-magazine/issue-49/coordinating-the-earthquake-response-lessons-from-leogane-western-haiti.

[33] Kerry Kennedy. (2010, July 26). *Haiti Relief Is not Charity: A Rights-based Approach to Aid.* Inter Press Service (IPS). www.ipsnews.net/2010/07/haiti-relief-is-not-charity-a-rights-based-approach-to-aid/ (accessed on May 10, 2013).

[34] Bhattacharjee and Lossio (2011), *supra* note 24, pp. 20–21.

[35] "Corporate response is declared when robust international aid and coordination is expected, and by declaring the Haiti earthquake a 'corporate response' the management was able to ensure that the entire organization rallied behind supporting the response and this gave managers authority to draw on support from various departments and units whenever needed" (ibid., p. 50).

[36] Ibid., p. 9.

damages created by the earthquake,[37] OCHA mobilized its staff resources for rapid deployment and by the end of the second week after the earthquake OCHA's in-country staff had increased from seven to sixty-five.[38]

Critical factors in the early response were the volume of funds by donors and the speed of disbursement. Overall, the response to the earthquake in the first three months was successful in quickly mobilizing aid, setting up cluster coordination and assembling important resources in the form of funds, military assets and staff.[39]

A factor complicating OCHA's role was the relationship between OCHA's humanitarian mandate and MINUSTAH's long-term mission in the country. Clear guidance did not exist regarding how in times of major crises, OCHA's humanitarian role interfaces with those of the mission.[40] Initially, MINUSTAH refused to engage in the early humanitarian response activities because the mission felt that such activities were not covered by its mandate. Only when the mandate was amended on January 19, 2010, did it begin to make its logistical capacities available.[41]

OCHA, for its part, some argue, did not appreciate the complexity of the disaster and did not deploy experienced senior leaders to the country. The Humanitarian Coordinator (HC) – the person who should be increasing the effectiveness of the humanitarian response and aid delivery – had to play the roles of both the Resident Coordinator and the Deputy Special Representative of the secretary-general of MINUSTAH at the same time. Given the competing demands of these roles, not all attention could be devoted toward coordination of humanitarian activities.[42]

37 Ibid., p. 1, in the Terms of Reference: "[T]he seaport was damaged, all staff, relief supplies, and operational assets and supplies had to be flown in via a single runaway airport in Port au Prince. Shortage of fuel and water supplies and damaged infrastructure hampered the response."

38 Ibid., p. 21.

39 Ibid., p. 9.

40 Ibid., pp. 10–11.

41 Binder, Grunewald and Georges (2010), *supra* note 16, p. 24 with more references.

42 Melanie Teff and Emilie Parry. (2010, October 2). Haiti: Still Trapped in the Emergency Phase. *Refugees International*, Field Report, 1 www.refugeesinternational.org/policy/field-report/haiti-still-trapped-emergency-phase (accessed on April 15, 2013). Suggestions to prevent such a triple role in another incident include the identification and training of a small group of experienced and senior intercluster coordinators with high facilitation and strategic thinking skills who can be readily deployed in complex emergencies when clusters are deployed (Bhattacharjee and Lossio (2011), *supra* note 24, p. 11) and "the swift appointment of a Deputy Humanitarian Coordinator, the delegation of the incumbent's other responsibilities to an alternative person, or the appointment of a separate HC as the situation requires" (IASC (2010), *infra* note 43, p. 24).

Despite these challenges, OCHA's dedicated staff managed to facilitate and support a massive mobilization of humanitarian response by the international community for the delivery of aid.[43] The Haitian community largely viewed the initial humanitarian response (i.e., a period of about three months) as timely and relevant.[44]

Shortcomings and Challenges

Limited Understanding of the Context Due to Lack of Consultation

IASC states that "it is imperative that a dialogue is established with the Government, development actors, communities, and above all the disaster-affected population."[45] Cluster evaluation uses the term "ownership" to define the role of local governmental authorities and civil society organizations in the coordination of humanitarian response for their country. "Ownership is important because it can help mitigate the typical capacity-reducing effect of international humanitarian assistance or even support the strengthening of local capacities and help ensure that gains achieved through the response are sustainable beyond the crisis phase."[46] Contrary to this knowledge, OCHA 2010 evaluations unanimously conclude that participation of national actors or affected populations in the humanitarian response was extremely limited.[47] Despite the overall commitment to "build back better," the UN's work in response to the earthquake crisis was regarded by some as "highly exclusive."[48] The international humanitarian community also had a very limited understanding of how to cooperate closely with Haitians from the onset of the response. In the following, these challenges will be analyzed in more detail.

[43] IASC. (2010, July 5). Response to the Humanitarian Crisis in Haiti – following the 12 January 2010 Earthquake, Achievements, Challenges and Lessons to Be Learned, Tranblemanntè 2010 nan peyi Ayiti, 1 available at www.humanitarianinfo.org/IASC/pageloader.aspx?page=content-news-newsdetails&newsid=143 (accessed on May 5, 2013); see also Bhattacharjee and Lossio (2011), *supra* note 24, p. 10.

[44] Paul O'Hagan, Kat Love and Angela Rouse. (2010, October). An Independent Joint Evaluation of the Haiti Earthquake Humanitarian Response. *CARE, Save the Children and the Emergency Capacity Building Project*. 4. www.alnap.org/pool/files/1192.pdf (accessed on May 3, 2013).

[45] IASC (2010), *supra* note 43, p. 25.

[46] OCHA. (2011, February). *Evaluations Synthesis Report*, 5 OCHA Occasional Policy Briefing Series, 16. https://ochanet.unocha.org/p/Documents/OCHA%20Evaluations%20Synthesis%20Report%202010-latest.pdf (accessed on May 10, 2013).

[47] Ibid., pp. 15–16.

[48] Binder, Grunewald and Georges (2010), *supra* note 16, pp. 38 and 41.

Limited Situation Analysis and Needs Assessment Although the undertaking of a needs assessment was recognized as a priority,[49] the Rapid Initial Needs Assessment (RINAH) was only ready six weeks after the incident.[50] Moreover, the assessment report did not provide data disaggregated by communal section, but only compared the larger Port-au-Prince area with the rest of the country, making these data interesting from a global perspective but "unusable by people in the field, who had to make operational decisions based on needs on the ground."[51] The RINAH focused only on needs, and failed to analyze the context, local capacities and constraints of the response. Instead, biased assumptions, such as the view that there was no local capacity whatsoever, or that the security situation was tense, were reinforced. By contrast, actors with good field presence found that there was still significant local capacity, that the security situation in most areas was calm, and that what seemed to be camps were actually "settlements that were closely connected to the dynamics and structures of the neighborhood and the city."[52] This weak assessment of the humanitarian situation delayed the response and led to significant gaps in geographical and sector-based coverage.[53]

Furthermore, OCHA's field offices did not take advantage of the presence of MINUSTAH civil affairs officers who had "good local knowledge and long-standing relations with local authorities" in the provinces.[54] As a result, the international community's contextual knowledge was very limited and it remained in most cases unaware of existing local capacities and initiatives by the affected population.[55]

[49] Bhattacharjee and Lossio (2011), *supra* note 24, p. 44.

[50] OCHA. (2011, July 31). OCHA's Management Response Plan (MRP) to Internally Mandated Evaluation of OCHA Response to the Haiti Earthquake, available at https://ochanet.unocha.org/p/Documents/Haiti_Internal_Evaluation_31JUL2011.pdf (accessed on May 5, 2013).

[51] See Julmy (2011), *supra* note 32, p. 28.

[52] Binder, Grunewald and Georges (2010), *supra* note 16, p. 46.

[53] Bhattacharjee and Lossio (2011), *supra* note 24, p. 9. For details, see Binder, Grunewald and Georges (2010), *supra* note 16, p. 45: "It [The Rapid Initial Needs Assessment] lacked in-depth analysis to prepare an adequate response strategy, such as cluster level needs, the response capacity of organisations and government to operate against the priorities, and the existing vulnerabilities and gaps. This caused disappointment at various levels, including the HC who was unable to convey a clear picture of needs to senior officials in Haiti, nor use it for the PDNA process."

[54] Bhattacharjee and Lossio (2011), *supra* note 24, p. 29.

[55] OCHA (2011), *supra* note 46, p. 5 with reference to Binder, Grunewald and Georges (2010), *supra* note 16, p. 42.

The Post Disaster Needs Assessment (PDNA) from March 2010 jointly conducted by the UN, the World Bank, the European Commission and the Government of Haiti received some harsh criticism as well. A group of local and Dominican NGOs known as "Ayuda a Haiti," for instance, was disappointed by the process, which was, in their words, "characterized by an almost total exclusion of Haitian social actors and civil society organizations, and by a very limited participation by uncoordinated representatives of the Haitian state." The NGOs felt the main goal of the paper was to attract international funding.[56] It was further observed that there was a lack of cooperation with the humanitarian community, leading to devastating gaps in the emergency and recovery phase. This was illustrated by the failure to draw a crucial correlation between the Safer Shelter Strategy[57] and the government's planned development hubs and buffer zones[58] in the PDNA process. The lack of coordination between the humanitarian community, represented by OCHA, and the PDNA process could be traced to linguistic differences[59] and the distance between the PDNA quarters and Logistics Base where the cluster meetings were held.[60] These barriers will be examined more closely in connection with the organization of the cluster system.[61] It suffices at this point to emphasize that in order to get a sufficient understanding of a complex post-disaster situation, not only a needs assessment but also capacity assessments have to be established in coordination and cooperation with the government, development actors and the local population.[62]

56 Ayuda a Haiti. (2010, March 18). *Movimientos sociales haitianos denuncian su exclusión total en conferencia de donantes*, available at http://plataforma-ayuda-haiti.blogspot.hk/2010/06/movimientos-sociales-haitianos.html (accessed on April 15, 2013) (in Spanish). For an English translation, see Center for Economic and Policy Issues (CEPR). (2010, March 19). Haitian NGOs Decry Total Exclusion from Donors' Conferences on Haitian Reconstruction. www.cepr.net/index.php/blogs/relief-and-reconstruction-watch/qhaitian-ngos-decry-total-exclusion-from-donors-conferences-on-haitian-reconstructionq (accessed on April 15, 2013).

57 See UNOPS. (2011). Rebuilding Haiti, One Year On, 8–10. www.unops.org/SiteCollectionDocuments/rebuilding_haiti_unops_EN_web.pdf (accessed on April 30, 2013).

58 Jean Max Bellerive. (2010, March). Haiti Earthquake PDNA: Assessment of Damage, Losses, General and Sectoral needs. Annex to the Government of the Republic of Haiti. (2011, March). *Action Plan for National Recovery and Development of Haiti*, 45–48. Retrieved from www.kirkensnodhjelp.no/contentassets/ee77fa84ec654fb2a01ac3ea8f72bd98/haiti_action_eng.pdf.

59 The humanitarian work was conducted mostly in English while the PDNA work was conducted in French.

60 IASC (2010), *supra* note 43, p. 28.

61 See *infra*, at II. (b) Limitations of the Cluster Approach.

62 Compare Binder, Grunewald and Georges (2010), *supra* note 16, p. 45.

Insufficient Consultation with the Disaster-Affected Population While the Haitian police and UN peacekeepers were absent until several days after the earthquake, the Haitian population began forming camps within hours after the earthquake. In the absence of authority, survivors also formed security brigades and newly homeless medical workers set up impromptu clinics.[63] The interagency real-time evaluation (RTE) confirmed numerous accounts of collective solidarity by the population while facing major constraints such as limited knowledge of first aid, rubble blocking streets and absence of electricity.[64]

However, these efforts were found not to be supported by the UN relief operation. The Haiti RTE observed that "the affected population was largely excluded from the design and implementation of the response."[65] There was a severe lack of communication with the local population while at the same time all means of providing first-aid in natural disaster situations, above all food, water, housing and medicine, were strictly controlled.[66]

Inequitable Distribution

Another drawback caused by the lack of understanding of the context and insufficient communication with local actors was the inequitable distribution of resources. During the first weeks of the response, the bulk of the aid brought to western Haiti was distributed in spontaneous settlements while ignoring areas where people had set up temporary structures in front of their houses. Certain communes in proximity to each other received different amounts of aid[67] from uncoordinated organizations. Some camps were completely neglected.[68] Such differences in agency packages did not

[63] Reed Lindsay. (2010). Haiti's Excluded. *The Nation*. 290(18), 18.

[64] Binder, Grunewald and Georges (2010), *supra* note 16, p. 26.

[65] Ibid., p. 41; see also the film accompanying the report where Haitians express their opinions about the disaster response at www.urd.org.

[66] Ibid., pp. 91–92.

[67] For example, the commune of Leogane received more aid than the nearby commune of Gressier.

[68] Lindsay (2010), *supra* note 63, p. 20. This can be partially explained by the practice of agencies that chose not to participate in cluster meetings owing to their own unrestricted funding (O'Hagan, Love and Rouse (2010), *supra* note 44, p. 25). See also Mark Schuller. (2010, October). *Unstable Foundations: Impact of NGOs on Human Rights for Port-au Prince's Internally Displaced People*, 18, http://ijdh.org/wordpress/wp-content/uploads/2010/10/Report-unstable-foundations-final-2.pdf (accessed on May 8, 2013), finding dramatically better outcomes for camps managed by an NGO. See also The LAMP for Haiti Foundation

only create poor conceptions of the international humanitarian community but also caused secondary population movements: people quickly understood that if they wanted to receive relief items, they needed to move to the camps. At the same time, camps that received less aid shrank in size while at the same time the ones that had received more grew.[69] In addition, spontaneous settlements suddenly appeared near towns and on the sides of roads, in places where aid workers could not fail to notice them.[70] Although cluster leads regularly underscore the importance of ensuring that cluster partners distribute aid equitably from the outset of an emergency response, these incidents demonstrate that equitable distribution was not properly discussed until it was already too late.[71]

Insufficient Coverage Despite Sufficient Resources

Multiple evaluations also concluded that international aid agencies were primarily focused on providing emergency assistance to displaced people in Port-au-Prince at the expense of assisting communities outside the capital, which contributed to population migration to the capital.[72] In Haiti, the urban population is regularly strongly attached to its rural place of residence via families or small businesses. As a result, people are highly mobile and very sensitive to "push and pull" factors, particularly in periods of disaster.[73] Despite significant resources and early identification of the needs of host families and communities in rural areas, the humanitarian community was limited in its support. The agriculture sector received limited, if any, funding. At the same time the flow of resources to the urban sector worked as an incentive for traditionally rural NGOs to provide aid in urban areas.[74]

et al. (2010). *Neglect in the Encampments: Haiti's Second-Wave Humanitarian Disaster*, 1, available at http://ijdh.org/archives/10671: concluding that food distributions one month after the earthquake were "sporadic, infrequent and apparently arbitrary."

69 The number of camps in Leogane started to increase, while in Gressier it decreased.

70 See Julmy (2011), *supra* note 32, p. 28; see for more details Jessica Leeder. (2010, May 8). Fake Encampments Spring Up in Haiti. *The Globe & Mail*, available at www.theglobeandmail.com/news/world/fake-encampments-spring-up-in-haiti/article1320052/ (accessed on May 12, 2013).

71 See Julmy (2011), *supra* note 32, p. 28.

72 IASC (2010), *supra* note 43, pp. 19, 21; O'Hagan, Love and Rouse (2010), *supra* note 44, p. 4; see also Katherine Haver and Nicole Rencoret. (2011, February). Haiti Earthquake Response: Mapping and Analysis of Gaps and Duplications in Evaluations, 17, www.alnap.org/resource/6063.aspx (accessed on May 5, 2013).

73 Binder, Grunewald and Georges (2010), *supra* note 16, pp. 20–21.

74 Ibid., p. 48.

The lack of support by the aid community to people who left urban areas to live with their relatives in the countryside resulted in a massive influx of people into Port-au-Prince. Hence, of the hundreds of thousands of people who left Port-au-Prince to return to their home provinces many returned, taking their families with them.[75] The failure to acknowledge the dynamics of the urban and the rural population flows in volatile contexts created severe challenges for relief efforts.[76]

Security

Another challenge in the disaster relief operations was what some regarded as ill-founded concerns about security. Haiti was classified by the UN as a "non-family duty station," which stood in contrast with development actors who had considered Haiti a relatively calm posting in recent years. Security concerns for post-earthquake Haiti were based more on existing protocols and past experience than on actual security incidents.[77] As a result, the UN security and safety measures unnecessarily spent vast resources to protect humanitarian convoys during distributions and created further obstacles to communication and coordination between Haitian communities and humanitarian workers.[78] The major relief aid agencies, for instance, often ignored the Haitian-established camp committees and made resource disbursements conditional on the presence of UN or US troops.[79]

Ignorance of Real Needs of the Population

The international humanitarian community also missed opportunities to find solutions that would take into account the real needs of the population. With regard to shelter, unlike the situation in post-tsunami Indonesia, living location and conditions were imposed on Haitians more than once. The Camp Coordination and Camp Management (CCCM) cluster, which is central to

[75] O'Hagan, Love and Rouse (2010), *supra* note 44, p. 4; see also Haver and Rencoret (2011), *supra* note 72, p. 17.

[76] Ibid.

[77] O'Hagan, Love and Rouse (2010), *supra* note 44, p. 24.

[78] Patrick Duplat and Emilie Parry. (2010, March 2). Haiti: From the Ground Up. *Refugees International Field Report*, 2. www.refugeesinternational.org/policy/field-report/haiti-ground (accessed on May 10, 2013).

[79] Lindsay (2010), *supra* note 63, p. 20, recounting a witnessed One World Food Program distribution being canceled at the last minute because not enough peacekeepers could be mobilized to provide security.

ensuring that protection of camp residents' rights are mainstreamed by all the agencies working in the camps, was led by the International Organization for Migration (IOM). IOM, not being a protection-based agency,[80] had only three junior protection officers and no links with local protection officers to help it to gain a better understanding of the cultural context and the threats facing displaced people.[81] This flawed security information led, inter alia, to a group of international NGOs insisting on the relocation of more than 1,000 displaced people from a tent city considered dangerous to a barren, windswept area known as Canaan. The well-intentioned relocation championed by actor Sean Penn, whose humanitarian group managed the tent city, was seriously questioned by local residents. One resident described the common frustration as follows: "We did not decide to come here. [...] They decided for us. There is nothing to do here: no activities, no work [...] all we have are the shelters. You can't eat a shelter."[82]

Even three years after the earthquake people were still living in camps and eventually regularly faced evictions by landowners. Interviews suggest that residents were "rarely, if ever, offered a seat at the negotiating table between the IOM and the landowner."[83] Such a participatory approach[84] has been

[80] For details, see Benton J. Heath. (2012, October 21). Accountability in the United Nations Humanitarian System: The Consequences of Institutional Choice in Disaster Response, paper presented at ASIL 2012 Midyear Meeting, October 20–21, 15–16, available at www.asil.org/midyearmeeting2012/pdfs/papers/Heath-Humanitarian-ASIL%20final-2012-1.pdf (accessed on April 15, 2013): "[T]he unique normative outlook of IOM, and its relative newness in large-scale humanitarian operations, make[s] it reasonable to suppose that the dynamics of institutional choice constitute at least one cause of the realities facing displaced persons in Haiti today."

[81] Teff and Parry (2010), *supra* note 42, p. 2.

[82] Deborah Sontag. (2012, August 15). Years after Haiti Quake, Safe Housing Is a Dream for Many. *The New York Times*, available at www.nytimes.com/2012/08/16/world/americas/years-after-haiti-quake-safe-housing-is-dream-for-multitudes.html?pagewanted=all (accessed on May 10, 2013).

[83] Ellie Happel. (2012, March 1). "Returning to Zero": Forced Evictions in Haiti's Displaced Persons Camps, rabble.ca, http://rabble.ca/blogs/bloggers/roger-annis/2012/02/%E2%80%98returning-zero-forced-evictions-haitis-displaced-persons-camps (accessed on April 16, 2013).

[84] The General Comment no. 7 of the UN Committee on Economic, Social and Cultural Rights (1997) defines forced evictions as follows: "The permanent or temporary eviction, against their will and without the provision of legal or other protection, of persons, families or communities from their homes or from land that they occupy." In practice, meeting these requirements involves adopting a number of concrete procedural protective measures. For the instant analysis it is in particular necessary to consult communities affected by evictions in advance with the aim of not only securing their informed consent but, where possible, their active participation in developing and implementing a sustainable resettlement plan (see Rhodri C. Williams. (2011, December). *From Shelter to Housing: Security of Tenure*

shown, time and again, to assist humanitarian relief organizations in providing more efficient solutions.[85] This can be illustrated by the following two examples of the WASH cluster.

The WASH cluster stands for water, sanitation, hygiene. To ensure that the disaster-affected population had safe drinking water, a group of NGOs installed a large number of bladder tanks at IDP sites in the first weeks after the earthquake. However, when a survey was conducted at a later stage, they realized that communities were hesitant about drinking trucked water because people had become used to purchasing water following a successful pre-earthquake government campaign to create safe water awareness.[86] This insight led them to change their approach and support private- and public-sector water vendors instead while looking for solutions to enable the poorest members to purchase water.[87]

In relation to sanitation, the WASH cluster's approach was to import portable toilets, which needed to be desludged every other day. After a short time, the practice became prohibitively expensive. Also, people soon started complaining about the unbearable smell caused by the inability of service providers to keep up with demand due to a shortage of desludging tankers and chronic traffic congestion. In contrast, the international NGO Oxfam realized that they could build on the pre-earthquake, largely slum practice of "flying latrines" whereby people disposed of excreta in plastic bags. Hence, this technique was systematized by distributing biodegradable plastic bags, which could be thrown away afterward. This approach even received positive feedback from people who had flush toilets before the earthquake.[88]

and Integration in Protracted Displacement Settings. A thematic report from the Norwegian Refugee Council, 16, available at www.nrc.no/?did=9642916 (accessed on May 15, 2012)).

85 Margaret L. Satterthwaite. (2011, May 6). Indicators in Crisis: Rights-Based Humanitarian Indicators in Post-earthquake Haiti. *N.Y.U. Journal of International Law and Politics*. 43, 79; NYU School of Law, Public Law Research Paper No. 11–26, available at SSRN: http://ssrn.com/abstract=1833530 (accessed on May 12, 2013).

86 Jane Cocking and Andy Bastable. (2010, October). Water, Sanitation and Public Health Reflections on Oxfam's Experience. *Humanitarian Exchange Magazine*. 48, 20, 21: "The survey revealed that people were continuing to buy water in small plastic bags or from water kiosks, as they had done prior to the earthquake. While agencies initially hoped that providing treated tankered water would have a significant health impact, the majority of people used it only for washing and cooking, and did not drink it."

87 Ibid., p. 21.

88 Ibid., pp. 21–22. For another anecdote about smaller organizations in Jacmel that repacked kits donated by a larger NGO with inadequate feminine toiletries and child care products, see Manolia Charlotin. (2010, March 11). Connecting with a Voice from Haiti's Grassroots. *Boston Haitian Reporter*. www.bostonhaitian.com/columns/2010/connecting-voice-haitis-grassroots (accessed on May 12, 2013).

The two examples illustrate that when local populations are consulted about local habits and practices before resource distribution decisions are made, this enables the development of a strategy aimed at optimizing community behavior instead of relying on ill-informed approaches that proved inadequate for a highly populated urban setting. The plastic bag approach was not only far more welcomed by the urban Haitians but was also more time- and cost-efficient.

Lessons Learned: The Need for a More Inclusive Approach

While OCHA responded to its weak situation assessment with the appointment of an Assessment Coordinator for Haiti in October 2010,[89] it also recognized that a more inclusive approach was needed. It has been noted that a more adequately conducted needs assessment "could have preempted or at least reduced population movements, thereby avoiding additional needs and vulnerabilities arising later on."[90] However, a much more important lesson learned was to build on preexisting local relationships that facilitated the crucial inclusion of local capabilities in both needs assessment and the relief process.[91] With local relationships in place, numerous challenges could have been at least partially avoided,[92] leading to not only greater efficiency but also human dignity.[93]

Interaction and Coordination with Government

The evaluation of the OCHA response to the earthquake concluded that "[m]ost clusters worked almost to the exclusion of the Government in their deliberations and planning."[94] This practice was a continuation of the power balance before the earthquake. Since international NGOs received more funding during the aid relief than the government (which received approximately 1 percent of all funding),[95] the latter was further

[89] Bhattacharjee and Lossio (2011), *supra* note 24, p. 44: This lesson was also implemented in the response to the floods in Pakistan in October 2010 where an intercluster coordination group on assessment was formed and an Assessment Coordinator was appointed early on in the response.

[90] IASC (2010), *supra* note 43, p. 17.

[91] O'Hagan, Love and Rouse (2010), *supra* note 44, p. 32.

[92] See Charlotin (2010), *supra* note 88.

[93] Satterthwaite (2011), *supra* note 85, p. 79.

[94] Bhattacharjee and Lossio (2011), *supra* note 24, p. 32.

[95] Associated Press (AP). (2010, January 27). Haiti Government Gets 1 Cent of U.S. Aid Dollar: Another 33 Cents Is Going to the U.S. Military for Security and Search Efforts. www.nbcnews.com/id/35103622/ (accessed on May 9, 2013).

marginalized.[96] Many observed that only a strong government could provide public health and public education services.

Most post-disaster assessments have suggested that a better approach for OCHA would have been to work more closely with both national and local government entities to increase coverage.[97] Cooperation with municipal governments can serve to strengthen local structures and counteract marginalization.[98] The mayor of Saint Marc, for instance, identified specific needs to increase city services, housing, extension of cultivated land and infrastructural development following the population influx. If such insights had been taken into account in OCHA's coordination work, the needs of displaced people could have been better identified and met.[99] The exceptional practice of the WASH and health programs that moved their cluster meetings to government premises and ensured that these were being cochaired by government authorities proved highly successful and led to a high level of participation by local NGOs[100] and government.[101]

Exclusion of Haitian NGOs

The final evaluation of OCHA's relief efforts in post-earthquake Haiti noted that "OCHA's ability to coordinate and relate to local NGOs and humanitarian players [...] was an issue in OCHA's response to the Myanmar cyclone two years ago, and not much appears to have changed since then."[102] Another report emphasized that:

> [e]ven though local capacity was severely reduced, there were existing networks that could have been better built upon to inform and shape the initial response. Instead, INGOs used their international relationships and looked outside of Haiti for quick fixes bringing in large numbers of expatriate staff which often lacked French skills and had no experience in Haiti whatsoever.[103]

96 O'Neill (2010), *supra* note 31.

97 Bhattacharjee and Lossio (2011), *supra* note 24, p. 32.

98 Clarine Clermont et al. (2011, March). Urban Disasters – Lessons from Haiti, Study of Member Agencies' Responses to the Earthquake in Port au Prince, Haiti, January 2010. *Report for the Disasters Emergency Committee* (DEC), 7, available at www.dec.org.uk/sites/default/files/files/Evaluations/Haiti/DEC-Haiti-urban-study.pdf (accessed on May 14, 2013).

99 Duplat and Perry (2012), *supra* note 78, p. 3.

100 Bhattacharjee and Lossio (2011), *supra* note 24, p. 32.

101 For example, in the Philippines and Ethiopia, see Elizabeth Ferris and Sara Ferro-Ribeiro. (2012, March). *Protecting People in Cities: The Disturbing Case of Haiti*, 9, available at www.brookings.edu/research/articles/2012/03/protection-haiti-ferris (accessed on May 14, 2013).

102 Bhattacharjee and Lossio (2011), *supra* note 24, with reference to evaluations of the response to Cyclone Nargis in Myanmar.

103 O'Hagan, Love and Rouse (2010), *supra* note 44, p. 32.

Yet other commentators found that the response was designed to replace local actors instead of supporting them.[104] While time pressure may explain some aspects of the approach, it could have been avoided by establishing relationships with the local community before the earthquake. If OCHA did not have the resources in Haiti for such "preliminary work," it could have consulted MINUSTAH or made use of its connections to well-established international NGOs who, for their part, had long-standing local relationships. The advantages of such an approach are obvious when looking at the practice of international NGOs with strong local ties. These organizations "benefitted from crucial assistance in designing, informing and implementing major operational responses."[105]

Many Haitian-led organizations could have been supported to play a larger role in reconstruction efforts in both planning and implementation strategies.[106] However, policy decisions regarding which projects to fund and how to distribute aid were primarily made by international actors.[107] Haiti's NGOs received only 0.4 percent of the international aid.[108] "This was partially due to paternalistic tendencies of foreign aid institutions, fear of government corruption, and a lack of communication between Haitian NGOs and international donors."[109]

Exclusion of Grassroots Movements and Civil Society

While Haitian grassroots organizations that sprouted in a wide number of sectors such as education, agriculture or microfinance constitute a vital part of Haitian society,[110] and many members of the Haitian civil society are capable of mobilizing the public and taking action for the common

104 Binder, Grunewald and Georges (2010), *supra* note 16, p. 46.

105 O'Hagan, Love and Rouse (2010), *supra* note 44, p. 30.

106 See Lucy Davis. (2012, January 10). *Haiti Progress Report January-December 2011*, 13, www.oxfam.org/en/policy/haiti-progress-report (accessed on May 13, 2013), quoting Esline Belcome, the president of a local water committee established by Oxfam, who explains that "[a]n outsider wouldn't have the same interest in managing things as we do. We want to plant trees. We want to form our own company to collect and remove the rubbish, and to then employ young people who cannot find work. If we could expand this business, we could get more contracts to remove waste in other sites. This is our community now, and we should be responsible. I feel happy and proud to be involved in this work, despite our difficulties here."

107 Shore (2010), *supra* note 21.

108 Kathie Klarreich and Linda Polman. (2012, November 12). The NGO Republic of Haiti: The International Humanitarian Effort to Help the Devastated Country Has Left Out Its People. *The Nation*. 11, 12.

109 Shore (2010), *supra* note 21.

110 Innocent (2010), *supra* note 17, p. 23.

good of Haitian citizens,[111] nevertheless, "due to their relatively low level of international visibility however, they have often been overlooked or marginalized in development efforts."[112] An OCHA staff member noted that: "We do not interact with local NGOs or government, forget about interacting with communities."[113]

The gap between large relief operations and the actual needs of communities highlights the need for closer collaboration with disaster-affected populations[114] in order to improve facilitation of humanitarian efforts and provide better protection for particularly vulnerable groups such as women or children.[115]

Harm to the Private Sector

OCHA's "relations with the private sector (both local and international) were very limited[,] [...] at least in the first two months after the earthquake."[116] Again, the assumption was that the disaster eradicated all local capacities. Quite to the contrary, private transport systems enabled survivors to leave Port-au-Prince to travel to their home provinces. Vendors sold food and water on the streets the day after the earthquake.[117] Studies have found that in most urban centers there is often a regular and established system of trade that is revived and vibrant within a short time-span following a disaster and should be used as a first point of reference.[118]

In regard to shelter construction, Haitian firms felt their local technical expertise and knowledge could have been used during the initial stages of reconstruction. However, despite findings of a technical evaluation that confirmed that "knowledge of context and caliber of people met was impressive," they were excluded from these efforts.[119] Instead, the imported "HousAlls" did not only take months to arrive but were inappropriate in the heat. Within the same time frame and for a comparable cost,

[111] Haiti Equality Collective (2010), *supra* note 14, p. 49.
[112] Innocent (2010), *supra* note 17, p. 23.
[113] Bhattacharjee and Lossio (2011), *supra* note 24, p. 32.
[114] Ibid., p. 22.
[115] Haiti Equality Collective (2010), *supra* note 14, p. 9.
[116] See Julmy (2011), *supra* note 32, p. 27; see also Clermont et al. (2011), *supra* note 98, pp. 9–10.
[117] O'Hagan, Love and Rouse (2010), *supra* note 44, p. 27.
[118] Ibid., pp. 29–30; Clermont et al. (2011), *supra* note 98, pp. 9–10.
[119] O'Hagan, Love and Rouse (2010), *supra* note 44, p. 4; see also Clermont et al. (2011), *supra* note 98, p. 14.

the humanitarian community could have explored construction "with materials available on the local market using local skills."[120]

Some members of the Haitian private sector were particularly struggling due to the widespread and free availability of goods and services. Since the funds going into post-earthquake Haiti came predominantly from bilateral and private donors,[121] the state received many inappropriate in-kind donations, including bottled water, hardware materials and pharmaceuticals that were already locally available.[122]

The influx of foreign rice, for instance, meant that the price of rice, which was already significantly low due to the prior two decades of American free trade policies, further plummeted. At the same time, the rural farming population was hurt by foreign aid centered on the earthquake-affected areas.[123] This led the then-president, René Préval, to call on the United States to "stop sending food aid" so that the local economy could recover and create jobs.[124]

Urban and rural professionals, including small businesses selling food and drinks, private pharmacists and doctors and small hotel owners, were also negatively affected by misplaced foreign aid.[125] The health care market in particular was disturbed, namely by the impact of the ongoing provision of free medical services that never existed previously on this scale in Haiti.[126] Often local doctors and nurses were ignored by incoming international medical teams, even in their own medical centers.[127] As a consequence, Haitian health care providers became increasingly hostile to what they saw as unfair competition.[128] Hence, while ordinary people were delighted at the

[120] Ibid.

[121] Binder, Grunewald and Georges (2010), *supra* note 16, p. 36.

[122] O'Hagan, Love and Rouse (2010), *supra* note 44, pp. 29–30.

[123] See, for the example of l'Artibonite, Adam Davidson and Caitlin Kenney. (2010, June 11). How Foreign Aid Hurts Haitian Farmers. www.npr.org/blogs/money/2010/06/10/127750586/how-foreign-aid-is-hurting-haitian-farmers (accessed on May 3, 2013).

[124] Kim Ives. (No date). Haiti Reconstruction: Factories, not Fields. North American Congress on Latin America (NACLA), https://nacla.org/node/6547 (accessed on May 3, 2013).

[125] O'Hagan, Love and Rouse (2010), *supra* note 44, p. 21.

[126] Ibid., p. 4.

[127] Clermont et al. (2011), *supra* note 98, p. 14.

[128] Luc Evrard and Pierre Salignon. (No date). Haiti Cannot Wait! Humanitarian Practice Network, Blog: The Humanitarian Space, available at www.odihpn.org/index.php?option=com_k2&view=item&layout=item&id=3128 (accessed on May 10, 2013): "Paradoxically, the poor have never been so well cared for, while the rich, previously the only ones with access to the full range of health care, are now going abroad for medical treatment." For a more detailed analysis in French of the effects of foreign aid on the Haitian health sector, see Luc Evrard. (2011, January). Haiti: Sortir de la dépendance humanitaire.

availability of free medical assistance, the government and private health care sector saw this practice as undermining the long-term future of health care provision in Haiti.[129] Indeed, the establishment of humanitarian dispensaries, mobile clinics and hospitals undermined the health care system so strongly that many private facilities were forced to shut down.[130]

Limitations of the Cluster Approach

The OCHA's Cluster Approach fell short of its intended results in a number of areas. John Holmes, head of OCHA at the time of the disaster, acknowledged the slow pace of activating several clusters.[131] In regards to cooperation with local capacity, an internal evaluation highlighted that:

> the interface between clusters and government-led coordination mechanisms was weak and there was no clear guidance on how the two related to each other and ensured coherence between humanitarian response and recovery/development work.[132]

Some recounted that the government, whose services were effectively substituted by the Cluster Approach, even had trouble accessing the cluster meetings.[133] For instance, a Haitian government official who was sent to a food cluster meeting was barred from entering because she did not carry a passport.[134]

Also, most meetings not only took place in the UN log base far away from the center of town, but also restricted access to people who had

Revue Humanitaire. 27, 27–30, available at www.medecinsdumonde.org/Publications/Livres/Recit-Haiti-sortir-de-la-dependance-humanitaire (accessed on May 10, 2013).

129 O'Hagan, Love and Rouse (2010), *supra* note 44, p. 4.

130 Evrard and Salignon (n.d.), *supra* note 128; see also for a good overview of the impact of free international aid Clermont et al. (2011), *supra* note 98, pp. 9–10.

131 Colum Lynch. (2010, February 17). Top U.N. Aid Official Critiques Haiti Aid Efforts in Confidential Email. Turtle Bay/Foreign Policy, http://turtlebay.foreignpolicy.com/posts/2010/02/17/top_un_aid_official_critiques_haiti_aid_efforts_in_confidential_email (accessed on April 15, 2013).

132 Bhattacharjee and Lossio (2011), *supra* note 24, p. 26.

133 Maura R. O'Connor. (2011, January 7). Does International Aid Keep Haiti Poor? *Slate*, available at www.slate.com/articles/news_and_politics/dispatches/features/2011/does_international_aid_keep_haiti_poor/the_un_cluster_system_is_as_bad_as_it_sounds.html (accessed on April 15, 2013); see also Ansel Herz. (2010, March 30). Haiti: Looking More and More Like a War Zone, IPS, www.ipsnews.net/2010/03/haiti-looking-more-and-more-like-a-war-zone/ (accessed on May 11, 2013), recounting the story of the mayor of Cite Soleil and a camp committee member from Leogane who were nearly blocked from entering the base.

134 Lindsay (2010), *supra* note 63, p. 21.

an appointment or belonged to accredited organizations. However, the desk where one had to register to become accredited was located within the log base. This UN policy effectively shut out all the representatives of camps of internally displaced people (IDP) and local NGOs.[135] Some have noted that the highly bureaucratic cluster system simply does not work well in places like Haiti that require flexibility and adaptation.[136]

The strict rules of access could partly be explained by the major challenge of cluster cooperation aimed at coordinating the "massive influx of international NGOs with varying capacity, levels of professionalism and resources."[137] More than 1,000 organizations flooded in to provide aid during the early emergency response,[138] many having no idea about clusters or the role of OCHA, and what professional humanitarianism meant.[139] The number of agencies that participated in early meetings, often exceeding 200, overwhelmed the UN cluster system.[140] Since the OCHA staff was new to the country,[141] it was unrealistic to expect OCHA to meet the interests of such diverse participants. Cluster meetings therefore worked on the principle of the lowest common denominator, and at their best, only served as platforms for information exchange in the early phase.[142] Only some cluster lead agencies reacted creatively to this situation by splitting the two key functions of the clusters, information sharing and strategy development, into separate meetings.[143]

In addition, the fact that cluster meetings were predominantly held in English instead of the local language, that is, French or Creole, negatively impacted levels of local participation.[144] In contrast, the positive

[135] Nona Lambert and Sabina Carlson. (2010). The Virtual Field: Remote Crisis Mapping of the Haitian Earthquake, *The Fletcher Journal of Human Security*. 25 (87), 87.

[136] Herz (2010), *supra* note 133. See also Satterthwaite (2011), *supra* note 85, p. 79, quoting an advocate she interviewed: "[T]he whole cluster [system] is ingeniously set up to insulate the people making the decisions from the information they need to make the decisions they are making."

[137] Binder, Grunewald and Georges (2010), *supra* note 16, p. 33.

[138] O'Hagan, Love and Rouse (2010), *supra* note 44, p. 25.

[139] Bhattacharjee and Lossio (2011), *supra* note 24, p. 27.

[140] Binder, Grunewald and Georges (2010), *supra* note 16, p. 33.

[141] As mentioned earlier, OCHA had only seven staff members, including the HoO, prior to the earthquake.

[142] Bhattacharjee and Lossio (2011), *supra* note 24, p. 27.

[143] The information-sharing cluster was open to all actors while the lead agency, key cluster members and in some cases the government met as a so-called baby cluster to decide on strategic implementation issues (Binder, Grunewald and Georges (2010), *supra* note 16, p. 33).

[144] Bhattacharjee and Lossio (2011), *supra* note 24, p. 31.

impact of local language use was demonstrated by the experience of the gender-based violence working group that coordinated with local NGOs from the moment the language of consultation switched to French.[145] Despite this progress, many local representatives who participated in cluster meetings felt that their voices and perspectives were not sufficiently valued and that cluster meetings were too disconnected from the reality outside of the UN compound. Hence, many society leaders abandoned cluster meetings to work with communities and camp members directly where communication would not be an issue, while facing severe resource constraints.[146] Ruth Derilus of the Haiti Response Coalition, a progressive organization uniting Haitian NGOs, described the paradoxical situation as follows: "The organizations that have aid distribute it poorly, and those who can distribute the aid well don't have any."[147]

Reconstruction and Recovery

While some have suggested that long-term funding continues to be necessary for Haiti's long-term development, arguably more important than funding is the need for genuine local procurement and participation,[148] particularly in reconstruction and development efforts.[149]

Observers have noted that the aspirations and expectations of the disaster-affected population are very different in the transition phase to development. Strong mechanisms must be built in to ensure that local players are treated as equal partners during the decision-making and implementation process.[150]

[145] Ibid., p. 32.

[146] Teff and Parry (2010), *supra* note 42, p. 3.

[147] Lindsay (2010), *supra* note 63, p. 19; see also Satterthwaite, *supra* note 85, p. 82: "Is it wise, one might ask, for Haitians to spend a great deal of (unpaid) time consulting with INGOs about how best to implement a project, or would that time be better spent engaging in civic action and working to influence the country's future?"

[148] Schuller (2010), *supra* note 68, p. 26, with reference to William Easterly (2006). *The White Man's Burden: Why the West's Effort to Aid the Rest Have Done So Much Ill and So Little Good*. The Penguin Press.

[149] CEPR. (2010, March 17). Haitian Government Must Not be Bypassed in Relief and Reconstruction Efforts, www.cepr.net/index.php/blogs/relief-and-reconstruction-watch/haitian-government-must-not-be-bypassed-in-relief-and-reconstruction-efforts (accessed on May 9, 2013); see also Shore (2010), *supra* note 21.

[150] See Julmy (2010), *supra* note 32, p. 27.

> The current situation requires substantial connection to and communication with the Haitian population to ensure that the rehabilitation and recovery efforts are relevant, appropriate and empowering.[151]

Quick but less sustainable solutions like delivery of free health care services met the short-term humanitarian imperative, but in the long term were more damaging than more complex, localized strategies (i.e., working with existing services).[152] Even though the aforementioned harmful consequences of displacing local labor through the influx of foreign aid existed before the earthquake, the distrust of NGOs strongly grew after the disaster. Graffiti around metropolitan areas read "aba [tout] ONG" or "ONG vole" (i.e., down with [all] NGOs / NGOs are thieves),[153] indicating that Haitians were well aware that only an incremental portion of foreign aid made it to the ground,[154] while the majority of aid worked its way back into the pockets of foreign donors.[155]

Although the transition from relief to reconstruction and recovery is of paramount importance in any disaster response, there was no clear guidance on how the clusters led by the UN would seamlessly flow into the recovery/reconstruction phase led by the government.[156] A common opinion in Haiti is that humanitarian activities and programs are financially unsustainable and are not helping Haitians achieve their own goals so that they can move forward from a state of emergency.[157] This is illustrated by the "cash for work" programs, which were initially appreciated by many[158]

151 Ibid.

152 Clermont et al. (2011), *supra* note 98, p. 16. However, it has been shown that these seemingly conflicting goals are not always mutually exclusive (see *infra*, at II (b) 0.)

153 Schuller (2010), *supra* note 68, p. 33.

154 Lindsay (2010), *supra* note 63, p. 20: "Of all the money sent, only an incremental amount, about 10 percent, actually makes it to the ground. The rest is spent on foreign experts, hotels, car rentals, hotel conferences."

155 Innocent (2010), *supra* note 17, p. 30, stating the foreign donors use the money for "staff salary and associated personnel costs, contracts awarded to foreign firms, and purchase of foreign materials such as supplies and parts."

156 Bhattacharjee and Lossio (2011), *supra* note 24, p. 32. A first step could be to establish an indicative time frame for the clusters to gradually transfer their functions to the government (OCHA (2011), *supra* note 50, p. 7).

157 O'Hagan, Love and Rouse (2010), *supra* note 44, p. 3.

158 The cash for work programs began just days after the earthquake and have employed up to 8,000 Haitians per day nationwide, providing much needed income to strengthen the autonomy of those individuals (IOM. (No date). IOM Fact Sheet, Haiti Earthquake Displacement and Shelter Strategy, 5, www.iom.int/jahia/webdav/shared/shared/mainsite/published_docs/brochures_and_info_sheets/IOMFactSheet.pdf (accessed on April 30, 2013)).

but steadily declined in relevance and appropriateness. For instance, a group of fishermen who joined the program following the loss of their fishing supplies ultimately really just wanted to be able to function independently with the help of low-interest financial loan services. As concerns about decreasing levels of self-sufficiency, especially among the youth, are growing,[159] the establishment of livelihoods that do not rely on perceived handouts becomes crucial.[160]

While it is imperative to provide basic services in moments of crisis, without robust mechanisms for strengthening public systems in Haiti, aid will continue to de-capacitate Haitian systems.[161] Hence, the government, which was itself severely affected by the earthquake, requires more support by the humanitarian community so that it can overtake the tasks of the cluster system and lead the reconstruction efforts.[162] In addition, Haitian private contractors, NGOs, grassroots organizations and civil society at large need to be at the heart of both the operative and decision-making processes. The explicit purpose of foreign aid workers must be "working themselves out of a job by empowering citizens to take over without reliance on external donations."[163] However, the localization of redevelopment decisions in order to eventually break the cycle of foreign dependency has not (yet) become reality.[164]

Policy Recommendations

The head of OCHA following the aftermath of the Haitian earthquake noted that "[t]he humanitarian community simply cannot afford not to work with national and local structures, to the fullest extent possible, however daunting and complex an operation may be."[165] This key recommendation

[159] Many Haitians feel trapped in a cycle of aid that increases dependency on it (O'Hagan, Love and Rouse (2010), *supra* note 44, p. 21).

[160] Ibid., p. 21.

[161] Satterthwaite (2011), *supra* note 85, p. 78.

[162] University of Haiti and Tulane University's Disaster Resilience Leadership Academy. (2011, January). *Haiti Humanitarian Aid Evaluation Structured Analysis Summary Report*, 29–30, available at www.drlatulane.org/groups/haiti-humanitarian-aid-evaluation (accessed on May 5, 2013).

[163] Rick Cohen. (2012, December 5). Clinton: NGOs (Nonprofits) Uniquely Useful in Networks. *Nonprofit Quarterly*. www.nonprofitquarterly.org/philanthropy/21455-clinton-ngos-nonprofits-uniquely-useful-in-networks.html (accessed on May 5, 2013).

[164] Shore (2010), *supra* note 21.

[165] John Holmes. (2010, October). Learning the Lessons of Haiti. *Humanitarian Exchange Magazine*. 48, 1, 3.

can be broken down into the following sub-recommendations. Local capacity assessment and participatory and community-based approaches should be used not only in the sectoral needs assessment but also during the analysis, planning, monitoring and response stages.[166]

Second, in regards to communication and consultation with the disaster-affected community, the UN should ensure that the input of the supported populations is comprehensive and targeted.[167] Methods need to be developed that allow entities to identify the most vulnerable in a disaster operation and enable them to distinguish between those directly and indirectly affected by the disaster (i.e., the rural population supporting their relatives) and those suffering from more systemic forms of deprivation.[168] Response to disasters on the scale experienced in Haiti require decentralized relief and recovery strategies[169] in small geographically defined units instead of through central command. This approach requires building strong relationships with individuals in the respective communities.[170]

Third, OCHA should seek to cooperate and coordinate first and foremost with governmental institutions instead of heavily relying on international NGOs that regularly lack understanding of the local context, including cultural awareness and language skills.[171] To reach this goal, cluster meetings ought to be held in governmental premises and coordinators may be sufficiently briefed on the local context and required to have the competence to facilitate building relationship with the government and municipalities.[172]

Fourth, local NGOs, grassroots organizations and organized camp leadership must be brought into the recovery, transition and implementation planning processes.[173] The appointment of so-called civil society liaison officers might help to bridge the gap between the UN and civil society movements.[174]

166 See OCHA (2011), *supra* note 46, p. 16.

167 O'Hagan, Love and Rouse (2010), *supra* note 44, p. 4.

168 Holmes (2010), *supra* note 165, p. 3.

169 Teff and Parry (2010), *supra* note 42, p. 4.

170 See Ferris and Ferro-Ribeiro (2012), *supra* note 101, p. 14, pointing out that the protection cluster developed a more decentralized approach to coordination to enable a more efficient, integrated and timely response to protection cases at the community level. The approach has successfully facilitated the inclusion of local government. By the same token, when Oxfam switched to this method, *communities welcomed the possibility to know individual staff members and express their opinions much more freely, leading to a more accountable and appropriate response* (Cocking and Bastable (2010), *supra* note 86, p. 22).

171 See *supra*, at II (b) 0. Interaction and Coordination with Government.

172 OCHA (2011), *supra* note 50, p. 2.

173 Ibid., Annex 2 p. 9.

174 Teff and Parry (2010), *supra* note 42, p. 4.

Fifth, aid workers should take local capacity into account and collaborate wherever possible with local commercial providers. At the same time, the humanitarian community needs to be careful to not compete unfairly with the local private sector.[175] In regards to local procurement, humanitarian practitioners would benefit from both assessment of existing local capacity and clearer mechanisms for engaging with the private sector to support the provision and distribution of assistance.[176] For instance, a systematic "Haiti first" policy could be implemented, committing UN agencies and international NGOs to procure locally whenever possible.[177] In regards to unfair competition with the local private sector, cluster lead agencies should hold special meetings to analyze the negative side effects of free services and goods in the respective private sectors and develop common mitigation strategies[178] and look for effective and sustainable methods to support and collaborate with local talent.

Sixth, "UN cluster meetings must be accessible to civil society and camp leadership, both in terms of location, entry, and language."[179] For any relief effort to benefit the most vulnerable, a reduction of bureaucratic, legal and administrative impediments is necessary. One possible approach to make cluster meetings more inclusive would be to embed clusters within technical ministries.[180] Accordingly, this would facilitate the cluster inclusion in the government structure as the ultimate goal. Alternatively, clusters could be co-led by the government.[181] An even more inclusive approach would be to train civil society leaders in the relevant skills of humanitarian cluster administration to ultimately enable them to co-lead every cluster.[182] In order to make cluster sizes more manageable, intercluster mechanisms could be used to encourage clusters to initially form smaller but representative membership of operational actors for both strategic planning and operational program coordination.[183]

Finally, the perennial challenge of balancing short-term needs with long-term solutions and strengthening linkages between relief and longer-term recovery and development requires further research.[184] In

[175] See *supra* note 24, p. 61.
[176] See Julmy (2011), *supra* note 32, p. 27.
[177] See Clermont et al. (2011), *supra* note 98, p. 10.
[178] OCHA (2011), *supra* note 46, p. 17.
[179] Teff and Parry (2010), *supra* note 42, p. 4.
[180] Ibid.
[181] See Bhattacharjee and Lossio (2011), *supra* note 24, p. 31.
[182] Satterthwaite (2011), *supra* note 85, pp. 79–80.
[183] Bhattacharjee and Lossio (2011), *supra* note 24, p. 27.
[184] Holmes (2010), *supra* note 165, p. 3.

this regard, initiatives such as the People First Impact Method (P-FIM)[185] or the ECB Project's Good Enough Guide[186] provide measures for greater community-based work. These methodologies can help improve communication with communities and facilitate appropriate, responsive and self-reliant processes.[187] Progressio's Advocacy Coordinator for Latin America and the Caribbean, Lizzette Robleto, sums this lesson up:

> Haitian people from all layers of Haitian society must be consulted at every stage of their country's reconstruction and renewal – now and long into the future.[188]

Looking Ahead

During post-earthquake relief efforts, social networks and social media, including grassroots public information mediums, were increasingly used to communicate and coordinate activity.[189] A noteworthy grassroots initiative was the Ushahidi Haiti Project (UHP), a crisis-mapping organization initiated to transmit citizen-generated, geographically referenced data to humanitarian response actors.[190] Another newly developed and successful program was the OpenStreetMap, a free interactive map that humanitarian organizations and affected persons could view and edit and link to geographic data.[191] These technological tools allowed volunteers from the Haitian diaspora to assist the humanitarian community with administrative tasks far from the location of the emergency.[192] Another initiative established by a group of international organizations[193] and supported by OCHA was the Communicating with

[185] See P-FIM, ©People First Impact Method 2010, www.p-fim.org/ (accessed on May 13, 2013).

[186] ECB, Emergency Capacity Building, *The Good Enough Guide*, www.ecbproject.org/the-good-enough-guide/the-good-enough-guid (accessed on May 13, 2013).

[187] O'Hagan, Love and Rouse (2010), *supra* note 44, p. 28.

[188] Progressio. (2010, April 12). Three Months On: Haiti Must not Miss Opportunity to Build "Just and Inclusive Society." Press Release, available at www.progressio.org.uk/blog/news/three-months-haiti-must-not-miss-opportunity-build-%E2%80%9Cjust-and-inclusive%E2%80%9D-society (accessed on April 15, 2013).

[189] OCHA. (2012). Coordination to Save Lives. History and Emerging Challenges, Policy and Studies Series, 18, https://ochanet.unocha.org/p/Documents/Coordination%20to%20Save%20Lives%20History%20and%20Emerging%20Challenges.pdf (accessed on May 7, 2012).

[190] Lambert and Carlson (2010), *supra* note 135, p. 87.

[191] OCHA (2012), *supra* note 189, p. 17.

[192] Ibid., p. 18.

[193] Save the Children, IFRC, OCHA, Thomson Reuters Foundation, BBC World Service Trust and IMS.

Disaster Affected Communities (CDAC) Network.[194] It was established in Haiti to advise humanitarian agencies on outreach and communication between the humanitarian community and certain sectors of the affected population.[195]

The advantage of these newly established techniques lies in their ability to allow two-way communication and facilitate the sharing of information on needs and capabilities[196] and as a result, facilitate civil society's involvement in coordination.[197] Among the many challenges that lie ahead is to thoroughly include these mostly volunteer-driven initiatives in the humanitarian system in order to harness their full potential.[198]

Conclusions

OCHA's "Transformative Agenda" of 2012 strives to improve "OCHA's own field effectiveness by strengthening advocacy and building stronger partnerships with governments, regional organizations, private companies, civic groups and technology experts."[199] Even though it has been demonstrated in numerous evaluations that inclusion of local capacity in the relief, recovery and reconstruction phase increases the likelihood of positive outcomes,[200] often, these "lessons learnt are simply either ignored or not acted upon." Indeed, "[l]ow levels of engagement with local people and limited cooperation with the local authorities [is] still the most common behavior."[201]

194 CDAC Network. (No date). *Communicating with Disaster Affected Communities*, www.cdacnetwork.org/public/about/cdac-haiti (accessed on May 13, 2013).

195 Binder, Grunewald and Georges (2010), *supra* note 16, p. 37.

196 Compare OCHA (2012), *supra* note 189, p. 18.

197 Dennis King. (2010, October). The Haiti Earthquake: Breaking New Ground in the Humanitarian Information Landscape. *Humanitarian Exchange Magazine*, 48, 23, 24–25.

198 OCHA (2012), *supra* note 189, p. 18. As a first step, the Harvard Humanitarian Initiative, in partnership with OCHA, the UN Foundation and the Vodafone Foundation, took stock of the innovative information-sharing initiatives used in Haiti in the joint publication *Disaster Relief 2.0*, a report on the future of information sharing in humanitarian situations.

199 OCHA. (2012). History and Challenges. 8, http://ochanet.unocha.org/p/Documents/Coordination%20to%20Save%20Lives%20History%20and%20Emerging%20Challenges.pdf (accessed on May 10, 2013).

200 OCHA (2011), *supra* note 46. Many of the challenges in Haiti were challenges that the humanitarian community has faced before and has documented in publicly available evaluations. However, agencies on the ground did not incorporate enough of the learning from relief experiences in previous similar disasters, such as the Bam earthquake in Iran (O'Hagan, Love and Rouse (2010), *supra* note 44, p. 25).

201 Binder, Grunewald and Georges (2010), *supra* note 16, p. 55.

While community-based organizations are often not engaged as operating partners much less consulted, it is nothing new in post-disaster relief in Haiti.[202] However, the case of Haiti should raise particular concerns because not only did the humanitarian community have much to learn in the urban environment of Port-au-Prince, but the beneficiaries were easy accessible, there were no conflicts or significant security concerns and "few logistics or linguistic barriers."[203] A Haitian-led recovery and reconstruction process, multiple studies suggest, would lead to a more effective transition from relief to recovery, reconstruction and ultimately development.[204] It would also have helped to avoid the ongoing challenges resulting from lack of community engagement, including limited understanding of the local context, limited situation analysis, inequitable distribution of resources, insufficient coverage of affected areas, nonalignment of resources with actual needs and harm to the local private sector, including Haitian construction companies, medical staff, pharmacists, rice farmers and food vendors, who were driven out due to the availability of free aid-supported alternatives.

202 Lindsay (2010), *supra* note 63, p. 20, referring to the situation in the 2008 floods in Gonaives. For an interesting comparison of the disaster relief discourse in the earthquake in Haiti with Hurricane Katrina in New Orleans in the United States see Heather Laursen. (2011). *Non-profit Disaster Relief Discourse of the American Red Cross in Hurricdne Katrina and Haiti.* (Master's thesis, Carleton University), noting on page 6 that victims are portrayed as a homogenized, uneducated mass of colonial "others" in need of much more fundamental and extensive expertise, instruction and intervention.

203 IASC (2010), *supra* note 43, p. 25.

204 Compare Duplat and Perry (2012), *supra* note 78, p. 2.

PART III

State-Led Response

6

Theory and Practice of State-Led Response

Introduction

In examining case studies of state-led post-disaster response efforts, we begin this unit by first reviewing existing insights regarding effective engagement with local populations. In many cases, state-led efforts such as the response to Hurricane Katrina and the Japan Tsunami of 2011 take place in economically well-resourced states, where existing state disaster response mechanisms are in place, albeit in most cases, overwhelmed by the size and scale of such disasters. With respect to local community engagement, existing research provides insights into the importance of capacity on the part of the state for: (1) information management and communications, (2) community assessment and planning, (3) establishing trust between state and local communities, (4) statutory measures and (5) monitoring and evaluation.

Information Management and Communications

The importance of information management by state actors in a crisis cannot be underestimated.[1] Information continues to be the most valuable commodity during emergencies. Information is the main element in the damage and needs assessment process and is the basis for coordination and decision making in emergency situations.[2] It impacts how national and international resources are mobilized.[3] It is essential for after-action analysis, evaluation and lessons learned. And in order to engage local communities properly, the "technical operations in highly

1 Susan Arroyo, Martha Rodriguez and Ricardo Prez. (2009). *Information Management and Communication in Emergencies and Disasters Manual for Disaster Response Teams*, Washington, DC: Pan American Health Organization, 13.

2 See Daniel Farber. (2011). Symposium Introduction: Navigating the Intersection of Environmental Law and Disaster Law. *Brigham Young University Law Review*, 1783–1820.

3 See Arroyo, Rodriguez and Prez (2009), *supra* note 1.

charged political and social situations must be accompanied by good public communication and information strategies that take all stakeholders into account."[4]

Good public communication and good information strategies imply several things. First, there must be clear communication standards for the organization managing post-disaster relief efforts. The standards need to be focused on creating trust and transparency,[5] two main challenges of communication with the local communities, and to ensure the information is clear, reliable and reflects the most urgent needs of the population, as well as to make sure the information is consistently updated.[6]

In order for national authorities to properly convey the risk to local populations and collaborate in post-disaster relief efforts, clear and efficient communication is necessary.[7] Information is perhaps the most valuable commodity in enabling a community to form its own recovery plan and drive its own recovery process.

The media has a powerful role to play in deciding what news to broadcast to the general public. It is a powerful instrument for changing attitudes and behavior in relation to health and the environment. These are critical issues in the post-emergency period. Keeping media attention and involvement after the crisis passes keeps the public mobilized around the relevant issues.[8]

Community Assessment and Planning

Several key lessons in relation to community assessment and planning were learned following the US national response to Hurricane Katrina. The National Response Framework (NRF), which stems from the National Response Plan (NRP), represents "an effort to create a common method of emergency planning among all emergency management stakeholders, including the local community. Its creation marked the first time there was a concerted effort to develop a common strategy in planning, response, recovery, and mitigation by local, state, and federal governments as well as community stakeholders and NGOs."[9]

[4] Ibid.
[5] Ibid., pp. 22–24.
[6] Ibid., p. 40.
[7] Ibid., p. 90.
[8] Ibid., p. 40.
[9] G. Bobby Kapur and Jeffrey Smith. (2011). *Emergency Public Health: Preparedness and Response*. Sudbury: Jones & Bartlett, p. 49.

The NRF "created ... a bottom-up design, [placing primary] responsibility for preparation and planning ... on local communities, businesses, NGOs, and individual households. It placed the responsibility for funding, development, and implementation on these groups while providing the foundation upon which to build these emergency management plans."[10] The local communities and other stakeholders used several methods to complete their assessment of vulnerability, including a systems-based strategy to identify components of infrastructure vulnerability, including communications, water, transportation, information technology and energy, as well as interdependencies between these components.[11]

Local education and disaster planning is critical to facilitating timely response and saving lives. For example, the California Education Code requires schools to conduct regular earthquake drills. Also, governmental organizations may distribute preparedness instructions, such as the LA Fire Department's free *Earthquake Preparedness Handbook*, which assists in preparing individuals for an earthquake by recommending that households keep three days' worth of water, food and supplies on hand, and understand how to shut off gas and electricity lines to a home. International bodies such as the Red Cross and Red Crescent societies also engage in emergency public health communication. In addition, having a clear plan and division of roles within a community is crucial, particularly during the initial response phase before the government and international bodies can come in. This includes plans for collaborating on freeing survivors from hazardous areas and beginning first aid.[12]

Research has found that engaging local communities through a community-based emergency management planning process includes:[13] identifying who must be at the table for successful and sustained community-based emergency management.[14] A team approach brings increased creativity, knowledge and experience to each phase of emergency management planning. A team-developed plan, which includes multiple viewpoints and reflects shared goals, is more likely to be successfully implemented in the community.[15]

[10] Ibid., p. 50.
[11] Ibid., p. 51.
[12] Ibid., pp. 384–387.
[13] Joint Commission Resources Inc. et al. (2005). *Standing Together: An Emergency Planning Guide for America's Communities*, p. 6. Retrieved from www.jointcommission.org/assets/1/18/planning_guide.pdf.
[14] Ibid., p. 9.
[15] Ibid., p. 9.

Studies stress the importance of utilizing existing social capital (i.e., relationships). Such studies suggest that communities should carefully and creatively examine their current assets and expand upon them to best capitalize on their investment in preparedness.[16] A key asset is the relationships that already exist among potential planning partners in the community; these relationships can serve as an important platform for building response capability.

Effective integration of the contributions of volunteers and nongovernmental organizations into the broader national effort was a key lesson learned from Hurricane Katrina.[17] Studies found that this integration would be best achieved at the state and local levels, prior to disaster incidents: state and local governments must engage NGOs in the planning process, credential their personnel and provide them the necessary resource support for their involvement in a joint response.[18]

Over the course of the Hurricane Katrina response, a significant capability for response resided in organizations outside of the government. Nongovernmental and faith-based organizations, as well as the private sector, all made substantial contributions. Faith-based, nonprofit and other nongovernment and volunteer organizations continued to provide essential support to Hurricane Katrina victims. For example, in Harris County, Texas, the Citizen Corps Council – a volunteer organization under the auspices of DHS – coordinated private-sector contributions and mobilized 60,000 volunteers.

Establishing Trust between State and Local Communities

In examining the role of collaboration between the nation-state and local communities in crisis response, some key challenges include overcoming resource constraints, disparities in financial resources and trust between the local communities and the government, all of which affect how the national government engages the local population in the wake of natural disasters.[19]

[16] Ibid., pp. 9–10.

[17] U.S. Executive Office of the President et al. (2006). *The Federal Response to Hurricane Katrina: Lessons Learned.* Government Printing Office, pp. 63–64. Retrieved from http://library.stmarytx.edu/acadlib/edocs/katrinawh.pdf.

[18] Ibid.

[19] U.S. Department of Homeland Security, Federal Emergency Management Agency. (2012). *Crisis Response and Disaster Resilience 2030: Forging Strategic Action in an Age of Uncertainty.* Washington, DC, p. 3.

States in particular need to "develop emergency management capabilities to address dynamic and unprecedented shifts in local and regional population characteristics and migratory flows. This will require close dialogue with community leaders to better understand local needs, including new vulnerable populations and emergency operating challenges related to issues like aging infrastructure."[20]

Studies have also suggested that in order to make information more useful and accessible, the government should "practice omni-directional knowledge sharing.[21] This means employing all relevant forums, networks (including sensitive and classified), and technologies so that information created and distributed by government remains relevant to the public in complex information and media environments. And it will mean staying abreast of the rapidly evolving world of social networks and knowing how to leverage their power and influence."[22]

The question of "dynamic partnerships" with the local communities and national governments includes a recognition of the need to "empower individuals, neighborhoods, and communities to play a greater role throughout all phases of disasters.[23] It is well understood that regardless of the situation, the public will be involved, as first responders, as eyewitnesses, providing updates, serving as information nodes, or relaying critical information to authorities. Engagement with communities offers an opportunity to partner with individuals and organizations in life-saving and life-sustaining actions to strengthen their role in emergency management.[24] The question is whether the emergency management community will succeed in building a constructive relationship with the public to empower them as a full partner in realizing mission success."[25]

Statutory Measures

Apart from community management, the state can also employ statutory measures to engage local communities in disaster relief and promote cross-agency collaboration.[26] For example, in 2006, the United States amended

[20] Ibid., p.13.
[21] Ibid.
[22] Ibid.
[23] Ibid., pp. 18–19.
[24] Ibid.
[25] Ibid.
[26] See: Farber (2011), *supra* note 2.

the Public Health Service Act with respect to public health security and all-hazards preparedness and response.[27] The amendment contains provisions for the recruitment and deployment of volunteers to a public health emergency.[28]

During a public health emergency, the secretary has the authority to activate and deploy willing members of the corps to areas of need, taking into consideration the public health and medical expertise required, with the concurrence of the state, local or tribal officials from the area where the members reside.[29]

Monitoring and Evaluation

The importance of the state's role in monitoring and evaluation following recovery efforts has been identified as a key lesson following the 1995 Kobe earthquake.[30] After the earthquake, the city of Kobe and the surrounding region established processes to assess and report on recovery progress. These jurisdictions required periodic external reviews over ten years on the progress made toward achieving recovery goals.[31] As a result of one of these reviews, the city of Kobe gained insight into unintended consequences of how it relocated elderly earthquake victims, which subsequently led to a change in policy.[32] Past recovery experiences – including practices that promote effective collaboration – offer potentially valuable lessons for future catastrophic events. FEMA has taken some steps to facilitate the sharing of such experiences among communities involved in disaster recovery.[33] A key goal is to build on and systematize the sharing of this information so that recovery lessons are better captured and disseminated for use in the future.[34]

[27] U.S. Government Printing Office. (2006). Pandemic and All-Hazards Preparedness Act. *Public Law 109–417*, at 2856. Retrieved from www.gpo.gov/fdsys/pkg/PLAW-109publ417/pdf/PLAW-109publ417.pdf.

[28] Ibid.

[29] Ibid., p. 2857.

[30] Stanley J Czerwinski. (2010). *Disaster Recovery: Experiences from Past Disasters Offer Insights for Effective Collaboration after Catastrophic Events.* Darby, PA, USA: DIANE Publishing, pp. 6–8. Retrieved from www.gao.gov/new.items/d09811.pdf.

[31] Ibid.

[32] Ibid.

[33] Ibid.

[34] Ibid.

Conclusion

These lessons from national communities in collaborating with local populations in relief efforts provide helpful insights into the importance of local education and planning, access to accurate and timely information and setting up an agreed plan to engage local communities to participate in their recovery process. This can be achieved through community assessment and planning, establishing trust between state and local communities and continuous monitoring and evaluation.

7

The Thai Flood of 2011

Introduction

The case of Thailand's flood in 2011 highlights lessons learned for state governments seeking to engage with local populations in post-disaster relief efforts. It demonstrates the importance of land use planning, accountability and transparency and establishing clear lines of communication with local communities. It also highlights that in state-driven approaches to disaster management, due to resource and geographical limitations, a single domestic government may not be able to give sufficient and timely assistance to everyone in need. Hence empowering local communities to address problems at the local level while the government coordinates central planning appears to be an effective approach in some cases.[1]

Thailand is highly vulnerable to natural disasters and is ranked the seventh most flood-prone country in the world.[2] While natural disasters occur almost annually, Thailand faced one of its worst floods in 2011. Following months of excessive and persistent rainfall brought about by successive powerful monsoons, the flood, which was regarded as the worst in more than half a century,[3] swamped the country between July 2011 and January 2012.[4] The flood hit the northern and central areas initially but

[1] Suthichai Yoon. (2011, October 20). Community-Based Approach Needed for Next Big Flood. Retrieved from www.nationmultimedia.com/opinion/Community-based-approach-needed-for-next-big-flood-30168060.html.

[2] World Bank Group. (2012a). *Thai Flood 2011: Rapid Assessment for Resilient Recovery and Reconstruction Planning*. Retrieved from www.gfdrr.org/sites/gfdrr.org/files/publication/Thai_Flood_2011_2.pdf.

[3] Ibid.

[4] Gabrielle Iglesias. (n.d.). *Lessons on Resilience from the 2011 Central Thailand Floods*. Retrieved from www.asiapacificadapt.net/adaptationforum2012/sites/default/files/Gabrielle%20Iglesias_Panel6B_Iglesias.pdf.

the run-off, having breached a few dams, drained south and devoured Bangkok, the capital of the country.[5]

The extent of the devastation was extraordinary: more than 6 million hectares of land in sixty-six of the country's seventy-seven provinces,[6] including seven major industrial estates,[7] were inundated; more than 13 million people were affected;[8] the death toll was more than 800.[9] The country's economy, in particular the manufacturing and agricultural sectors, was severely hampered. As outputs contracted by 12 percent quarter on quarter, annual gross domestic product (GDP) growth plummeted from 7.8 percent in 2010 to 0.1 percent in 2011.[10] It was estimated that the country's total GDP declined by up to 2 percent as a result of the flooding.[11] The total loss and damage was estimated to be THB 1.43 trillion (or US$ 46.5 billion).[12]

Local canals were clearly unable to handle the heavy rainwater, thus floodwater persisted over months, severely hindering the daily operations of residents as infrastructure was extensively damaged.[13] Locals had to find ways to maneuver across waist- and chest-high water levels after scavenging and salvaging what was left of personal belongings.[14] In some areas, individuals had to tow children and supplies on boats to safety over distances of more than a kilometer.[15]

5 BBC. (2011, October 22). Thailand Floods: Crisis "to Last Four to Six Weeks." Retrieved from www.bbc.co.uk/news/world-asia-pacific-15413818.

6 World Bank Group (2012a), *supra* note 2.

7 Pisit Leeahtam and Cynn Treesraptanagul. (2012, April 12). After the Floods: Thailand's Long Road to Recovery. *East Asia Forum*. Retrieved from www.eastasiaforum.org/2012/04/12/after-the-floods-thailand-s-long-road-to-recovery/.

8 World Bank Group (2012a), *supra* note 2.

9 Guy Carpenter. (2012, October 28). Thailand Flood 2011: Executive Summary. *CaptialIdeas*. Retrieved from www.gccapitalideas.com/2012/10/28/thailand-flood-2011-executive-summary/.

10 Leeahtam and Treesraptanagul (2012), *supra* note 7.

11 Asian Development Bank. (2011, November 21). News Release: ADB Gives Emergency Support to Thailand after Worst Floods in over 50 Years. Retrieved from http://th.one.un.org/presscentre/documents/Thailand_EmergencyAssistanceforFlooding_NR.pdf.

12 World Bank Group (2012a), *supra* note 2.

13 WFP Thailand. (2011). WFP Special Operation (200372): *Provision of Logistics Support to the Government of Thailand's Response to Floods in 28 Districts*. Available at: http://one.wfp.org/operations/current_operations/project_docs/200372.pdf

14 S. Roughneen. (2011, October 10). Inside the Thailand Flood Zone. *The Diplomat*. Retrieved from http://thediplomat.com/2011/10/10/inside-the-thailand-flood-zone/.

15 Ibid.

National Response

The Institutional Setting

The Thai government has been aware that Thailand is prone to natural disasters, and it has been proactive in enhancing its disaster management capacity. In 2002, the Department for Disaster Prevention and Mitigation (DDPM) was established under the Ministry of Interior to coordinate disaster management.[16] To date, it operates in all seventy-seven provinces and has eighteen regional centers.[17]

In 2007, the Disaster Prevention and Mitigation Act (DPMA)[18] was passed to empower and to achieve better coordination among different actors within the country's disaster management mechanism.[19] In particular, the DPMA:

(1) extends the scope of management activities to all types of disasters;[20]
(2) nominates the National Disaster Prevention and Mitigation Committee (NDPMC), a national multisectoral body chaired by the prime minister or the deputy prime minister, to be the coordinating body for policy formulation;[21]
(3) designates the DDPM as the central government unit in relation to the execution and operation of disaster prevention and mitigation activities;[22]
(4) orders the formulation of disaster prevention and mitigation plans at both national[23] and provincial[24] levels, as well as one that is specially tailored for the Bangkok metropolitan area;[25] and

16 Dan Sparks. (2011, November 8). Thailand's Worst Floods in 50 Years: International Response and Preparing for Future Disasters. Retrieved from www.globalhumanitarianassistance.org/thailands-worst-floods-in-50-years-international-response-and-preparing-for-future-disasters-3271.html.

17 World Bank Group. (2011, December 13). The World Bank Supports Thailand's Post-floods Recovery Effort. Retrieved from www.worldbank.org/en/news/feature/2011/12/13/world-bank-supports-thailands-post-floods-recovery-effort.

18 Disaster Prevention and Mitigation Act B.E. 2550 [A.D. 2007]. Retrieved from http://photo-journ.com/wp-content/uploads/2011/11/Disaster-Prevention-and-Mitigation-Act.pdf.

19 World Bank Group (2011), *supra* note 17.

20 Disaster Prevention and Mitigation Act, Section 4, *supra* note 18.

21 Ibid., Sections 6 and 7.

22 Ibid., Section 11.

23 Ibid.

24 Ibid., Section 15.

25 Ibid., Section 32.

(5) clearly identifies the responsible authorities and persons for disaster management tasks at all levels.[26]

Examples of responsible authorities include the Thai Meteorological Department (TMD), which issues weather forecasts and disaster warnings, and the Royal Irrigation Department (RID), which manages hydraulic facilities such as drainage canals, sluices and dams and so on.

Responses to the 2011 Floods

Emergency Responses

Section 31 of the NDMPA provides that the prime minister has full capacity to command and to direct all government agencies and local administrations to take measures to deliver emergency relief and to assist people who are affected. Owing to the severity of the floods, this section was invoked by Prime Minister Yingluck Shinawatra on October 21, 2011, to take control of the emergency response.

In addition, in response to the floods in 2011, the Flood Relief Operations Center (FROC), chaired by the justice minister, was set up on October 21, 2011, to replace its predecessor, the Emergency Operation Center, which coordinates emergency response and delivery of aid.[27]

Other government departments and ministries were also involved in the initial emergency response. For example:

(1) The Ministry of Social Development and Human Security established more than 2,400 shelters nationwide;[28]
(2) The Bangkok Metropolitan Administration established an additional 175 shelters for residents of the country's capital;[29]
(3) The Ministry of Public Health set up emergency clinics in the affected areas;[30]
(4) The Royal Thai Army mobilized its personnel to assist with flood water management, distribution of aid and supplies to the people affected and so on.[31]

[26] Ibid., Chapter 6.
[27] World Bank Group (2012a), *supra* note 2, Annex 24.
[28] Ibid.
[29] Ibid., Annex 24.
[30] Ibid.
[31] Ibid.

Immediate Recovery

In order to facilitate recovery, the Bank of Thailand reduced the interest rate to 3 percent. In addition, the Thai government approved three financial decrees, totaling THB 700 billion (US$ 22.5 billion), for rehabilitation and long-term water management systems. More specifically, the Thai government put forward a stimulus package that provided a range of measures and financial support, targeting the affected population.[32]

For instance, in respect of the flood-affected households, the Thai Government made available a cash grant of THB 5,000 per household, with the possibility of an additional THB 2,000 for those that required additional support.[33] Furthermore, they were entitled to household recovery allowances, which were capped at THB 200,000 for partially damaged houses, and THB 300,000 for completely destroyed houses.[34]

To make the country's economy more disaster-resilient, the Thai government made available a range of financial measures and incentives, including a debt moratorium, low-interest loans, and other loan arrangements with the aim of providing affected sectors such as agriculture and farming the capital to invest in recovery projects.[35]

A national disaster fund was pledged by the local government to support flooding victims by providing natural disaster risk coverage.[36] It was estimated that up to THB 500 billion (US$ 16.1 billion) worth of losses could be insured.[37] Various investment projects were initiated to allow for more long-term infrastructure to be built that will hopefully prevent future flooding and better management of areas along the Chao Phraya River Basin.[38] Such investments were not limited nationally, however; overseas sources also contributed to these projects, including funds from Japan.[39]

External Support

The sheer scale and magnitude of the floods and the massive displacement caused by the widespread flooding attracted much international attention

[32] World Bank Group (2012a), *supra* note 2.

[33] Ibid.

[34] Ibid.

[35] Ibid.

[36] AON Benfield. (2011). *Thailand Floods Event Recap Report*. Chicago: Impact Forecasting LLC.

[37] Ibid.

[38] Ibid.

[39] Ibid.

and response. By the end of 2011, the Thai government had received more than US$ 2 million in donations from other countries and international nongovernmental organizations.[40] Moreover, through working closely with both the national and local authorities, international organizations were able to provide assistance to those who were affected and displaced by the floods.

The United Nations

The United Nations extended its assistance to Thailand by providing relief items such as cooking equipment, insecticide-treated mosquito nets, generators and solar-powered lamps in evacuation centers;[41] supplying basic and emergency health kits and other medical equipment to mobile clinics and other health facilities;[42] delivering locally purchased supplies to the affected families via the Ministry of Public Health (MOPH);[43] distributing pamphlets and educating the public on how they can protect their health during emergencies;[44] providing items for water purification (such as chlorine drops), alcohol hand-wash gel and garbage bags to improve the water, sanitation and hygiene situation and help prevent the spread of communicable diseases;[45] setting up child-friendly spaces in shelters for children to enjoy a safe place for recreation and receive psychosocial support;[46] and distributing "school in a box" kits, which contained teaching and learning supplies such as notebooks, pencils, rulers, chalks, markers, maps and posters, through the Ministry of Education so that lessons could continue while schools were being repaired or refurbished.[47]

[40] Church World Service Asia/Pacific. (2011, December 2). *Thailand Floods: Situation Report and Emergency Appeal.* Retrieved from www.cwsasiapacific.org/wp-content/uploads/2012/01/2011.12.02-CWS-ACT-Thai-Flood-Sit-Rep.web_.pdf.

[41] UNESCO Bangkok. (2011, November 22). UN Lends Full Support for Thailand Flood Response. Retrieved from www.unescobkk.org/news/article/un-lends-full-support-for-thailand-flood-response/.

[42] United Nations Country Team in Thailand. (2011, November 18). Press Release: UN Lends Full Support for Thailand Flood Response. Retrieved from www.un.or.th/presscentre/documents/111118UNCTPressReleaseonflooding.pdf.

[43] UNICEF. Press Release (2011, November 10). UNICEF Provides 300,000 Water, Sanitation, Hygiene Items for Flood Victims. Retrieved from http://www.unicef.org/media/media_60473.html.

[44] Ibid.

[45] Ibid.

[46] United Nations Country Team in Thailand (2011), *supra* note 42.

[47] Ibid.

International Organization for Migration (IOM)

The International Organization for Migration (IOM) also worked closely with other organizations, other countries and the Thai government to provide immediate assistance to the affected population. For instance, it collected donations from international organizations and communities, including the United States Agency for International Development (USAID), the United Nations Office for the Coordination of Humanitarian Affairs (OCHA) and the governments of Australia, Germany and Israel;[48] procured emergency equipment, including boats, life vests, pumps, generators, water purifiers and water treatment kits; and delivered the same to DDPM for distribution.[49]

Furthermore, to overcome unnecessary bureaucracy and to reach the flood victims more quickly, it distributed food, mosquito nets, hygiene items and medical supplies and so on directly to the affected migrant population.[50]

Thai Red Cross

Similar to other international organizations, the Thai Red Cross distributed food and nonfood items, including relief kits, bottled water, food packs, ready-to-eat meals and medical kits in the affected areas.[51]

In addition, it deployed and operated: sixteen flat-bottom boats in six provinces, working alongside authorities to evacuate communities that were at risk; three water purification trucks in two provinces; and three mobile health units, which consisted of a medical doctor, a pharmacist and a nurse, in two provinces using a flat-bottom boat to reach isolated communities.[52]

ActionAid

ActionAid worked closely with local authorities to distribute necessities such as food and basic medicine to high-risk families who had been displaced.[53]

[48] International Organization for Migration. (2012, March). *Overview of IOM's Flood Relief Efforts during the Thai Flood Crisis 2011/12*, 2012. Retrieved from www.iom.int/jahia/webdav/shared/shared/mainsite/activities/countries/docs/thailand/Overview-IOM-Flood-Response-Thailand-March-2012.pdf.

[49] Ibid.

[50] Ibid.

[51] World Bank Group (2012a), *supra* note 2.

[52] Ibid.

[53] ActionAid. (2011, October 27). *Thailand Floods – ActionAid's Response*. Retrieved from www.actionaid.org.uk/103061/thailand_floods___actionaids_response.html (accessed on January 13, 2013).

Unfortunately, despite such efforts, due to geographical difficulties many were still not reached.[54]

Local Participation

In the aftermath of the floods, the Thai government engaged local communities for the purpose of flood management. During the five-day Workshop on the Development of a National Strategy for Integrated Flood Management for Thailand in March 2012, it was recognized that community participation was central in improving preparedness, emergency responses and recovery actions.[55]

Nonetheless, while the government identified a few potential problems in involving local communities, such as insufficient or inefficient communication and limited knowledge and expertise in flood prevention and management,[56] the community-based approach seemed to have been implemented successfully and effectively, building on local leaders' own initiatives as demonstrated by the following examples.

In Tambon Bangrakam, Banglane District, Nakhon Pathom Province

Learning from their experience in the 2006 flood that severely damaged their homes and farmland, the local community leaders of Tambon Bangrakam in Banglane district, Nakhon Pathom province realized that they could not merely wait for and count on the government to cope with the natural disaster.[57] And as they knew the local terrain and social network better than anyone else who could have come to their aid, they decided to make their own antiflood plan.[58] They acknowledged that it would be more efficient to collaborate with others, and joined forces with leaders of nearby provinces such as Chai Nat, Suphan Buri and Samut Sakhon to form a small-scale, local antiflood alliance.[59]

Through collaboration, the local disaster network worked out preparation, emergency response, evacuation and recovery plans.[60] It set aside

[54] Ibid.

[55] Thai Meteorological Department and World Meteorological Organization. (2012). *Report: Workshop on the Development of a National Strategy for Integrated Flood Management for Thailand*. Retrieved from www.apfm.info/pdf/Reports/THAILAND_IFM_REPORT_MARCH_2012.pdf.

[56] Ibid.

[57] Yoon (2011), *supra* note 1.

[58] Ibid.

[59] Ibid.

[60] Ibid.

certain areas for evacuation, erected embankments to protect roads vital for communications and heavily populated areas, diverted and released excessive water into vacant farmland, and preserved those lands on which crops had not been harvested.[61] As a result, the flooding was confined to about three to five centimeters above the road surface, which was manageable for the affected villagers. Further, loss and damage were minimized, and the recovery and rehabilitation process was facilitated.[62]

In the Province of Pathum Thani

The local communities in the province of Pathum Thani were located in the low-lying area by the Chao Phraya River, which was about forty-six kilometers from Bangkok.[63] The floodwater inundated homes and farmland of the villagers in October 2011; the water level was over two meters and food supplies were limited.[64] The situation was worsened by the fact that pregnant women and babies needed urgent attention and some of the elderly populations refused to leave their homes and move to evacuation centers.[65]

Chaluay Kawaonag, the chairperson of a local committee, then took the lead and worked with leaders from twenty-eight neighboring communities to cope with the floods.[66] They drew up the daily plan to feed the 3,050 households in the area, along with the thousands of outsiders stranded by the floods. They gathered boats to bring people to safe quarters like the local temple, to relay messages to the municipality that in addition to relief kits, medicines and milk powder were needed. They also requested assistance to resolve burglaries and conflicts in the evacuation camps.[67]

Following a joint study process with community members to understand local needs, they worked to advance the following goals:[68] to educate the populations on undertaking urgent renovations, such as raising the floors of their houses through government loans;[69] to work with local

[61] Ibid.

[62] Ibid.

[63] UN Women. (2012, January 3). Leadership in Communities: Thai Women Preparing for Natural Disaster. Retrieved from www.unwomen.org/2012/01/leadership-in-communities-thai-women-preparing-for-natural-disasters/.

[64] Ibid.

[65] Ibid.

[66] Ibid.

[67] Ibid.

[68] Ibid.

[69] Ibid.

authorities to ensure that boats were available and functional to transport pregnant women and the disabled to safety;[70] and to create a designated community center nearby, for the many who would not evacuate their homes.[71] It was believed that through community participation, they were able to "[accept] nature, but [cope] better."[72]

Private-Sector Collaboration

Anecdotal reports revealed that the private sector had provided significant support to local communities and community-based organizations;[73] it attempted to provide as much of its services as possible to the affected regions. Citibank and Thanachart Bank, for example, opened accounts and services to allow donation deposits.[74] Advanced Info Service (AIS) provided free telephone services worth THB 30 million to those in affected regions.[75] Chevrolet Sales Thailand offered delivery of supplies to schools in selected regions over a two-week period.[76]

Coca-Cola donated more than US$ 2 million to "reunite to relieve and rebuild Thailand" by providing emergency relief and rehabilitation to flood victims.[77] As part of the project, the company supported Habitat for Humanity Thailand to rebuild schools and homes; committed 5 million bottles of water for relief agencies; partnered with the Thai Red Cross and Habitat for Humanity Thailand to operate mobile kitchens and deliver bottled water and food.[78] Further, the company put on hold TV commercials and other advertising materials for all Coca-Cola brands and redirected them to raise money and to recruit volunteers.[79]

[70] Ibid.
[71] Ibid.
[72] Ibid.
[73] World Bank Group (2012a), *supra* note 2.
[74] The Nation Thailand. (2011, October 13). Private Sector's Supports. Retrieved from www.nationmultimedia.com/business/Private-sectors-supports-30167574.html.
[75] Ibid.
[76] Ibid.
[77] Coca-Cola. (2011, November 21). The Coca-Cola System Donates More Than 2 Million USD for Flood Victims in Thailand. Retrieved from www.coca-colacompany.com/press-center/company-articles/the-coca-cola-system-donates-more-than-2-million-usd-for-flood-victims-in-thailand.
[78] Ibid.
[79] Ibid.

Outcome

The floods eventually receded in January 2012 and, although there were reservations about Thailand's long-term growth,[80] the country's economy gradually recovered. For example, the number of tourist arrivals rose to 1.95 million in January 2012, representing a 9.5 percent increase from December 2011. Moreover, by April 2012, 70 percent of the 800 flood-hit industrial operators supported by the Thailand Board of Investment had resumed operations.[81]

Overall the response appeared optimistic and positive, yet from the local perspective, there were shortfalls as the damage exceeded relief efforts and many people consequently suffered as a result.[82] As mentioned earlier, there were many physical constraints, such as geographical difficulties, limiting the access of support and relief reaching those affected. Even with the Thai government and international aid working together, some areas were left unattended and neglected due to limited manpower and the large numbers of victims.[83] In some areas, relief work simply came too late. Food and supplies usually benefited only those who lived near the distribution points, whereas those with the greatest need, furthest away from distribution points, were unable to be reached by relief teams to receive supplies.[84]

Although private firms and neighboring countries donated boats in an attempt to assist, the boats, unfortunately, did not come with outboard engines.[85] Therefore, assistance in the form of engine provision from local firms was requested by the government to ensure the relief operations could go forward.[86] It is evident that little communication and coordination occurred between disaster relief teams and organizations. This consequently led to duplication of work in some areas,[87] suggesting even more inefficient resources use.

[80] See, for example, Credit Suisse. (2012, February 13). Thailand's Post-flood Recovery: Turning the Tide. Retrieved from https://doc.research-and-analytics.csfb.com/docView?language=ENG&format=PDF&document_id=804818550&source_id=em&serialid=%2FuPFdB3n5KRuP7HWRGJetxYWrNJETP4p9yMKQXENObY%3D.

[81] Leeahtam and Treesraptanagul (2012), *supra* note 7.

[82] Regina Quadir. (2012, February 14). The Great Flood of 2011, Thailand: A Firsthand Account. *Centers for Disease Control and Prevention*. Retrieved from http://blogs.cdc.gov/publichealthmatters/2012/02/the-great-flood-of-2011-thailand-a-firsthand-account-3/.

[83] Ibid.

[84] Ibid.

[85] WFP Thailand (2011), *supra* note 13.

[86] Ibid.

[87] Quadir (2012), *supra* note 82.

It is clear from the tragic experience that floods of such magnitude can never be anticipated or fully prepared for. Even with massive amounts of relief efforts and support from various bodies in the aftermath, many human and physical issues hinder the potential influence of aid to the affected.

Lesson Learned

A number of lessons were learned regarding state–local engagement following the aftermath of the Thai flood in 2011. These lessons included the importance of risk assessment and knowledge dissemination, emergency management and coordination and community-based planning, discussed in further detail as follows.

Risk Assessment and Dissemination of Knowledge

Risk assessment is crucial to the prevention and planning of response to natural disasters. While it can be conducted by the government using advanced technologies, community-based assessments that engage local residents who possess knowledge of the disaster-prone terrain have been found to be more useful and effective.[88]

Moreover, the results of risk assessments must be communicated to the public. Sometimes people base their decisions such as whether to leave home and move to an evacuation center on their experience of floods in the past. For example, during the 2011 floods, some people were convinced that they did not need to leave their homes because the water reached only the first floor last time.[89] They turned out to be wrong when the rising water isolated them and the relief personnel, short of boats and supplies, couldn't reach them.[90] As one official noted, "people will not evacuate when they can, and want to evacuate when it is not possible."[91]

Hence, in addition to conducting timely and comprehensive risk assessments, it is very important to share information with the public and make

[88] Ministry of Finance, Royal Thai Government and The World Bank. (2012, January 18). *Thailand Flooding 2554 Rapid Assessment for Resilient Recovery and Reconstruction Planning*. Retrieved from www.undp.org/content/dam/thailand/docs/UNDP_RRR_THFloods.pdf.

[89] Yoon (2011), *supra* note 1.

[90] Ibid.

[91] Ministry of Finance, Royal Thai Government and The World Bank (2012), *supra* note 88.

sure that they understand the implications so that vulnerability to future risks can be reduced.[92]

Emergency Management and Coordination

According to the National Disaster Prevention and Management Plan, more than ten ministries and organizations were designated as key disaster management agencies.[93] In addition, adhoc national disaster response committees were set up. For example, the Emergency Operation Center was set up on August 22, 2011, but was replaced shortly by the Flood Relief Operation Center (FROC) on October 21, 2011, due to its ineffectiveness.[94] In the absence of a clear definition of roles and responsibilities, and without good coordination and communication, efforts were duplicated and valuable resources were wasted.[95]

It was also noted that there was a lack of coordination on flood prevention and management planning across administrative areas; there was conflict within and between communities that border different administrative zones.[96] Better coordination and communication could have resulted in more effective and efficient relief responses and recovery.

Urban Vulnerability

The flooding in 2011 was so widespread that many urban and suburban areas that had not had any flooding problems for more a decade were deluged.[97] This had two implications: first, the land use planning was done without giving any due consideration to flood prevention or floodwater management (meaning that the density of the settlements was high, there was no room for the absorption or retention of excessive water etc.); and second, the communities in those areas lacked experience in dealing with flooding and hence they were less resilient and adaptive to the situation.[98] Therefore, better land use planning and public awareness are needed to improve preparedness of urban communities and thereby reduce vulnerability to disasters.[99]

[92] Ibid.
[93] Ibid.
[94] Ibid.
[95] Ibid.; Quadir (2012), *supra* note 82.
[96] Ministry of Finance, Royal Thai Government and The World Bank (2012), *supra* note 88.
[97] Ibid.
[98] Ibid.
[99] World Bank Group (2011), *supra* note 17.

Community-Based Approach

Community-based responses can complement and extend the reach of government plans as local communities possess knowledge of the terrain and the needs of the people. Further, they are in a better position to deploy local resources and utilize social networks. Not only does a community-centered response help raise public awareness, it also allows the development of a stronger sense of responsibility and ownership.[100]

Through the provision of training and support,[101] and partnerships with local nongovernmental and civil society organizations, community members can engage in training, coordinating and preparing for disaster risk management.[102]

Policy Recommendations

Drawing on lessons learned from the 2011 flood in Thailand, the following policy recommendations can be considered for future disaster response planning.

Capacity Assessment and Resources Mapping at the Local Level

The Thai government, local government authorities and agencies, nongovernmental organizations, civil society institutions and local communities should be engaged in assessing[103] both risks and local capacity and in identifying the resources available to respond to future disasters.[104] This enables communities to plan ahead and seek assistance in advance where there is inadequacy.

Relief management through tracking skills, expertise and inventory in post-disaster regions has been found to be a critical element in recovery efforts. Tools such as open data platforms, data-sharing protocols among the involved institutions, crowd-sourcing tools and OpenStreetMap are useful in this regard and can be deployed.[105]

100 Ministry of Finance, Royal Thai Government and The World Bank (2012), *supra* note 88.
101 Thai Meteorological Department and World Meteorological Organization (2012), *supra* note 55.
102 Ibid.
103 World Bank Group (2012a), *supra* note 2.
104 Ibid.
105 Ibid.

Moreover, in planning cities, towns and villages, the Thai government, both national and local, is encouraged not only to focus on social and economic needs but also to invest in flood protection measures such as better drainage systems and buffer zones between rivers and settlements.[106] Critical infrastructure that is highly vulnerable and situated in high-risk areas should be relocated.[107]

In addition, the differences between urban and rural areas should be noted given that working with urban areas is usually more complex and time-consuming than working with rural areas. Thus when devising relevant risk reduction or recovery plans, regard should be given to the unique needs in urban and rural areas.[108]

Improve Accountability and Transparency

Transparency and accountability are vital to the success of recovery projects. They are necessary in the management and usage of funds, as well as in the progress and results of the projects. It has been proposed[109] that: information on available programs, resources and levels of assistance be made public and accessible to beneficiaries on a timely basis; complaints mechanisms be established; stringent community validation processes be used to confirm lists of eligible beneficiaries for the measures (especially where cash transfer is involved); and partnerships with civil society organizations, research institutions and the media be established to allow effective monitoring by independent third parties.

Establish Clear Lines of Communication

While it is not uncommon to have multiple actors involved in the disaster management process, it is essential to set up a communication strategy that provides clear and consistent messages in a timely manner.[110] It is, therefore, suggested that an integrated, united, single-command authority be established so that relief work and other recovery and rehabilitation projects may

[106] Ibid.

[107] Nokeo Ratanavong. (2012, February 20–22). *Thailand Floods Damage and Loss Assessment: Lessons Learned*. Retrieved from www.itu.int/ITU-D/asp/CMS/Events/2012/emergencyworkshop/Nokeo_Ratanavong.pdf.

[108] World Bank Group (2012a), *supra* note 2.

[109] Ibid.

[110] Ibid.

be planned and carried out in a more effective manner.[111] In addition, both formal and informal communication channels should be streamlined.[112]

Integrated Early Warning System

The Thai government has been encouraged to develop an effective and structured forecast and warning system in order to alert the public to any potential hazards and disasters as early as possible so that they will have sufficient time to prepare themselves.[113]

Promote a Culture of Learning and Develop a Capacity for Resilience

Experiences of resilient communities are helpful in building capacity among surrounding communities. Therefore, regional reflection gatherings to share and exchange useful experience can be organized so that communities can learn from one another in relation to experiences on how to organize human resources, and minimize loss and damage during disasters.[114]

Conclusion: Adopting a Community-Based Approach

In the context of a domestic-led approach to disaster management, due to resource and geographical limitations, a single domestic government may not be able to give sufficient and timely assistance to everyone in need. Hence, empowering local communities to address problems at the local level while the government coordinates central planning and coordination appears to be an effective approach.[115]

As local communities develop more advanced skills and capabilities in relation to planning, relief and recovery work, this will improve the overall level of response to disaster risks. The engagement of local communities can also improve accountability and transparency of recovery projects.

[111] Iglesias (n.d.), *supra* note 4.
[112] World Bank Group (2012a), *supra* note 2.
[113] Iglesias (n.d.), *supra* note 4.
[114] World Bank Group, *supra* note 2.
[115] Yoon (2001), *supra* note 1.

8

Japan's Tohoku Earthquake and Tsunami 2011

Introduction

This chapter will examine the state-led response of Japan following the Tohoku Earthquake and Tsunami of 2011. Like the case in Thailand, the primary response to the 2011 tsunami in Japan was led by the national government. Local communities played an important role in contributing to volunteer local reconstruction efforts, building repair, senior care and reuniting families through online forums.[1] This chapter will explore lessons learned in Japan's state engagement with local communities in post-disaster relief work.

Throughout history, Japan has suffered a number of massive earthquakes, including the 1923 Kanto Earthquake[2] and the 1995 Hanshin Earthquake,[3] both of which caused major damage and loss of lives.[4] In response to the propensity for natural disasters, Japan has been developing its disaster response measures through policies, organizations and research. In spite of a long history of devastating earthquakes, a new

[1] While localized relief initiatives were widespread, at the same time scholars have highlighted significant shortcomings and challenges in relation to Japan's state compensation policy. See, for example, Eric A. Feldman. (2013). Fukushima: Catastrophe, Compensation, and Justice in Japan. *DePaul Law Review*. 62, 335; Daniel Farber. (2012). Introduction: Legal Scholarship, the Disaster Cycle, and the Fukushima Accident. *Duke Environmental Law & Policy Forum*. 23, 1; Joel Rheuben. (2014). Government Liability for Regulatory Failure in the Fukushima Disaster: A Common Law Comparison. *Pacific Rim Law & Policy Journal*. 23, 113; Harold S. Yun. (2015). Fukushima and New Zealand v. France Nuclear Tests: Can Japan Be Brought to the International Court of Justice for Damages Caused by the Fukushima Plants? *Minnesota Journal of International Law*. 24, 387.

[2] C. D. James and C. Cameron (2002). The 1923 Tokyo Earthquake and Fire. National Information Service for Earthquake Engineering. Retrieved from http://nisee.berkeley.edu/kanto/tokyo1923.pdf.

[3] International Recovery Platform (IRP). (2008). Great Hanshin-Awaji Earthquake, 1985. Retrieved from www.recoveryplatform.org/assets/file/irp_casestudies/irp-cs-8-jpn.pdf.

[4] M. Denawa. (2005). Behind the Accounts of the Great Kanto Earthquake of 1923. Retrieved from http://library.brown.edu/cds/kanto/denewa.html.

committee for reconstruction has been formed following each disaster since relief and recovery work straddle several levels of government.

The Incident

The Great Tohoku Earthquake took place on March 11, 2011, at midday at a magnitude of 9.0 on the Richter scale, the largest ever recorded in the history of Japan. The epicenter was located offshore near Sendai, approximately 231 miles northeast of Tokyo.[5] The earthquake was preceded by foreshocks as strong as 7.2 on the Richter scale and three relatively large aftershocks measuring more than 6.0.[6] The massive earthquake sent energy churning up a devastating tsunami that swept over cities along the east coast of Japan. As a result, there were around 18,700 casualties.[7] Around 6,000 were injured, 475,000 evacuated and 3,200 confirmed missing.[8] As a result of the fifteen-meter-high tsunami, three nuclear reactors at Fukushima were struck, causing a meltdown.[9] When the quake hit, eleven reactors at four nuclear power plants in the region were automatically shut down although no significant damage was found.[10]

Impact

The Tohoku Earthquake caused a large-scale, multifaceted impact, including a tsunami, blackout and nuclear emergency, which will be described in greater detail subsequently.

Waves measuring 10 to 38.9 meters high were recorded along the eastern coast of Japan.[11] The seacoast area of Iwate, Miyagi and Fukushima

[5] Multidisciplinary Center for Earthquake Engineering Research (MCEER). (2013). The Great Tohoku, Japan Earthquake & Tsunami: Facts, Engineering, News & Maps. Retrieved from http://mceer.buffalo.edu/infoservice/disasters/Honshu-Japan-Earthquake-Tsunami-2011.asp#3.

[6] Ibid.

[7] Daniell and Vervaeck. (2011). CATDAT Yearly Review of Damaging Earthquakes in 2011, available at: http://earthquake-report.com/2012/01/09/catdat-damaging-earthquakes-database-2011-annual-review/.

[8] MCEER (2013), *supra* note 5.

[9] World Nuclear Association (WNA). (2013). Fukushima Accident 2011. Retrieved from www.world-nuclear.org/info/Safety-and-Security/Safety-of-Plants/Fukushima-Accident-2011/#.

[10] Ibid.

[11] National Oceanic and Atmospheric Administration (NOAA). (2012). March 11, 2011 Japan Earthquake and Tsunami. National Geophysical Data Centre (NGDC). Retrieved from www.ngdc.noaa.gov/hazard/tsunami/pdf/2011_0311.pdf.

prefectures that were closest to the epicenter suffered the most. Buildings and infrastructure were damaged as a result.

Road and railway systems to the Tohoku region were severely damaged, causing the transportation of supplies to be delayed. More than 463 roads, 43 bridges, 7 railways and 5 embankments were destroyed.[12] Food and water rationing took place in many parts of the region. Some areas were completely cut off from fresh water.[13] As the major hub for freight shipment and passenger transport, Sendai Airport was severely affected, and distribution of goods and human mobility were significantly hampered.[14]

There was a full-scale blackout in Sendai and major areas of the Tohoku region. Medical facilities were running on stored electricity and critical patients had to be relocated to other facilities. The daily minimum temperature was close to zero degrees Celsius.[15]

While the earthquake did not affect the nuclear plant structure, two tsunami waves hit the plant, submerging and damaging seawater pumps for cooling purposes. The tsunami also drowned the diesel generator, causing a blackout. The Emergency Core Cooling System took over for a short period of time; however, soon afterward, the reactors were susceptible to a hydrogen explosion and subsequently a meltdown. The region had to be evacuated, employees of the plant were allowed a choice of staying on the job or leaving, and nationwide radiation readings were regularly announced on TV and in the daily newspapers. As there were clear signs of radiation contamination, water and food became a great concern to the public both in the immediate region and across the nation.[16] As a result of radiation, food and water were at risk of contamination.

About 30 percent of Japan's total energy comes from nuclear power plants. As a result of the automatic shutdown of plants in the affected area, supply to the nation became heavily affected. Rationing of electricity took

[12] OCHA (2011, March 13). Japan: Earthquake & Tsunami - Situation Report No. 2. Asia-Pacific Regional Office, OCHA. Available at: http://reliefweb.int/sites/reliefweb.int/files/resources/289B1BF0F9F6B4C7C12578520045004D-Full_Report.pdf

[13] Geography Association (GA). (2011). Japan Tsunami – March 2011. Retrieved from www.geography.org.uk/resources/japantsunami.

[14] National Institute for Research Advancement (NIRA). (2011, September). Indexes for Recovery and Reconstruction following the Great East Japan Earthquake. Retrieved from www.nira.or.jp/pdf/1102english_report.pdf.

[15] S. Shibahara (2011), The 2011 Tohoku Earthquake and Devastating Tsunami. *Tohoku J Exp Med.* 223(4), 305.

[16] World Nuclear Association (WNA). (2011). The Situation at Fukushima (report). Available at: http://www.world-nuclear.org/features/fukushima/situation-at-fukushima/.

place nationwide with areas scheduled for power outages for three to six hours on a rotating basis.[17]

Many undersea cables connecting Japan to Asia and other parts of the world were damaged. Cable systems between Tokyo and Sendai suffered most of the damage.[18]

As a result of the tsunami, a tremendous amount of debris washed onto shore in the affected region, as well as debris washed away by waves and ocean current. The tsunami waves carried large amounts of sediment that was deposited along its path. Corrosion and degradation resulted from the seawater contact. Waste contamination also resulted from water that engulfed the affected region.[19]

Casualties

An estimated 244,000 people were housed in 1,900 temporary evacuation centers located in northeastern and eastern Japan. More than 27,500 people were confirmed dead or unaccounted for. Approximately 64 percent of the deaths were elderly people.[20]

National Response

As Japan is prone to natural disasters, the enactment of the Disaster Countermeasures Basic Act (DCBA) in 1961 was considered a turning point in the system of management. The DCBA defined the protection of national land, citizens' lives, livelihoods and damaged property as national priorities. It specified the national-level framework for disaster management.[21] In the event of a disaster, specific laws came into effect.

[17] *Japan Times*. (2011). Tohoku Joins Tepco in Rationing Power. Retrieved from www.japantimes.co.jp/news/2011/03/16/news/tohoku-joins-tepco-in-rationing-power/#; Nautilus Institute for Security and Sustainability (NISS). (2011). After the Deluge: Short and Medium-Term Impacts of Reactor Damage Caused by the Japan Earthquake and Tsunami. Retrieved from www.jpri.org/publications/friends/SRJapanReactors.pdf.

[18] O. Malik. (2011). In Japan, Many Undersea Cables are Damaged. *Gigaom*. Retrieved from http://gigaom.com/2011/03/14/in-japan-many-under-sea-cables-are-damaged/.

[19] UNEP. (2012). Managing Post-disaster Debris: The Japan Experience. Retrieved from www.unep.org/pdf/UNEP_Japan_post-tsunami_debris.pdf.

[20] OCHA, (2011, March 25). Japan: Earthquake & Tsunami - Situation Report No. 13. Asia-Pacific Regional Office, OCHA. Available at: http://reliefweb.int/sites/reliefweb.int/files/resources/F84BF143778FD115C125785E0045E9C6-Full_Report.pdf.

[21] MOFA. (2011). Post Disaster Response Stages: Emergency Response (kinkyuushien 緊急支援) – Search and Rescue (First 72 Hours); Immediate Response (shinsaishien 震災支援) – Provision of Food and Water Supply (First 80 Days); Restoration (fukkyou 復旧) – Restoration of Utilities and Basic Infrastructure (3 Years Post-disaster); Reconstruction

The DCBA covers all phases of disaster management and stipulates management councils at three levels: national – Central Disaster Management Council; Prefectural – Local Disaster Management Council; and Municipal Disaster Management Councils.[22] The DCBA defines the organization, duties and conditions of these headquarters for disaster control in cases of emergency.[23]

In March 2005, as a result of the 1996 Hanshin Earthquake, the Central Disaster Management Council (CDMC) established an "earthquake disaster management reduction" program. Estimations of expected hazard levels of earthquakes and tsunamis for the Tokai Earthquake Tonankai and Nankai Earthquakes, Tokyo Inland Earthquakes and Chubu and Kinki Regions Inland Earthquakes were conducted. The CDMC attempted to replicate the earthquakes and tsunamis experienced over the past few hundred years in the stated regions, and carried out a modeling exercise based on future assumptions.[24] In spite of these efforts, the Tohoku Earthquake with a magnitude of 9.0 caused by the "interlocking of several epicentral areas in the Japan Trench" was beyond the earthquake and tsunami hazard assumptions as the two events occurred simultaneously as a "tsunami earthquake."[25]

Emergency Response

Immediately after the earthquake hit, the Japanese government held the National Committee for Emergency Management, headed by the prime minister (PM), to identify key priorities for emergency response operation in affected areas, namely, the Prefecture of Iwate, Miyagi and Fukushima.[26]

(fukkou 復興) – Reconstruction and Recovery from Impact of Disaster (Self-Sustaining Growth); Revitalization (saisei 再生) – Revitalizing Livelihoods and Economic Growth.

[22] E. Nazarov. (2011). Emergency Response Management in Japan: Final Research Report. Asian Disaster Reduction Centre. Retrieved from www.adrc.asia/aboutus/vrdata/finalreport/2011A_AZE_Emin_FRR.pdf; COGJ-DM, Cabinet Office, Government of Japan: Disaster Management. (2011). Disaster Management in Japan. Retrieved from www.bousai.go.jp/1info/pdf/saigaipanf_e.pdf.

[23] Ibid.

[24] COGJ-DM (2011), *supra* note 23.

[25] G20 Disaster Risk Management Report. (2012). *Improving the Assessment of Disaster Risks to Strengthen Financial Resilience: A Special Joint G20 Publication by the Government of Mexico and the World Bank.* Washington, DC: International Bank for Reconstruction and Development, p. 197.

[26] WHO Western Pacific Region. (2011, March 12). *Japan Earthquake and Tsunami – Situation Report No. 03*, p. 4. Available at: www.who.int/kobe_centre/emergencies/east_japan_earthquake/situation_reports/sitrep3_12mar2011.pdf?ua=1 (accessed on February 24, 2015).

Thousands of troops, planes and ships were mobilized and sent to these areas and emergency specialist teams from a number of countries were deployed to help rescue survivors.[27] The government also declared a State of Atomic Power Emergency as a result of the uncertainties in relation to the Fukushima nuclear power plants. Thousands of residents within a ten-kilometer radius of the plants were immediately evacuated as the PM recognized a "small amount" of radioactive material in the air.[28]

Nuclear emergency needs were addressed by the Japan Red Cross as it was supplied with special equipment to deal with nuclear, chemical and biological disasters.[29] Efforts to cool the Fukushima Daiichi Nuclear Power Plant continued through March and Special Defence Force helicopters and police deployed water cannons to spray seawater onto the nuclear power plant in an attempt to cool the plant's reactors.[30]

Search and rescue remained a high priority for the first three days following the earthquake.[31] Around 100,000 troops were deployed to lead the relief efforts.[32] Firefighters, police, the National Police Agency, the Japan Self-Defence Force, the Coast Guard and Fire and Disaster Management Agencies were major actors in the search and rescue efforts. A week after the disaster struck, search and rescue operations continued to find survivors, totaling 26,000 survivors by March 18.[33]

Evacuation centers were set up in affected areas of Miyagi, Fukushima, Ibaraki, Iwate, Tochigi and Aomori to accommodate the 371,800 people displaced by the event.[34] Due to adverse winter weather, relief efforts were greatly hampered. A week after the event, many of the evacuees fell ill

[27] Ibid.

[28] OCHA, No.1 (2011, March 12). Japan: Earthquake & Tsunami - Situation Report No. 1. Asia-Pacific Regional Office, OCHA. http://reliefweb.int/sites/reliefweb.int/files/resources/60C5286F730C9B6449257851004A922B-Full_Report.pdf.

[29] International Federation of Red Cross and Red Crescent Societies. (2011, March 15). *Japan: Earthquake and Tsunami – Information Bulletin No. 3*, p. 3. Available at: www.ifrc.org/docs/appeals/rpts11/JPeq15031103.pdf (accessed on February 24, 2015).

[30] International Atomic Energy Agency. (2011, March 18). *Fukushima Nuclear Accident Update Log*. IAEA Briefing on Fukushima Nuclear Emergency (18 March 2011). Available at: www.iaea.org/newscenter/news/fukushima-nuclear-accident-update-log-25 (accessed on February 24, 2015).

[31] OCHA. (2011, March 18). Japan: Earthquake & Tsunami - Situation Report No. 7. Asia-Pacific Regional Office, OCHA. Available at: http://reliefweb.int/sites/reliefweb.int/files/resources/C85BCD0DEBF49372C1257857003DE0B5-Full_Report.pdf\.

[32] International Federation of Red Cross and Red Crescent Societies, *supra* note 29, p. 1.

[33] *Supra* note 31, p. 1.

[34] Ibid.

because of freezing weather and had diarrhea and other illnesses caused by sanitation and lack of clean water.[35]

Medical assistants, including doctors and nurses, were met by disaster medical assistant teams and the Japan Red Cross. The Red Cross had almost 2,700 nurses trained to provide psychosocial support. Volunteers were also mobilized through the Red Cross in supporting distribution of relief items, supporting the displaced, clearing debris and assisting in medical transportation.[36] From March 17, the minister of state for disaster management announced that services for people living in evacuation centers would be prioritized and the Ministry of Health, Labour and Welfare (MHLW) would take the lead in providing essential health services for the elderly, children and women. Treatments for post-traumatic stress disorder among the affected population and the rescue teams were also made available.[37]

Key supplies such as food, water, blankets, light and fuel were mobilized and transported through joint efforts between the government and the private sector.[38] OCHA No.6 reported that approximately 2.5 million households remained without water on March 17. The logistics of food and supply delivery were organized by evacuation centers that would send requests to municipalities. The prefecture would then consolidate these requests and liaise with the national government. These items would then be consolidated at the Japan Self-Defence Force (JSDF) sites and transported to the area by the JSDF. Distribution of items was done by municipalities and/or the JSDF.[39]

The Reconstruction Agency (RA) was established on February 10, 2012, with a ten-year mandate to carry out reconstruction in the affected areas. The RA was created under the terms set out in the Basic Act on

[35] World Health Organization. (2012). *The Great East Japan Earthquake: A Story of Devastating Natural Disaster, a Tale of Human Compassion*, p. 40. Available at: www.wpro.who.int/publications/docs/japan_earthquake.pdf (accessed on February 24, 2015).

[36] Japan Red Cross Society. (2011, April 13). *Japan: Earthquake and Tsunami – Operations Update No. 1*, p. 5. Available at: http://reliefweb.int/sites/reliefweb.int/files/resources/full%20report_48.pdf (accessed on February 24, 2015).

[37] WHO (2012), *supra* note 35.

[38] OCHA. (2011, March 15). Japan: Earthquake & Tsunami Situation Report No. 4. Asia-Pacific Regional Office, OCHA. Available at: http://reliefweb.int/sites/reliefweb.int/files/resources/B695CD6B9CF47956C12578540048D0D6-Full_Report.pdf.

[39] See Chart 1: Distribution of Relief Items to the Evacuation Centers, OCHA, (2011, March 20). Japan: Earthquake & Tsunami - Situation Report No. 9. Asia-Pacific Regional Office, OCHA. Available at: http://reliefweb.int/sites/reliefweb.int/files/resources/9180D35ADC66A3FCC125785900421328-Full_Report.pdf.

Reconstruction in succession of the "Reconstruction Headquarters in Response to the Great East Japan Earthquake."[40] The RA works closely with national and local governments and the private sector to supervise a wide spectrum of activities. In addition to reconstructing the living circumstances of those affected, RA acts to promote "local economic revival through tax and investment incentives and other measures, and provide support to public-private reconstruction related initiatives in the region."[41]

Immediate Response

The immediate response to post-earthquake issues such as shelter, medical care, food, sanitation, debris removal and nuclear containment were addressed, as will be discussed in more detail in this section.

Temporary shelters across seven prefectures housed approximately 430,000 evacuees. Prefectures in vicinities not affected by the emergency offered to take some of the evacuees.[42]

Hospitals in the affected areas were unable to function due to a lack of medicines, fuel and water.[43] Lack of electricity and poor communication prevented hospitals from getting additional support. The challenge of keeping patients alive without water and electricity remained in the second week after the disaster.[44] Some hospitals reported having to reduce the number of meals and procedures provided.[45]

Meals were delivered to the evacuation centers and hospitals in the affected area and the Ministry of Agriculture, Forestry and Fisheries of Japan requested the private sector to increase production of food products, such as rice, bottles of water, bread, instant noodles, formula milk, snacks and instant food.[46] The crippled transportation system remained a hindrance to providing food and medical supplies to the affected areas a week after the disaster.[47]

40 Ibid.

41 Ibid.

42 OCHA, No.6.

43 WHO (2012), *supra* note 35.

44 OCHA, No.7.

45 OCHA, No.8.

46 OCHA, No.6.

47 WHO Western Pacific Region. (2011, March 19). *Japan Earthquake and Tsunami – Situation Report No. 10*, p. 5. Available at: www.who.int/entity/kobe_centre/emergencies/east_japan_earthquake/situation_reports/sitrep10_19mar2011.pdf?ua=1 (accessed on February 24, 2015).

During the first week after the event, coordination and transportation of nonfood and food items was a major challenge. A rolling power outage had also affected production of basic livelihood items.[48] The government of Japan called for gasoline, paraffin oil, portable stoves, plastic plates and utensils, toothbrushes, diapers, sanitary napkins, clothes, blankets, batteries, candles, medicines, masks, soaps and portable latrines.[49] Fuel remained limited as six out of nine oil factories remained closed and 700 additional tankers were ordered to deliver fuel to the affected areas.[50]

During the first week after the event, 1.6 million households were without water in twelve prefectures. This number reached 1.8 million on March 18.[51] The MHLW coordinated with 245 water supply companies for emergency water supply.[52]

By the end of the first week after the event, Disaster Medical Assistance Teams (DMAT) operating in disaster zones decreased from 100 to 30.[53] Medical assistance was replaced by health worker teams.[54] Church World Service (CWS) reported that health conditions among evacuees were stabilized, but "a lot of cases of flu and chronic diseases" remained.[55]

One week after the disaster, a massive cleanup effort was undertaken to restore vital infrastructure. Tohoku Expressway and Sendai Airport, which were submerged, reopened for emergency vehicles, airplanes and helicopters.[56]

The situation at the Fukushima Daiichi Nuclear Power Plant remained critical until March 19 when electrical power to the plant was restored.[57] Radiation dose rates across forty-seven Japanese cities were made known

48 OCHA, No.6.

49 Ibid.

50 OCHA, No.7.

51 Ibid.

52 OCHA, No.6.

53 WHO Western Pacific Region. (2011, March 17). *Japan Earthquake and Tsunami – Situation Report No. 08*, p. 9. Available at: www.who.int/kobe_centre/emergencies/east_japan_earthquake/situation_reports/sitrep8_17mar2011.pdf?ua=1 (accessed on February 24, 2015).

54 OCHA, No.6.

55 Church World Service (CWS). (2011, April 21). "Still Humanitarian Gaps in Japan Relief," says Church World Service. Retrieved from http://reliefweb.int/report/japan/'still-humanitarian-gaps-japan-relief'-says-church-world-service.

56 OCHA, No.7.

57 WHO Western Pacific Regional Office. (2011). *Japan Earthquake and Tsunami Situation Report No. 10*. See also WHO Western Pacific Regional Office (2012). The Great East Japan Earthquake. Geneva: WHO Press. Available at: www.wpro.who.int/publications/docs/japan_earthquake.pdf.

to the public.[58] By March 23, 83,778 people were evacuated from the twenty-kilometer zone around the Fukushima Daiichi Nuclear Power Plant.[59]

Restoration

In the period following the immediate aftermath of the earthquake, the government of Japan began to engage in restoration efforts. These efforts focused on housing, electricity and health care provision, as will be discussed in this section.

Temporary housing development began by March 19. The Ministry of Land, Infrastructure, Transportation and Tourism estimated 8,800 homes were needed in Iwate, 10,000 in Miyagi and 14,000 in Fukushima for the short term. The government of Japan requested a consortium of constructors to build at least 30,000 in two months.[60] The challenge in constructing temporary housing in Tohoku was the mountainous landscape and hence a lack of suitable construction sites.

A special Task Force for Livelihood Support of the Affected Population made 40,500 government apartments available in addition to the 19,500 public housing units offered for displaced families, making a total of approximately 60,000 apartments.[61]

The affected population relied on meals delivered by the day, and blankets and diapers continued to be in high demand. The population relied heavily on bottled water.[62] Twelve days after the disaster hit, half a million people remained without electricity, and those without water supply totaled 2.1 million.[63]

Medical assistance was reported to have shifted from emergency assistance to providing general health care to affected populations in the evacuation centers.[64] Preventative measures to stop the spread of infectious disease, post-traumatic stress disorder, gastric ulcers, pneumonia, cardiac infection, cerebral stroke, treatment of chronic diseases and provision of

58 OCHA, No.8.

59 OCHA, No.12.

60 OCHA, No.8.

61 OCHA, No.13.

62 Center for Excellence in Disaster Management & Humanitarian Assistance. (2011, March 21). Japan Earthquake and Tsunami Update, p. 7. Available at: https://community.apan.org/cfs-filesystemfile.ashx/__key/telligent-evolution-components-attachments/01-4865-00-00-00-06-21-96/Japan-Earthquake-and-Tsunami-Update-03232011.pdf (accessed on February 25, 2015).

63 OCHA, No.12.

64 *Supra* note 62.

artificial dialysis were identified as medical needs in the second week after the disaster.[65] The MHLW relaxed several regulations to facilitate medical assistance, such as allowing medical institutes to sell or contribute medicine without permission from the prefectural government.[66] The Ministry of Education, Culture, Sports, Science and Technology decided to dispatch 144 clinical psychotherapists to affected schoolchildren in Miyagi and Fukushima and the MHLW also coordinated the dispatch of child welfare specialists to affected areas.[67] On a second visit to Miyagi Prefecture two weeks after the disaster, OCHA, the World Food Programme, USAID's Disaster Assistance Response Team, the Cabinet Office, with support from the NGO Peace Boat and local government, visited three out of 144 evacuation centers, two official centers and one unofficial, and reported significant humanitarian needs that were not being met because of coordination and logistical issues. The biggest concern was the extremely poor conditions at the evacuation centers. Diarrhea, which is a prime indicator for deteriorating sanitary conditions, was steadily on the rise along with nausea and gastroenteritis.[68]

The MHLW coordinated the deployment of a range of medical professionals, including care managers, child welfare specialists and psychologists from across the country to Iwate (more than forty-two teams), Miyagi (more than eighty-eight teams) and Fukushima (more than five teams).[69] Thirty-eight Japan Red Cross Society teams, thirty-three Japan Medical Association teams and eight All Japan Hospital Association teams were also in operation. According to a survey conducted in Iwate, 60 percent of evacuation centers required mental health assistance for evacuees. Many people experienced irritation, anxiety and sleeping disorders such as sleepwalking. Overcrowded conditions were also a contributing factor.[70]

As a result of radioactive materials found in vegetables in Fukushima Prefecture, the government ordered residents not to consume vegetables or drink tap water and milk in Fukushima and the neighboring prefecture, Ibaraki.[71] Radiation exceeding the standard was also detected from

65 OCHA, No.8.

66 Ibid.

67 COE-DMHA, 2011. P8.

68 WHO, *supra* note 35, p. 31.

69 OCHA, No.14.

70 Ibid.

71 International Atomic Energy Agency. (2011, March 25). *Fukushima Nuclear Accident Update Log*. IAEA Briefing on Fukushima Nuclear Accident (25 March 2011). Available at: www.iaea.org/newscenter/news/fukushima-nuclear-accident-update-log-37 (accessed on February 25, 2015).

seawater collected sixteen kilometers from Fukushima Daiichi.[72] Seawater and water table contamination due to a partial meltdown was a high risk. The government of Japan considered "lowering the standards for radiation found in food in Japan as current criteria [were] viewed as too strict and out of line with international standards."[73]

In Miyagi alone, the debris amounted to 15 million to 18 million tons – equivalent to twenty-three years' worth of waste for the prefecture while its capacity to dispose of waste was 0.8 million tons per year. Authorities estimated that debris removal would take at least three years and would not include cars and boats.[74]

Farmers in the Fukushima region who usually begin farming rice and soya in April were asked to postpone planting crops until the radiation level of the soil was fully analyzed and determined to be safe.[75]

The Tokyo Metropolitan Government deployed about 1,000 officials to Miyagi and Iwate to reinforce prefectural government offices to support emergency response. At least 100 officers were stationed in the affected region each day from April to the end of May to support the provision of nonemergency services and the management of evacuation centers.[76] The Japan Platform took a leading role with support from JANIC to coordinate assistance demands with local and international NGOs. The NGOs consortia facilitated information sharing and coordinated needs from the field.[77]

External Support

Emergency Response

Immediately after the earthquake, the government of Japan accepted offers of assistance from 130 countries and thirty-three international

[72] International Atomic Energy Agency. (2011, March 21). *Fukushima Nuclear Accident Update Log.* IAEA Briefing on Fukushima Nuclear Accident (21 March 2011). Available at: www.iaea.org/newscenter/news/fukushima-nuclear-accident-update-log-32 (accessed on February 25, 2015).

[73] OCHA, No.13.

[74] Earthquake Engineering Research Institute. (2011, August). *Learning from Earthquakes.* EERI Special Earthquake Report – August 2011, p. 16. Available at: www.eqclearinghouse.org/2011-03-11-sendai/files/2011/03/Japan-SocSci-Rpt-hirez-rev.pdf (accessed on February 25, 2015).

[75] OCHA, No.13.

[76] OCHA, No.14.

[77] Ibid.

organizations, and agreed to the deployment of the UNDAC (UN Disaster and Assessment) team.[78] Relief items were accepted from fifteen countries.[79] Close to 700 NGOs and other organizations offered assistance.[80] Telecoms San Frontiers (TSF) sent a team to assess the communications infrastructure and provide emergency telecommunications assistance.[81] All international dispatches arrived in Japan within the first two days.[82] The seven-member UNDAC team arrived in Tokyo on the second day to assist with the coordination of search and rescue, and to offer assistance in assessments and environmental hazard analysis.[83]

Funding and pledges were received from more than forty-five countries and aid organizations and private individuals contributed a total of US$ 145 million to the government of Japan, the Red Cross, international NGOs and other partners[84] to support search and rescue operations and to provide medical services and relief items.[85] The Japanese Red Cross Society received more than $249 million.[86]

Emergency responses included rescue teams and rescue support and supplies. Members of rescue teams included medics, search and rescue teams, search and rescue dogs and specialists.[87] Supplies were in the form of relief goods (blankets, rubber boots and gloves, tents, emergency lights, portable toilets, footwear), cans of water and equipment (nuclear tests, search and rescue).[88]

Pledges, donations and in-kind donations were largely facilitated by the Japanese and US Red Cross, World Vision, Mercy Corps and Global

[78] Center for Excellence in Disaster Management & Humanitarian Assistance. (2011, March 23). *Japan Earthquake and Tsunami Update*, p. 2. Available at: https://community.apan.org/cfs-filesystemfile.ashx/__key/telligent-evolution-components-attachments/01-4865-00-00-00-06-21-96/Japan-Earthquake-and-Tsunami-Update-03232011.pdf (accessed on February 25, 2015).

[79] Ibid.

[80] OCHA, No.12.

[81] OCHA, No.1.

[82] OCHA, No.2.

[83] UN News Centre. (2011, March 14). "Japan: UN Stepping up Assistance in Wake of Quake and Tsunami." Available at: www.un.org/apps/news/story.asp?NewsID=37762#.VO-CFy77eio (accessed on February 25, 2015).

[84] COE-DMHA, 2011.

[85] OCHA, No.12; Financial Tracking Services (FTS). (2011). Japan 2011: Total Humanitarian Funding, List of All Humanitarian Pledges, Commitments & Contributions in 2011. Retrieved from http://fts.unocha.org/reports/daily/ocha_R10c_C105_Y2011_asof___1303211530.pdf.

[86] COE-DMHA, *supra* note 84.

[87] OCHA, No.2.

[88] Ibid.

Giving.[89] Immediately after the disaster in March 2011, a total of US$ 722 million in monetary and in-kind donations was received and US$ 412 million was pledged from around the world.[90]

Immediate Response

International NGOs not involved with search and rescue were urged to wait until search and rescue operations were finished before commencing their work. One week after the event, some thirteen NGOs began providing assistance in the affected region. These included Médecins Sans Frontières (MSF), Turkish Red Crescent, the Switzerland Humanitarian Aid Response Team, Save the Children and Plan International.[91] Two weeks after the disaster, MSF and Save the Children focused their efforts on getting to especially remote areas and on providing specialist help to the elderly and children.[92]

Around 5,300 US service men and women supported the disaster relief effort, including eight military ships, aircraft carriers, transport aircraft and more than 100 military helicopters, which were repositioned to northern Japan to assist ongoing humanitarian efforts. Relief operations included delivery of food, water and other relief supplies.[93]

At the request of OCHA, Crisis Commons put together a Japan Data Profile wiki containing data sources relevant to the earthquake and tsunami response.[94]

A week after the disaster and with the nuclear threat unresolved, a large number of embassies in Japan started advising foreign nationals residing in Tokyo to evacuate to western or southern Japan or temporarily move out of the country. The Immigration Bureau reported that approximately 10,000 foreign nationals left the country following the earthquake.[95]

The International Atomic Energy Agency (IAEA) posted official updates on the nuclear power plants. The World Health Organization also posted radiation-related health risks. Meteorologists worked closely with regional specialized meteorological centers in Beijing, Tokyo and Obninsk to

[89] FTS (2011), *supra* note 86.
[90] Ibid.
[91] OCHA, No.6.
[92] OCHA, No.8.
[93] OCHA, No.6.
[94] Ibid.
[95] Ibid.

monitor the situation and to develop predictions and trajectories a regarding the spreading of the contaminants with its cross-border implications.[96]

Civil Society Participation

The government of Japan coordinated with civil society and private-sector entities to provide targeted resources to communities affected by the earthquake and tsunami.

At the request of the government of Japan, All Nippon Airways (ANA) was asked to provide support for the transport of humanitarian personnel and relief items free of charge by air.[97]

Japan's Federation of Economic Organizations organized a relief items hotline to link affected populations with private-sector and charity organizations. In response to specific requests for items such as rice, instant food, toilet paper, gloves, flashlights, diapers and powdered milk such items were sent to designated locations.[98]

At the request of the Ministry of Agriculture, Forestry and Fisheries, thirty-seven private-sector companies offered 2.4 million meals and 300,000 liters of water. The Japanese Consumers' Co-operative Union delivered a total of 1.3 million nonfood and food items to the affected area.[99]

The World Food Programme collaborated with the TNT parcel delivery service in assisting the transportation of 60,000 blankets to the affected areas. The International Telecommunication Union also dispatched emergency telephone equipment to the region, including satellite phones with GPS devices to assist in rescue operations.[100]

The Association for Aid and Relief Japan (AAR) organized soup kitchens in coordination with Ingram Co. Ltd. As a result, approximately 16,650 meals were provided in forty-eight locations.[101]

In-kind goods were largely collected and delivered through the AAR. Around 65,000 people in 600 institutions benefited from the AAR. AAR in cooperation with the Adventist Development and Relief Agency (ADRA

96 OCHA, No.8.

97 OCHA, No.6.

98 OCHA, No.8.

99 OCHA, No.6.

100 Ibid.

101 Association for Aid and Relief Japan (AAR). (2011, June 10). Three Months since the Great East Earthquake: Activity Report. Retrieved from http://reliefweb.int/report/japan/three-months-great-east-japan-earthquake-activity-report.

Japan) delivered relief supplies and other daily necessities to families in temporary and leased housing.[102]

Small projects sprang up through the collaborative efforts of NGOs, NPOs and the private sector that provided additional assistance. The "Let's Bring Hot Springs to the Disaster Zone!" project brought hot water baths to 500 to 600 evacuees every day through the collaboration between Manyo Club Co. Ltd., Ascendia Ltd., other companies and the AAR.[103]

Google Japan erected Google Person Finder (Google PF) and the Google Crisis Response (Google CR) system. Although mobile connectivity was a major problem immediately after the event, by the morning of March 12, 2011, 25,000 persons reported their safety on Google PF. Google began using technology for Google Maps to map the results of the earthquake and tsunami. This mapping project was of tremendous assistance to the humanitarian aid community.[104]

Local Participation

In working with local communities, the government of Japan established a "volunteers coordination unit" under the cabinet secretary's office that coordinated the activities of volunteer groups and NPOs in support of the earthquakes/tsunami victims in close consultation with relevant ministries to facilitate the exchange of information among organizations.[105]

A network of NGO and volunteer organizations, the "Japan Civil Network for Disaster Relief in East Japan," was formed to facilitate the communication and exchange of information among organizations working in the Tohoku area to support survivors.[106] A Web site (www.jpn-civil.net/) was created where individuals can access information on the activities of each organization. Inter-agency meetings between national and international NGOs were regularly scheduled to facilitate information exchange and relief support and organization.

The AAR coordinated with local construction companies as well as the Council of Social Welfare and other related organizations in repairing buildings and facilities for senior care and people with disabilities.[107] The AAR

[102] Ibid.

[103] Ibid.

[104] Google Crisis Response. (2012, March 7). 3/11: Google Crisis Response Began. Retrieved from www.google.org/crisisresponse/kiroku311/chapter_01.html.

[105] OCHA, No.6.

[106] OCHA, No.15.

[107] AAR (2011), *supra* note 102.

also installed ten container housing units in the town of Onagawa in Miyagi Prefecture and moved evacuees who had been in evacuation centers.[108]

The day after the incident, twenty-seven FM radio broadcasting channels sprang up and established a network to channel information to and from disaster zones as radio signals were more reliable in disaster zones. According to a survey conducted in August 2011, sources of information were distributed in the following manner: 58.6 percent radio, 34.0 percent newspaper and 26.6 percent television. People across the nation relied on these sources for information on the incident, survivor reports and information for daily living such as electricity rationing and water supply.[109] The reliance on radio networks was also a result of severe damage to telephone networks (29,000 mobile signal stations were down; 1,900,000 landlines suffered damage).[110]

Information Technology

Information technology played an important role in state relief efforts in Japan. It served as a means of coordinating and connecting individuals following the earthquake and tsunami. For example, Telecom for Basic Human Needs (BNH) was a major engine behind connecting individuals in the Tohoku disaster. BHN is an NPO that aims to support access to information through information communication technology by bridging divides across various levels – individuals, households and geographic locations. BHN facilitated the setup of local radio stations as stated earlier, and set up Internet access and TV telecom at shelter homes. These networks were essential for all parties in the affected zones.

Social networking services (SNS) such as Mixi, Twitter and Facebook played a significant part in information sharing.[111] Within two days after the disaster, a Yahoo Japan mobile information site was accessible by the mobile telecommunication network. The site allowed people to post short

[108] Ibid.

[109] H. Ichimura. (2012). The Current State and Challenges: Temporary Radio Broadcasting Stations for the Great East Japan Earthquake Disaster. *Regional Society and Communication Media in Japan, No. 154*. Institute of Economic and Political Studies, Kansai University. Retrieved from www.kansai-u.ac.jp/Keiseiken/books/sousho154.htm.

[110] Ibid. Electricity outage across 4,861,200 households was also a contributing factor. As of February 2012, twenty of these channels were still serving the community.

[111] M. Imase. (2012, December). Lessons Learnt from "Information Flow" during the Great East Japan Earthquake and Local Participation: The Case of Outlying Islands Urato in Shiogama City. Civic Action Clearinghouse. Retrieved from http://sicnpo.jp/saigai110311/imase-urado2012.pdf.

messages on a digital message board. Individuals, for example, reported their whereabouts and the conditions of the location.[112] Within four to seven days, individuals were using Twitter, Mixi, Facebook and personal blogs as venues for communication. Various medical and relief requests were made through social networks. This was particularly critical in the outlying islands off of Shiogama City.[113]

Google's philanthropic arm, Google.org, developed several tools to help in consolidating and sharing humanitarian information. Google CR and Google PF were Google's signature projects. In one report, Google CR reported that Tweets about an earthquake preceded the announcement on NHK, which occurred one minute after the quake.[114] Another report noted that Twitter was most effective in information dissemination as each Tweet was limited to 140 characters, stamped with time and place. Within one hour from the minute the earthquake had occurred, in Tokyo alone, there were more than 1,200 tweets.[115] Twitter immediately started an official blog titled "Tohoku-Pacific Earthquake" that consolidated all tweets with tags related to the incident so that users could search and consolidate information efficiently.[116] According to a survey on the use of Twitter (n = 655) and Facebook (n = 248) in relation to the earthquake and within seventy-two hours after the incident, 83.5 percent used Twitter as a way to collect information, and 56 percent used Facebook as means to check the safety of friends and acquaintances.[117] As many as 47.5 percent used Twitter to share information, and 46.8 percent used Facebook as a means to collect information.[118] The function of sharing Tweets helped spread messages and in some cases led to rescue. While accurate information was conducive to relief efforts, inaccurate information also caused problems (Google CR, July 20, 2012).[119]

Social networking systems have also effectively facilitated volunteer activities, acceptance and distribution of in-kind donations and monetary donations. Tasukeai.jp was founded immediately after the disaster with the

112 Ibid.

113 Ibid.

114 Google CR (2012), *supra* note 105.

115 Y. Yoshitsugu. (2011). Roles of Social Media at the Time of Major Disasters Observed in the Great East Japan Earthquake: Twitter as an Example. *NHK Broadcast Media Research and Analysis July 2011*, p. 19. Retrieved from www.nhk.or.jp/bunken/summary/research/report/2011_07/20110702.pdf.

116 Ibid.

117 Ibid., p. 21.

118 Ibid.

119 Ibid., p. 21.

goal of acting as a portal of information to help individuals in the region. Its name, tasukeai, in Japanese means "mutual help."[120] The site tasukeai.jp had a digital bulletin board where individuals relayed information regarding specific supply and assistance needs in the area. Tasukeai worked in cooperation with the Reconstruction Agency, a national entity.[121]

While telephone and mobile network lines were disrupted during the earthquake, Internet connectivity that runs on a different network was relatively uninterrupted. Internet connectivity enabled the use of SNS such as Twitter, and allowed some to use Skype as an alternative to telephone.[122] According to data from the company, the number of Skype application downloads jumped from 3.09 million to 3.53 million during the week after the earthquake on March 11.[123] This data, however, did not indicate whether these were numbers within Japan or worldwide.

Two months after the disaster, the coordination of volunteers at Tasukeai.jp spun off to become Volunteerinfo.jp, an NPO dedicated solely to the purpose of coordinating volunteering efforts. It was subsequently absorbed into the "AP Bank Tohoku Volunteer Program" that is run in collaboration with an international NGO, SEEDS Japan. Volunteerinfo.jp continues to act as a consolidator of volunteering information and has further played a role in restoration of tourism in the Tohoku region by combining voluntary efforts with tourism.[124]

Online information sharing, facilitated by sites such as Google Japan, provided a venue for individuals to document, remember and revitalize disaster-ridden areas. Google built a Web site, www.miraikioku.com, to serve as a database of images before and after the event by using accumulated street view images. The site also invites people to submit photos, videos and messages for individuals they have lost.[125]

Outcome

The government of Japan provided 1 million JPY to each family whose home was lost in the disaster.[126] The government also set guidelines for debris removal. Temporary entry to private land for debris removal was

[120] Ibid., p. 22.
[121] Ibid.
[122] Ibid.
[123] Ibid.
[124] Ibid.
[125] Ibid.
[126] OCHA, No.15.

allowed without the permission of the owner. Vehicles and vessels were relocated to different locations and disposed of if owners did not reclaim them. Personal mementos were temporarily stored.[127]

Lessons Learned

Preparedness

The Central Disaster Management Council (CDMC) conducted a damage scenario in 2005, but the damages caused by the 2011 disaster far exceeded anything envisaged in the scenario due to the height of the tsunami, the inundation area and the human and material damage caused. The G20 DRM Report noted that:

> Enormous damage was caused by factors for which qualitative but not quantitative scenarios had been created. These factors included tsunami fires; missing people; and destruction caused by the shaking of the earthquake and the tsunami to substations and power lines, water intakes, water purification and sewage treatment plants and oil storage tanks (with emphasis).[128]

As a result, the CDMC will reassess the scenario methods, take into account the differences in estimated and actual damages incurred and analyze the relationship between regional characteristics and the shaking generated by the earthquake.[129]

Principles for conducting earthquake and tsunami hazard assumptions for the future will be reassessed and "the largest-possible mega earthquakes and tsunamis should be considered from every possible angle."[130] Research and analysis explaining mechanisms that trigger earthquakes and tsunamis must include research from an extensive period of time, including research data "from seismology, geology, archaeology, and history, as well as tsunami deposits on land and ocean floor, the geology of coastal terraces, and biological fossils, among others."[131]

Local socioeconomic conditions need to be assessed and accounted for in planning and response.[132] A database of information compiled at the

[127] OCHA, No.13.
[128] G20 DRM Report (2012), *supra* note 25, p. 198.
[129] Ibid., p. 196.
[130] Ibid.
[131] Ibid., p. 196.
[132] OECD. (2006). OECD Studies in Risk Management Report. Paris: OECD Publications. Available at: www.oecd.org/japan/37378001.pdfp. 25.

prefectural level can offer critical information about the type of needs in a given area under different emergency conditions. However, in some cases "using social data" and sharing such data with humanitarian aid agencies and organizations may be "impeded by privacy laws and [the lack of] training in using existing social data."[133]

Disaster risk awareness is an important element in community preparation efforts.[134] In surveys carried out by the Cabinet Office of Japan regarding disaster prevention, a high percentage of homes took measures to prepare for a major earthquake after the Great Hanshin-Awaji Earthquake in 1995, but the preparedness fell progressively in subsequent surveys in 1999 and even more dramatically seven years onward in 2002.[135] Preparedness was reflected by the measures taken such as having secured furniture, radio and flashlight, stored food and drinking water and a plan for contacting family members.[136]

State Engagement with Local Actors

Established coordination mechanisms between governmental authorities and public- and private-sector organizations foster a more effective coordination of relief efforts.[137] During the 2011 disaster, Japanese NGOs and NPOs were (along with government expert teams) frontline contributors to relief activities, interacting with affected communities through mobilization of funding, volunteers and commitments to community support.[138] However,

> There was no functional coordinating mechanism among the various government organizations, civil society, and the private sector, to help avoid

[133] Ibid.

[134] K. Suganuma. (2006). Recent Trends in Earthquake Disaster Management in Japan. *Quarterly Review*, 19, 91. Retrieved from www.houseoffoust.com/edano/Scribble_Japan_Earthquake/pdfs%5CSTTqr1907.pdf.

[135] Ibid.

[136] Ibid.

[137] International Federation of Red Cross and Red Crescent Societies. (2012, February 13). *Preparing for and Responding to Large Scale Disasters in High Income Countries.* Report: Findings and Lessons Learned from the Japanese Red Cross Society's Response to the Great East Japan Earthquake and Tsunami, p. 10. Available at: http://ifrc.org/docs/Evaluations/Evaluations%202012/AsiaPacific/JPTsunamiEarthquake12_report.pdf (accessed on February 25, 2015).

[138] Federica Ranghieri and Mikio Ishiwatari (Eds.). (2014). *Learning from Megadisasters – Lessons from the Great East Japan Earthquake*, p. 128. Available at: https://books.google.com.hk/books?id=J2YJBAAAQBAJ&printsec=frontcover#v=onepage&q&f=false (accessed on February 25, 2015).

> duplication and confusion in relief-and-response activities. Coordinating was required at all levels and all phases.[139]

A framework for interorganization cooperation with governmental authorities at both local and national levels is instrumental in sharing information, coordinating relief efforts and understanding changing community needs.[140] Without a mechanism, the capacities of local governments to conduct disaster management may be overstretched.[141]

Communicating timely and accurate information to affected populations is of paramount importance. The government of Japan was particularly criticized for its failure to convey timely updates on the radiation situation, creating distrust of official information and exacerbating health and safety fears among the public.[142] Panda (2012) noted that while the government was balancing "competing priorities of informing the public about an evolving situation and reducing fear," in emergency situations, the dissemination of timely but incomplete information may be more desirable than otherwise.[143]

Arrangements for particular protection of special or vulnerable groups must be organized in advance. Two-thirds of the deaths during the 2011 disaster occurred among people over the age of sixty, despite elderly citizens accounting for only 30 percent of the population affected by the disaster.[144] While Sendai City in Miyagi established thirty "welfare shelters" providing special care services for the disabled and the elderly, at most centers, special needs groups had to utilize ordinary facilities.[145] A lack of gender sensitivity in relation to privacy for female evacuees was also cited as a source of inconvenience.[146] Anticipation of special needs is integral to effective management of evacuation centers, and by extension, fulfills the needs of evacuees.

139 Ibid., p.130.

140 Ibid., p.131.

141 Ibid.

142 The Heritage Foundation. (2012, April 26). *One Year Later: Lessons from Recovery after the Great East Japan Earthquake*, p. 18. Available at: http://thf_media.s3.amazonaws.com/2012/pdf/sr108.pdf (accessed on February 25, 2015).

143 Rajaram Panda. (2012, January 1). Japan's Disaster Response Management: Lessons for the World. *Journal of Defence Studies*. 6 (1), p. 64. Available at: www.idsa.in/~idsa/system/files/jds_6_1_RajaramPanda.pdf (accessed on February 25, 2015).

144 The World Bank. (2012). *Learning from Megadisasters – Knowledge Notes (Executive Summary)*. Available at: http://wbi.worldbank.org/wbi/Data/wbi/wbicms/files/drupal-acquia/wbi/drm_exsum_english.pdf (accessed on February 25, 2015).

145 Ranghieri and Ishiwatari (2014), *supra* note 139, p. 157.

146 World Bank (2012), *supra* note 145, p. 10.

Strength of the Triangle: National-Municipal, Local, International

Led by the PM, the government of Japan established an emergency response team immediately after the disaster and within a day, the Ministry of Defense ordered deployment of the country's military, the Japan Self-Defence Forces, the National Police Force and the Fire and Disaster Management Agency. Furthermore, national and international NGOs moved quickly in organizing relief efforts that included the Japanese Red Cross that serves as an auxiliary to the government for disaster relief.[147] While the government of Japan responded swiftly, shortages of fuel, food and sanitary supplies continued due to massive interruptions in access to the affected area.

> [T]he most vulnerable populations – small children, the aged, the poor, and pets – suffered disproportionately because of the difficulty in evacuating or reaching them.[148]

Carafano (2012) noted the people of Japan demonstrated a "culture of preparedness," "remarkable resilience and discipline with no reports of rioting or large-scale disruptions."[149] He further commented that "the character and resolve demonstrated by the population generally served the nation well," although "in some coastal communities, residents were so confident in their response measures for tsunamis they had become complacent and were overwhelmed by the massive scale of destruction."[150]

Communication and People

The greatest difference between the 2011 Tohoku Earthquake and the 1995 Hanshin-Awaji Earthquake was the way people were able to communicate through Internet, computer and mobile networks. According to a consumer report, 76 percent of households in Japan own a personal computer and 83 percent of households use the computer as a communication tool.[151] In a report on the use of the Internet as of January 2011, 93.8 percent of people were identified as Internet users as compared to

147 J. J. Carafano. (2011). *The Great Eastern Japan Earthquake: Assessing Disaster Response and Lessons for the United States*. Washington, DC: The Heritage Foundation, p. 2.
148 Ibid., p. 2.
149 Ibid., p. 4.
150 Ibid.
151 Yoshitsugu (2011), *supra* note 116.

less than 3.3 percent before 1997.[152] Ensuring undisrupted access to these networks could enhance dissemination and exchange of information including search and rescue, and coordination of relief goods and support. Nonetheless, the availability of electricity supply and resilience of networks following the earthquake posed challenges and also revealed the potential for ICT to play a significant role in humanitarian aid response.

While Japan is technologically advanced, it still relies heavily on formal early warning systems, evacuation plans and alerts. In 2011, the government employed a variety of mechanisms ranging from traditional warning sirens to social media tools such as Twitter.[153] Despite the existence of social media and ICT tools, the government found that the sharing of accurate information in a timely manner was difficult. Carafano and others have pointed out how the use of social media can be problematic in times of crisis.

> One challenge is the constant question of information assurance – knowing whether the data are precise and reliable. During a large-scale crisis in particular, information can be spotty as communication systems are down and officials have difficulty collecting information and providing situational awareness.... Social media can compound [errors], as rumors, perfidy, and faulty information can be widely dispersed with great speed.[154]

Other challenges are accuracy and authenticity of government information. As social media also transforms formal journalism to "public journalism" through crowd-sourcing, in some cases misinformation can have disastrous effects.[155]

Policy Recommendations

In any large-scale disaster, individuals are the front line in any catastrophic event. Some studies have recommended empowering individuals and communities through training and capacity building.[156] Since coordination occurs at the municipal level in Japan, having a local team of trained

152 Ibid.

153 D. S. Abraham. (2011, March 16). How Bad Communication Is Undermining Japan's Crisis Response. *The Atlantic*. Retrieved from www.theatlantic.com/international/archive/2011/03/how-bad-communication-is-undermining-japans-crisis-response/72573/.

154 Carafano (2011), *supra* 148, p. 7.

155 Ibid., p. 8.

156 Ibid.

disaster responders formed by local residents may help provide a focal point for coordinating volunteering efforts. Since community residents have local knowledge and can often be the most important source for collecting and disseminating information, building capacity among local residents can be vital. The private sector can also play an important role in supporting recovery efforts.

In addition, investment in enhancing scientific research tools that can help communities better understand potential risks and effects of disasters is critical.[157]

Recent research has suggested that the creation of hazard maps and knowledge regarding their effective use at the municipal and local levels are critical as "municipalities are the primary agents for the implementation of disaster management measures."[158] Hazard maps should provide information of damage risk, evacuation sites and escape routes, and can be useful when considering improvements and retrofits of facilities for preventative and emergency measures.

Social policies should also promote education and awareness among citizens to build understanding of how to minimize risk and damage. Distribution of safety informative materials and regular drills at the community level are important. Such communication must be carried out in a way that is nonthreatening in order to encourage a preventative and preparatory attitude rather than fear. The identification and training of community members to identify risks and take mitigation measures may be considered.[159]

Conclusion

Japan's primary response to the 2011 tsunami was led by the national government. Local communities played an important role in contributing to volunteer efforts, local reconstruction efforts, building repair, senior care and reuniting families through online forums. While throughout history, Japan has suffered a number of massive earthquakes, including the 1923 Kanto Earthquake[160] and the 1995 Hanshin Earthquake,[161] the major

[157] G20 DRM Report (2012), *supra* note 25.

[158] Suganuma (2006), *supra* note 135, p.105.

[159] Christchurch Engineering Lifelines Group (1997). *Risks & Realities: A Multi-disciplinary Approach to the Vulnerabiliyt of Lifelines to Natural Hazards.* Christchurch: Centre for Advanced Engineering, University of Canterbury

[160] James and Cameron (2002), *supra* note 2.

[161] IRP (2008), *supra* note 3.

difference facilitating national coordination with local response efforts in 2011 was the introduction of online communication tools through Internet, computer and mobile networks. Ensuring undisrupted access to these networks no doubt will assist in the dissemination and exchange of information, including search and rescue, and coordination of relief goods and support.

9

Hurricane Katrina

Introduction

Katrina was an extraordinarily powerful and deadly hurricane that struck the United States during the 2005 Atlantic hurricane season.[1] Like the response to Thailand's flood of 2011 and Japan's earthquake and tsunami of 2011, the response to Hurricane Katrina in the United States was largely led by state agencies. Similar lessons were learned in state–local coordination, including the need for adequate planning and back-up communications systems, clear lines of coordination, information sharing and logistics capacity. In addition, particular issues unique to the United States, including the existence of racial prejudice and discrimination, exacerbated suffering through often delayed and insufficient response.

Considering the scope of its impact, Katrina was one of the most devastating natural disasters in US history[2] and presents yet another example of a state-led response. The "track" of Hurricane Katrina's path was a tropical depression formed on August 23 about 200 miles southeast of Nassau in the Bahamas.[3] Moving northwestward, it became tropical storm Katrina

[1] U.S. Senate Committee on Homeland Security and Government Affairs (2006). *Hurricane Katrina: A Nation Still Unprepared.* Washington, DC: U.S. Government Printing Office. Available at www.gpoaccess.gov/serialset/creports/katrinanation.html (accessed on April 10, 2013), p. 2; Richard D. Knabb et al. (2005, December). *Tropical Cyclone Report Hurricane Katrina, August 23–30, 2005.* National Hurricane Center. Updated September 14, 2011, p. 1. Available at www.nhc.noaa.gov/pdf/TCR-AL122005_Katrina.pdf (accessed on April 6, 2013); see also the overview of the National Oceanic and Atmospheric Administration (NOAA) at www.nhc.noaa.gov/outreach/history/#katrina (accessed on April 18, 2013); William L. Waugh. (2006). The Political Costs of Failure in the Katrina and Rita Disasters. *The ANNALS of the American Academy of Political and Social Science.* 604(10), p. 13.

[2] Eric S. Blake et al. (2011). *The Deadliest, Costliest and Most Intense United States Tropical Cyclones from 1851 to 2010 (and Other Frequently Requested Hurricane Facts).* National Climatic Data Center, National Hurricane Center. National Oceanic and Atmospheric Administration, p. 5. Available at www.nhc.noaa.gov/pdf/nws-nhc-6.pdf (accessed on April 5, 2013).

[3] U.S. Senate Committee on Homeland Security and Government Affairs (2006), *supra* note 1, p. 22; Knabb et al. (2005), *supra* note 1, p. 2; White House. (2006). *The Federal Response to Hurricane Katrina: Lessons Learned,* White House, Washington, DC, p. 1. Available at

the following day.[4] The storm moved through the northwestern Bahamas on August 24–25, and then turned westward toward southern Florida.[5] Tropical storm Katrina became a hurricane on August 25 just before making landfall in southern Florida, where it caused the first fatalities and damage.[6] At that time, Hurricane Katrina was a Category 1 hurricane on the Saffir-Simpson Hurricane Scale.[7] On August 26, Hurricane Katrina moved southwestward across southern Florida into the eastern Gulf of Mexico.[8] Katrina then strengthened significantly, reaching Category 5 intensity on August 28.[9] On the morning of August 29, 2005, Hurricane Katrina made landfall, at the upper end of Category 3 intensity, on the coast of southeast Louisiana and Mississippi.[10] Continuing northward, the hurricane made a second landfall near the mouth of the Pearl River at the Louisiana/Mississippi border.[11] Katrina weakened rapidly after moving inland over southern and central Mississippi[12] and became a

http://georgewbush-whitehouse.archives.gov/reports/katrina-lessons-learned/ (accessed on April 26, 2013); Andrea M. Quenette and Robert S. Littlefield. (2007). Crisis Leadership and Hurricane Katrina: The Portrayal of Authority by the Media in Natural Disasters. *Journal of Applied Communication Research*. 35(1) 26, p. 30.

4 See again the overview of NOAA, *supra* note 1.

5 Quenette and Littlefield (2007), *supra* note 3, p. 30.

6 Knabb et al. (2005), *supra* note 1, p. 2.

7 The Saffir-Simpson Hurricane Wind Scale is a 1 to 5 rating based on a hurricane's sustained wind speed. This scale estimates potential property damage. Hurricanes reaching Category 3 and higher are considered major hurricanes because of their potential for significant loss of life and damage. Categories 1 and 2 storms are still dangerous, however, and require preventative measures. Categories 4 and 5 hurricanes are considered major hurricanes while the term "super typhoon" is reserved for Category 5 tropical cyclones that sustain winds exceeding 150 mph. Refer for more specific details to the National Hurricane Center Web site at www .nhc.noaa.gov/aboutsshws.php (accessed on April 15, 2013). See also the Saffir-Simpson Team's report at www.nhc.noaa.gov/pdf/sshws.pdf (accessed on April 15, 2013) and Blake et al. (2011), *supra* note 2, p. 3.

8 Knabb et al. (2005), *supra* note 1, p. 3.

9 U.S. Senate Committee on Homeland Security and Government Affairs (2006), *supra* note 1, p. 52.

10 Katrina turned to the northwest and then north, with the center making landfall near Buras, Louisiana, at 1110 UTC August 29 with maximum winds estimated at 125 mph. See Knabb et al. (2005), *supra* note 1, p. 3 and U.S. Senate Committee on Homeland Security and Government Affairs (2006), *supra* note 1, pp. 21 and 53; U.S. Department of Homeland Security, Office of Inspector General. (2006). *A Performance Review of FEMA's Disaster Management Activities in Response to Hurricane Katrina*. Washington, DC: U.S. Government Printing Office p. 4. Available at www.dhs.gov/xoig/assets/mgmtrpts/OIG_06-32_Mar06.pdf (accessed on April 14, 2013).

11 This occurred at 1445 UTC August 29 with maximum winds estimated at 120 mph (Category 3). See the overview of NOAA, *supra* note 1.

12 It had become a Category 1 hurricane by 1800 UTC August 29. See Knabb et al. (2005), *supra* note 1, p. 4.

tropical depression over the Tennessee Valley on August 30.[13] Eventually, on August 31, what remained of Hurricane Katrina was absorbed and dissipated over the eastern Great Lakes.[14]

The damage and loss of life this massive hurricane inflicted in Louisiana and Mississippi were staggering, with significant effects extending into the Florida panhandle, Georgia and Alabama.[15] It was the deadliest hurricane to strike the United States since the Palm Beach–Lake Okeechobee hurricane of September 1928.[16] The number of fatalities known to be either directly or indirectly related to Katrina totaled 1,833.[17] This includes 1,577 fatalities in Louisiana, 238 in Mississippi and 14 in Florida.[18] Four additional deaths occurred in Georgia and Alabama.[19] This makes Katrina the third deadliest hurricane to strike the United States.[20] Data provided indicate that more than 1.2 million people along the northern Gulf Coast from southeastern Louisiana to Alabama were under some type of evacuation order, but it is not clear how many people actually evacuated.[21] Hurricane Katrina caused catastrophic damage in southeastern Louisiana and southern Mississippi. Storm surge along the Mississippi coast caused total destruction of many structures, with the surge damage extending several miles inland.[22] Similar damage occurred in portions of southeastern Louisiana southeast of New Orleans.[23] The surge overtopped and breached levees in the New Orleans

[13] This occurred at 1200 UTC August 30. See Knabb et al. (2005), *supra* note 1.

[14] The depression continued northeastward and transformed into an extratropical low pressure system by 0000 UTC August 31. See Knabb et al. (2005), *supra* note 1.

[15] See the overview of NOAA, *supra* note 1.

[16] The Palm Beach–Lake Okeechobee hurricane was responsible for at least 2,500 deaths and was the second deadliest hurricane to strike the United States. See the overview of NOAA, *supra* note 1; see also table 2 in Blake et al. (2011), *supra* note 2, p. 7.

[17] See U.S. Department of Homeland Security, *supra* note 10, p. 4; Patrick Sharkey. (2007). Survival and Death in New Orleans: An Empirical Look at the Human Impact of Katrina. *Journal of Black Studies*. 37(4), p. 482, pp. 487–490; Roger D. Congleton. (2006). The Story of Katrina: New Orleans and the Political Economy of Catastrophe. *Public Choice*, 127(1–2), p. 5.

[18] Knabb et al. (2005), *supra* note 1, p. 11; Blake et al. (2011), *supra* note 2, p. 5.

[19] Knabb et al. (2005), *supra* note 1, p. 11.

[20] See table 2 in Blake et al. (2011), *supra* note 2, p. 7. The Galveston Hurricane of 1900 was responsible for at least 8,000 deaths and remains first on the list. See also figure 1.1 in White House (2006), *supra* note 3, pp. 6 and 8–9. See also Lee Clarke. (2006, June 11). *Worst Case Katrina*. Available at http://understandingkatrina.ssrc.org/Clarke/ (accessed on April 2, 2013).

[21] Joanne M. Nigg et al. (2006). Housing Hurricane Katrina and the Flooding of New Orleans: Emergent Issues in Sheltering and Temporary. *The ANNALS of the American Academy of Political and Social Science*. 604, p. 113, pp. 115–117.

[22] Knabb et al. (2005), *supra* note 1, p. 12.

[23] Ibid.

metropolitan area, resulting in the inundation of much of the city and its eastern suburbs.[24] Wind damage from Katrina extended well inland into northern Mississippi and Alabama. The hurricane also caused wind and water damage in Miami-Dade and Broward Counties. The damage was estimated at US$ 108 billion in the New Orleans area and along the Mississippi.[25] This made Katrina the costliest US hurricane on record.[26]

In addition to its ensuing death and destruction, Hurricane Katrina put to the test the preparedness of federal agencies and Gulf Coast communities to deal with a natural disaster of this magnitude.[27]

National Response

Disaster response and planning, at the time Hurricane Katrina hit the United States, was delineated in the National Response Plan (NRP).[28] This was a national plan to respond to emergencies such as natural disasters or

24 U.S. Senate Committee on Homeland Security and Government Affairs (2006), *supra* note 1, pp. 53–56; U.S. Department of Homeland Security (2006), *supra* note 10, p. 4; Louise K. Comfort. (2006, March). Cities at Risk: Hurricane Katrina and the Drowning of New Orleans. *Urban Affairs Review*. 41, p. 501; Kulwinder Banipal. (2006). Strategic Approach to Disaster Management: Lessons Learned from Hurricane Katrina. *Disaster Prevention and Management*. 15(3), 484–485; Tun Lin Moe. (2010). Cleanup after Katrina: An Analysis on Policy, Process, Priorities, Problems, and Politics. *Disaster Prevention and Management*. 19(3), 314–315.

25 Blake et al. (2011), *supra* note 2, p. 5. The Policy Research Working Paper of the World Bank refers to indirect economic losses amounting to $42 billion compared to $107 billion of direct economic losses in Louisiana. See Stephane Hallegatte and Valentin Przyluski. (2010, December). *The Economics of Natural Disasters: Concepts and Methods, Sustainable Development Network*. The World Bank, p. 19. Available at www-wds.worldbank.org/external/default/WDSContentServer/IW3P/IB/2010/12/21/000158349_20101221155640/Rendered/PDF/WPS5507.pdf (accessed on April 8, 2013). Initial estimates indicated that the economic losses from Hurricane Katrina could be more than $200 billion. See Raymond J. Burby. (2006). Decisions for Hazardous Areas. Hurricane Katrina and the Paradoxes of Government Disaster Policy: Bringing About Wise Government. *The ANNALS of the American Academy of Political and Social Science*. 604, 171.

26 Blake et al. (2011), *supra* note 2, p. 5; Knabb et al. (2005), *supra* note 1, p. 13; White House (2006), *supra* note 3, pp. 7–8; Burby (2006), *supra* note 25.

27 ANSI Homeland Security Standards Panel (HSSP). (2007, March). *Lessons Learned from Hurricane Katrina and the Role for Standards and Conformity Assessment Programs*. ANSI Publication, p. 5. Available at www.ansi.org/hssp (accessed on May 5, 2013).

28 See CRS Report for Congress. (2006, November 15). *Federal Emergency Management Policy Changes after Hurricane Katrina: A Summary of Statutory Provisions*. Congressional Research Service, p. 31. Available at www.crs.gov (accessed on May 4, 2013); U.S. Congress Select Bipartisan Committee. (2006). *A Failure of Initiative: Supplemental Report and Document Annex*. Washington, DC: U.S. Government Printing Office, p. 131. Available at www.gpoaccess.gov/serialset/creports/katrinasupp.html (accessed on April 15, 2013); White House (2006), *supra* note 3, pp. 13–14.

terrorist attacks. It came to effect in December 2004, and was superseded by the National Response Framework in March 2008.[29]

The Disaster Management Structure

Pursuant to the NRP, disaster response and planning was first and foremost a local government responsibility.[30] When local government exhausts its resources, it then requests specific additional resources from the county level. The request process proceeds similarly from the county to the state to the federal government as additional resource needs are identified.[31] This shapes a "federal vs. state" structure that is often referred to as a "pull vs. push" system.[32]

The "pull" system term is used to describe the federal government's assistance in response to requests of the states or local governments via the states.[33] It, therefore, relies on states to request assistance from the federal government, and the resources the federal government provides in any disaster response are intended to supplement the resources of the state and local governments. As a general rule, the federal government responds to most natural disasters when the affected state(s) requests help because the disaster is of such severity and magnitude that an effective response is beyond the capabilities of the state and local governments.[34] In reality, states can make these requests even before disaster strikes because of the near certainty that federal assistance will be necessary.[35] On the other side, the federal government's assistance can be provided without waiting for specific requests from the state or local governments.[36] This is considered a "push" system.[37]

Apart from the two-level structure of federal versus state and local government response, states can prior to, or in addition to, seeking assistance from the federal government request assistance from other states. This

[29] See www.fema.gov/national-response-framework (accessed on May 2, 2013). The text of the National Response Framework is available at www.fema.gov/library/viewRecord.do?id=7371 (accessed on May 1, 2013).

[30] U.S. Senate Committee on Homeland Security and Government Affairs (2006), *supra* note 1, p. 79.

[31] U.S. Congress Select Bipartisan Committee (2006), *supra* note 28, p. 30.

[32] Ibid.

[33] FEMA. *A Guide to the Disaster Declaration Process*, available at www.fema.gov/pdf/rrr/dec_proc.pdf (accessed on April 25, 2013).

[34] Ibid.

[35] U.S. Congress Select Bipartisan Committee (2006), *supra* note 28, p. 31.

[36] White House (2006), *supra* note 3, p. 14.

[37] FEMA, *supra* note 33.

possibility is provided by participation in the Emergency Management Assistance Compact (EMAC), an interstate mutual aid agreement among member states to provide assistance after disasters overwhelm the affected state's capacity.[38] EMAC was created in 1996[39] and provides the legal framework for states to request a series of resources apart from interstate assistance.[40] They can, for instance, request temporary shelters and cargo aircraft, which may be available from other member states.[41]

In order to better understand the federal and local governments' response to Hurricane Katrina, it is important to examine the national framework for emergency management in greater detail.[42] In the following section, the federal authorities will be briefly delineated. Furthermore, specific reference will be made to the state and local emergency management of Louisiana and the city of New Orleans. This is explained as Louisiana and especially the New Orleans metropolitan area were hit severely and the most significant number of deaths occurred in New Orleans, which flooded as the levee system failed.[43]

Federal Framework for Emergency Management

When Hurricane Katrina hit, the disaster response and planning was conducted under the NRP. The NRP designates the following federal authorities as responsible for the coordination, response to and recovery from most major disasters, incidents or emergencies.

The Department of Homeland Security The Department of Homeland Security (DHS) is a cabinet department of the US federal government, created in response to the September 11 attacks.[44] It was created by the Homeland Security Act of 2002 (HAS), which transformed several federal

[38] See EMAC's official Web site at www.emacweb.org/ (accessed on May 3, 2013).

[39] Congress approved the creation of EMAC in 1996, building on the earlier efforts of the Southern Regional Emergency Compact that Florida and sixteen other states created in 1993 after experiencing dissatisfaction with the state and federal response to Hurricane Andrew in 1992. The National Emergency Management Association, the professional association of state emergency managers, administers the compact.

[40] Importantly, this assistance can, and often does, come from participating states' National Guards.

[41] U.S. Congress Select Bipartisan Committee (2006), *supra* note 28, p. 31.

[42] Ibid.

[43] Ibid.

[44] For the functions and the divisions of DHS, see www.dhs.gov/ (accessed on May 5, 2013).

agencies, programs and offices to create the DHS.[45] Amidst its agencies are the Federal Emergency Management Agency and the US Coast Guard, which are mainly entrusted with the coordination of responses following a natural disaster, such as Hurricane Katrina.

The Federal Emergency Management Agency The Federal Emergency Management Agency (FEMA) coordinates the federal government's role in preparing for, preventing and, mitigating the effects of, responding to and recovering from all domestic disasters, whether natural or man-made, including acts of terror.[46] FEMA was established in 1979 in an effort to consolidate many of the federal policies related to the management of emergencies, including preparedness, mitigation, disaster response and recovery.[47] With the creation of the DHS, Congress, in March 2003, placed FEMA within this new department.[48] The DHS comprised three directorates, created by the HSA. One of these three directorates[49] is the Emergency Preparedness and Response (EPR) Directorate. Specifically, the HSA placed FEMA – with the exception of its terrorism preparedness functions – into the EPR Directorate along with a number of additional entities and functions.[50] The three directorates of the DHS were abolished by a July 2005 reorganization and their responsibilities were transferred to other departmental components.[51] After the 2005

45 U.S. Congress Select Bipartisan Committee (2006), *supra* note 28, p. 29.

46 White House (2006), *supra* note 3, pp. 16–17. For more information, see www.fema.gov/ (accessed on April 27, 2013). For the history of FEMA, see also www.highbeam.com/topics/fema-hurricane-katrina-t10093 (accessed on May 2, 2013) and Pamela Denise Reed. (2007). From the Freedmen's Bureau to FEMA: A Post-Katrina Historical, Journalistic, and Literary Analysis. *Journal of Black Studies*. 37(4), 555, 559–563.

47 Among other agencies, FEMA absorbed: the Federal Insurance Administration, the National Fire Prevention and Control Administration, the National Weather Service Community Preparedness Program, the Federal Preparedness Agency of the General Services Administration and the Federal Disaster Assistance Administration activities from the US Department of Housing and Urban Development. Civil defense responsibilities were also transferred to the new agency from the Defense Department's Defense Civil Preparedness Agency.

48 U.S. Congress Select Bipartisan Committee (2006), *supra* note 28, p. 30.

49 The other two were the Border and Transportation Security Directorate and the Information Analysis and Infrastructure Protection Directorate.

50 Moreover, EPR also assumed responsibility for the Department of Health and Human Services' Office of Emergency Preparedness, which manages the National Disaster Medical System, a network of federal, state, local, private-sector and civilian volunteer medical and support personnel who augment local medical providers during disasters.

51 U.S. Congress Select Bipartisan Committee (2006), *supra* note 28, p. 30.

reorganization, FEMA reports directly to the secretary of the DHS.[52] Last on October 4, 2006, the post-Katrina Emergency Reform Act reorganized FEMA with the aim of strengthening its preparedness mission.[53]

For most major disasters or emergencies, DHS (via FEMA) establishes a Regional Response Coordination Center (RRCC) using staff from the regional offices it maintains, in order to coordinate the initial relief activities.[54] Furthermore, FEMA established a multiagency coordination center called the Joint Field Office (JFO) to direct the relief efforts of the federal, state and local officials. Moreover, during an incident of national significance, the secretary of the DHS may designate a Principal Federal Official (PFO) to act as the secretary's representative in overseeing and executing incident management responsibilities.[55] At the same time, the president of the United States can designate a Federal Coordinating Officer (FCO) to direct all federal assistance in the affected area.[56]

The US Coast Guard The US Coast Guard is a military, multi-mission, maritime service. Among the main responsibilities of the Coast Guard is to develop, establish, maintain and operate rescue infrastructure under and over the high seas and waters of the US jurisdiction.[57] By the time Hurricane Katrina struck, oversight was placed within the DHS and continues today.[58] The US Coast Guard is renowned for its search and rescue (SAR) capabilities, whether near the shore or hundreds of miles at sea.[59] To better direct its activities, the Coast Guard is organized into sectors. The sectors that were most affected by Katrina were

52 CRS Report for Congress (2006), *supra* note 28, p. 8.

53 Ibid.

54 White House (2006), *supra* note 3, pp. 17–18.

55 U.S. Congress Select Bipartisan Committee (2006), *supra* note 28, p. 37.

56 Pursuant to the Stafford Act, the president of the United States can issue an emergency or a major disaster declaration in case of incidents, such as major disasters or emergencies, that overwhelm or are likely to overwhelm state and local resources. If the president issues an emergency or major disaster declaration, he must also designate a Federal Coordinating Officer (FCO). See White House (2006), *supra* note 3, p. 15.

57 See www.uscg.mil/ (accessed on April 27, 2013); U.S. Government Accountability Office. (2006). *Coast Guard: Observations on the Preparation, Response, and Recovery Missions Related to Hurricane Katrina*. Washington, DC: U.S. Government Accountability Office p. 8. Available at www.gao.gov/new.items/d06903.pdf (accessed on April 10, 2013).

58 U.S. Congress Select Bipartisan Committee (2006), *supra* note 28, p. 41.

59 White House (2006), *supra* note 3, p. 38.

those that fell within the boundaries of Sector New Orleans and Sector Mobile, Alabama.[60]

The Department of Defense In the event of a natural disaster or emergency, the NRP stipulates that the Department of Defense (DOD) may be asked to provide assistance to the DHS and FEMA in an attempt to save lives and lessen the amplitude of the catastrophe.[61] Before examining the authorities within the DOD who are charged with the duty of providing assistance, it is important to refer to the distinction the DOD makes between "homeland security" and "homeland defense." In this regard, "homeland security" refers to response to threats and violence, including terrorism, whereas "homeland defense" is linked to the military protection against external threats and aggression with the aim of securing the safety of the domestic population.[62] The distinction between homeland security and homeland defense is important as the DOD is a lead agency only as regards to homeland defense.[63] Thus, the DOD's support can be triggered mainly for homeland defense matters. Homeland defense in the case of great disasters will consist of military response in the areas affected and will be normally provided only when local, state and other federal resources are overwhelmed. This designates the military response the DOD provides as a resource of "last resort."[64]

The Assistant Secretary of Defense for Homeland Defense As stated earlier, the DOD is the lead agency in the area of homeland defense (HD).[65] The department's activities in homeland defense are coordinated and led by the Assistant Secretary of Defense for Homeland Defense (ASDHD).[66] The DOD's military support of civil authorities is a last resort option and is triggered when the Lead Federal Agency (LFA) responding to an incident or natural disaster requests assistance. More specifically, when

[60] See www.uscg.mil/history/katrina/katrinaindex.asp (accessed on May 4, 2013).

[61] U.S. Congress Select Bipartisan Committee (2006), *supra* note 28, p. 39. For more details, see www.defense.gov/about/ (accessed on May 2, 2013).

[62] U.S. Senate Committee on Homeland Security and Government Affairs (2006), *supra* note 1, p. 468.

[63] In the context of homeland security, the DOD operates only in support of a civilian-led federal agency, referred to as Civil Support (CS).

[64] U.S. Congress Select Bipartisan Committee (2006), *supra* note 28, p. 39.

[65] See DOD. *Organizations and Functions of the Department of Defense*, available at http://odam.defense.gov/omp/Functions/Organizational_Portfolios/Organization_and_Functions_Guidebook.html (accessed on May 10, 2013).

[66] Ibid.

natural disasters occur and a military response is anticipated, the DHS (via FEMA) will be the LFA and will have the option to request assistance from the DOD. The request for assistance is made through a request for the appointment of a Defense Coordinating Officer (DCO) who will serve as the single DOD point of contact within the disaster area.[67] In order to designate a DCO, the ASDHD has to coordinate with another authority of the DOD, the Northern Command.

The Northern Command Within the DOD, the Northern Command (NORTHCOM) is the coordinating command for domestic terrorism and national disaster incidents.[68] Northern Command carries out civil support missions with forces assigned as required from all the armed services, typically through the creation of a joint task force (JTF). The civil support responsibilities the Northern Command carries out reside with the Joint Director of Military Support.[69]

The process for requesting DOD active duty forces has several layers of review. In the case of natural disasters, when local, state and other federal resources are overwhelmed, the LFA can request the DOD's support. The lead federal agency for natural disasters is FEMA, who through the FCO will request the DOD to designate a DCO.[70] Within the DOD, the Assistant Secretary of Defense for Homeland Defense will evaluate the request and if approved,[71] he will forward it to the Joint Director of Military Support, who will in turn provide NORTHCOM with the appropriate orders. Therefore, when the magnitude of the disaster is great, a JTF will be created and a DCO will serve as task force commander. As indicated, the DCO will serve as the single point of contact for DOD resources. The DCO does not, however, have operational control of the US Army Corps of Engineers or National Guard personnel operating in state active duty.[72]

The aforementioned process is carved out to maximize the DOD's coordination with FEMA and state governments. However, there are two

[67] U.S. Senate Committee on Homeland Security and Government Affairs (2006), *supra* note 1, p. 468.
[68] White House (2006), *supra* note 3, p. 42.
[69] U.S. Congress Select Bipartisan Committee (2006), *supra* note 28, p. 40.
[70] Ibid.
[71] Requests are submitted to the Office of the Secretary of Defense (OSD), where they are evaluated by the Assistant Secretary of Defense for Homeland Defense (ASDHD) according to the following criteria: legality, readiness, lethality, risk, cost and appropriateness.
[72] U.S. Congress Select Bipartisan Committee (2006), *supra* note 28, p. 39.

exceptions. First, if the president of the United States directs otherwise, the request for military assistance from the DOD can be direct and must not necessarily originate from the lead federal agency.[73] Second, when a natural disaster is anticipated and it is almost certain that military assistance will be necessary, NORTHCOM can designate a DCO prior to a DHS/FEMA request. The designation of a DCO at this stage is done informally and is justified for early assessment of the needs of the affected area.[74]

Local Emergency Management and the Specific Emergency Management Framework of Louisiana and New Orleans

In most situations, disaster management is subject to a process of escalation beginning from the local level and culminating at the state level, as incidents grow or as it becomes known that an incident has overwhelmed local capabilities.[75]

Local governments – cities, towns, counties or parishes – and the officials who lead them are responsible for both the development of emergency management frameworks and the response plans needed when disasters or other emergencies strike.[76] Pursuant to the NRP, depending on the terms of the state or local laws, local officials have "extraordinary powers" to, among other things, order evacuations. In addition, local officials may suspend local laws and order curfews.[77]

At the state level, note that a state's chief executive, the governor, is responsible for public safety and plays a key role in the emergency management framework.[78] The governor is vested with a wide range of emergency management responsibilities, including requesting federal assistance when it is clear that state resources are or will be overwhelmed. Governors also serve as the commanders in chief of their state military forces, and particularly the National Guard when in a state of active duty. The National Guard is the United States' first military responder to events within the United States and is the only force that has the unique dual role of providing forces at both the state and federal levels.[79] The National

[73] White House (2006), *supra* note 3, p. 42.

[74] U.S. Congress Select Bipartisan Committee (2006), *supra* note 28, p. 40.

[75] U.S. Senate Committee on Homeland Security and Government Affairs (2006), *supra* note 1, p. 79.

[76] U.S. Congress Select Bipartisan Committee (2006), *supra* note 28, p. 45.

[77] Ibid.

[78] U.S. Senate Committee on Homeland Security and Government Affairs (2006), *supra* note 1, p. 79.

[79] Ibid.

Guard abides by two oaths, one to the governor and one to the president of the United States.[80] In fact, governors historically rely on the National Guard to serve in disaster relief tasks when great disasters or emergencies arise. In these cases, the National Guard serves under the governors' commands.

Last governors are responsible for implementing mutual interstate agreements as well as requesting interstate aid through EMAC as indicated earlier.[81] Governors are assisted in their disaster management duties by state emergency management agencies. These agencies report to their governors and are entrusted with coordination alongside other state agencies as well as local emergency response departments to plan for and respond to potential or imminent disasters or emergencies.[82]

Emergency Management Framework of Louisiana The Louisiana Homeland Security and Emergency Assistance and Disaster Act outlines the specific responsibilities of key state entities and emergency responders and provides for the coordination of activities among state agencies and local and federal governments. These will be delineated in the following section.

The Governor Louisiana law entrusts the governor with "overall responsibility for emergency management in the state."[83] The governor is authorized, for instance, to declare a disaster or emergency and coordinate delivery of all emergency services during this disaster or emergency. In his emergency management duties, the governor of Louisiana is seconded by the Louisiana Office of Homeland Security and Emergency Preparedness (LOHSEP).[84] By making a disaster declaration as just indicated, the governor of Louisiana activates the state's emergency response and recovery program, which is under the command of the LOHSEP director. Note that the governor of Louisiana can delegate his authority to direct emergency operations to the state

[80] More specifically, the governor has command and control of the National Guard, either in state active duty or Title 32 status, unless units are federalized. If federalized under Title 10, the National Guard falls under the command and control of the president.

[81] See earlier for discussion of disaster management structure at page 15.

[82] Ibid.

[83] U.S. Congress Select Bipartisan Committee (2006), *supra* note 28, p. 49.

[84] See www.gohsep.la.gov/ (accessed on April 18, 2013).

adjutant general, who usually serves both as director of LOHSEP and as commander of the National Guard.[85]

The Louisiana Office of Homeland Security and Emergency Preparedness Louisiana's lead agency for emergencies is LOHSEP.[86] LOHSEP is placed within the Military Department and under the authority of the governor and the adjutant general of the state and is responsible for emergency preparedness and homeland security in the state of Louisiana.[87] LOHSEP also prepares and maintains the Emergency Operation Plan (EOP), which establishes the state's disasters and emergencies management structure. More specifically, the EOP stipulates the various phases of emergencies and disasters, being preparedness, response, recovery and prevention (mitigation). The EOP also delineates the role of FEMA when federal relief is sought.

The National Guard Within Louisiana's emergency management framework the National Guard can be called to serve under the governor's commands. In particular, Louisiana's commander of the National Guard generally serves both as director of LOHSEP and the adjutant general of the state.[88]

Emergency Management Framework of the City of New Orleans The Emergency Management Framework of the City of New Orleans is provided in the City of New Orleans Comprehensive Emergency Management Plan (NOCEMP).[89] This plan is consistent with the State of Louisiana Emergency Operational Plan carved out by LOHSEP. As at the state level the governor is entrusted with "overall responsibility for emergency management in the state," likewise the NOCEMP stipulates that the "City government bears the initial responsibility for disaster response and relief."[90] This means that the mayor of the City of New Orleans is responsible for the implementation of the NOCEMP. In these duties, the

85 U.S. Congress Select Bipartisan Committee (2006), *supra* note 28, p. 49.

86 Before 2003, LOHSEP was known as the Government's Office of Homeland Security and Emergency Preparedness. It was created in 1950, and since its creation it was variously assigned to the Department of Public Safety, the Military Department and finally the Governor's Office.

87 U.S. Senate Committee on Homeland Security and Government Affairs (2006), *supra* note 1, pp. 79–80.

88 White House (2006), *supra* note 3, p. 55.

89 U.S. Congress Select Bipartisan Committee (2006), *supra* note 28, p. 49.

90 Ibid.

mayor is seconded by the New Orleans Office of Emergency Preparedness (NOOEP).[91]

If the magnitude of the disaster renders it clear that the resources of the City of New Orleans will be overwhelmed, then the mayor may request state and/or federal assistance through LOHSEP.[92] In this regard, NOOEP will coordinate with LOHSEP to better deal with the disaster or emergency.[93]

The Specific Role of the American Red Cross

The American Red Cross (ARC) is an independent, nongovernmental organization.[94] It is the only nongovernmental organization with lead agency responsibilities under the NRP.[95] It is a "federal instrumentality" due to its charter requirements to carry out responsibilities delegated by the federal government.[96] The stated mission of the ARC is to "provide relief to victims of disasters and help people prevent, prepare for, and respond to emergencies."[97] In a presidentially declared disaster or emergency, the ARC, pursuant to the NRP, is coordinated by FEMA with the aim of better responding to emergencies and disasters. More specifically, the ARC functions as the primary organization in coordinating the use of mass care resources and is the lead agency in dealing with mass care, housing and human services.[98]

The Federal and Local Governments' Responses

The National Hurricane Center issued multiple dire warnings when it tracked Katrina as it gained intensity and crossed the Gulf of Mexico. On August 26, 2005,[99] the National Hurricane Center predicted that Hurricane Katrina's track had shifted and was headed for southeast Louisiana and New Orleans.[100] The landfall was at that time anticipated to be of a Category 4 hurricane.[101]

91 Ibid.
92 Ibid.
93 Ibid.
94 See more information at www.redcross.org/ (accessed on April 15, 2013).
95 U.S. Congress Select Bipartisan Committee (2006), *supra* note 28, p. 42.
96 Ibid.
97 Ibid.
98 Ibid.
99 By 5:00 p.m. See U.S. Department of Homeland Security (2006), *supra* note 10, p. 5.
100 White House (2006), *supra* note 3, p. 55.
101 U.S. Congress Select Bipartisan Committee (2006), *supra* note 28, p. 59; U.S. Government Accountability Office. (2005). *Hurricane Katrina: Providing Oversight of the Nation's*

Federal Government's Pre-landfall Responses

Even before Hurricane Katrina shifted toward Louisiana, FEMA emergency response teams began coordinating with the Gulf Coast states to preposition commodities and personnel in the areas expected to be hit.[102] In addition, quantities of ice, water, ready-to-eat meals, and other commodities were pre-staged among other areas of Florida, Georgia, Texas, Mississippi and Louisiana. At the same time, the US Coast Guard began prepositioning resources in a ring around the expected impact zone and activated more than 400 reservists.[103] On August 27, the US Coast Guard moved its personnel out of the New Orleans region prior to the mandatory evacuation. The same day, the Corps of Engineers positioned teams and supplies in Alabama, Louisiana and Mississippi.[104]

Before the hurricane made landfall, the president of the United States, George W. Bush, declared a state of emergency in selected regions of Louisiana, Alabama and Mississippi, authorizing FEMA to begin preparing for the impact of Katrina.[105] The same day, the National Hurricane Center (NHC) upgraded the storm alert status and issued hurricane warnings over the stretch of coastline between Morgan City, Louisiana, and the Alabama–Florida border. On Saturday, August 27, the National Weather Service warned that levees could be topped in New Orleans, causing catastrophic flooding.[106] By August 28, when the magnitude of Hurricane Katrina had become evident, the NHC extended the storm-warning zone to cover most of the Louisiana coastline.[107]

On August 27, FEMA assigned NORTHCOM the mission of establishing Barksdale Air Force Base in Louisiana as a federal operational staging area. On August 28, 2005, NORTHCOM established a JTF

Preparedness, Response, and Recovery Activities. Washington, DC: Government Accountability Office. Available at www.gao.gov/new.items/d051053t.pdf (accessed on April 20, 2013).

102 More specifically, FEMA activated its National Response Coordination Center (NRCC) in Washington, DC, and Regional Response Coordination Centers (RRCC) in Atlanta, Georgia, and Denton, Texas.

103 U.S. Department of Homeland Security (2006), *supra* note 10, p. 5; U.S. Government Accountability Office. (2006). *Coast Guard, supra* note 57, p. 6.

104 U.S. Congress Select Bipartisan Committee (2006), *supra* note 28, p. 59.

105 More specifically, federal emergency declarations were issued for Louisiana on August 27, 2005, and for Mississippi and Alabama on August 28, 2005. Richard T. Sylves. (2006). President Bush and Hurricane Katrina: A Presidential Leadership Study. *The ANNALS of the American Academy of Political and Social Science*. 604, 26–27.

106 Sylves (2006), *supra* note 105.

107 Knabb et al. (2005), *supra* note 1, p. 3.

Katrina[108] to coordinate the military response to the natural disaster. JTF Katrina was based on Camp Shelby in Mississippi and US Army Lieutenant General Russel L. Honoré was appointed as commander.[109]

Local Governments' Pre-landfall Responses

During Hurricane Katrina, the governors of Alabama, Mississippi and Louisiana requested that all National Guard forces deployed to their states operate under Title 32 status. This request was granted retroactively to August 29 by the secretary of defense.[110] Under Title 32, the governors were in command of all National Guard assets and actions during Hurricane Katrina. Several evacuation orders were issued and state officials coordinated the contraflow of the state of Louisiana with the states of Mississippi and Texas, since Louisiana interstates fed into these states.[111] Up to 1.2 million Louisiana residents followed the evacuation orders and evacuated themselves in their private vehicles; however, it later became apparent that thousands of residents, particularly in New Orleans, did not evacuate or seek shelter, but remained in their homes.[112]

Specifically for the state of Louisiana, on Friday, August 26, Louisiana Governor Blanco authorized the mobilization of the Louisiana National Guard (LANG).[113] The LANG went on alert, participating in preparation missions[114] and staging equipment and on August 27 it had been fully activated.[115] On the same day, Governor Blanco wrote to President Bush, declaring a state of emergency in Louisiana due to Hurricane Katrina. Coordination also began in the area of search and rescue through EMAC. Meanwhile, on August 28, evacuations began; however, although buses were available to transport those dependent

108 Initially known as Joint Task Force Katrina-Forward.

109 Ibid.

110 White House (2006), *supra* note 3, p. 25 *et seq.*

111 U.S. Government Accountability Office. (2006). *Disaster Preparedness: Preliminary Observations on the Evacuation of Hospitals and Nursing Homes due to Hurricanes.* Washington, DC: U.S. Government Accountability Office. p. 12 *et seq.* Available at www.gao.gov/new.items/d06443r.pdf (accessed on April 15, 2013); U.S. Government Accountability Office. (2006). *Disaster Preparedness: Preliminary Observations on the Evacuation of Vulnerable Populations due to Hurricanes and Other Disasters.* Washington, DC: U.S. Government Accountability Office. p. 2 *et seq.* Available at www.gao.gov/new.items/d06790t.pdf (accessed on April 13, 2013).

112 Ibid.

113 U.S. Congress Select Bipartisan Committee (2006), *supra* note 28, p. 67.

114 The LANG participated in a number of preparation missions, including law enforcement, traffic control, shelter support and security, and securing operations at the Superdome.

115 By Saturday, August 28, the day prior to landfall, the LANG had prepositioned 9,792 MREs and 13,440 liters of water at the Superdome, the "shelter of last resort."

on public transportation, not enough bus drivers were available.[116] This was due to the fact that Governor Blanco did not sign an emergency waiver to allow any licensed driver to transport evacuees on buses. On Saturday, August 27, the New Orleans Regional Transit Authority (RTA) fueled up its fleet and got ready to face the hurricane. On Sunday, August 28, Governor Blanco asked President Bush, prior to landfall, to declare an expedited major disaster for the State of Louisiana. President Bush made this major disaster declaration the next day.[117]

In the city of New Orleans, Mayor Ray Nagin ordered the first mandatory evacuation of the city only on August 28, nineteen hours before landfall.[118] In the city of New Orleans, several refuges of last resort were established for citizens who could not leave.[119] Specifically, the Louisiana Superdome, which is a sports and exhibition stadium, was used to shelter and provide food and water to approximately 26,000 people.[120]

American Red Cross Pre-landfall Response

The American Red Cross (ARC) began preparations two days before Katrina made landfall on the Gulf Coast.[121] On August 27, the ARC reported to the DHS that it had every resource at its disposal, including personnel, equipment and materials, in anticipation of Katrina's landfall. By August 28, when the magnitude of Katrina was well known, the ARC announced that a center would be set up to coordinate and deliver mass care services.[122]

Meta-landfall Response

Katrina made landfall by 6:10 a.m. on Monday, August 29. Later that morning levees began to overtop and breach in the city of New Orleans, causing catastrophic flooding and many casualties. The failure of the levee system was not known to the DHS and the White House until early Tuesday morning. Communications began to fail around Monday

[116] Heather McKillop. (2005, December).The Aftermath of Katrina. American Anthropological Association. *Anthropology News*. Available at www.aaanet.org/press/an/1205/AN2005Dec_mckillop.pdf.

[117] U.S. Senate Committee on Homeland Security and Government Affairs (2006), *supra* note 1, p. 68.

[118] U.S. Congress Select Bipartisan Committee (2006), *supra* note 28, p. 64.

[119] Nigg et al. (2006), *supra* note 21, p. 117 *et seq.*

[120] Ibid., p. 113.

[121] Stephen Zuckerman and Teresa Coughlin. (2006, February). *Initial Health Policy Responses to Hurricane Katrina and Possible Next Steps*. The Urban Institute. Available at www.urban.org/afterkatrina/ (accessed on April 7, 2013).

[122] Ibid.

afternoon.[123] Search and rescue operations started around this time with the Coast Guard initiating action. Of the 60,000 people stranded in New Orleans, the Coast Guard rescued more than 33,500.[124] Through the JTF Katrina that had been established in Mississippi, approximately 58,000 National Guard personnel, coming from all fifty states, were activated to deal with Katrina's aftermath. The Department of Defense also activated volunteer members of the Civil Air Patrol. As Katrina made landfall, the Red Cross had staffed all the emergency operation centers (state and federal) in Alabama, Louisiana, Florida, Mississippi, Georgia, South Carolina and Tennessee.[125]

On August 30, 2005, Michael Chertoff, secretary of the DHS, officially decided to take over the federal, state and local operations.[126] Michael Chertoff designated Michael D. Brown, head of FEMA, as the Principal Federal Official (PFO) to lead the federal response to Katrina. In Louisiana, Governor Blanco refused the take-over of DHS/FEMA, indicating that her National Guard could manage. In fact, a lack of planning and coordination led to the replacement of Michael D. Brown as the PFO by Coast Guard Vice Admiral Thad W. Allen.[127]

Michael D. Brown promised Louisiana Governor Kathleen Blanco that 500 buses would arrive within hours to begin evacuations from the Superdome in New Orleans. On the same day, the mayor of the city of New Orleans, Ray Nagin, opened the Morial Convention Center as an additional shelter of last resort.[128] Federal officials were not aware of that until later in the week. The buses Brown promised, arrived on Thursday and evacuations were not completed until Saturday, September 3. Of the trailers requested for shelter support by FEMA, only one-fifth were supplied. Therefore, an enormous housing shortage was created. This shortage was also driven by the fact that many local areas voted not to allow trailers or lacked the necessary utilities required prior to the placement of trailers.[129] FEMA, however,

123 Claire H. Procopio and Steven T. Procopio. (2007). Do You Know What It Means to Miss New Orleans? Internet Communication, Geographic Community, and Social Capital in Crisis. *Journal of Applied Communication Research*. 35(1), 67–68.

124 Congress recognized the Coast Guard's response with an official entry in the Congressional Record, and the Armed Service was awarded the Presidential Unit Citation.

125 U.S. Congress Select Bipartisan Committee (2006), *supra* note 28, pp. 69–70.

126 U.S. Senate Committee on Homeland Security and Government Affairs (2006), *supra* note 1, p. 69.

127 Ibid, p. 70.

128 Ibid., p. 364.

129 Daniel P. Aldrich and Kevin Crook. (2008, September 1). Strong Civil Society as a Double-Edged Sword: Siting Trailers in Post-Katrina New Orleans. Available at http://ssrn.com/abstract=960497 (accessed on April 20, 2013).

also provided rental assistance and paid for hotel costs of 12,000 individuals and families displaced by Katrina. In sum, FEMA provided housing assistance to more than 700,000 families and individuals.[130]

In the weeks following the catastrophe, agencies from as far as California, Michigan and New York provided support to Louisiana and New Orleans. The support comprised manpower and equipment as well as law enforcement aid.[131] After Katrina moved away on August 30, 2005, some residents of the city of New Orleans began entering stores mainly in search of food and water. Confusion was created when the media reported murders, thefts, carjackings and rapes that later proved inaccurate in the majority of the cases.[132] Over the first week of September 2005, law and order was gradually restored in the city of New Orleans. However, the aftermath of the catastrophic Hurricane Katrina led evacuees to seek refuge in all fifty states.[133]

Engaging with Local Populations in Relief Efforts

This section will focus on the effectiveness of the relief efforts and the coordination of response. First, the effectiveness of federal, state and local governments' response will be addressed to examine how all levels of government engaged with local populations in providing relief. Second, the response of NGOs as well as the response of private individuals will be examined.

Effectiveness of Federal, State and Local Governments' Response

A large portion of the problems that arose in dealing with the aftermath of Hurricane Katrina were caused by inadequate planning and back-up

[130] U.S. Department of Homeland Security (2006), *supra* note 10, p.13.

[131] A number of arrests were made throughout the affected area, including some near the New Orleans Convention Center. A temporary jail was constructed of chain link cages in the city train station.

[132] Ibid.

[133] Most evacuees had stayed within 250 miles (400 km), but 240,000 households went to Houston and other cities more than 250 miles (400 km) away, and another 60,000 households went more than 750 miles (1,200 km) away. See Anthony Oliver-Smith. (2006, June 11). *Disasters and Forced Migration in the 21st Century*. Available at http://understandingkatrina.ssrc.org/Oliver-Smith/ (accessed on April 8, 2013). Refer also to Elizabeth Fussell. (2006, June 11). *Leaving New Orleans: Social Stratification, Networks, and Hurricane Evacuation*. Available at http://understandingkatrina.ssrc.org/Fussell/ (accessed on April 7, 2013).

communications systems at various levels.[134] More specifically, the response elucidated that there was not an effective network of cooperation or effective hierarchy but rather confusion over the chain of command.[135]

This lack of coordination was underscored in the pre-Katrina landfall as well as the meta-Katrina landfall. Despite adequate warning fifty-six hours before landfall, Governor Blanco and Mayor Nagin delayed ordering a mandatory evacuation in New Orleans until nineteen hours before landfall.[136] By the time the evacuation took place, evacuees were ordered to shelters of last resort that lacked provisions for food, water, security or sanitary conditions.[137] Moreover, the lack of an effective hierarchy was highlighted as several federal authorities were only announcing their presence to state and local governments without acting under specific orders. Also, the Louisiana National Guard said it was there to "support" while on Saturday, September 3, it was apparent that no central command post existed to inform people when they would be evacuated from the city of New Orleans.[138]

In addition, the capacity of the disaster relief network was weakened, and investigation conducted after the severe disaster found that FEMA and the ARC were not capable of fully supporting the massive number of Gulf Coast victims due to the lack of a sophisticated logistics capacity.[139]

The former head of FEMA testified before a US House subcommittee in late September 2005. When asked why President Bush's declaration of a state of emergency on August 27 had in fact not included any of Louisiana's

[134] Sylves (2006), *supra* note 105, p. 32.

[135] Donald P. Moynihan. (2007). *From Forest Fires to Hurricane Katrina: Case Studies of Incident Command Systems*. IBM Center for the Business of Government, p. 18. Available at www.businessofgovernment.org/report/forest-fires-hurricane-katrina-case-studies-incident-command-systems (accessed on April 10, 2013); Judy Whitehead. (2005, December). The Neoliberal State in Disaster Management. American Anthropological Association, *Anthropology News*. Available at www.aaanet.org/press/an/1205/AN2005Dec_whitehead.pdf (accessed on April 10, 2013).

[136] Moynihan (2007), *supra* note 135, p. 14.

[137] See Jacob L. Vigdor. (2007, April). The Katrina Effect: Was There a Bright Side to the Evacuation of Greater New Orleans? Working Paper 13022, National Bureau of Economic Research. Available at www.nber.org/papers/w13022 (accessed on April 10, 2013).

[138] Ibid.

[139] U.S. Government Accountability Office. (2006). *Hurricanes Katrina and Rita: Coordination between FEMA and the Red Cross Should Be Improved for the 2006 Hurricane Season*. Washington, DC : U.S. Government Accountability Office, p. 7. Available at www.gao.gov/new.items/d06712.pdf (accessed on May 6, 2013); Charles Perrow. (2006, June 11). *Using Organizations: The Case of FEMA*. Available at http://understandingkatrina.ssrc.org/Perrow/ (accessed on April 6, 2013).

coastal parishes, whereas the coastal counties were included in the declarations for Mississippi and Alabama, Brown testified that Louisiana Governor Blanco had not included those parishes in her initial request for aid. However, just after the hearing, Blanco released a copy of her letter, which showed she had requested assistance for "all the southeastern parishes including the City of New Orleans," but it was clear that her request was not adequate and in some sense erroneous.[140]

Last, the overall response to Katrina ignited outrage about race and inequality in the United States.[141] Some have noted that the response was delayed due to the effects of centuries of neglect and racism that had affected the population of New Orleans.[142]

Effectiveness of NGOs and Private Individuals' Response

As soon as Katrina made landfall, a network of volunteers, including NGOs[143] and charities, began providing aid to the residents of New Orleans

140 U.S. Senate (2006), *supra* note 1, p. 591.

141 See the following articles in the special issue of the *Journal of Black Studies* about Hurricane Katrina: Troy D. Allen. (2007). Katrina: Race, Class, and Poverty: Reflections and Analysis. *Journal of Black Studies*. 37(4), 466; Jason David Rivera and DeMond Shondell Miller. (2007). Continually Neglected: Situating Natural Disasters in the African American Experience. *Journal of Black Studies*. 37(4), 502; Ismail K. White et al. (2007). Feeling the Pain of My People: Hurricane Katrina, Racial Inequality, and the Psyche of Black America. *Journal of Black Studies*. 37(4), 523; Patric R. Spence et al. (2007). Crisis Communication, Race, and Natural Disasters. *Journal of Black Studies*. 37(4), 539; DeMond Shondell Miller. (2007). Book Review: Come Hell or High Water: Hurricane Katrina and the Color of Disaster. *Journal of Black Studies*. 37(4), 568. See also Nils Gilman. (2006, June 11). What Katrina Teaches about the Meaning of Racism. Available at http://understandingkatrina.ssrc.org/Gilman/ (accessed on April 5, 2013).

142 See Sandra Crouse Quinn. (2006). Hurricane Katrina: A Social and Public Health Disaster. *American Journal of Public Health*. 96(2), 204, and Robert R. M. Verchick. (2006, November). Risk, Fairness, and the Geography of Disaster. Available at http://ssrn.com/abstract=2214079 (accessed on April 14, 2013); Jon Hanson and Kathleen Hanson. (2006). The Blame Frame: Justifying (Racial) Injustice in America. Harvard Public Law Working Paper, No. 08-47, *Harvard Civil Rights-Civil Liberties Law Review*. 41, 413, 416; Susan L. Cutter. (2006, June 11). The Geography of Social Vulnerability: Race, Class and Catastrophe. Available at http://understandingkatrina.ssrc.org/Cutter/ (accessed on April 5, 2013). Refer also to Dorian T. Warren et al. (2006, June 11). Katrina's Political Roots and Divisions: Race, Class, and Federalism in American Politics. Available at http://understandingkatrina.ssrc.org/FrymerStrolovitchWarren/ (accessed on April 8, 2013).

143 The American Red Cross, America's Second Harvest (now known as Feeding America), Southern Baptist Convention, Salvation Army, Oxfam, Common Ground Collective, Burners Without Borders, Emergency Communities, Habitat for Humanity, Catholic Charities, Service International, "A River of Hope," The Church of Jesus Christ of Latter-day Saints, and many other charitable organizations provided help to the victims of the storm.

and the surrounding parishes. Many of these volunteers were not allowed into New Orleans by the National Guard for several days after the hurricane hit because of safety concerns. However, some smaller organizations and individuals ignored the access restrictions and provided assistance.[144]

As communications deteriorated, volunteers from amateur radio emergency services provided communications in areas where the communications infrastructure had been damaged or totally destroyed.[145] In fact, the grid of amateur radio operators was quickly developed to locate more than 25,000 survivors and in some places, such as Hancock County in Mississippi, amateur radio operators provided the only communications into or out of the area.[146]

As was seen from the response of volunteers, relief efforts lacked coordination with the federal, state and local authorities. Even the ARC despite its tremendous efforts was found to lack a logistics capacity designed to face disasters of Katrina's magnitude.[147] While the efforts of volunteers lacked coordination, their involvement was important especially in dealing with Katrina's aftermath. NGOs, charities and private individuals continued to provide housing, financial and even emotional and spiritual support[148] more than six months after the storm. NGOs and charities raised more than US$ 4 billion in donations by the public, which was used to provide for the affected population in various ways.[149]

Outcome

In dealing with the outcome of the overall response to Hurricane Katrina, the US Congress Select Bipartisan Committee noted that even though "all people involved, at all levels of government, were trying their best to save lives and ease suffering, their best just wasn't good enough."[150] Similarly, a

144 Ibid.

145 For example, Salvation Army pastoral care counselors were on hand to address the emotional and spiritual needs of 277,000 individuals.

146 Ibid.

147 Ibid.

148 Ibid.

149 U.S. Government Accountability Office. (2005). *Hurricanes Katrina and Rita: Provision of Charitable Assistance*. Washington, DC: U.S. Government Accountability Office, p. 3. Available at www.gao.gov/new.items/d06297t.pdf (accessed on April 25, 2013). The American Red Cross received more than half of the donations. Also, corporate donations to the relief efforts were announced to be around US$ 409 million, and were expected to exceed $1 billion.

150 U.S. Congress Select Bipartisan Committee (2006), *supra* note 28, p. 359.

report from a US Senate Committee found that Katrina led to "an undermining of confidence in our governments' ability to plan, prepare for, and respond to national catastrophes."[151] Of the 1,500 fatalities in Louisiana, the majority was caused by the failure of the levee system and the serious delay of the evacuation of the city of New Orleans.[152] In this regard, responders were warned about the potential effects of a great disaster several days before Katrina's landfall. A tropical depression was already observed by August 23, 2005, and in spite of adequate warnings regarding Katrina's magnitude two days before landfall, the evacuation of the city of New Orleans was not ordered until nineteen hours before Katrina made landfall.[153]

In sum, the response system failed and the confusion over the chain of command left tens of thousands without basic supplies.[154] Government responders seemed unable to provide basic protection from the ravages of nature and the weakening of the emergency relief network was largely caused by the weaknesses of its hubs. This in turn was due to the absence of a back-up plan as communications deteriorated and specific orders were not given because of the nonexistence of an effective hierarchy.[155]

Lessons Learned

The response to Hurricane Katrina was not about some individual's "failure of initiative. It was about organizational and societal failures of initiative."[156] As a general comment, the overall response indicated governmental failures and in some cases incompetence of officials.[157] With the aim of better understanding how effectively the national response

[151] U.S. Senate Committee on Homeland Security and Government Affairs (2006), *supra* note 1, p. 585.

[152] Sharkey (2007), *supra* note 17, p. 485 *et seq.*

[153] U.S. Congress Select Bipartisan Committee (2006), *supra* note 28, p. 64.

[154] Ibid.

[155] Ibid.

[156] Ibid., p. 359.

[157] Donald F. Kettl. (2006). *Is the Worst Yet to Come? The ANNALS of the American Academy of Political and Social Science.* 604, 273, 282. In its report, the White House enumerated critical challenges in the following: National Preparedness, Integrated Use of Military Capabilities, Communications, Logistics and Evacuations, Search and Rescue, Public Safety and Security, Public Health and Medical Support, Human Services, Mass Care and Housing, Public Communications, Critical Infrastructure and Impact Assessment, Environmental Hazards and Debris Removal, Foreign Assistance, Non-governmental Aid, Training, Exercises, and Lessons Learned, Homeland Security Professional Development and Education, Citizen and Community Preparedness. See White House (2006), *supra* note 3, p. 51 *et seq.*

engaged with local populations in providing relief, the lessons learned from Hurricane Katrina will be examined.

Tardy and Ineffective Response Combined with Levee System Structural Failures

Even though the magnitude of Katrina was known through continuous warnings, these warnings went unheeded and the potential for destruction was not given the attention needed.[158] Especially for the city of New Orleans, the risk of breaching and overtopping of levees was not taken seriously. In fact, the critical period of preparation and response for Hurricane Katrina, which lasted just more than a week, was not at the level required and thus timely evacuations did not take place. Especially in the days immediately before Katrina made landfall, government officials demonstrated unreasonable delay in decision making.[159] The example centers on the mayor of the city of New Orleans as well as the governor of Louisiana. Mayor Nagin, despite being adequately informed of Katrina's magnitude more than two days before landfall, ordered a mandatory evacuation of the city of New Orleans only nineteen hours before Katrina hit. At the time the evacuation was made, evacuees were ordered to shelters of last resort where the lack of funding for sanitation revealed the insufficiency of planning.[160] Furthermore, the Louisiana Office of Homeland Security

[158] Enrico Quarantelli. (2006, June 11). Catastrophes Are Different from Disasters: Some Implications for Crisis Planning and Managing Drawn from Katrina. Available at http://understandingkatrina.ssrc.org/Quarantelli/ (accessed on April 5, 2013); Andrew Lakoff. (2006, June 10). From Disaster to Catastrophe: The Limits of Preparedness. Available at http://understandingkatrina.ssrc.org/Lakoff/ (accessed on April 8, 2013).

[159] William Carwile. (2005, August). Unified Command and the State-Federal Response to Hurricane Katrina in Mississippi. *Homeland Security Affairs*. 1(2), pp. 4–7. Available at www.hsaj.org/?article=1.2.6 (accessed on April 15, 2013); Michael Greenberger. (2005, October). The Role of Federal Government in Response to Catastrophic Health Emergencies: Lessons Learned from Hurricane Katrina. University of Maryland School of Law, Legal Studies Research Paper, No 2005–52, p. 6. Available at http://papers.ssrn.com/sol3/papers.cfm?abstract_id=824184 (accessed on April 14, 2013); Stephen M. Griffin. (2006, March). Stop Federalism Before It Kills Again: Reflections on Hurricane Katrina. *Public Law and Legal Theory Research Paper Series*, Research Paper No. 06-04, Tulane University School of Law. Available at http://ssrn.com/abstract= 894470 (accessed on April 20, 2013); Margaret B. Takeda and Marilyn M. Helms. (2006). Bureaucracy, Meet Catastrophe: Analysis of Hurricane Katrina Relief Efforts and Their Implications for Emergency Response Governance. *International Journal of Public Sector Management*. 19(4), 397, 402–403.

[160] For more details see the report of the U.S. Department of Health and Human Services, Office of Inspector General. (2006). *Nursing Home Emergency Preparedness and Response*

and Emergency Preparedness (LOHSEP) failed to ensure that Louisiana agencies could respond in a timely manner as it did not adequately inform them of their emergency relief obligations. This is indicative of the absence of long-term planning in the emergency response system of Louisiana.[161] Another aspect was the failure to coordinate state and local resources. Moreover, Governor Blanco submitted an inadequate request for assistance to the president and thus did not seek sufficient assistance from the federal government.[162]

On the other hand, the DHS failed to act according to the urgency of the situation and the federal government's preparation for the landfall of Katrina was at best tardy.[163] For instance, the DHS secretary appointed a Principal Federal Official only thirty-six hours after Katrina's landfall. Federal officials delayed considerably in gaining situational awareness about the levee breaches and the subsequent flooding. These officials did not act despite the many reports, which even though not definite, clearly indicated the failure of the levee system.[164] FEMA's response indicated that its director, Michael D. Brown, did not give adequate directions for the prepositioning of critical resources and personnel and also failed to communicate and coordinate with the DHS secretary. However, the DHS secretary should have also been more active in the preparations for Katrina's landfall. His failure to do so underscored that he falsely relied on the reassurances he received, and he did little to make sure that other federal agencies were preparing to provide assistance to the DHS, if required.[165]

The tardy and ineffective response was combined with the structural flaws of the levee system. Had the levee system not failed, hundreds of fatalities would have been prevented.[166] Several engineering analyses indicated that the levees protecting the city of New Orleans were not built to withstand severe hurricanes of Katrina's magnitude. These analyses also

during Recent Hurricanes. Washington, DC: U.S. Government Printing Office. Available at www.oig.hhs.gov/oei/reports/oei-06-06-00020.pdf (accessed on April 12, 2013).

161 Ibid.

162 U.S. Senate (2006), *supra* note 1, p. 591.

163 Charles Perrow. (2005, August). Using Organizations: The Case of FEMA. *Homeland Security Affairs*. 1(2), 2. Available at www.hsaj.org/?article=1.2.4 (accessed on April 5, 2013).

164 Ibid.

165 Ibid.

166 Gary M. Feinman and Field Museum. (2005, November). The Dangers of Ignoring the Evidence: Hurricanes, Hazards and Survival. American Anthropological Association, *Anthropology News*. Available at www.aaanet.org/press/an/1105/Feinman_Fisher.htm (accessed on April 17, 2013).

revealed uncertainty over which authority was responsible for key issues such as levee system repairs. This further shed light on the fact that none of the relevant authorities had a response plan to levee system failures.[167] Moreover, despite the failure of the levee system, if the evacuation of New Orleans had started in a more timely manner, many deaths could have been avoided. Last, the government responses indicated that the outcomes from previous emergency preparedness exercises were ignored or inadequately applied.[168] In particular, in 2004, the federal government had sponsored a planning exercise with participation of all levels of government in order to test the preparedness to deal with severe hurricane impacts. This was the so-called Hurricane Pam exercise, which resulted in draft plans that were incomplete and inadequately applied when Katrina struck.[169]

Confusion over the Chain of Command Combined with the Breakdown of Communications

The tardy and ineffective response noted earlier was confounded by the confusion over the chain of command and the deterioration of communications as Katrina made landfall.[170] The paralyzing of communications hampered situational awareness and revealed the absence of a back-up plan in communications.[171] More specifically, the electronic systems federal and state authorities used were incompatible and whenever assistance was requested, these requests needed to be transferred from the state system to the federal system manually. This further revealed that FEMA did not have at its disposal the necessary tools to track the status of supplies and other vital equipment needed across the Gulf Coast. Furthermore, the deterioration of communications impeded the search and rescue efforts and in some areas, amateur radio operators provided the only means of communications into or out of these areas.[172] Among other impacts caused by the absence of back-up plans of communications

167 Ibid.

168 Ibid.

169 U.S. Congress Select Bipartisan Committee (2006), *supra* note 28, pp. 81–83.

170 Moynihan (2007), *supra* note 135, p. 22.

171 See for a complete analysis Procopio and Procopio, *supra* note 123, p. 67, and Damion Waymer and Robert L. Heath. (2007). Emergent Agents: The Forgotten Publics in Crisis Communication and Issues Management Research. *Journal of Applied Communication Research*. 35(1), 88, 92 *et seq.*

172 Ibid.

were that the federal authorities were not immediately informed of the dire situation of the shelters of last resort and the buses intended to evacuate these shelters were delayed considerably.[173]

The failure of effective leadership is underscored by the fact that Hurricane Katrina mobilized approximately 50,000 troops of the National Guard, which is the largest number of National Guard deployment in the history of the United States.[174] However, the relief efforts of these troops were not coordinated with NORTHCOM. In particular, when Katrina made landfall in New Orleans, neither the federal nor the state and local governments exerted anything other than partial control of the response.[175] In fact, none of these officials took charge and efforts to establish a unified command were undermined as state and local emergency infrastructure was destroyed. The duplicative and uncoordinated responses of all levels of government were pervasive. In this regard, the DHS secretary did not invoke the Catastrophic Incident Annex (CIA) of the NRP.[176] Pursuant to the CIA of the NRP, the federal government had the authority to take proactive initiative before landfall; however, it is doubtful whether this would have sufficed to mitigate Katrina's impact. In any case, DHS delayed significantly in becoming fully engaged in the relief efforts. Had it engaged sooner, the impact of Katrina could have been dealt with more efficiently.[177]

Inadequate Planning to Confront Katrina-Magnitude Hurricanes

The inadequate planning to confront Katrina-magnitude hurricanes was apparent in all levels of government. What is especially important is that the "Hurricane Pam" exercise was not taken into account as seriously as it should have been and the state and local governments left shelter and

173 U.S. Government Accountability Office. (2007). *Observations on DHS and FEMA Efforts to Prepare for and Respond to Major and Catastrophic Disasters and Address Related Recommendations and Legislation*. Washington, DC: U.S. Government Accountability Office, pp. 5 and 9 *et seq*. Available at www.gao.gov/new.items/d07835t.pdf (accessed on April 15, 2013).

174 Peter Burns and Matthew O. Thomas. (2006, March). The Failure of the Nonregime: How Katrina Exposed New Orleans as a Regimeless City. *Urban Affairs Review*. 41, 517, 521–522; Lynn E. Davis et al. (2007). *Hurricane Katrina: Lessons for Army Planning and Operations*. Santa Monica, CA: RAND Corporation. Available at www.rand.org/pubs/monographs/2007/RAND_MG603.pdf (accessed on April 18, 2013).

175 Ibid.

176 U.S. Senate (2006), *supra* note 1, pp. 168–169; White House (2006), *supra* note 3, p. 18.

177 Burns and Thomas (2006), *supra* note 174, pp. 521–522; Davis et al. (2007), *supra* note 174.

housing plans incomplete and at best haphazard.[178] In the next paragraph specific attention is paid to FEMA's overwhelmed logistics.

The response to the catastrophe caused by Hurricane Katrina showed that FEMA was not only inadequately prepared but also that FEMA's logistics were not prepared to face hurricanes like Katrina.[179] Furthermore, FEMA was inadequately staffed and its workforce lacked training. One reason for this is that FEMA was reorganized many times since 1995 and temporary staff were used in permanent positions.[180] This left FEMA with a workforce under-trained for serious catastrophes. While individual officials within FEMA promoted catastrophic planning and management, the outcomes of the "Hurricane Pam" exercise were not fully endorsed. In addition, a fragmented human resource management structure, continuous reorganizations and limited funding contributed to the overall challenges faced.[181]

State Engagement with Local Actors

FEMA was made responsible for the emergency delivery of human services pursuant to the Emergency Support Function 6 (ESF-6) Annex to the NRP, entailing support for special needs populations, counseling and other immediate and short-term assistance in the aftermath of disaster.[182] However, due to the absence of a single point of access for such assistance, a large number of Hurricane Katrina victims encountered high levels of bureaucracy and inefficiencies in seeking support for their needs.[183] An integrated, consumer-oriented assistance system providing support at both the federal and state levels should be coordinated by the Department of Health and Human Services to ensure adequate support for disaster victims.[184]

178 Michael McGuire and Debra Schneck. (2010). What if Hurricane Katrina Hit in 2020? The Need for Strategic Management of Disasters, pp. 202–203. Available at www.indiana.edu/~spea/research/focus_newsletter/mcguire_katrina.pdf (accessed on April 10, 2013).

179 U.S. Government Accountability Office (2007), *supra* note 173, p. 11.

180 U.S. Government Accountability Office. (2006). *Statement by Comptroller General David M. Walker on GAO's Preliminary Observations Regarding Preparedness and Response to Hurricanes Katrina and Rita*. Washington, DC: U.S. Government Accountability Office, p. 5. Available at www.gao.gov/new.items/d06365r.pdf (accessed on May 2, 2013).

181 Ibid.

182 White House. (2006, February). *The Federal Response to Hurricane Katrina: Lessons Learned*, "Chapter 5: Lessons Learned." Available at http://georgewbush-whitehouse.archives.gov/reports/katrina-lessons-learned/ (accessed on February 25, 2015).

183 Ibid.

184 Ibid.

A lack of interagency coordination resulted in significant difficulties finding shelter for evacuees after the hurricane had caused mass destruction. While the Department of Housing and Urban Development (HUD) held "extensive expertise and perspective on large-scale housing challenges," it did not work in liaison with FEMA until relatively late in the relief efforts.[185] Meanwhile, Gulf Coast inhabitants – some of whom had not evacuated due to physical disability or other circumstances – encountered delays and inefficiencies in the relocation process undertaken by the federal government.[186] A key failing of FEMA was its inability to identify available housing sites and to utilize units available from other federal agencies – for instance, Veterans Affairs (VA) – for displaced persons.

Failure of state and local officials in Louisiana, Mississippi and Alabama to utilize the Emergency Alert System (EAS) mechanism to communicate disaster updates contributed to public affairs officers' lack of access to timely, accurate information.[187] Compounded by the dissemination of conflicting information by officials at the federal, state and local levels, individuals and media outlets came under the perception that government sources lacked credibility.[188] An integrated public communications plan, developed by the Department of Homeland Security, should be designed to properly inform and create public trust at all stages of a disaster.[189]

Policy Recommendations

The aftermath of Hurricane Katrina made clear that the US national emergency response scheme required development in order to bolster preparedness as well as future response to major disasters. The US Congress and the Senate issued voluminous reports alongside the White House's report.[190]

[185] Ibid.

[186] Ibid.

[187] Ibid.

[188] Ibid.

[189] Ibid.

[190] Apart from these reports, see also the big volumes issued by ANSI Homeland Security Standards Panel (HSSP), *supra* note 27; Federal Financial Institutions Examination Council. (2006, June 15). *Lessons Learned from Hurricane Katrina: Preparing Your Institution for a Catastrophic Event*. Available at www.ffiec.gov/katrina_lessons.htm (accessed on April 10, 2013); U.S. Government Accountability Office. (2006). *Hurricane Katrina: GAO's Preliminary Observations Regarding Preparedness, Response, and Recovery*. Washington, DC: U.S. Government Accountability Office Available at www.gao.gov/new.items/d06442t .pdf (accessed on May 3, 2013); U.S. Department of Homeland Security, Office of Inspector General. (2006). *A Performance Review of FEMA's Disaster Management Activities in Response to Hurricane Katrina*. Washington, DC: U.S. Government Printing Office, especially

Their recommendations found their way into the Emergency Reform Act, which on October 4, 2006, reorganized FEMA with the aim of strengthening its preparedness mission. Furthermore, the NRP was superseded by the National Response Framework on March 22, 2008.[191] The second edition of the National Response Framework was updated in 2013 and seeks to provide the framework for both national preparedness as well as community cooperation in times of emergencies and disasters.[192] The majority of the recommendations made are synopsized as follows.

Clarify the Responsibilities of Disaster Management Authorities and Avoid Duplication

The uncertainties over the chain of command as well as the absence of a clear hierarchy played a central role in the overall disaster management response. In this regard, the recommendations indicated that first and foremost, the DHS had to work with the NRP to avoid duplication in relief efforts.[193]

p. 187 *et seq.* Available at www.dhs.gov/xoig/assets/mgmtrpts/OIG_06-32_Mar06.pdf (accessed on April 14, 2013). From relevant articles, see among others Christopher Bellavita. (August 2005). Changing Homeland Security: An Opportunity for Competence. *Homeland Security Affairs.* 1(2). Available at www.hsaj.org/?article=1.2.5 (accessed on April 7, 2013); Amy Donahue and Robert Tuohy. (2006, July). Lessons We Don't Learn: A Study of the Lessons of Disasters, Why We Repeat Them, and How We Can Learn Them. *Homeland Security Affairs.* 2(2). Available at www.hsaj.org/?article=2.2.4 (accessed on April 12, 2013); Laura Steinberg et al. (2011, February). Baton Rouge Post-Katrina: The Role of Critical Infrastructure Modeling in Promoting Resilience. *Homeland Security Affairs.* 7. Available at www.hsaj.org/?article=7.1.7 (accessed on April 15, 2013); Banipal (2006), *supra* note 24; Moe (2010), *supra* note 24; Elizabeth A. Weeks. (2006). Lessons from Katrina: Response, Recovery and the Public Health Infrastructure. *DePaul Journal of Health Care Law.* 10(2), 251; David J. Gottlieb. (2006). Katrina Consequences: What has the Government Learned? *Loyola Law Review.* 52, 1113; Iris Young. (2006). Katrina: Too Much Blame, Not Enough Responsibility. *Dissent.* 53(1), 41; Richard Forgettee et al. (2009). Before, Now, and After: Assessing Hurricane Katrina Relief. *Population Research and Policy Review.* 28(1), 31; Robert Greenstein. (2005, October 20). *Meeting the Basic Needs of Hurricane Katrina Victims: Recommendations to Federal Policymakers.* Center on Budget and Policy Priorities. Available at www.cbpp.org (accessed on April 20, 2013); *Hurricane Katrina: GAO's Preliminary Observations Regarding Preparedness, Response, and Recovery.* Washington, DC: Government Accountability Office, 2006. Available at www.gao.gov/new.items/d06442t.pdf (accessed on May 3, 2013).

191 For more details, see FEMA. (2013, May). *Overview of the National Planning Frameworks.* Available at www.fema.gov/library/viewRecord.do?id=7361 (accessed on April 28, 2013); FEMA. (2013, May). *Information Sheet National Response Framework.* Available at www.fema.gov/library/viewRecord.do?id=7373 (accessed on April 27, 2013).

192 See www.fema.gov/national-response-framework (accessed on May 2, 2013).

193 U.S. Department of Homeland Security (2006), *supra* note 10, p. 25. See also Waugh (2006), *supra* note 1, p. 12.

Subsequently, FEMA needed to clarify the roles of the Principal Federal Official and the roles of other officials such as the Federal Coordinating Officer.[194] To achieve more precise distinction between the roles and responsibilities of various officials and authorities, it was proposed that FEMA should establish a working group to better coordinate emergency relief preparedness and response. Especially, it was suggested that FEMA should cooperate on one hand with the other divisions of DHS, such as the US Coast Guard and on the other hand with the Department of Defense's relative entities such as NORTHCOM.

Enhance the Capabilities, Training and Preparedness of FEMA and the DHS

Another factor of paramount importance was the need for greater training of FEMA's staff.[195] FEMA was therefore asked to develop a more intense and comprehensive training scheme to train both existing and new personnel as well as to ensure that all DHS staff were fully aware of their responsibilities under the National Response Plan. In parallel, FEMA was instructed to establish a more comprehensive human resource recruitment program and augment the number of its permanent staff. FEMA was also instructed to implement an organizational chart where clarity of each official's responsibilities would be an indispensable part.[196] Furthermore, it was suggested that the DHS and FEMA ought to provide states with more comprehensive and multifaceted training and FEMA should provide this kind of training to more national centers and contractors to reinforce national capabilities. The need to design a disaster workforce plan was also highlighted.[197] This plan would provide a source for permanent, temporary and reserve staff that could be called on to respond to various

[194] Larry Irons. (2005, August). Hurricane Katrina as a Predictable Surprise. *Homeland Security Affairs*. 1(2), 14. Available at www.hsaj.org/?article=1.2.7 (accessed on April 15, 2013).

[195] U.S. Department of Homeland Security (2006), *supra* note 10, p. 60; U.S. Government Accountability Office. (2006). *Hurricane Katrina: Better Plans and Exercises Needed to Guide the Military's Response to Catastrophic Natural Disasters*. Washington, DC: U.S. Government Accountability Office, p. 35. Available at www.gao.gov/new.items/d06643.pdf (accessed on May 3, 2013); U.S. Government Accountability Office. (2006). *Expedited Assistance for Victims of Hurricanes Katrina and Rita: FEMA's Control Weaknesses Exposed the Government to Significant Fraud and Abuse*. Washington, DC: U.S. Government Accountability Office, pp. 4–6. Available at www.gao.gov/new.items/d06655.pdf (accessed on May 3, 2013).

[196] Ibid.

[197] U.S. Department of Homeland Security (2006), *supra* note 10, p. 61; Ben Depoorter. (2006). Horizontal Political Externalities: The Supply and Demand of Disaster Management. *Duke Law Journal*. 56(3), 101, passim; Marla Nelson et al. (2007). Planning, Plans, and People: Professional Expertise, Local Knowledge, and Governmental Action in

emergencies. Another aspect of this plan would be the design of a case management scheme that would be responsive to the needs of applicants and a system that would automate the training, selection and deployment of responders.[198]

In order to enhance its capabilities, FEMA was instructed "to place priority on analysis of new methods and technology to verify damage, occupancy, and ownership, when traditional methods of inspection are not responsive in the timely provision of assistance."[199]

Recognize the Importance of Local Governments in Disaster Prevention

Even if the federal response system was greatly enhanced, the Katrina response made clear that any emergency preparedness and response scheme should fully integrate state and local government officials.[200] This is elucidated by the evacuation of New Orleans. The tardiness of local officials to order a mandatory evacuation of the city proved detrimental as the city was not evacuated and the levee system failed catastrophically. The timely order of evacuations is apparent when taking into consideration how difficult it was to convince the elderly residents of New Orleans to leave.[201] Furthermore, it was recommended that the DHS should develop a scheme to assess the capability of state and local authorities to respond to severe disasters without federal assistance.[202] To better assess the needs and priorities of states and localities, it was suggested that an advisory council be constituted. This council would be made up of state, local officials and first responders who would ensure that necessary actions are organized and implemented with regard to emergency planning and preparedness.[203]

Post-Hurricane Katrina New Orleans. *The University of New Orleans. Cityscape: A Journal of Policy Development and Research*. 9(3), 23, 35–37.

198 Ibid.

199 U.S. Senate Committee on Homeland Security and Government Affairs (2006), *supra* note 1, p. 620.

200 Bill Bytheway. (2007, March 15). The Evacuation of Older People: The Case of Hurricane Katrina. Available at http://understandingkatrina.ssrc.org/Bytheway/ (accessed on March 25, 2013); and Joseph Scanlon. (2006, June 11). Two Cities, Two Evacuations: Some Thoughts on Moving People Out. Available at http://understandingkatrina.ssrc.org/Scanlon/ (accessed on April 5, 2013).

201 Ibid.

202 Pamela Winston et al. (2006). *Federalism after Hurricane Katrina: How Can Social Programs Respond to a Major Disaster*. Washington, DC: The Urban Institute. Available at www .urban.org/UploadedPDF/311344_after_katrina.pdf (accessed on April 24, 2013).

203 U.S. Department of Homeland Security, *supra* note 10, p. 190; Sheila R. Zedlewski. (2006, February). Building a Better Safety Net for the New New Orleans. Washington, DC: The Urban Institute. Available at www.urban.org/afterkatrina/ (accessed on April 7, 2013).

Develop and Sustain Back-up Plans for Communications

The complete deterioration of the communications as well as the incompatibility of the federal and local electronic systems could not be foreseen. It was recommended that the DHS use new technologies to establish back-up plans as well as to design an information management system that would allow responders to track and share information more openly and more efficiently.[204] The DHS was also instructed to standardize the format and methodology of information collecting procedures. Last, it was recommended that FEMA should equip responders with communications equipment designed to sustain severe circumstances.[205]

Enhance the Logistics Capacity of FEMA

A considerable amount of resources were lost because FEMA's logistics capacity was overwhelmed. Therefore, it was suggested that FEMA redesign its logistics with the aim of standardizing and streamlining the resource ordering and tracking process.[206] To better implement this, FEMA was instructed to design its resource tracking system in order to be efficiently informed of whether resources were ordered, delivered or provided. In particular, FEMA should design this tracking system by including a contract mechanism in order to directly order federal resources.[207]

The ordering of evacuees to shelters of last resort as well the dire situation of these shelters led to several recommendations in regard to alternative housing.[208] It was suggested that FEMA should design and implement a housing resource plan that would be able to identify any available

[204] See also the discussion made by Marsha L. Vanderford et al. (2007). Emergency Communication Challenges in Response to Hurricane Katrina: Lessons from the Centers for Disease Control and Prevention. *Journal of Applied Communication Research*. 35(1), 9; George L. Daniels and Ginger Miller Loggins. (2007). Conceptualizing Continuous Coverage: A Strategic Model for Wall-to-Wall Local Television Weather Broadcasts. *Journal of Applied Communication Research*. 35(1), 48.

[205] Ibid.

[206] U.S. Department of Homeland Security (2006), *supra* note 10, p. 190.

[207] U.S. Senate Committee on Homeland Security and Government Affairs (2006), *supra* note 1, p. 621.

[208] U.S. Government Accountability Office (2006), *supra* note 111, p. 8 *et seq.*; William L. Waugh. (2006). Shelter from the Storm: Repairing the National Emergency Management System after Hurricane Katrina. *The ANNALS of the American Academy of Political and Social Science* 604, 288, passim.

resource and avoid potential duplication by establishing clear roles and responsibilities for the housing of affected populations.[209]

Review the Levee System

The staggering death toll in New Orleans was the result, on one hand of the belated evacuation, and on the other hand of the failure of the levee system.[210] When the levees failed, surges flooded the city and caused considerable fatalities. In this regard, serious recommendations were made for FEMA to develop a surge plan. Furthermore, it was suggested that the American Society of Civil Engineers (ASCE) External Review Panel (ERP) should be entrusted with the task of evaluating the levee system in Louisiana as well as review its design and operation.[211] Under federal law, the responsibility of the design and construction of Louisiana's levee system fell to by the US Army Corps of Engineers (USACE), and it was suggested that the process of evaluation should be independent of USACE.[212] Furthermore, it was suggested that state statutes governing the levee systems should be reviewed to ensure the enhancement of flood control projects as well as the regular inspection of the levee districts.[213]

Develop a Framework to Better Integrate Private-Sector Resources

The aftermath of Hurricane Katrina found NGOs and the private sector ill-integrated in the response system.[214] Many private companies

209 See John K. Pierre and Gail S. Stephenson. (2008). After Katrina: A Critical Look at FEMA's Failure to Provide Housing for Victims of Natural Disasters. *Louisiana Law Review*. 68(2). Available at http://digitalcommons.law.lsu.edu/lalrev/vol68/iss2/6 (accessed on April 26, 2013).

210 See Douglas A. Kysar and Thomas Owen McGarity. (2006). Did NEPA Drown New Orleans? The Leeves, The Blame Game, and The Hazards of Hindsight. Cornell Legal Studies Research Paper No. 06-024. Available at http://ssrn.com/abstact=928869 (accessed on April 17, 2013).

211 Ibid.

212 U.S. Senate Committee on Homeland Security and Government Affairs (2006), *supra* note 1, p. 621; Peter Dreier. (2006, March). Katrina and Power in America. *Urban Affairs Review*. 41, 528, 533; Philip J. Weiser et al. (2006, May 15). Toward a Next Generation Architecture for Public Safety Communications. Available at http://papers.ssrn.com/sol3/papers.cfm?abstract_id=903151 (accessed on April 25, 2013).

213 Comfort (2006), *supra* note 24, p. 514.

214 See Steven Horwitz. (2008, March). Making Hurricane Response More Effective: Lessons from the Private Sector and the Coast Guard during Katrina. *Mercatus Policy Series*. Global Prosperity Initiative. Available at www.mercatus.org/globalprosperity (accessed on April 19, 2013).

provided assistance that saved the lives of many individuals. However, no system existed that could effectively integrate the private sector's resources into the response efforts. In this regard, it was recommended that a framework be developed to better integrate the private sector's involvement.[215]

The development and coordination with the private sector in relief efforts will be examined in the chapters that follow.

Conclusion

Like the response to Thailand's flood of 2011 and Japan's earthquake and tsunami of 2011, the response to Hurricane Katrina in the United States was largely led by state agencies. Similar lessons were learned in state–local coordination, including the need for adequate planning and back-up communications systems, clear lines of coordination, information sharing and logistics capacity. In addition, particular issues unique to the United States, including the existence of racial prejudice and discrimination, exacerbated suffering through often delayed and insufficient response. Recognizing the importance of local governments in disaster prevention, key steps forward include integrating state and local government officials in the response team, and developing an advisory council to better assess needs and priorities for future natural disasters.

[215] U.S. Congress Select Bipartisan Committee (2006), *supra* note 28, pp. 343–354.

PART IV

Examining Public–Private Partnerships

10

Myanmar's Cyclone Nargis of 2008

Introduction

This section will examine how public–private partnerships alongside state and national responses helped address the after effects of Cyclone Nargis in some villages in Myanmar. While the Cyclone Nargis disaster of 2008 can be characterized in some respects as an interventionist response that conflicted directly in some cases with domestic preferences, selected regions and territories within Myanmar provide innovative case studies of public–private partnerships.

On May 2 and 3, 2008, Cyclone Nargis, a category 3 cyclone, struck the coast of Myanmar, making landfall in the Ayeyarwady Division, approximately 250 km southwest of Yangon. The cyclone affected more than fifty townships, mainly in Yangon and Ayeyarwady Divisions. The damage was most severe in the Irrawaddy Delta region, where the effects of the extreme winds were compounded by a twelve-foot (3.6-meter) storm surge.[1] The disaster was the worst natural disaster in Myanmar as of that time, killing at least 140,000 people and leaving 3 million in urgent need of assistance.[2] The cyclone caused widespread destruction to homes and infrastructure such as roads, jetties, water and sanitation systems, fuel supplies and power stations. A large number of water supplies was contaminated and food stocks were damaged or destroyed.[3] The disaster also inundated paddy land with seawater, leaving many people in a situation of food insecurity. In early June, 55 percent of households had one day of food stock or

[1] "A Report Prepared by the Tripartite Core Group Comprised of the Government of the Union of Myanmar, the Association of Southeast Asian Nations and the United Nations with the Support of the Humanitarian and Development Community: Post Nargis Joint Assessment," July 2008, p. 1, § 1.1. Available at: http://unic.un.org/imucms/userfiles/yangon/file/post-nargis_joint_assessment_all_pages.pdf (accessed on July 19, 2013).

[2] Jonathan Head. (2012, December 21). Rebuilding Burma's Cyclone-Hit Irrawaddy Delta. *BBC News*, Irrawaddy Delta, Burma. Available at www.bbc.co.uk/news/world-asia-20778768 (accessed on July 19, 2013).

[3] See *supra* note 1, p. 1, § 1.2.

less. After the cyclone, the population of Myanmar also faced an increasing risk of acute malnutrition and micronutrient deficiencies, particularly among infants, young children and pregnant women: Consumption of fish and eggs dropped by 25 percent; consumption of vegetables and fruits decreased by 9 percent; and the disruption of infant feeding practices posed a major threat to the survival, nutrition and development of children under the age of five.[4]

The Village Track Assessment (VTA), which is a survey of households, key informants (e.g., teachers, village leaders) and focus groups in the worst affected townships conducted across thirty townships over ten days in early June 2008,[5] indicated that the cyclone damaged close to 75 percent of health facilities in the affected townships. Almost all the destroyed facilities were primary health facilities, including station hospitals, rural health centers and subcenters, impacting access to health services.[6] This was at a time when more than 65 percent of households surveyed reported health problems among household members during the fifteen days preceding the survey in early June 2008. As many as 23 percent of households reported mental problems among household members due to the cyclone. There was also the danger of a rise in gastrointestinal diseases.[7]

The education sector also suffered as a result of Cyclone Nargis. An estimated 50 to 60 percent of public schools were destroyed or damaged according to government administrative data, UN agencies and the VTA survey. Administrative data show that 43–48 percent of schools were either totally or severely damaged; the VTA shows 63 percent of schools damaged in the thirty most severely affected townships.[8]

Private-Sector Collaboration

Private-sector collaboration played an important role in the aftermath of Cyclone Nargis. A number of entities collaborated with local governments and community members to contribute to the reconstruction work through the provision of food and nonfood items, psychosocial support, medical supplies, cremation and funeral services and housing assistance. Examples of these collaborations will be explored in this section.

[4] Ibid., p. 7, § 2.2.1.
[5] Ibid., p. 5, § 2.1.
[6] Ibid., p. 5, § 2.1.
[7] Ibid., p. 8, § 2.2.2.
[8] Ibid., p. 9, § 2.2.3.

ActionAid Myanmar (AAM), with the support of ActionAid (international), worked both through partnerships with local NGOs[9] and through direct implementation of projects in disaster risk reduction (DRR).[10] Part of AAM's relief efforts in Myanmar was to provide food and nonfood items and psychosocial support to those affected by the cyclone.[11]

The Adventist Development and Relief Agency (ADRA), working in partnership with the World Food Programme (WFP), provided emergency funds for immediate disaster relief, and food assistance and medical supplies to communities in the Irrawaddy Delta region. As of May 14, 2008, ADRA had distributed twenty-five metric tons of rice and power biscuits to an estimated 50,000 internationally displaced persons in Labutta, a rice-trading town in the delta, which had become a refuge for thousands of people. It then expanded its response in the aftermath of the cyclone, committing additional resources and funds.[12]

The American Jewish World Service (AJWS) had long-standing partnerships with grassroots organizations in the region. Through this network, the AJWS was able to identify and provide emergency support to local welfare organizations and religious institutions that were responding to the needs of the people of Myanmar. The AJWS provided food, water, cooking equipment, shelter, clothing and health services to those who needed them most. Funds were used to provide cremation and funeral services for the victims of the cyclone.[13]

AmeriCares, another nonprofit international disaster relief and humanitarian aid organization,[14] was one of the first relief groups allowed into Myanmar. Within forty-eight hours of the first airlift's arrival, fifteen tons of aid was delivered to communities affected by the disaster. The emergency medical teams of AmeriCares provided health care in the affected areas. On average, each team saw around 100 survivors per day. One year

[9] ActionAid. Believing in Community Capacity: A Reflection on the Response to Cyclone Nargis. Available at http://187.45.205.122/Portals/0/Docs/mianmar%20Report%20FINAL.pdf (accessed on January 4, 2016).

[10] Ibid., p. 7.

[11] Ibid., pp. 5–7.

[12] Hearly Mayr and Nadia McGill. (2008, May 14). May 14: ADRA Expands Emergency Relief in Myanmar. Available at www.adra.org/site/News2?page=NewsArticle&id=9197 (accessed on August 1, 2013).

[13] American Jewish World Service. (2008, May 6). Burma (Myanmar) Reels from Cyclone Nargis. Available at http://ajws.org/who_we_are/news/archives/features/burma_reels_from_cyclone_nargis.html (accessed on August 1, 2013).

[14] See https://twitter.com/AmeriCares (accessed on August 1, 2013).

after the disaster, AmeriCares continued to provide medicines and supplies to those who still needed help.[15]

Architecture for Humanity[16], working with the Association of South East Asian Nations (ASEAN), has been working with a number of construction professionals in Myanmar and Thailand in rebuilding after the cyclone.[17] Asia Children's Mission (ACM)[18] brought basic necessities to the villages, including household goods, blankets, clothes and food. At the request of Buddhist monks and other community leaders, ACM sent thirty Christian Myanmar schoolteachers into the region, which helped with the reopening of fourteen primary schools.[19]

The Avaaz organization,[20] which had built a strong relationship with monks and civil society groups in Myanmar, donated $1.6 million to distribute to aid groups in order to purchase rice, medicine, fuel and other supplies required to rescue, house and feed the survivors of the cyclone.[21]

CARE International (CARE)[22] supplied food provided by the World Food Programme.[23] CARE also distributed nonfood items (NFIs) supplied by Save the Children (SCF) and the Malaysian Red Crescent Society

[15] AmeriCares. (2009, May 2). Myanmar Remembers Anniversary of Deadly Cyclone Nargis. Available at www.americares.org/who-we-are/newsroom/news/myanmar-burmese-cyclone-nargis-anniversary.html (accessed on August 1, 2013).

[16] A nonprofit design services firm founded in 1999; for more information, see: http://architectureforhumanity.org/about (accessed on August 1, 2013).

[17] Architecture for Humanity. Cyclone Nargis Rebuilding in Myanmar. Available at http://architectureforhumanity.org/myanmar# (accessed on August 1, 2013).

[18] For information about Asia Children's Mission's story, see www.asianchildrensmission.org/about-acm/the-story-of-acm/ (accessed on August 1, 2013).

[19] Asian Children's Mission. Cyclone Nargis Relief. Available at www.asianchildrensmission.org/portfolio/cyclone-nargis-relief/ (accessed on August 1, 2013).

[20] A global web movement launched in 2007 with the aim to organize citizens of all nations "to close the gap between the world we have and the world most people everywhere want". For more information, see Avaaz. "About Us." Available at www.avaaz.org/en/about.php (accessed on August 1, 2013).

[21] Avaaz. Burma Cyclone Aid Report: Avaaz Members from 124 Countries Donate $2,000,000 to the Burmese People. Available at www.avaaz.org/en/burma_aid_report/ (accessed on August 1, 2013).

[22] Care International (CI) is "a confederation composed of twelve national Members, each being an autonomous non-governmental organisation in its own right. CI Members in North America, Europe, Asia and Australia carry out a range of project-related, advocacy, fundraising, and communications activities in support of CARE's relief and development programmes in over 65 countries worldwide"; see: www.alnap.org/members/108.aspx (accessed on August 1, 2013).

[23] For more information on the World Food Programme, see www.wfp.org/about/mission-statement (accessed on August 1, 2013).

Humanitarian Aid (MRCS), agricultural materials and established WASH activities[24] in early June through August 2008.[25]

Habitat for Humanity (Habitat)[26], in partnership with World Concern,[27] built and repaired more than 1,700 basic houses in eighteen communities in Ayeyarwady Delta. Habitat provided experts in design, construction and project management as part of the Seattle-based World Concern's Cyclone Emergency Response and Recovery project. Habitat also helped supervise the construction of jetties and the repair of roads through a cash-for-work program funded by World Concern. Habitat's approach was to build basic cyclone-resilient structures so that the structures would last even if another cyclone struck. Habitat received funding from the Jersey Overseas Aid Commission, part of the UK-related Channel Islands, the Hong Kong Christian Council and Baptist World Aid.[28]

Other examples include Caritas, which supplied more than 100,000 people with basic food staples, around 40,000 people with nonfood items and thousands of other families with household hygiene and sanitation kits[29] and supplies and cash grants.[30] Other entities that provided support included the Disaster Emergency Committee[31] and the International Federation of Red Cross and Red Crescent Societies.[32]

24 Water, sanitation services and good hygiene are termed as "WASH" in the humanitarian community. See European Commission. Humanitarian Aid and Civil Protection: Water, Hygiene and Sanitation (WASH). Available at http://ec.europa.eu/echo/files/aid/countries/factsheets/thematic/wash.pdf (accessed on August 1, 2013).

25 Bjorn Ternstorm, Makiba Yamato, Sandy Myint and U. K. M. Lwin. (December 2008). Evaluation of CARE Myanmar's Cyclone Nargis Response. Available at www.alnap.org/resource/5651.aspx (accessed on August 1, 2013).

26 For information about Habitat for Humanity's mission statement and principles, see www.habitat.org/how/mission_statement.aspx (accessed on August 1, 2013).

27 For information about World Concern's mission statement and principles, see www.worldconcern.org/aboutus/ (accessed on August 1, 2013).

28 Habitat for Humanity. Myanmar. Available at www.habitat.org/sites/default/files/cp_Myanmar_pdf.pdf (accessed on August 1, 2013).

29 Caritas. Myanmar on Cyclone Nargis Anniversary. Available at www.caritas.org/activities/emergencies/MyanmarOneYear.html (accessed on August 1, 2013).

30 Emergency Response. (2009, October 16). Cyclone Nargis Response Timeline. *Direct Relief.* Available at www.directrelief.org/2009/10/cyclone-nargis-response-timeline/ (accessed on August 1, 2013).

31 Disaster Emergency Committee. (2008). Myanmar (Burma) Cyclone Appeal. Available at www.dec.org.uk/2008-myanmar-burma-cyclone-appeal (accessed on August 1, 2013).

32 A list of agencies providing health intervention may be found at www.who.int/hac/crises/mmr/myanmar_who_what_where.pdf (accessed on August 1, 2013).

The Myanmar Baptist Convention (MBC)[33] also contributed to the relief efforts by setting up a temporary Emergency Relief and Rehabilitation Central Committee (NRRCC). Local churches, associations and partners of MBC began to provide assistance upon hearing the news. MBC's NRRCC had assisted 14,160 beneficiaries as of April 15, 2009. Recovery inputs included food and housing items as well as providing agriculture and fishing supplies to the affected churches and communities.[34]

Further, according to the TCG 2008 Report, the Myanmar business community also contributed substantially to relief and construction post-cyclone. For example, large construction and engineering firms, in close cooperation with the GoUM and village and township elders, gave priority to the renovation and rebuilding of hospitals and schools and the construction of relief camps. As of July 2008, the Myanmar business community had contributed a total of US $ 68.13 million to help the people of Myanmar.[35]

A Myanmar Village Response

The story of one village's response to the cyclone in Myanmar reflects an example of how community-based partnerships and collective decision making building on existing structures of collaboration led to the saving of many lives and a rapid and efficient recovery process. Following the cyclone, one village outside of Rangoon reported that 100 of its community's homes were completely destroyed, all its rice stocks were washed away and about twenty people were killed with another twenty missing.[36]

In an initial conversation with an individual working in the area, she shared some of her impressions regarding the response of the community following Cyclone Nargis. Following the cyclone, "the Local Assembly ... gathered and decided to host everyone in the village and near-by villages in the center as it was the less damaged building in the area. They then organize themselves to provide food and water for all people specially children and the elderly. They begin to assess the damage in properties and the

[33] For more information, see www.oikoumene.org/en/member-churches/myanmar-baptist-convention (accessed on August 1, 2013).

[34] Reliefweb. (2009, April 15). Myanmar: One year after Cyclone Nargis. Available at http://reliefweb.int/report/myanmar/myanmar-one-year-after-cyclone-nargis (accessed on August 1, 2013).

[35] See *supra* note 1, pp. 41–42, § 5.1.1., ¶ 15.

[36] See http://ireport.cnn.com/docs/DOC-20779.

number of people affected and lives lost."[37] According to a CNN report, the principle that all are "members of one human family whatever race, nationality or creed"[38] animated efforts at collective decision making in the community.

In consultation with the villagers, the decision was made to "begin a plan to reconstruct the homes damaged and everyone young and old capable of helping took turns to offer their help, cooking, building, carrying things etc."[39] At the same time external support was requested for "the farmers who lost all their crops and were in very dire condition, not having anywhere to sleep. In consultation with the national body a plan was made. The situation was very critical because there was not even drinking water or food for people and the relief agencies were [unable to reach the area]. It was the prompt assistance of the [community] that alleviated most of the pain and distress by hosting everyone and providing water and rice soup to everyone for two days and in that way prevented even more deaths."[40]

In addition, "some grants were acquired [for] one or two tractors to help clear up the debris from the land and begin preparing the land [for] their crops. The [community] made a roster for the farmers to take turns using the tractor for a period of time and a committee supervised [its implementation]. The farmers also received loans to buy seeds with a term of payment with no interest."[41]

The community has now largely recovered due in large part to the strong community-based consultation skills developed through regular community gatherings, a service orientation, ongoing capacity-building efforts and an emphasis on unity that existed prior to the cyclone.

Domestic Response

In addition to public–private partnerships facilitated by local and international NGOs, the Government of the Union of Myanmar (GoUM) established the National Natural Disaster Preparedness Central Committee (NDPCC) chaired by the prime minister, General Thein Sein. A meeting of the NDPCC was held on the morning of May 3, 2008, with the aim of

[37] Interview, Respondent Village, June 15, 2013.
[38] See *supra* note 36.
[39] See *supra* note 37.
[40] Ibid.
[41] Ibid.

formulating and implementing an immediate response to the cyclone.[42] Ten Emergency Disaster Response Sub-committees were formed to deal with: (1) News and Information; (2) Emergency Communication; (3) Search and Rescue; (4) Assessment and Emergency Relief; (5) Confirmation of Loss and Damages; (6) Transportation and Route Clearance; (7) Natural Disaster Reduction and Emergency Shelter Provision; (8) Health Care; (9) Rehabilitation and Re-construction; and (10) Security.

Individual ministers were assigned to each of the townships affected by the cyclone. The prime minister also opened an office in Yangon to provide close supervision and support to the NDPCC.[43] The GoUM's approach and priorities[44] were: rebuilding of houses by the townspeople; reconstruction of hospitals, schools and markets; repairing of roads and bridges; reconstruction of communication; restoration of electricity; resettling and construction of villages washed away by the storm surge; construction of damaged houses in village tracts; rehabilitation of drinking water sources; resuscitation of business enterprises, factories and workplaces for employment generation; revival of agriculture and rural industries to restore basic livelihoods of the villagers; revival of the fishery industry for restoring employment and earning opportunities for village folk; rehabilitation of rice mills; restoration of salt production facilities; restoration of the means of production for fruits, vegetables and livestock by the rural population.

On May 4, 2008, the GoUM indicated informally that it would be open to international assistance and then formally in a briefing to the United Nations (UN) and diplomats on May 5. However, the authorities took no immediate steps to facilitate the issuing of visas for international humanitarian staff.[45] Even those who were able to get into Myanmar to help had to hide in paddy fields when sending out materials to those who needed help. If they went into a village, they would not be able to stay long as

[42] See *supra* note 1, § 5.1.1., ¶ 6.

[43] See *supra* note 1, pp. 38–39, § 5.1.1., ¶ 7.

[44] Ibid., pp. 39–40, § 5.1.1., ¶ 9.

[45] CTV News. (2008, May 6). Aid Starting to Trickle into Burma: Agencies. Available at www.ctvnews.ca/aid-starting-to-trickle-into-burma-agencies-1.293822 (accessed on August 1, 2013); Julie Belanger and Richard Horsey. (2008, December). Negotiating Humanitarian Access to Cyclone-Affected Areas of Myanmar: A Review. In Humanitarian Practice Network Managed by Humanitarian Policy Group. *Humanitarian Exchange*. 41, 2. Available at www.odihpn.org/humanitarian-exchange-magazine/issue-41 (accessed on July 26, 2013).

they would be arrested and possibly sent out if the army caught them.[46] Although local staff did not face the same difficulties, there was a shortage of key staff with experience in responding to major disaster situations since it was the first time a disaster on this scale struck Myanmar. The absence of international staff also meant that local staff had to work for extended periods without rotation and with insufficient organizational support.[47] According to a BBC reporter's account one month after the cyclone,[48] he was told by a local young man that the village where he came from – a village in the Irrawaddy Delta region devastated by the cyclone – a village that was, by then, only water – had seen no aid organizations nor had it received any help.[49]

Global Response

On May 23, 2008, the UN secretary-general's meeting with Myanmar's Senior General Than Shwe produced an agreement to allow all humanitarian aid workers, regardless of nationality, into the affected areas. Greater access into the country was then possible,[50] even though some villages still received no help.[51] The World Bank (the Bank) would not give any financial aid or loans to Myanmar because the military-ruled country had been in arrears with the Bank for a decade.[52] However, even at an early stage of the disaster, many countries were willing to provide aid to Myanmar. These

46 Paul Danahar. (2008, May 8). Eyewitness: No Help after Cyclone. *BBC News*, Southern Burma. Available at http://news.bbc.co.uk/2/hi/asia-pacific/7389576.stm (accessed on July 27, 2013).

47 Belanger and Horsey (2008), *supra* note 45.

48 Matt Prodger. (2008, June 2). Storm Victims' Misery Turns to Fury. *BBC News*, Rangoon. Available at http://news.bbc.co.uk/2/hi/asia-pacific/7430867.stm (accessed on July 28, 2013).

49 Voravit Suwanvanichkij, Mahn Mahn, Cynthia Maung et al. (2009, May). *After the Storm: Voices from the Delta*, 2nd edn. Executive Summary 1. Available at www.jhsph.edu/research/centers-and-institutes/center-for-public-health-and-human-rights/locations/asia/BurmaCyclone.html (accessed on July 30, 2013).

50 United Nations. (2008). Myanmar: Revised Appeal – Cyclone Nargis Response Plan. Consolidated Appeal. Available at http://ochadms.unog.ch/quickplace/cap/main.nsf/h_Index/Revision_2008_Myanmar_FA/%24FILE/Revision_2008_Myanmar_FA_VOL1_SCREEN.pdf?OpenElement (accessed on July 28, 2013).

51 Prodger (2008), *supra* note 48.

52 Die Welt. (2008, May 20). World Bank Won't Give Loan to Myanmar. Available at www.welt.de/english-news/article2014183/World-Bank-wont-give-loan-to-Myanmar.html (accessed on July 29, 2013).

countries included Canada,[53] Bangladesh,[54] India,[55] Italy,[56] Thailand,[57] the United Kingdom[58] and the United States.[59] As early as May 9, 2008, the UN launched a flash appeal for additional aid.[60]

Local Participation

On May 25, 2008, at the ASEAN-UN International Pledging Conference, agreement was reached to form a Tripartite Core Group (TCG) to coordinate relief efforts. TCG consisted of the GoUM, the UN and ASEAN.[61] The TCG provided a mechanism for rapid needs assessment and the framework for international response.[62] Local participation was, therefore, facilitated by the tripartite group.

Other than through the GoUM, the TCG 2008 report indicates that the Tatmadaw (Myanmar Armed Forces) provided substantial assistance in the overall relief and early recovery effort. The Tatmadaw was responsible

[53] Foreign, Affairs, Trade and Development Canada. (2008). Project Profile for Burma Cyclone Nargis – Adventist Development and Relief Agency Canada Appeal. Available at www.acdi-cida.gc.ca/cidaweb%5Ccpo.nsf/projEn/M012846001 (accessed on August 1, 2013); Foreign, Affairs, Trade and Development Canada. (2008). Project Profile for Burma Cyclone Nargis – Care Canada Appeal. Available at www.acdi-cida.gc.ca/cidaweb/cpo.nsf/vWebCCEn/08FB8A4B672EF18985257452003739FD (accessed on August 1, 2013).

[54] *BBC News*. (2008, May 9). Bangladesh Aid Arrives in Burma. Available at http://news.bbc.co.uk/2/hi/7391550.stm (accessed on July 30, 2013).

[55] For example, Sanjoy Majumder. (2008, May 16). India Sends Doctors to Burma. *BBC News*, Delhi. Available at http://news.bbc.co.uk/2/hi/south_asia/7405602.stm (accessed on July 30, 2013); Indrani Bagchi. (2008, May 18). India Works to End Myanmar's Isolation. *The Times of India*. Available at http://articles.timesofindia.indiatimes.com/2008-05-18/india/27750799_1_naypyidaw-myanmarese-myanmar-government (accessed on July 30, 2013).

[56] World Food Programme. (2008, May 7). Cyclone Nargis: Italian Government Dispatches Aid for Myanmar Population from Brindisi Base. Available at www.wfp.org/stories/cyclone-nargis-italian-government-dispatches-aid-myanmar-population-brindisi-base (accessed on July 30, 2013).

[57] See note 17.

[58] *BBC News*. (2008, May 15). UK Gives £12m More Aid to Burma. Available at http://news.bbc.co.uk/2/hi/uk_news/7403324.stm (accessed on July 30, 2013).

[59] U.S. Government Accountability Office. (2011, July). Burma: UN and U.S. Agencies Assisted Cyclone Victims in Difficult Environment, but Improved U.S. Monitoring Needed. Report to Congressional Committees. Available at www.gao.gov/products/GAO-11-700 (accessed on July 30, 2013).

[60] See *supra* note 1, p. 49, § 5.1.2.2.

[61] See *supra* note 1, foreword.

[62] Silva Ferretti. (2009, July 6). *Evaluation of ActionAid's Response to Cyclone Nargis, Myanmar*, p. 6. Available at www.actionaid.org/publications/evaluation-actionaids-response-cyclone-nargis-myanmar (accessed on August 1, 2013).

for the maintenance of law and order, search and rescue, evacuation of the injured, setting up of camps for the displaced, collection, identification and burial of the dead, loading and unloading of relief goods, and generally helping in the distribution of relief assistance to the distressed. They also provided emergency medical care in the affected areas.[63] However, some reports indicated that the Tatmadaw was largely thought to be corrupt and ineffective.[64] The Emergency Assistance Team-Burma (EAT), which was a group of health workers from the community-based organizations (CBOs) in cyclone-affected areas,[65] conducted ninety in-depth interviews: thirty-three among relief workers and health care providers in the affected areas, fifty-seven among survivors of the cyclone. Many interviewees believed that the GoUM and the army's relief efforts fell short in the delivery of aid.[66]

Outcome

Because of government, community and humanitarian agencies' effort to improve access to food, health care, disease-prevention activities, clean water and sanitation, the physical health of the people living in Ayeyarwady Delta and Yangon Division stabilized two years after the cyclone.[67] Around three-quarters of the respondents of the TCG's IV Periodic Review (PR) indicated that they could reach a health facility within one hour. Access to health facilities was much improved.[68]

As to the adequacy of water supply in the affected area, more than 40 percent of the 1,400 surveyed households in the fourth periodic review indicated that they had a protected water source within their compound, while 56 percent accessed a nearby unprotected well, a public tap, a tube well, spring, pond, dug well or standpipe.[69] Compared

[63] See *supra* note 1, pp. 40–41, § 5.1.1., ¶ 13.

[64] See *supra* note 2; Head (2008).

[65] Ibid.

[66] See *supra* note 49. Ibid., Executive Summary, p. 3.

[67] "The Fourth and Final Report Prepared by the Tripartite Core Group Comprised of Representatives of the Government of the Union of Myanmar, the Association of Southeast Asian Nations and the United Nations with the Support of the Humanitarian Community," July 2010, p. 13, § 2.1. Available at www.google.com.hk/url?sa=t&rct=j&q=&esrc=s&source=web&cd=1&ved=0CCoQFjAA&url=http%3A%2F%2Fwww.themimu.info%2FRCC%2FTCG%2FPost-Nargis%2520Periodic%2520Review%2520IV%2520Report.pdf&ei=QUD6UbHCJY7OkAW2k4CgBg&usg=AFQjCNEOd9exw7L0xjTRfJj5_GP6EL0g2Q (accessed on August 1, 2013).

[68] Ibid., p. 13, § 2.1.1.

[69] Ibid., p. 27, § 2.2.1.

to the results of PR III – which indicated only about 8 percent had a protected water source within their compound and 21 percent had to access a nearby unprotected well, a public tap or a standpipe[70] – the adequacy of water supply was much improved within the half-year period. PR IV also indicated better sanitation compared with PR II and PR III.[71]

Over time, food security improved to the extent that the bulk of the population no longer needed food aid, but food insecurity was still present. PR IV findings are similar to those of PR III.[72]

Two years after the cyclone, livelihood recovery remained weak. Pre-cyclone owners of assets in major livelihood categories (draught animals, small animals, boats of all types and fishing gear of all types) now had far fewer assets than before the disaster.[73]

The education participation rate among children aged five to ten years declined slightly to 84 percent in PR IV as compared to 86 and 90 percent in PR II and PR III, respectively.[74] The most common reason children did not attend school was because they had to work. This was the case for 19 percent of boys and 16 percent of girls. Education costs were also a factor, although improvements were made in accessibility and availability of teachers.[75]

Shelter recovery was also limited. Preparedness scores remained low in some areas of the coast hit hardest by the cyclone as many of these households had to rebuild without assistance.[76] Shelter preparedness on average ranked 2.59 out of 7 protective features critical to the protection from severe winds and storms. In PR IV 82 percent of household heads indicated that they did not view their dwellings as capable of protecting members against storms. Only 1 percent of PR IV respondents indicated that they were completely prepared for another disaster. Awareness of community emergency preparedness plans was limited.[77]

[70] "A Report Prepared by the Tripartite Core Group Comprised of Representatives of the Government of the Union of Myanmar, the Association of Southeast Asian Nations and the United Nations with the Support of the Humanitarian and Development Community," January 2010. Available at http://reliefweb.int/report/myanmar/myanmar-post-nargis-periodic-review-iii (accessed on August 1, 2013).

[71] See *supra* note 67, pp. 31–38, § 2.2.2.

[72] Ibid., p. 39, § 2.3.

[73] Ibid., p. 78.

[74] Ibid., p. 71.

[75] Ibid., p. 75, § 3.1.2.

[76] Ibid., p. 78.

[77] Ibid., pp. 91–92.

Conclusion and Lessons Learned

Among the lessons learned from Cyclone Nargis was the importance of timely and unified response. In particular international visa access and a clear organizational response structure are key factors in contributing to a timely response.[78] The Myanmar village experience demonstrated the importance of community-based partnerships building on existing structures of collaboration and consultation. In the case example, community cohesion and existing capacity for consultative decision making led to the saving of many lives and a rapid and efficient recovery process.

It is clear from the Cyclone Nargis experience that local participation should not be underestimated in responding to a crisis.[79] For at least the first two or three weeks of the disaster, external help was not able to reach the affected areas. Therefore, working in partnerships with local communities was crucial.[80] Working with local partners in a relationship based on learning, consultation and reflection is critical. Therefore, partnering with local communities may be seen as a form of knowledge transfer. Having a functioning humanitarian country team and close coordination and mapping program are also important components of an effective response program.[81]

Another lesson learned was that creative negotiation approaches and flexible adaptation are needed in response to restricted situations such as not being able to gain access to affected areas. ASEAN and the TGC were successful in building trust with the GoUM and then gaining access for international humanitarian workers. Alternative coordination methods could also be used; for example, UNICEF, the only organization with a formal agreement with the Ministry of Education to carry out emergency education activities, was able to bring other partners in through the UN cluster system.[82]

78 See *supra* note 57, pp. 13, 34.

79 Kerren Hedlund and D. M. Su. (2008, December). Support to Local Initiatives in the Nargis Response: A Fringe versus Mainstream Approach. In Humanitarian Practice Network Managed by Humanitarian Policy Group. *Humanitarian Exchange*. 41, p. 19. Available at www.odihpn.org/humanitarian-exchange-magazine/issue-41 (accessed on July 26, 2013).

80 "Humanitarian Partnerships Following Cyclone Nargis in Myanmar." Prepared by Mercy Malaysia with Input from Partners in Myanmar, June 30, 2008. Available at www.google.com.hk/url?sa=t&rct=j&q=&esrc=s&source=web&cd=1&ved=0CCoQFjAA&url=http%3A%2F%2Fwww.globalhumanitarianplatform.org%2Fdoc00003010.doc&ei=tm76UeDMMomqkQXI34DoCQ&usg=AFQjCNGNloZj2-511WHEaa8VDC6M8tgL7w (accessed on August 1, 2013).

81 U.S. Government Accountability Office (2011), *supra* note 59, p. 43.

82 Ibid., p. 37.

Coordination may be improved by using standard reporting and information-sharing forms and increasing support for field staff. This can be done by establishing local resource centers and NGO liaison officers at field locations and by increasing visits from Rangoon-based leadership. It was also found that the Myanmar Information Management Unit and cluster-managed resources were helpful in information management.[83]

Most importantly, perhaps, Cyclone Nargis highlighted the importance of disaster preparedness. The shortage of experienced personnel in Myanmar immediately after the cyclone meant that it was difficult to meet all response needs.[84] Moreover, it is clear that response to natural disasters such as Cyclone Nargis is extremely costly and that a disaster risk reduction approach is much preferred.

Policy Recommendations

Studies have proposed a shift in the focus from disaster response to disaster risk reduction in order to minimize damage in affected communities. Strengthening the organizational structure of humanitarian organizations alongside clear lines of coordination is critical. Partnerships between local and international agencies benefit local agencies, international entities and, most importantly, people in the affected areas.

83 Ibid., p. 39.
84 Ibid., p. 43.

11

Public–Private Partnerships through Crowd-Sourced Governance

Introduction

A growing number of public–private partnerships are emerging; among them are those involved in the development of crowd source technology for humanitarian relief efforts fueled by local participation and knowledge. Many of the technological developments for humanitarian relief are spontaneous and post-disaster, such as the responses to Hurricane Katrina, the Haiti earthquake and the Japan tsunami. The growing use of crowd source technology such as crowd mapping and resource tracking being universally accessible, collaboratively designed, subject to ongoing improvement and responsive to on-the-ground needs reflects in many respects the emerging UN governance mechanisms developed to support the creation of such technology.[1]

The UN has recognized the importance of such technologically enhanced global partnerships. Especially in light of the UN Millennium Development Goals (MDGs), developed in 2000, Resolution 56/76 was passed in 2001 encouraging the development of partnerships by providing greater opportunities for collaboration among the private sector, nongovernmental organizations (NGOs) and civil society so as to contribute toward the realization of global development objectives.[2] In particular, especially in the technology sector, the UN has recognized the ability of the private sector to contribute not only financial and human resources but also access to technology, management expertise and support.[3]

[1] For complete discussion, see S. Ali. (2014). Crowd Sourced Governance in a Post-disaster Context. *International and Comparative Law Quarterly*. 64(1), 211–226.

[2] UN Resolution. (2001). A/RES/56/76. Towards Global Partnerships. Available at www.unglobalcompact.org/docs/issues_doc/un_business_partnerships/A_RES_56_76.pdf (accessed on March 18, 2014).

[3] Ibid.

Technology Collaboration for Humanitarian Relief at the UN

The UN has adopted two main strategies to facilitate humanitarian relief efforts. First, through the direct use of some its key bodies (and through the coordination of the UN/UN-related organizations such as the UN Office for the Coordination of Humanitarian Affairs (OCHA) and the Inter-Agency Standing Committee (IASC)) to provide humanitarian relief; second, through the work of the UN Foundation, which promotes and provides support through partnerships with the private sector.

Given the number of UN agencies and private partnerships working in the area of humanitarian technology development for post-disaster relief, the UN has developed mechanisms to coordinate their collective efforts. They include the Emergency Relief Coordinator (ERC), the IASC and the Humanitarian Field Coordination and Information Management mechanisms.[4]

Inter-agency Standing Committee

The IASC is a unique inter-agency forum "for coordination, policy development and decision-making involving the key UN and non-UN humanitarian partners"[5] at the global, regional and country levels. It "plays a key role in preventing gaps and duplications in humanitarian response with real-time evaluations and feedback mechanisms to improve the quality of assistance."[6]

Relevant to the issue of utilizing technology in humanitarian aid, the IASC has developed a set of guidelines to help national authorities and humanitarian organizations exchange data, thereby improving the effectiveness of humanitarian response. These guidelines "outline the common datasets needed for response in humanitarian emergencies, as well as the governance model for the management of the data (i.e., accountability and responsibility).[7] These guidelines also recognize the primary

[4] OCHA, Reference Guide Phase II. (2009), pp. 87–89 available at http//ochanet.unocha.org/p/Documents/Reference%20Guide%20-%20Phase%20II%20-%20Final.pdf (accessed January 4, 2016).

[5] IASC. About the Inter-Agency Standing Committee. Available at www.humanitarianinfo.org/iasc/pageloader.aspx?page=content-about-default (accessed on March 18, 2014).

[6] OCHA. (2012). *Inter-Agency Standing Committee*. 2. Available at https://docs.unocha.org/sites/dms/documents/120229_oom-iasc_eng.pdf.

[7] ISCA. (2010). *Guidelines on Common Operational Datasets in Disaster Preparedness and Response*. Requested by the 77th IASC Working Group Meeting; IASC Endorsed on November 2, 2010. 1. Available at www.humanitarianresponse.info/system/files/documents/files/iasc_guidelines_on_common_operational_datasets_in_disaster_preparedness_and_response_2010-11-01.pdf.

role of the state affected by the disaster to organize, coordinate and implement humanitarian assistance within its territory.[8] To this effect, these guidelines aim to ensure that the Common Operational Datasets (CODs) support national information systems and standards, build local capacities and maintain appropriate links with relevant government, state and local authorities.[9]

UN Foundation and Partners

Apart from sole and direct action by UN bodies, the United Nations Office for Partnerships (UNOP) serves as a gateway for partnership opportunities with the UN. The UNOP provides Partnership Advisory Services and Outreach to a variety of entities, as well as manages the United Nations Fund for International Partnerships (UNFIP).[10] In establishing public–private collaboration for humanitarian action, the UN works according to the guiding principles of:[11] promoting cooperative relationships with government; building local capacity; focusing on existing needs and systematic reporting, monitoring and evaluation.

The bulk of UNOP's work is funded and mandated by the UNFIP, which focuses on technology partnerships among other areas of concern. The UNOP's focus on technology partnerships has direct implications for the support of open source governance development programs at the grass roots. For example, the UN Partnership Annual Report 2010 highlighted the UN Foundation's achievements in its technology partnerships with mobile phone operators such as Vodafone to strengthen the humanitarian efforts of the UN through the use of wireless technology. The initiative focuses on mobile health initiatives for development and emergency response communications to support disaster relief and aims to "harness the ubiquity of mobile communications to address pressing challenges in the developing world."[12]

[8] Ibid.

[9] Ibid.

[10] UNOP. Welcome to the United Nations Office for Partnerships. Available at www.un.org/partnerships/ (accessed on March 18, 2014).

[11] World Economic Forum and OCHR. (2007). Guiding Principles for Public-Private Collaboration for Humanitarian Action. Available at www.un.org/partnerships/Docs/Principles%20for%20Public-Private%20Collaboration%20for%20Humanitarian%20Action.pdf (accessed on March 18, 2014).

[12] UN Foundation. *UN Partnership Annual Report 2010*, pp. 7–8. Available at www.un.org/partnerships/Docs/A_65_347.pdf (accessed on March 18, 2014).

The UNFIP also funds the Mobile Health (mHealth) for Development program to support health data collection in Africa using mobile devices. Funding also supports building an information communications technology (ICT) Humanitarian Emergency Platform that will standardize ICT response capabilities through the humanitarian community.[13]

Public–Private Partnerships: Disaster Relief 2.0

Reflecting expanded participation at the local level in coordinated state response, within the past ten years, several public–private partnerships have emerged in collaboration with UN agencies to provide mutual assistance in humanitarian response. Several of these partnerships have focused on the development of mobile and Internet technology for use in the post-disaster context. One such initiative involved a collaboration between the UNOP, the Vodafone Foundation and the Harvard Humanitarian Initiative following the 2010 Haiti earthquake. In reviewing the results of this collaboration, it was noted that "the rise of mobile phones, social networks, and open source crisis mapping tools is creating a new culture of community driven disaster preparedness and response. These tools can harness the power of mass collaboration to quickly aggregate and distribute information about urgent needs, using cloud-, crowd- and SMS-based technologies to gather, translate, geolocate, and publish information about urgent humanitarian needs."[14] Through this means, some have suggested that individuals and technical communities were better able to reach the aid community.[15]

In addition to the UN-Vodafone-Harvard collaboration, examples of partnerships to develop ICTs between the UN and businesses from the private sector include partnerships with Microsoft, Hewlett-Packard, Cisco, Nokia and Ericsson in developing mobile networks and ICT in various parts of the world.[16]

[13] Ibid.

[14] UN Foundation. (2011). *Disaster Relief 2.0*. Available at www.unfoundation.org/assets/pdf/disaster-relief-20-report.pdf (accessed on March 19, 2014).

[15] For summaries, see www.unfoundation.org/assets/pdf/disaster-relief-2-findings-1.pdf (accessed on March 19, 2014), www.trust.org/alertnet/blogs/technotalk/disaster-relief-20-how-technology-puts-people-at-the-heart-of-humanitarian-aid/ (accessed on March 19, 2014) or www.smartglobalhealth.org/blog/entry/technology-and-the-future-of-humanitarian-aid/ (accessed on March 19, 2014).

[16] See UN partnership stories in information and communications technologies, www.business.un.org/en/browse/partnership_stories/17?all_locales (accessed on March 19, 2014) and http://ochanet.unocha.org/p/Documents/OOM_PublicPrivPartnerships_English.pdf (accessed on March 19, 2014).

In the Asian region, the Asian Disaster Reduction and Response Network has coordinated efforts to engage with communications technology in order to attempt to "reshape both humanitarian response and communications in disaster response."[17]

In addition, a large number of organizations and businesses in the private sector contribute to the development of technology for humanitarian relief efforts. Some of their programs include the following:[18] Airtel, a private mobile operator in Bangladesh, has teamed up with the Campaign for Sustainable Rural Livelihoods, the Centre for Global Change and two international NGOs (Oxfam and CARE) to provide early weather warnings to fishermen at sea using GPS. The Map Kibera project, which uses hand held GPS devices to collect geographic information in Nairobi's largest slum, is providing important information on the availability and location of health, security, education and water and sanitation services.

Many of these projects are independent efforts; however, these often-local initiatives may sometimes be the most effective in achieving their purposes due to greater access and local knowledge. Médecins Sans Frontières (MSF),[19] provides emergency aid to victims of epidemic and natural disasters through the Access Campaign.[20] MSF is also responsible for the creation of Epicentre, an on-line World Health Organization collaborating center for research in epidemiology and response to emerging diseases.[21]

ICT4Peace

The ICT4Peace Foundation, a UN partner, was established in 2006[22] to promote "the practical realization in all stages of crisis

[17] Oliver Lacey-Hall, Head, Regional Office for the Asia & Pacific, OCHA. (2012). *Communication as Aid.* http://ochanet.unocha.org/p/Documents/OLH%20ADRRN%20Speech%20-%20Phnom%20Penh%20090212.pdf (accessed on March 19, 2014).

[18] IRIN. *Technology: IRIN's Pick of the Year 2011.* www.irinnews.org/Report/94565/TECHNOLOGY-IRIN-s-pick-of-the-year-2011 (accessed on March 19, 2014), and *Technology: IRIN's Pick of the Year 2010.* www.irinnews.org/Report/91414/TECHNOLOGY-IRIN-s-pick-of-the-year-2010 (accessed on March 19, 2014).

[19] MSF. About MSF. Available at www.msf.org/msf/about-msf/about-msf_home.cfm (accessed on March 19, 2014).

[20] Ibid.

[21] MSF. (2011). MSF Affiliated Organizations. Available at www.msf.org/msf/articles/2011/12/msf-affiliated-organisations.cfm (accessed on March 19, 2014).

[22] The World Summit of the Information Society (WSIS) Tunis Commitment 2005, para 36 states, "36. We value the potential of ICTs to promote peace and to prevent conflict which,

management."[23] Information and communications technology (ICT), ranging from the Web and the Internet through personal computers to the mobile web through smartphones and Short Message Service (SMS), is increasingly seen as an important vehicle for humanitarian relief. ICT4Peace focuses on the following issues:[24] raising awareness about the contribution and potential of ICT in crisis management; fostering the exchange of best practices in the field of ICT for crisis management; contributing to the establishment of broad principles derived from operational best practices, helping to integrate them into UN and multi-stakeholder processes and making ICT part of UN and global multi-stakeholder evaluation exercises.

Since 2007, ICT4Peace has provided "strategic input into how the UN system could interface with the burgeoning crisis mapping community to integrate, with appropriate and timely validation routines, crowd-sourced information into its decision and policymaking processes."[25]

SecondMuse

SecondMuse is an organization that facilitates collaborative innovation and assists individuals and organizations to access inspiration through one another, using breakthrough collaboration processes, supported by technology and social media to advance understanding and communication.[26] Currently, its main collaborative projects include: Random Hacks of Kindness (RHoK), LAUNCH, Understanding Risk, GEM and Power as Capacity.

As the Operational Lead Partner for RHoK, a joint initiative among Google, Yahoo!, Microsoft, NASA, HP and the World Bank, SecondMuse coordinates global volunteer efforts to develop software solutions that

inter alia, negatively affects achieving development goals. ICT can be used for identifying conflict situations through early-warning systems preventing conflicts, promoting their peaceful resolution, supporting humanitarian action, including protection of civilians in armed conflicts, facilitating peacekeeping missions, and assisting post conflict peace-building and reconstruction."

23 Daniel Stauffacher. (2011). *Strengthening Crisis Information Management*. Available at www.un.org/wcm/content/site/chronicle/home/archive/issues2011/thedigitaldividend/strengtheningcrisisinformationmanagement (accessed on March 19, 2014).

24 ICT4Peace. (2010). *The ICT4Peace Story*. Available at http://ict4peace.org/whoweare (accessed on March 19, 2014).

25 Stauffacher (2011), *supra* note 23.

26 SecondMuse. (2012). *What Are We Up To*. Available at www.secondmuse.com/ (accessed on March 19, 2014).

respond to challenges in the field of natural disaster risk and response.[27] A hackathon is a "unique forum for collaborative problem solving that results in concrete software solutions that can be implemented around the world to address critical challenges."[28] These challenges include helping recipients of the Supplemental Nutritional Assistance Program (SNAP) in Philadelphia,[29] shelter management and post-earthquake response.[30]

In June 2010, SecondMuse organized six international events bringing together more than 500 technologists from around the world to work together on software solutions, collaborating across time zones, international boundaries, oceans and language barriers to create innovative technology for vulnerable populations.[31] The process was facilitated by videoconferencing among event sites, live streaming to promote collaborative development of online tools, including wiki pages and IRC chat channels. Many of the applications developed through RHoK have already received support from governments, NGOs and international organizations and have been implemented to contribute to critical disaster risk assessment and response needs.[32]

In addition, SecondMuse has been collaborating closely with the Academy for Educational Development on the implementation of innovative programs using mobile phones, SMS and cloud technologies to gather and analyze important health information from rural populations.[33]

SecondMuse also collaborated on a project called *Understanding Risk* with the World Bank to engage thousands of technical experts and practitioners from more than 130 countries around the world in sharing their experiences in preparing for and responding to natural disasters. The collaborative online global community served as a forum to enable practitioners from diverse backgrounds and across disciplines to share ideas and to spur the development and use of new innovations and technologies in the field of disaster risk. The online collaboration led to the Understanding Risk Forum held at the World Bank, Washington, DC, in June 2010, where 400 world experts shared their work.[34]

[27] Random Hacks of Kindness. (2012). About. www.rhok.org/about (accessed on March 19, 2014).

[28] Ibid., p. 10.

[29] Ibid., p. 15.

[30] Ibid., p. 23.

[31] SecondMuse. (2010). *Google, Microsoft, Yahoo!, NASA, The World Bank*. Available at www.secondmuse.com/portfolio/view/RHoK1/ (accessed on March 19, 2014).

[32] Ibid.

[33] SecondMuse. (2010). *Technology's Potential in Social and Economic Development*. Available at www.secondmuse.com/en/portfolio/view/sms/ (accessed on March 19, 2014).

[34] For more, see www.understandrisk.org (accessed on March 19, 2014).

SecondMuse is also helping to architect and build an open source, global seismic risk modeling platform for *Global Earthquake Model*, known as GEM, a global collaborative effort bringing together national and international organizations and scientists to create open standards for calculating and communicating earthquake risk worldwide. The work started in 2009 and at the end of 2013, the first fully featured version of the model was launched. SecondMuse was contracted for IT systems architecture, engineering leadership and management of the engineering team responsible for development of the GEM platform.[35]

Among the achievements of RHoK is its significant growth in recent years. RHoK organized its first hackathon in December 2009 in Silicon Valley, California.[36] By December 2012, RHoK's hackathons were held in thirty cities.[37] This has enabled many around the world to participate and innovate through RHoK's coordination. For example, in Bogota, a shelter management system developed at RHoK was adopted by the national government and partners. In Santiago, the TweetTheTweet Twitter syntax developed at RHoK was used to track the aftermath of the 2010 earthquake.[38] Growth of the RHoK community can be seen from the increase in the number of RHoK events, from one in November 2009 to thirty in December 2012. The number of problem definitions has also increased from 11 in November 2009 to 176 in December 2012; and the number of solutions from 7 in November 2009 to 128 in December 2012.

RHoK events have enabled individuals from around the world to come together to develop creative solutions ("hacks") while using minimal resources in response to locally defined problems.[39] After each hackathon, RHoK identifies and supports projects with high potential for deployment and impact. Beginning in June 2012, RHoK partnered with Geeks Without Bounds and their Humanitarian Accelerator, "a new six-month program focusing on business development, technical execution and deployment of high potential humanitarian technology projects."[40] This is a major achievement in humanitarian action since organizations dealing with such challenges often lack the technical

[35] For more, see www.globalquakemodel.org (accessed on March 19, 2014).

[36] Random Hacks of Kindness. 2013 Report, p. 6. Available at http://open.nasa.gov/blog/2013/03/11/random-hacks-of-kindness-report-2013/ (accessed on March 19, 2014).

[37] Ibid., p. 10.

[38] Ibid., p. 23.

[39] Ibid., p. 10.

[40] Ibid., p. 14.

expertise to drive a software project forward. Technical expertise may be provided by RHoK through RHoK's Sustainability Projects,[41] including "First Responder"[42] and "Sheltr."[43]

RHoK "has gone from a small, focused hackathon to a vast and distributed global movement."[44] From the experiences of SecondMuse, lessons may be learned as to the importance of local collaboration and the use of technical knowledge in addressing global challenges.[45]

Policy Suggestions

It is clear that there is a shifting emphasis toward greater collaboration with the private sector in developing technology for humanitarian efforts. This trend reflects insights from new governance literature as discussed in Chapter 1 on expanded participation and partnership on the part of governments and non-state actors in solving public problems; a learning-focused orientation; and the role of the state as a convener, catalyst and coordinator. For instance, according to UNCTAD, in the realm of disaster response and development "much of the required investment will come from the private sector. Experience shows that the private sector has been the most innovative player and the major driving force behind e-business and ICT development."[46] Therefore, an "e-strategy" that merges public action with private-sector initiative in a mutually supportive manner will be most effective.[47] This chapter will conclude by commenting on suggestions for improving public–private collaboration in post-disaster open source technology development through (a) data management in public–private partnerships and (b) the engagement of stakeholders in building legitimacy and forging partnerships between international and local actors and (c) suggestions on enhancing the cooperation of international and public bodies (UN or governments) with the private sector.

[41] Ibid., p. 14.

[42] Ibid., p. 25.

[43] Ibid., p. 26.

[44] Ibid., p. 42.

[45] Ibid., p. 44.

[46] UNCTAD. (2004). *Partnership for Development: Information and Knowledge for Development*, pp. 6–7. Available at unctad.org/en/docs/td394_en.pdf (accessed on March 19, 2014).

[47] Ibid.

Data Collection and Data Management

With respect to data management, following the Haiti earthquake in 2010, several studies began to examine concrete suggestions regarding how disaster preparedness and crisis information management can be strengthened.[48] Some of these suggestions include: (1) the accelerated development and population of easily accessible *datasets with essential information shared* across UN and other aid agencies, to help identify, prepare for and mitigate disasters; (2) significantly *improving interoperability across all systems between UN agencies and other key platforms*; (3) *helping communities develop their own capacities and capabilities* for disaster early warning, prevention and resilience; and (4) *greater cooperation between governments and NGOs*, based on standard operating procedures governing information sharing to help aid work.[49]

In addition, with respect to data collection, research has suggested that the use of "simple, universal indicators and clear case definitions in easy-to-use formats; accuracy and consistency; focus on data that has clear and defined utility and use readily deployable and easily understood technology" (i.e., cell phones with SMS capacity) to facilitate data collection.[50]

With respect to data management some studies have recommended that organizations should streamline their data collection and dissemination systems and adopt a peer review system.[51] In terms of human resource management, recommendations include simplifying indicators and processes and using technologies familiar to personnel (e.g., cell phones).[52] The application of innovative technologies that are easy to use, durable and easily interfaced, yet secure and transmittable in real time has also been suggested as a means of increasing the quality of the data management process.[53] Suggestions also include using SMS and damage-resistant laptops powered by solar/gear power[54] since mobile phone infrastructure is generally inoperable in the days and in some cases weeks following a natural disaster.

[48] Stauffacher (2011), *supra* note 23.

[49] Ibid.

[50] Harvard University. *Humanitarian Health Conference 2007 – Final Report*, p.18. Available at http://hhi.harvard.edu/images/resources/files/hhc_2007_final_report.pdf (accessed on March 19, 2014).

[51] Ibid., pp. 18–19.

[52] Ibid., p. 19.

[53] Ibid., pp. 19–20.

[54] Ibid.

Addressing Legitimacy: Partnerships between International Bodies and Local Governments

Apart from technological and managerial improvements through data collection and processing, partnership with governments at the local level is another important mechanism not only for improving humanitarian coordination but also for addressing the broader question of enhancing the legitimacy of localized decision-making structures. As noted earlier, a key challenge facing new governance approaches is limited accountability and legitimacy absent state oversight.[55] Some have suggested that in order to benefit from devolution and decentralization,[56] the necessary conditions for success include (1) the broadest possible degree of stakeholder participation compatible with effective decision making, and (2) effective and informed monitoring.[57] The Cluster Approach developed by the OCHA encourages the UN to reflect on key challenges, especially in light of civil society involvement, including how to best build partnership with disaster-prone countries in disaster management that encompasses capacity building for preparedness and response; and how to ensure principled humanitarian action and accountability with the proliferation of humanitarian actors, including the military, the private sector and faith-based organizations.[58] While "progress has been made so far in the implementation of the cluster approach,"[59] greater attention can be focused on developing local capabilities to engage in joint assessment and planning in the context of disaster recovery.

Development of Private–Public Partnerships

Partnerships between the humanitarian community and the private sector are increasingly important in relief efforts.[60] John Holmes, the undersecretary-general for humanitarian affairs of OCHA underscored that humanitarian needs are continually rising and that current

[55] J. Solomon. (2008) Law and Governance in the 21st Century Regulatory State. *Texas Law Review.* 86, 819–856.

[56] Lisa T. Alexander. (2010). Reflections on Success and Failure in New Governance and the Role of the Lawyer. *Wisconsin Law Review Symposium Afterword.* 737–738.

[57] Ibid., pp. 740–741; see also S. Ali. 2010. Measuring Success in Devolved Collaboration. *Journal of Land Use and Environmental Law.* 26 (Fall).

[58] OCHA (2011), *supra* note 6, pp. 16–17.

[59] Ibid.

[60] World Economic Forum (n 1) 1.

international response capacities are being stretched thin. He emphasized that "engaging other actors such as the private sector is even more important at this time, including not only cash and resource based assistance, but expertise-based partnerships that mobilize the skills and talents of the private sector in support of humanitarian assistance."[61]

In addition, investment in national and local capacity for response, prevention and recovery; engagement of the private sector; humanitarian recovery as part of broader social and economic development aims; and regional and international readiness to address cross-border humanitarian issues are all key areas for further development.[62]

[61] Ibid.
[62] Ibid.

PART V

Survey Findings and Policy Recommendations

12

Governance and Humanitarian Aid Survey Data

Building on an examination of case studies exploring the dynamics of local engagement in response to natural disasters and a discussion of emerging crowd-sourced post-disaster technological collaboration tools, this chapter explores the attitudes and perceptions of practitioners working in the field of disaster response. The aim of the survey is to help provide insights into the dynamics, challenges and lessons learned from the perspective of those directly engaged in the work of post-disaster relief with particular attention to the dynamics of local engagement. The principal finding of this chapter, based on survey data and follow-up questions, is that there is a statistically significant correlation between the level of engagement with a local community and perceived effectiveness of response.[1]

The findings of this chapter echo recent insights from sociolegal scholars of disaster studies. In particular, "factors of inequality contribute to producing higher rates of vulnerability" in disaster contexts and usually reflect "the profound asymmetry that divides those who decide from those who will be affected by such decisions."[2] The origins and effects of disasters are "global and local at the same time,"[3] and reflect the "the humanitarian impulse (Sarat and Lezaun 2009) to care for people after disaster."[4] At the same time, "non governmental organizations have globalized the response to disaster." Yet the nature and quality of response vary. International "presence,"[5] whether it be "sheer, mere, or peer," gives rise to widely differing levels of engagement. Mere presence or "passively just

[1] For additional discussion, see S. Ali. (2015). Toward Peer Presence in Post-disaster Governance: An Empirical Study. *Hastings Journal of International and Comparative Law*. 38, 243.

[2] Valerio Nitrato Izzo. (2013). Law, State and the Politics of Catastrophes: A Critical Perspective on Epiphanies of Injustice and the Need for Protection. In Susan Steret (Ed.), *Disaster and Sociolegal Studies*, Onati Socio-Legal Series. New Orleans, LA: Quid Pro Books, p. 71.

[3] Ibid., p. 73.

[4] Ibid., p. 13.

[5] Kimberley Coles. (2007). *Democratic Designs: International Intervention and Electoral Practices in Postwar Bosnia-Herzegovina*. Ann Arbor: University of Michigan Press.

being there,"[6] falls somewhat short of sheer presence, meaning "social visibility" or "implicit and explicit show of international concern, resources and actions."[7] Peer presence "trains [community members]."[8] The survey findings of this chapter confirm recent scholarship identifying an overriding "sense of frustration felt by many internationals ... because their (implicit) model was not functioning according to plan: their presence was often not enough."[9]

The findings also speak to the growing literature on resilience, reflecting that "emergency response teaches people that they must rely on each other, and ... that those who respond first to claims in disaster are neighbors."[10] This literature of internalized self-governance posits that "people are to be ready to become someone new when disaster strikes."[11] It calls on policy makers to reflect on "who is the community" affected by displacement[12] and "allows the mobilizing for justice ... sometimes bringing partial compensation or regulatory improvement."[13] At the same time, the findings caution us away, as critics of resilience note, from an abdication of responsibility on the part of the state or a claw back of social welfare responsibilities.[14]

Summary of Findings

The findings of this chapter can be grouped into two areas. The first area reports on the correlation between post-disaster program effectiveness and level of engagement with local communities. Here the data suggest a statistically significant correlation between perceived program effectiveness and level of community engagement. The second part reports on insights from practitioners regarding the strengths and challenges of existing disaster relief programs. The findings here indicate that international

6 Ibid., p. 108.

7 Ibid., p. 92.

8 Ibid., p. 108.

9 Ibid., p. 102.

10 Susan Sterett (Ed.). (2013). *Disaster and Sociolegal Studies*, Onati Socio-Legal Series. New Orleans, LA: Quid Pro Books, p. 13.

11 Ibid. See Pat O'Malley. (2013). Uncertain Governance and Resilient Subjects in the Risk Society. In Susan Sterett (Ed.), *Disaster and Sociolegal Studies*, Onati Socio-Legal Series. New Orleans, LA: Quid Pro Books, p. 15.

12 S. Sterett and J. Reich. (2007). Prayer and Social Welfare: Race and Service after Hurricane Katrina. In H. Potter (Ed.), *Racing the Storm*. Lanham, MD: Lexington Books, pp. 135–156.

13 Sterett (2013), *supra* note 10, p. 4.

14 Brad Evans and Julian Reid. (2014). *Resilient Life: The Art of Living Dangerously*. Cambridge: Polity Press (Wiley).

institutions face the greatest challenge in effective engagement with local communities, while state agencies are in a somewhat better position to collaborate and coordinate on response planning. This finding supports case studies presented in Parts II and III of this book. Practitioner suggestions for improving the overall process of response are included in the final chapter that follows.

Survey Data Collection Method

Survey data was collected in order to gain insight into the dynamics of local involvement, if any, in the planning, implementation and distribution of humanitarian post–natural disaster aid and resulting challenges and lessons learned. While it must be noted that "the random nature of disasters and multiplicity of players makes comprehensive analysis difficult,"[15] and given the small sample size (n= 69) the purpose of the survey is not to provide for generalizable findings, but rather to offer insights into how some practitioners are learning from the challenges of effectively engaging with communities in the wake of disaster response.

The survey questionnaire contained a quantitative part asking for yes-no answers and numerical responses in the form of percentage estimates or evaluations according to a five-point scale, as well as a "supplemental" part containing qualitative, open-ended questions asking for personal observations, judgments and proposals.

The first part of the survey asked participants for background information on their organizational affiliations and the number of years they have worked in disaster aid. The second part of the survey examined the nature and extent, if any, of participants' collaboration with local communities in disaster relief. The final part examined the strengths and challenges of local collaboration and suggestions for improving the process of local engagement.

The sample pool consisted of humanitarian aid practitioners working in post-disaster response from more than eighteen countries and regions. The sample group was selected from contacts made with members of international humanitarian agencies and professional associations, including the Asia Foundation in Beijing, Oxfam in Boston, MA, USAID

[15] T. E. Drabek and D. A. McEntire. (2002). Emergent Phenomena and Multiorganizational Coordination in Disasters: Lessons from the Research Literature. *International Journal of Emergencies and Disasters* [online]. 20(2), 197–224. Available at http://ijmed.org/articles/574/download/ (accessed on October 29, 2012).

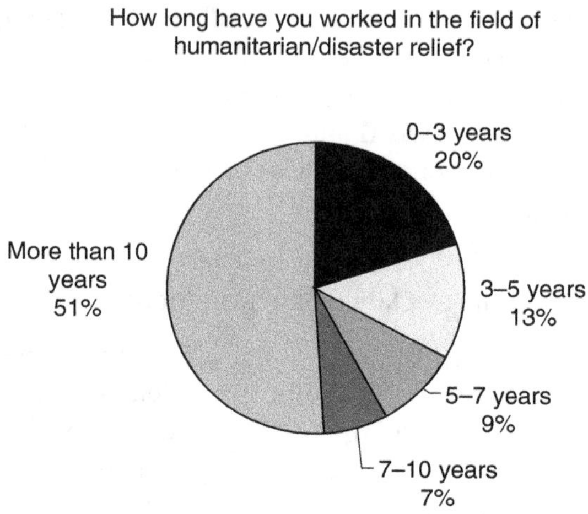

Figure 12.1 Years of experience.

in Washington, DC, RedR in India, the UN Office for the Coordination of Humanitarian Affairs in Geneva, UN Women in NY, UNDP in Bangkok, Thailand, the World Health Organization, Mercy Malaysia, the Cash Learning Partnership in Oxford, the Bill & Melinda Gates Foundation, Seattle, WA, the CDC in Atlanta, GA, Fundacion Macau, and individuals working at Red Cross centers in Yangon, Myanmar, Lijiang, Hainan and Shenzhen, PRC, Hong Kong, Houston, TX, Macau SAR, Istanbul, Turkey, Haifa, Israel, Kuala Lumpur, Malaysia, the International Committee for the Red Cross and Humanitarian and Disaster Aid research centers at Tufts University, Harvard University and UC Berkeley. Of the respondents, fifty-five worked for an international organization, nine worked for a private entity, three worked for a state agency, and seven worked for a public–private partnership organization. The majority of respondents (thirty-six) had more than ten years of experience (Figure 12.1).

The survey was conducted between April 2013 and November 2014. A total of seventy-one surveys was distributed in person and initiated via a web link portal and sixty-nine surveys were completed. The questions and survey links were distributed in person at humanitarian aid centers throughout the world, to members of the International Humanitarian and Development Professionals Group and attendees at the "Human Security: Humanitarian Perspectives and Responses" conference in Istanbul, Turkey and the "International Humanitarian Conference" in Kuala Lumpur, Malaysia in 2013.

Table 12.1. *Program effectiveness by level of engagement with local community, 2013–2014*

Response	Level of engagement		
	Highly engaged	*Minimally engaged*	Total
Very effective	39 (58%)	15 (22%)	(54)
Limited effectiveness	4 (6%)	9 (13%)	(13)
Total	(43)	(24)	67

Note: The association between program effectiveness and level of engagement is considered statistically significant according to Fisher's exact test: The two-tailed P value equals 0.0088; it is also significant according to the Chi Square test with Yates Correction (Chi Square = 6.132; P = 0.0133)

Program Effectiveness

Perhaps the most significant survey finding is the existence of a statistically significant correlation between program effectiveness and community engagement in disaster response (see Table 12.1). Those who self-report high levels of community engagement also perceive their relief programs to be more effective than those who report low levels of community engagement. This reflects a growing body of research that collaboration and active participation of multiple stakeholders, seen as the "core" principles of new governance,[16] and large-scale public challenges benefit from local decision making.[17] This is because experimentation, inclusion of local knowledge and collaboration between stakeholders can take place more readily in the community context.[18]

The Role of the Local Community in Disaster Relief Work

In examining the relationship between local actors in disaster relief work, the findings indicate that international institutions and private agencies face the greatest challenge in effective engagement with local communities, while state agencies are in a somewhat better position to collaborate

16 Ibid., pp. 4–5.

17 See Jerome Van der Heijden. (2013). Looking Forwards and Sideways: Trajectories of New Governance Theory. Amsterdam Law School Legal Studies, Research Paper No. 2013-04, p. 6.

18 Ibid.

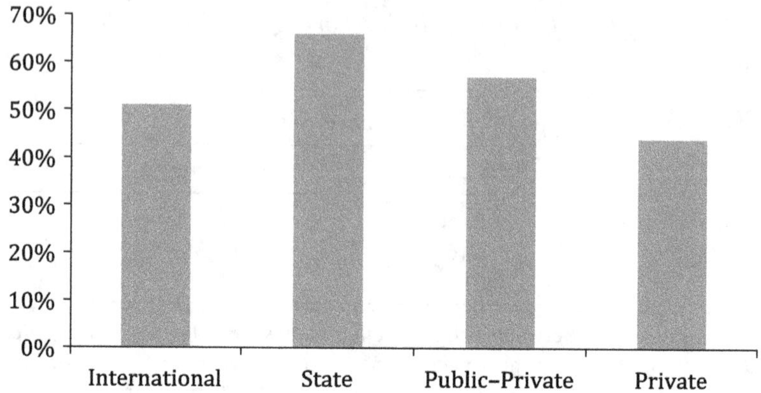

Figure 12.2 Reporting significant coordination with local community.

and coordinate on response planning. A total of 66 percent of state agency respondents reported a "primary" or "significant amount of collaboration" with the local community in disaster response while only 44 percent of private actors and 51 percent of international agencies reported that relief efforts were "primarily" or "significantly driven by local input" (see Figure 12.2).

These findings reflect the varying nature and quality of disaster response examined in scholarship on international "presence."[19] The findings indicate that international response has a greater tendency to reflect either "sheer" or "mere" presence (characterized by "social visibility," meaning "implicit and explicit show of international concern, resources and actions"[20]), while state response may more closely approximate "peer" presence (characterized by training of "[community members]."[21] Recent scholarship describes an overriding "sense of frustration felt by many internationals … because their (implicit) model was not functioning according to plan: their presence was often not enough."[22] This is also reflected in survey findings and follow-up questions discussed in greater detail in this chapter.

The findings on the varying proximity of collaborative relationships with local actors in relief work also reflect the aspirations of world community

[19] Coles (2007), *supra* note 5.
[20] Ibid., p. 92.
[21] Ibid., p. 108.
[22] Ibid., p. 102.

scholarship demonstrating how changing notions of community influence collective interest over "egoistic interests of individual states."[23] The concept of community designates interactions in which "participants in pursuit of their own objectives must regularly take account of the activities and demands of others."[24] Research underscores the link between perception and action through the observation that "it is the perception of interdependence in community process that leads participants to appreciate the relevance of pursuing common interests and motivates them to clarify it."[25] Here, the survey findings indicate that the challenge continues to be the need for a shift in perception of communities affected by disasters as "recipients of aid" to peer partners in planning and relief.

Local Collaboration

Relief aid workers noted that when local-based partnerships in planning take place, this has led to a number of positive outcomes, including more "effective communication,"[26] "better long term sustainability" and "ownership in work,"[27] "flexibility,"[28] "partnership,"[29] "trust"[30] and "good relationships with the community"[31] and a more "culturally accepted" approach.[32] In addition, such collaboration enables "the parties involved to work in harmony with one purpose or goal. Everyone feels part … of every resource."[33] Collaboration also enables "smart planning [and] effective communication."[34] Other positive outcomes include "transparency, commitment … team work"[35] and the ability to reach a "targeted population."[36]

23 Bruno Simma and Andreas L. Paulus. (1998). The "International Community": Facing the Challenge of Globalization. *European Journal of International Law*. 9, 266.

24 Myres S. McDougal, Michael W. Reisman and Andrew R. Willard. (1988). The World Community: A Planetary Social Process. *University of California at Davis Law Review. 21, 807.*

25 Ibid.

26 Disaster Aid Survey Respondent, January 13, 2014 6:15 p.m.

27 Disaster Aid Survey Respondent, January 13, 2014 5:51 p.m.

28 Disaster Aid Survey Respondent, November 18, 2013 3:07 a.m.

29 Disaster Aid Survey Respondent, November 06, 2013 11:52 a.m.

30 Disaster Aid Survey Respondent, November 05, 2013 4:44 a.m.

31 Disaster Aid Survey Respondent, January 13, 2014 4:43 p.m.

32 Disaster Aid Survey Respondent, January 13, 2014 4:35 p.m.

33 Disaster Aid Survey Respondent, December 05, 2013 8:26 p.m.

34 Disaster Aid Survey Respondent, February 02, 2013 3:21 a.m.

35 Disaster Aid Survey Respondent, December 01, 2013 3:27 a.m.

36 Disaster Aid Survey Respondent, November 28, 2013 7:48 p.m.

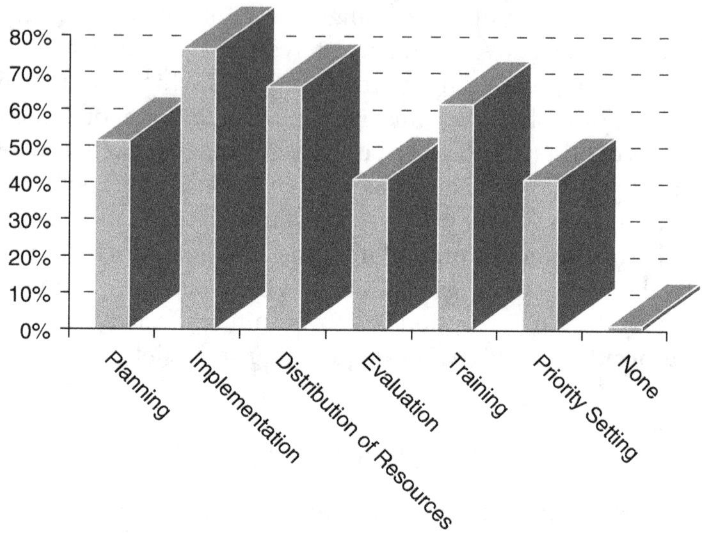

Figure 12.3 Nature of local collaboration.

This, in some cases, reflects the possibility for a shift beyond "mere presence" to something more akin to "peer presence."[37]

Nature of Collaboration

In describing the nature of collaboration with community members affected by disasters, respondents noted that perhaps the most significant area of collaboration is in "implementation" (52). This is followed by "distribution" (45), "training" (42), "planning" (35) and "priority setting" (28) in disaster relief (see Figure 12.3). This reflects recent scholarship indicating that "the legal framework of disaster response does not deal as well with long term recovery," but rather reflects a tendency to focus on "short term" efforts.[38]

Benefits of Collaboration: Efficiency, Access, Information and Resilience

Disaster aid workers shared their understanding of the key benefits of local collaboration. These benefits fell in the areas of greater efficiency,

[37] Coles (2007), *supra* note 5.

[38] Victor B. Flatt and Jeffrey J. Stys. (2013). Long Term Recovery in Disaster Response and the Role of Non-profits. In Susan Steret (Ed.), *Disaster and Sociolegal Studies*, Onati Socio-Legal Series. New Orleans, LA: Quid Pro Books, p. 216.

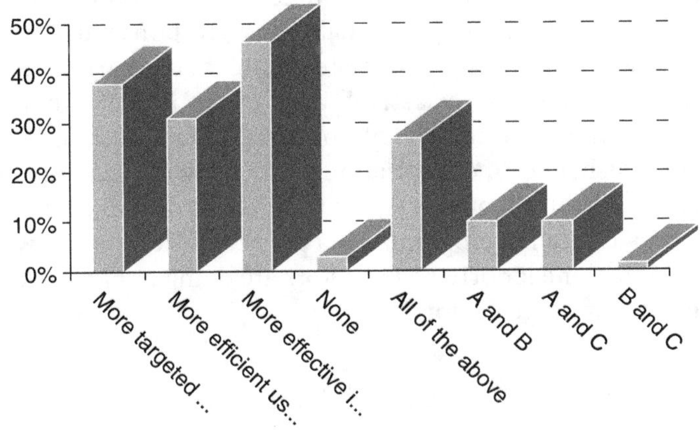

Figure 12.4 Benefits of local collaboration.

improved access, networking and collaboration, information sharing, integration of local knowledge and improved resilience, which will be discussed in greater detail in this section.

Summarizing the benefits of local collaboration (Figure 12.4), the most significant benefit highlighted was "more effective implementation" (33), followed by a "more targeted response/greater understanding of needs" (27). This was followed by "more efficient use of resources" (22) and "all of the above" (19).

Efficiency

Efficiency was identified as a key benefit of local collaboration. One aid worker noted that with "no expenses for expats, funding stays within the country, local and cultural specifics are respected, needs of target groups are properly addressed according to their needs instead of anticipating needs based on western staff needs assessments, which are usually of bad quality."[39] Collaboration also leads to "better understanding of needs and better and faster project implementation."[40] Considering questions of scale, being "a small yet effective" organization was considered a strength in "local response."[41]

[39] Disaster Aid Survey Respondent, October 28, 2013 6:40 p.m.
[40] Disaster Aid Survey Respondent, October 28, 2013 6:33 p.m.
[41] Disaster Aid Survey Respondent, May 04, 2013 8:12 p.m.

Collaboration also "minimizes resource wastage and promotes efficiency and cost effectiveness."[42] Collaborative response also draws on insights and local knowledge associated with "being part of response/ during and right after [a] disaster"[43] and "direct implementation and follow up."[44] It draws on the strength of "local volunteers" and provides for "well established local organizations."[45] Putting it succinctly, one aid worker observed: "if the purpose is to achieve maximum efficiency of a humanitarian assistance programs for a particular situation, it would be illusory to go it alone ignoring what actors are doing or capable of doing in complement of a global effort."[46]

Networking and Coordination

Respondents also noted increased strength in networking and coordination systems through collaboration with local community members. One aid worker noted, "we have bilateral relations with local actors … [which] link to wider coordination mechanisms which include international and local actors."[47] In practice, one aid worker described, "we work together in teams"[48] and the teams "make plans"[49] that "respect local initiatives."[50] Another respondent noted that her organization is "internationally and locally networked with government agencies (embassies, foreign affairs ministries, health departments, public universities), [the] public sector as well as other NGOs / INGOs."[51] Drawing on local volunteers through schools and universities provides a systematic way to coordinate with local resources. One respondent noted that her organization "involve[s] university students in [its] disaster preparedness programs."[52] Flexibility in coordination was also highlighted: "the primary idea is to find a mechanism for coordination to ensure optimization of work, relief and protection of lives."[53]

42 Disaster Aid Survey Respondent, November 20, 2013 11:59 p.m.
43 Disaster Aid Survey Respondent, October 29, 2013 6:56 p.m.
44 Disaster Aid Survey Respondent, October 28, 2013 9:27 p.m.
45 Disaster Aid Survey Respondent, October 28, 2013 8:17 p.m.
46 Disaster Aid Survey Respondent, July 16, 2013 9:33 p.m.
47 Disaster Aid Survey Respondent, October 28, 2013 11:24 a.m.
48 Disaster Aid Survey Respondent, January 13, 2014 6:07 p.m.
49 Ibid.
50 Disaster Aid Survey Respondent, January 13, 2014 5:51 p.m.
51 Disaster Aid Survey Respondent, January 13, 2014 5:26 p.m.
52 Disaster Aid Survey Respondent, January 13, 2014 5:05 p.m.
53 Disaster Aid Survey Respondent, February 02, 2013 3:02 p.m.

Information Sharing and Access

Access and sharing of information was another benefit noted in collaborative response. With local collaboration, aid workers "are able to access local communities quicker and with appropriate assistance. Local organizations also know the local dynamics and this helps us to integrate protection and gender concerns effectively into all programming."[54]

Additional strengths from localized response programs were evident in "information sharing... and promoting good practices."[55] Many programs are increasingly devoting significant attention to "vulnerability analysis and hazard mapping."[56] Some development-oriented NGOs noted that "we almost always provide support in regions where we are already deployed in development activities, so we tend to have relationships with the communities and local supply lines already established."[57] "Good communication" and "social media outreach and volunteer coordination" were noted as strengths alongside "having a road map clearly indicating all points of action [for] implementing the task."[58] Another noted that we "use a science base for response."[59]

Integration of Local Knowledge and Resilience

Some aid workers shared that they had seen improvement in listening skills and integration of local knowledge in planning and implementation of relief activities. One noted that he saw "better understanding of needs and better [and] faster project implementation."[60] Another noted greater "local wisdom integration in programming and priority setting [and] participation of community institutions in coordination, implementation, monitoring and evaluation."[61] An aid worker also noted greater "understanding of priorities and conditions [and] local knowledge of the area,"[62] including a "holistic approach and collaboration with locals."[63]

[54] Disaster Aid Survey Respondent, November 25, 2013 11:23 p.m.
[55] Disaster Aid Survey Respondent, January 13, 2014 4:18 p.m.
[56] Disaster Aid Survey Respondent, December 10, 2013 8:33 p.m.
[57] Disaster Aid Survey Respondent, December 05, 2013 8:15 p.m.
[58] Disaster Aid Survey Respondent, April 26, 2013 11:14 p.m.
[59] Disaster Aid Survey Respondent, May 10, 2013 4:13 a.m.
[60] Disaster Aid Survey Respondent, October 28, 2013 6:33 p.m.
[61] Disaster Aid Survey Respondent, October 28, 2013 10:59 a.m.
[62] Disaster Aid Survey Respondent, June 15, 2013 10:23 a.m.
[63] Disaster Aid Survey Respondent, May 22, 2013 3:29 a.m.

A key aim of localized response is the development of greater resilience and strength such that local communities "organize and drive the efforts, while 'outsiders' support in the ways requested by locals, [this] allows (and encourages) the full capacity of the local actors. Ownership and effectiveness are increased, which in turn leads to greater resilience."[64] Overall, the concept of resilience, understood as a "capacity to adapt and thrive in the face of challenge" (World Economic Forum 2008, p. ix), continues to be viewed largely as an objective of disaster response:

> in the past decade, programs of resilience, and particularly resiliency training, have been developed with the aim of creating subjects able to thrive and prosper under conditions of extreme uncertainty. They constitute a form of governance promoting a positive "freedom to."[65]

While numerous benefits can be associated with greater community resilience, from a policy perspective, some scholars have cautioned that such emphasis should not constitute an abdication of responsibility on the part of the state or a claw back of social welfare responsibilities.[66] The balancing of long-term policy aims of self-sufficiency with acute crisis support will need to remain at the forefront of policy research in years to come.

Challenges in Disaster Aid

Individuals working at all levels of disaster relief, whether it be within international entities, at state agencies, with local NGOs or in private–public partnerships, all faced a number of challenges in post-disaster response and coordination. These challenges include effective coordination and access to funding, information and resources in the context of volatile, cross-cultural and multilingual environments.

International Organizations

International respondents reported that perhaps the most significant challenge facing international entities was that of coordination – particularly given their distance from locally affected populations. In particular, survey participants noted difficulties in "networking national-scale NGO's in each country,"[67] integrating diverse viewpoints "with various

[64] Disaster Aid Survey Respondent, May 08, 2013 11:01 p.m.
[65] See O'Malley (2013), *supra* note 12, p. 23.
[66] Ibid., p. 36.
[67] Disaster Aid Survey Respondent, January 13, 2014 5:58 p.m.

worldviews and needs"[68] and achieving unity of action and movement "in the same direction"[69] while reconciling different "objectives and expectations,"[70] including "donors milestones"[71] with local "priority needs and expectations."[72] In addition, limitations were reported in "leadership and facilitation for coordination"[73] to achieve "shared objectives" and "harmony" among "diverse stakeholders and participants."[74] Given that, in many cases, "organisations are cumbersome and slow moving on policy changes, and decentralisation of authority,"[75] these challenges become even more difficult.

International aid workers also noted a crisis of funding. One respondent observed that "sustainable funding for our organizations general fund needs to be larger so we can operate optimally."[76] In addition to funding, financial oversight is another challenge. Several respondents noted "difficulties with overseeing the management of funds. Also, sometimes there can be bias in the selection of project beneficiaries as local partner staff choose areas of interest to them over more needy areas."[77] Relatedly, there was a need for more "efficient use of available resources."[78] In some cases, "resources are spent for established international NGOs, [they have a] monopoly of funding, spending and coordination among the established big organizations and UN. Local structures only serve as auxiliaries and are not taken serious[ly] in their expertise and possible contributions."[79] One respondent noted that because of "funding relationships, we miss opportunities for alternative collaborations" and "we tend to look for local actors who look/behave like us."[80] This participant also noted that "externally: national actors often feel alienated from international coordination systems."[81]

Accessing information, particularly in disaster areas, was another major challenge noted by international agencies.[82] This manifested itself in lack

68 Disaster Aid Survey Respondent, January 13, 2014 5:51 p.m.
69 Ibid.
70 Disaster Aid Survey Respondent, January 13, 2014 4:18 p.m.
71 Disaster Aid Survey Respondent, December 06, 2013 7:51 p.m.
72 Ibid.
73 Disaster Aid Survey Respondent, December 02, 2013 3:02 p.m.
74 Disaster Aid Survey Respondent, November 20, 2013 11:59 p.m.
75 Disaster Aid Survey Respondent, November 19, 2013 10:37 p.m.
76 Disaster Aid Survey Respondent, January 13, 2014 5:26 p.m.
77 Disaster Aid Survey Respondent, November 25, 2013 11:23 p.m.
78 Disaster Aid Survey Respondent, December 10, 2013 8:33 p.m.
79 Disaster Aid Survey Respondent, October 28, 2013 6:40 p.m.
80 Disaster Aid Survey Respondent, October 28, 2013 11:24 a.m.
81 Ibid.
82 Disaster Aid Survey Respondent, January 13, 2014 4:18 p.m.

of understanding of "the coordination mechanism"[83] and "lack of situational awareness."[84] Placing "institutional interest" above "beneficiaries interest"[85] can occur in situations where a particular project is funded by an entity with strict requirements on aid distribution absent awareness of local dynamics and requirements for capacity building:

> There is pressure to change our participatory approaches to fit UN and RC-driven systems. Also, when under an implementation contract from an external donor like WFP, the policies regarding rationalization of losses and thefts etc. can result in long term challenges for our development efforts. We are not free to require communities to police themselves, participate actively in their own distributions, and be responsive to such events. We try to work in a sustainable/community-based approach even in relief settings and strictly limit straight distribution, but this doesn't fit with other agencies' models.[86]

Effective functioning in volatile crisis environments directly impacted issues of "staffing," "security" and "coordination." For example, several survey participants noted that "accessibility to … insecure area[s]"[87] was a key challenge alongside "language barriers" and "lack of security to reach isolated areas" and underrepresentation of women.[88] One observed that "disasters usually happen in remote areas, not accessible by standard or common means of transport, making the final leg of the delivery of the primary items, be they medicine, food or other, difficult. The challenge is [to] make sure that the relief items are delivered by the available means of transpiration by ground or air."[89]

While the importance of local collaboration is generally understood, many practitioners highlighted challenges in its implementation. One respondent noted the difficulty of "finding relationships,"[90] particularly in light of "changing target area[s], beneficiaries and interventions."[91] Coordinating with "ALL actors present in the humanitarian arena"[92] and "coordination in general is a challenge as there is a lack of leverage to engage in coordination with local population[s], other organizations and

[83] Disaster Aid Survey Respondent, January 13, 2014 4:01 p.m.
[84] Ibid.
[85] Ibid.
[86] Disaster Aid Survey Respondent, December 05, 2013 8:15 p.m.
[87] Disaster Aid Survey Respondent, December 05, 2013 4:13 p.m.
[88] Disaster Aid Survey Respondent, November 29, 2013 4:51 p.m.
[89] Disaster Aid Survey Respondent, April 26, 2013 11:14 p.m.
[90] Disaster Aid Survey Respondent, November 06, 2013 11:52 a.m.
[91] Disaster Aid Survey Respondent, November 18, 2013 3:07 a.m.
[92] Disaster Aid Survey Respondent, November 17, 2013 7:40 p.m.

governments."[93] Offering an introspective assessment, one aid worker noted "we do not work [in a] participatory way when it comes to working with target groups. Often the response is based on experience."[94] Centralized coordination is another difficulty. As one respondent noted, there is "no one to create and host a platform to coordinate players on relief works. Not all players are willing to communicate with other players about their own programs."[95] These challenges required several international NGOs to "redefine the role of the organization in a distributed knowledge environment."[96] In addition, some noted incidents of "corruption" and "unfair recruitment" and "unfair distribution of resources."[97]

Cultural and language issues were also noted. One aid worker observed that "coordination operations have extremely high transactions costs. Cultural differences require careful negotiation. None of these operations are efficient. Usually, financing, resources and patience is inadequate. Lack of imagination and stereotypes also impair relief efforts."[98]

State Entities

For individuals working in state-led relief agencies, respondents noted a number of challenges in communications, access, resource support and institutional integrity in the provision of disaster aid. Echoing issues raised by international agencies, respondents noted challenges with the breakdown of communications, including "telephone lines,"[99] and lack of "mutual understanding due to language barriers."[100] In the context of "changing vulnerabilities"[101] aid workers faced challenges with "adaptation."[102] In some cases "occupation restrictions"[103] posed barriers to access. Several state respondents noted challenges in relation to "shortages and irregularity of funding"[104] and "lack of resources"[105] to address

93 Disaster Aid Survey Respondent, October 30, 2013 9:15 p.m.
94 Disaster Aid Survey Respondent, October 30, 2013 7:42 p.m.
95 Disaster Aid Survey Respondent, May 17, 2013 12:50 a.m.
96 Disaster Aid Survey Respondent, January 13, 2014 5:36 p.m.
97 Disaster Aid Survey Respondent, December 02, 2013 3:21 a.m.
98 Disaster Aid Survey Respondent, November 12, 2013 2:32 p.m.
99 Disaster Aid Survey Respondent, January 13, 2014 6:15 p.m.
100 Ibid.
101 Disaster Aid Survey Respondent, December 16, 2013 10:04 p.m.
102 Ibid.
103 Disaster Aid Survey Respondent, December 01, 2013 3:27 a.m.
104 Ibid.
105 Disaster Aid Survey Respondent, January 13, 2014 4:52 p.m.

needs in a "timely manner."[106] In some cases, state agencies can function on the basis of policies that "work against effectiveness [in cases where] local actors are both powerful and corrupt."[107]

Public–Private Partnerships

Similar to the challenges faced at the international and state levels, those working in the area of public–private partnerships faced difficulties in gaining accurate and "real information"[108] from the affected population. Some noted challenges with "tedious process"[109] and "politics on the ground."[110] Others faced challenges "convincing the local public and government to [get] involved in the programs"[111] and "getting all partners on board with response."[112] Similar to state agencies, "lack of resources"[113] both financial and human was also a common concern. One aid worker noted that she faced challenges getting "support from employees to understand volunterism and community service."[114] Another echoed challenges with "lack of resources and [man] power"[115] and "lack of recognition and assistance from relief agencies."[116]

Local Aid Workers and NGOs

Local aid workers noted a number of challenges in coordinating with local counterparts. A core element of this challenge seemed to lie in a tendency on the part of international entities to place external/international objectives/benchmarks over local needs. One respondent observed a general "bias towards international staff (mostly western)" and a "lack of seriousness when it comes to local staff issues."[117] Another noted that his organization faced challenges "navigating between competing local priorities and agendas of various actors; overcoming inclusion and exclusion errors;

[106] Ibid.
[107] Disaster Aid Survey Respondent, May 01, 2013 4:44 a.m.
[108] Disaster Aid Survey Respondent, January 13, 2014 6:07 p.m.
[109] Disaster Aid Survey Respondent, November 28, 2013 7:48 p.m.
[110] Ibid.
[111] Disaster Aid Survey Respondent, November 04, 2013 9:32 p.m.
[112] Disaster Aid Survey Respondent, May 07, 2013 7:21 p.m.
[113] Disaster Aid Survey Respondent, May 22, 2013 3:29 a.m.
[114] Disaster Aid Survey Respondent, January 13, 2014 5:43 p.m.
[115] Disaster Aid Survey Respondent, January 13, 2014 4:43 p.m.
[116] Disaster Aid Survey Respondent, June 15, 2013 10:23 a.m.
[117] Disaster Aid Survey Respondent, May 01, 2013 8:44 p.m.

managing/containing biases among actors and affected communities."[118] Challenges with "corruption" and "staying neutral" were also noted.[119]

At the same time, local protectionism may result in "local partners ... looking after their own benefit first" and therefore "priority setting is sometimes difficult."[120] Others viewed challenges arising from "weak local infrastructure, communication, poor budgeting, local hurdles,"[121] as well as "dealing ... with ... bureaucracy."[122] One aid worker noted, "in most situations, the challenge is to reconcile objectives and aspirations of the state on the territory of which the assistance is provided with those of the donors supporting ... other organizations, and indeed with each actor's own primary objectives. In the case of failed states, the challenge is to identify (or be recognized, as the case may be) as the most appropriate coordinator – the natural leader as it were."[123] In some cases, "official duty bearers (Governments), who have the primary role in assisting their people ... are all too often and easily left outside of the humanitarian system, and thus not being held accountable for failure to live up to their duty."[124]

Several local respondents highlighted the need for greater training in language,[125] cultural sensitivity and decision making on the part of aid workers. One noted that "finding 'outsiders'" who know how to listen to locals is always a challenge. While this is a learnable skill (and I teach it), it is shocking how many people don't see the need to listen."[126] Another observed that "organisations heavily depend on our trained international medical expert volunteers from Germany and Europe and at times that is a challenge because cultural issues ... cannot be fully trained ... so patience is needed for younger staff ... and empathy for older who always try to replicate old disaster situations in a new context."[127] The ability to make good decisions and set priorities[128] was also noted as requiring further development.

[118] Disaster Aid Survey Respondent, October 28, 2013 10:59 a.m.
[119] Disaster Aid Survey Respondent, October 28, 2013 6:33 p.m.
[120] Disaster Aid Survey Respondent, October 28, 2013 9:27 p.m.
[121] Disaster Aid Survey Respondent, October 28, 2013 11:39 a.m.
[122] Disaster Aid Survey Respondent, April 27, 2013 5:23 a.m.
[123] Disaster Aid Survey Respondent, July 16, 2013 9:33 p.m.
[124] Disaster Aid Survey Respondent, October 28, 2013 7:13 p.m.
[125] Disaster Aid Survey Respondent, October 28, 2013 8:17 p.m.
[126] Disaster Aid Survey Respondent, May 08, 2013 11:01 p.m.
[127] Disaster Aid Survey Respondent, October 28, 2013 6:42 p.m.
[128] Disaster Aid Survey Respondent, May 01, 2013 4:40 a.m.

In the context of emergency conditions requiring rapid response where international relief is requested, arriving at a community-driven response is perhaps among the greatest challenges in the localization of relief work. One relief worker observed that:

> Relief requires timely delivery of urgent basic services. Our approach is based on enabling the local community to be the key driver of its own development (we are primarily a "training" organization using projects to help the people realize what they can do once they accept to work together. We never want to create dependency. In relief, we have to contribute financially a lot more than what we would normally consider desirable. Another challenge is to mobilize sufficient resources from the surrounding villages in the state. We [have been able] however [to] react faster than most international agencies because we were already there and the money and goods that we got were local. Our resources came mostly from the ... rural area. Money from the government took forever and with so many strings attached that we will not repeat [that approach].[129]

Other local respondents generally echoed the challenge of "coordination"[130] and "lack of ... involvement in decision making and information sharing" and general difficulties "working together [in] the field."[131]

Local aid workers also identified "bad experiences"[132] with "top down policies"[133] that result in "each actor tak[ing] his own path and communities not being considered."[134] Some comments such as "some system is better than no system" and "the main issue is to create understanding of the system and its usage by all"[135] seem to imply a belief on the part of some that convincing local communities to simply accept and adopt an external system – which in many instances may not fit with local realities – reflects a form of "participation." In the absence of collaboration, often a response is designed in a way that is "not necessarily made to meet the real problems of beneficiaries but ... rather meet[s] the will and objectives of donors regarding bilateral cooperation."[136] While improvement has been noted, one respondent observed that "integration of local state and non state actors remains minimal."[137]

[129] Disaster Aid Survey Respondent, November 05, 2013 4:44 a.m.
[130] Disaster Aid Survey Respondent, April 25, 2013 9:25 p.m.
[131] Disaster Aid Survey Respondent, October 29, 2013 6:56 p.m.
[132] Disaster Aid Survey Respondent, January 13, 2014 5:36 p.m.
[133] Ibid.
[134] Ibid.
[135] Disaster Aid Survey Respondent, January 13, 2014 4:01 p.m.
[136] Disaster Aid Survey Respondent, October 30, 2013 6:37 p.m.
[137] Disaster Aid Survey Respondent, October 28, 2013 7:13 p.m.

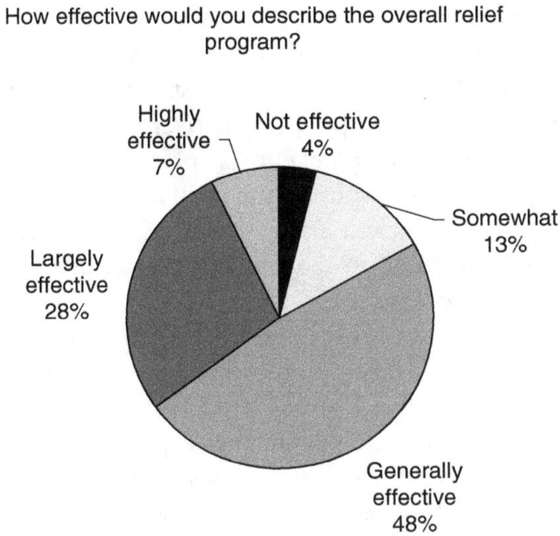

Figure 12.5 Program effectiveness.

Overall, the majority of survey participants viewed relief programs as "generally effective" (48 percent) or "somewhat effective" (13 percent). Only 7 percent viewed their relief program as "highly effective" (see Figure 12.5). These figures seem to indicate that while progress is being made in implementing collaborative, timely and targeted response programs, much remains to be learned about how such programs can be improved in the long term. The final section of this chapter examines suggestions relief workers made on improving the overall quality of disaster aid programs.

Conclusions

This chapter explored the attitudes and perceptions of practitioners working in the field of humanitarian aid and disaster response. The principal finding of this chapter based on survey data is that there is a statistically significant correlation between the level of engagement with a local community and perceived effectiveness of response. Given "the random nature of disasters and multiplicity of players makes comprehensive analysis difficult,"[138] and small sample size (n= 69), the purpose of the survey was

[138] Drabek and McEntire (2002), *supra* note 16.

not to provide generalizable findings, but rather to offer insights into how some practitioners are learning from the challenges of effectively engaging with communities in the wake of disaster response. Practitioners offered a number of suggestions for improving the overall quality of local–global coordination in humanitarian relief efforts, including local capacity building and training, logistical support at the local level, improvement in networking and coordination, initiating planning at the community level, accountability and information sharing and greater attention to cultural sensitivity and language.

The origins and effects of disasters are "global and local at the same time,"[139] and reflect the "the humanitarian impulse (Sarat and Lezaun 2009) to care for people after disaster."[140] At the same time, "non governmental organizations have globalized the response to disaster." Yet the nature and quality of response varies. "Presence"[141] at the international level is more often characterized by sheer and "mere" presence (involving "social visibility" and an "implicit and explicit show of international concern, resources and actions"),[142] while state action in some cases is moving toward greater peer presence (focused on "training [community members].")[143]

The findings also speak to the growing literature on resilience, reflecting that "emergency response teaches people that they must rely on each other, and ... that those who respond first to claims in disaster are neighbors."[144] At the same time, the findings reflect cautionary notes as described by critics of resilience policy that it not be a justification for an abdication of responsibility on the part of the state or a claw back of social welfare responsibilities,[145] or even a source of disempowerment.[146] The balancing of long-term policy aims of self-sufficiency with acute crisis support will need to remain at the forefront of policy research in years to come.

139 Ibid., p. 73.
140 Ibid., p. 13.
141 Coles (2007), *supra* note 5.
142 Ibid., p. 92.
143 Ibid., p. 108.
144 Sterett (2013), *supra* note 10, p. 13.
145 Ibid., p. 36.
146 Evans and Reid (2014), *supra* note 15.

13

Conclusions: Lessons Learned/Policy Suggestions

Our discussion of international, state and public-private relief efforts have provided insights into the importance of systematic efforts to meaningfully engage local populations in education, communications and planning in order to achieve sustainable, targeted and cost-effective outcomes. This concluding chapter summarizes key lessons from selected case studies and presents policy recommendations for improving the overall quality of local–global coordination in humanitarian relief efforts.

First, in examining case studies of international-led relief efforts, the distinctions between post-disaster approaches in Haiti and Indonesia provide some useful insights. While a variety of factors in Haiti, including high levels of social and economic inequality, poverty, malnutrition, unemployment and mortality,[1] all contributed to the challenges surrounding post-disaster relief efforts, these challenges were compounded by limited understanding of the local context, limited situation analysis, inequitable distribution of resources to earthquake-affected areas, nonalignment of resources with actual needs and harm to the local private sector. On the other hand, in Indonesia, following the 2004 tsunami where international institutions engaged individuals in a long-term process of decision making regarding redevelopment goals, resource use, materials and design through a "community-driven development strategy," projects achieved higher satisfaction and usage rates because they were developed on the basis of local knowledge of needs, resources and preferences. Local participation enabled quick response to the most urgent needs[2] and reduced the problem of marginalization.[3]

[1] Haiti Equality Collective. (2010). *Ensuring Haitian Women's Participation and Leadership in All Stages of National Relief and Reconstruction*. A Gender Shadow Report of the 2010 Haiti PDNA, 1. Available at www.genderaction.org/publications/2010/gsr.pdf (accessed on May 8, 2013).

[2] B. Dercon and M. Kusumawijaya. (2007). Two Years of Settlement Recovery in Aceh and Nias: What Should the Planners have Earned? 43rd ISOCARP Congress, Antwerp, Belgium.

[3] T. Ophiyandri, D. Amaratunga and C. Pathirage. (2010). Community Based Post Disaster Housing Reconstruction: Indonesian Perspective. CIB 2010 World Congress, May 10–13, 2010, Salford Quays, United Kingdom, p.13.

Second, in state-driven relief efforts, useful insights can also be drawn from comparing local engagement efforts in Japan and the United States following the Tohoku Earthquake and Tsunami of 2011 and Hurricane Katrina of 2005. The key differences in these cases lie in variation between what might be described as a centralized, robust, unified response in the case of Japan and a factionalized and overlapping response in the case of the United States.[4] These differing features and approaches impacted the quality of local collaboration. In Japan, because local coordination centers originated at the municipal level, information dissemination, private sector collaboration and the development of response innovation tools were relatively closely coordinated with state agencies.[5] In contrast, the United States' Hurricane Katrina of 2005 revealed challenges associated with overlap of duties and lack of clarity as to the chain of response, resulting in delays and inefficiencies in the response effort. This, combined with reported instances of racial prejudice, compounded suffering and weakened relief efforts.

Finally, in the area of public–private partnerships, helpful insights can be drawn by examining the response of a village community in Myanmar following Cyclone Nargis and the work of SecondMuse in grassroots crowd-designed open-data platforms for disaster response. These community decision-making approaches emphasizing partnership, collaboration, sharing of resources, efficiency and, local access to and creation of knowledge resulted in positive examples of harnessing the "power of mass collaboration" in the case of SecondMuse and timely, unified, efficient and rapid recovery in the case of a Myanmar village.

This chapter ends with policy suggestions derived from practitioner survey input aimed at improving the overall quality of local–global coordination in humanitarian relief efforts at the international, state and public/private levels. These suggestions fell in the categories of local capacity

[4] For discussion on fragmentation and adversarialism in the United States, see Robert A. Kagan. (2003). *Adversarial Legalism and American Government: The American Way of Life*. Harvard University Press.

[5] Scholars have also highlighted significant shortcomings and challenges in relation to Japan's compensation policy. See, for example, Eric A. Feldman. (2013). *Fukushima: Catastrophe, Compensation, and Justice in Japan. DePaul Law Review*. 62, 335; Daniel Farber. (2012). Introduction: Legal Scholarship, The Disaster Cycle, and the Fukushima Accident. *Duke Environmental Law & Policy Forum*. 23, 1; Joel Rheuben. (2014). Government Liability for Regulatory Failure in the Fukushima Disaster: A Common Law Comparison. *Pacific Rim Law & Policy Journal*. 23, 113; Harold S. Yun. (2015). Fukushima and New Zealand v. France Nuclear Tests: Can Japan be Brought to the International Court of Justice for Damages Caused by the Fukushima Plants? *Minnesota Journal of International Law*. 387.

building and training, logistical support at the local level, improvement in networking and coordination, initiating planning at the community level, accountability and information sharing and greater attention to cultural sensitivity and language.

Indonesia and Haiti: Recognizing the Importance of Local Knowledge and Institutions

In comparing lessons learned from Indonesia and Haiti with regard to the international coordination of relief efforts, some key lessons can be learned. Implementation of the community-driven development process (CDD) whereby local representatives engaged in a long-term consultation process to determine relief priorities, design and approaches led to advances in response time to the most urgent needs,[6] efficiency and reduction of marginalization.[7] In addition, projects adopting a CDD model were completed eighteen months ahead of schedule, produced more output than any other program and cost 56 percent less than programs adopting a conventional approach.[8]

It was through the crisis of Indonesia's tsunami in 2004 that the importance of local knowledge and institutions was demonstrated. Given the high degree of familiarity with the local environment, resources and talents, engaged community members were in a position to assess loss and damage. Reconstruction and development programs, customized to fit local norms, conditions, constraints and capacities, were found to be more efficient, effective and sustainable in the long term.[9]

Engagement with local governments had to be developed and sustained through regular contact and interaction. Skills and capabilities were developed through training, technical assistance and mentoring. International agencies that lacked contextual knowledge and local language skills benefited from the involvement of local governments.[10] Assisting national and local governments to build disaster management capacities rather than simply to deliver resources as requested at both national and local levels led to sustainable outcomes. Capacities were developed in the areas of planning, procurement, meeting facilitation, mediation and conflict resolution,

[6] Dercon and Kusumawijaya (2007), *supra* note 2.

[7] Ophiyandri, Amaratunga and Pathirage (2010), *supra* note 3.

[8] World Bank Group. (2009, December). *Five Years after the Tsunami: Continuing the Commitment to Reconstruction*, p. 23.

[9] Ibid.

[10] Ibid.

accounting and reporting, auditing, monitoring and evaluation. Further, communities' capacity to plan and carry out future self-help projects was improved. Following the implementation of World Bank CDD initiatives, improvement were made in terms of physical infrastructure and social capital beyond the pre-disaster level.[11]

An enabling environment was also fostered by increasing advocacy for freedom of expression, women's rights and vulnerable groups. Meeting facilities were provided, and village government offices were better enabled to plan for and coordinate these meetings through better execution and implementation of such programs.[12]

With greater participatory processes, greater transparency and accountability was achieved. In allowing participation and empowering communities to make decisions at different stages of the rebuilding process, continual transparency and accountability was achieved. This resulted in increased confidence and a sense of responsibility.[13]

As a result, in communities implementing the CDD approach in Indonesia, the occupancy rate for housing built by such programs was 97 percent, whereas that of similar houses built by other programs was more than 10 percent lower. Where local institutions were engaged directly in the rebuilding process, capacity was built, which was key to the true and sustainable recovery of the affected communities.[14] At the same time, in areas that did not directly and systematically draw on community input, many rebuilt homes had to be demolished and replaced by a new road.[15] Such incidents reflected poor levels of understanding regarding the needs of the community and also led to a waste of funds.[16]

In contrast, in Haiti, despite the approximately 3.5 billion dollars international aid inflow into Haiti[17] due to high levels of social and economic inequality, poverty, malnutrition, unemployment and mortality,[18]

[11] Ibid.

[12] Ibid.

[13] Ibid.

[14] Aceh Community Assistance Research Project. (2007). *The Acehnese Gampong Three Years On: Assessing Local Capacity and Reconstruction Assistance in Post-tsunami Aceh.*

[15] I. MacKinnon. (2008, August 15). Indonesia: Aceh Villagers Face Homelessness Again – in Name of Tsunami Aid from US government. *The Guardian.* Retrieved from www.guardian.co.uk/world/2008/aug/15/tsunami2004.naturaldisasters.

[16] J. Levs. (2012, April 11). Tsunami Scare Tests New Life-Saving Procedures. *CNN.* Retrieved from http://edition.cnn.com/2012/04/11/world/asia/indonesia-earthquake-differences/index.html.

[17] http://fts.unocha.org/reports/daily/OCHA_R24_E15939.XLS and source: http://fts.unocha.org/reports/daily/OCHA_R24_E15797.XLS

[18] Haiti Equality Collective (2010), *supra* note 1.

alongside an international engagement approach that reflected limited understanding of the local context, limited situation analysis, inequitable distribution of resources to earthquake-affected areas, nonalignment of resources with actual needs and harm to the local private sector who was driven out due to the availability of free international aid-supported alternatives, communities in Haiti continue to suffer from the effects of the disaster more than five years after the earthquake struck in 2010.

The head of OCHA following the aftermath of the Haitian earthquake noted that "[t]he humanitarian community simply cannot afford not to work with national and local structures, to the fullest extent possible, however daunting and complex an operation may be."[19] Local capacity assessment and participatory and community-based approaches should be used not only in the sectorial needs assessment but also during the analysis, planning, monitoring and response stages.[20]

In regards to communication and consultation with the disaster-affected communities, the UN should ensure that the input of the supported populations is comprehensive and targeted.[21] Methods need to be developed that allow entities to identify the most vulnerable in a disaster operation and enable them to distinguish between those directly and indirectly affected by the disaster (i.e., the rural populations supporting their relatives) and those suffering from more systemic forms of deprivation.[22] Response to disasters on the scale experienced in Haiti requires decentralized relief and recovery strategies[23] in small geographically defined units instead of through central command. This approach requires building strong relationships with individuals in the respective communities.[24]

[19] John Holmes. (2010, October). Learning the Lessons of Haiti. *Humanitarian Exchange Magazine*. 48, 1, 3.

[20] See OCHA. (2011, July 13). OCHA's Management Response Plan MR to Internally Mandated Evaluation of OCHA Response to the Haiti Earthquake, available at https://ochanet.unocha.org/p/Documents/Haiti_Internal_Evaluation_31JUL2011.pdf (accessed May 5, 2013).

[21] Paul O'Hagan, Katy Love and Angela Rouse. (2010, October). An Independent Joint Evaluation of the Haiti Earthquake Humanitarian Response. *CARE, Save the Children and the Emergency Capacity Building Project*, p. 4. Retrieved from www.alnap.org/pool/files/1192.pdf.

[22] Holmes (2010), *supra* note 19, p. 3.

[23] Melanie Teff and Emilie Parry. (2010, October 6). Haiti: Still Trapped in the Emergency Phase. *Field Report*, Refugees International, p. 4. Retrieved from www.refugeesinternational.org/policy/field-report/haiti-still-trapped-emergency-phase.

[24] See Elizabeth Ferris and Sara Ferro-Ribeiro. (2012, March). *Protecting People in Cities: The Disturbing Case of Haiti*. The Brookings Institute, p. 14. Retrieved from www.brookings.edu/research/articles/2012/03/protection-haiti-ferris, pointing out that the protection cluster developed a more decentralized approach to coordination to enable a more

International cooperation and coordination must engage first with governmental institutions instead of international NGOs given their understanding of local language, culture and context.[25] To reach this goal, cluster meetings ought to be held in governmental premises and coordinators may be sufficiently briefed on the local context and required to have the competence to facilitate building relationships with the government and municipalities.[26]

Local NGOs, grassroots organizations and organized camp leadership must be brought into the recovery, transition and implementation planning processes.[27] The appointment of civil society liaison officers can help to bridge the gap between the UN and civil society movements.[28] It is also suggested that aid workers take local capacity into account and collaborate wherever possible with local commercial providers. At the same time, the humanitarian community needs to be careful to not compete unfairly with the local private sector.[29] In regards to local procurement, humanitarian practitioners would benefit from both assessment of existing local capacity and clearer mechanisms for engaging with the private sector to support the provision and distribution of assistance.[30] For instance, a systematic "Haiti first" policy could be implemented, committing UN agencies and international NGOs to procure locally whenever possible.[31] In regards

efficient, integrated and timely response to protection cases at the community level. The approach has successfully facilitated the inclusion of local government. By the same token, when Oxfam switched to this method, *communities welcomed the possibility to know individual staff and express their opinions much more freely, leading to a more accountable and appropriate response*; Jane Cocking and Andy Bastable. (2010, October). Water, Sanitation and Public Health Reflections on Oxfam's Experience. *Humanitarian Exchange Magazine*. 48, 22.

25 Abhijit Bhattacharjee and Roberta Lossio. (2011, January). *Evaluation of OCHA Response to the Haiti Earthquake – Final Report*, p. 32. Retrieved from https://ochanet.unocha.org/p/Documents/Evaluation of OCHA Response to the Haiti Earthquake.pdf.

26 OCHA, Evaluations Synthesis Report, 5 OCHA Occasional Policy Briefing Series 16 (Feb. 2011) p. 2.

27 Ibid.

28 Teff and Parry (2010), *supra* note 23, p. 4.

29 O'Hagan, Love and Rouse (2010), *supra* note 21, p. 4.

30 See Stephanie Julmy. (2011, February). Coordinating the Earthquake Response: Lessons from Leogane, Western Haiti. *Humanitarian Exchange Magazine*. 49, 27. Retrieved from www.odihpn.org/humanitarian-exchange-magazine/issue-49/coordinating-the-earthquake-response-lessons-from-leogane-western-haiti.

31 See Clarine Clermont, David Sanderson, Anusha Sharma and Helen Spraos et al. (2011, March). Urban Disasters – Lessons from Haiti: Study of Member Agencies' Responses to the Earthquake in Port au Prince, Haiti, January 2010. *Report for the Disasters Emergency*

to unfair competition with the local private sector, cluster lead agencies should hold special meetings to analyze the negative side effects of free services and goods in the respective private sectors and develop common mitigation strategies[32] and look for effective and sustainable methods to support and collaborate with local talent.

In addition, "cluster meetings must be accessible to civil society and camp leadership, both in terms of location, entry, and language."[33] For any relief effort to benefit the most vulnerable, a reduction of bureaucratic, legal and administrative impediments is necessary. One possible approach to make cluster meetings more inclusive would be to embed clusters within technical ministries.[34] Accordingly, this would facilitate the cluster inclusion in the government structure as the ultimate goal. Alternatively, clusters could be co-led by the government.[35] An even more inclusive approach would be to train civil society leaders in the relevant skills of humanitarian cluster administration to ultimately enable them to co-lead every cluster.[36]

Finally, the perennial challenge of both balancing short-term needs with long-term solutions and strengthening linkages between relief and longer-term recovery and development requires further monitoring and evaluation.[37] In this regard, initiatives such as the People First Impact Method (P-FIM)[38] or the ECB Project's Good Enough Guide[39] provide measures for greater community-based work. These methodologies can help improve communication with communities and facilitate appropriate, responsive and self-reliant processes.[40] Progressio's advocacy

Committee (DEC), p. 10. Retrieved from www.dec.org.uk/sites/default/files/files/Evaluations/Haiti/DEC-Haiti-urban-study.pdf.

32 OCHA, *supra* note 26, at 17.

33 Teff and Parry (2010), *supra* note 23, p. 4.

34 Ibid.

35 Bhattacharjee and Lossio, supra note 25, p. 31.

36 Margaret L. Satterthwaite. (2011, May 6). Indicators in Crisis: Rights-Based Humanitarian Indicators in Post-earthquake Haiti. *N.Y.U. Journal of International Law and Politics*. 43, NYU School of Law, Public Law Research Paper No. 11–26, pp. 79–80. Retrieved from http://ssrn.com/abstract=1833530.

37 Holmes (2010), *supra* note 19, p. 3.

38 See P-FIM, ©People First Impact Method. 2010. Available at www.p-fim.org/ (accessed on May 13, 2013).

39 ECB, Emergency Capacity Building, The Good Enough Guide. Available at: www.ecbproject.org/the-good-enough-guide/the-good-enough-guid (accessed on May 13, 2013).

40 O'Hagan, Love and Rouse (2010), *supra* note 21, p. 28.

coordinator for Latin America and the Caribbean, Lizzette Robleto, sums this lesson up:

> Haitian people from all layers of Haitian society must be consulted at every stage of their country's reconstruction and renewal – now and long into the future.[41]

Japan and the United States: Centralization and Fragmentation

Through examination of state-driven relief efforts, in particular comparing the response of Japan and the United States to recent disasters, the difference between a centralized state policy as in the case of Japan[42] and a factionalized, divergent response clouded at times by prejudice as in the case of the United States demonstrates the important role of state institutions in coordinating with local actors. These differing features and approaches impacted the quality of local collaboration.

Since post-disaster coordination occurs at the municipal level in Japan and links up directly with state agencies, having a local team of trained disaster responders formed by local residents helped provide a focal point for coordinating volunteering efforts in the Tohoku Earthquake and Tsunami of 2011.[43] Since community residents could draw on local knowledge and provide a direct source for disseminating information, drawing on this capacity among local residents was vital. The private sector also played an important role in supporting recovery efforts by investing in enhanced scientific research tools to help communities better understand potential risks and effects of disasters.[44]

[41] Progressio. (2010, April 12). Three Months On: Haiti Must Not Miss Opportunity to Build "Just and Inclusive Society." Press Release. Available at www.progressio.org.uk/blog/news/three-months-haiti-must-not-miss-opportunity-build-%E2%80%9Cjust-and-inclusive%E2%80%9D-society (accessed on April 15, 2013).

[42] Scholars have also highlighted significant shortcomings and challenges in relation to Japan's compensation policy. See, for example, Eric A. Feldman (2013). Fukushima: Catastrophe, Compensation, and Justice in Japan. *DePaul Law Review* 62, 335; Daniel Farber. (2012). Introduction: Legal Scholarship, the Disaster Cycle, and the Fukushima Accident. *Duke Environmental Law & Policy Forum* 23, 1; Joel Rheuben. (2014). Government Liability for Regulatory Failure in the Fukushima Disaster: A Common Law Comparison. *Pacific Rim Law & Policy Journal* 23, 113; Yun, *supra* note 5.

[43] J. J. Carafano (2012). *The Great Eastern Japan Earthquake: Assessing Disaster Response and Lessons for the United States*. Washington, DC: The Heritage Foundation, p. 8.

[44] G20 Disaster Risk Management Report. (2012). *Improving the Assessment of Disaster Risks to Strengthen Financial Resilience: A Special Joint G20 Publication by the Government of*

The localized creation of hazard maps and knowledge regarding their effective use at the municipal and local level was also critical.[45] Social policies that promoted education and awareness among citizens helped build understanding of how risk and damage could be minimized. Distribution of safety information materials and regular drills at the community level were also important in the preventative and preparatory stages of response.

In contrast, the United States' Hurricane Katrina of 2005 revealed challenges associated with overlap of duties and lack of clarity as to the chain of response resulting in delays and inefficiencies. This is not to say that civic engagement was not robust among local residents. In particular, following Katrina, observers have noted that "now [residents] show up in force when policy is being made and the city's future is being charted."[46] Coordination, however, between state and local agencies remains an area for continued learning. National-level agencies had to clarify the National Response Plan to avoid duplication in relief efforts, while emergency management agencies required greater clarification of internal roles and responsibilities.[47] Following a review of the response efforts, a working group was recommended to better coordinate emergency relief preparedness and response among various officials and authorities, including FEMA, the DHS, the US Coast Guard and the Department of Defense's related entities, such as NORTHCOM.[48] A more intense and comprehensive training scheme to train both existing and new personnel as well as to ensure that staff were fully aware of their responsibilities was developed as a result.[49] Such training programs, it is suggested, can be supplemented

Mexico and the World Bank. Washington, DC: International Bank for Reconstruction and Development.

45 K. Suganuma. (2006). Recent Trends in Earthquake Disaster Management in Japan. *Quarterly Review*. 19, 91, p.105. Retrieved from www.houseoffoust.com/edano/Scribble_Japan_Earthquake/pdfs%5CSTTqr1907.pdf.

46 Rebecca Solnit. (2015, August). In the Shadow of the Storm. *Harpers Magazine*, Archive.

47 See William L. Waugh. (2006). The Political Costs of Failure in the Katrina and Rita Disasters. *The ANNALS of the American Academy of Political and Social Science*. 604, 10, 12.

48 Larry Irons. (2005, August). Hurricane Katrina as a Predictable Surprise. *Homeland Security Affairs*. 1(2), 14. Available at www.hsaj.org/?article=1.2.7 (accessed on April 15, 2013).

49 U.S. Government Accountability Office. (2006). *Hurricane Katrina: Better Plans and Exercises Needed to Guide the Military's Response to Catastrophic Natural Disasters*. Washington, DC: U.S. Government Accountability Office, p. 35. Available at www.gao.gov/new.items/d06643.pdf (accessed on May 3, 2013); U.S. Government Accountability Office. (2006). *Expedited Assistance for Victims of Hurricanes Katrina and Rita: FEMA's Control Weaknesses Exposed the Government to Significant Fraud and Abuse*. Washington, DC: U.S. Government Accountability Office, pp. 4–6. Available at www.gao.gov/new.items/d06655.pdf (accessed on May 3, 2013).

with programs to raise awareness about prejudices and stereotypes that have resulted in clouded decision making and ineffective relief efforts.

The importance of local governments in disaster prevention was thus recognized. Emergency preparedness and response schemes should be fully integrated with state and local government officials.[50] National agencies should, in the future, develop a scheme to assess the capability of state and local authorities to respond to severe disasters without federal assistance. The design of a case management scheme that would be responsive to the needs of applicants and systematize the training, selection and deployment of responders is also necessary.[51] Priority can be placed on analysis of new methods and technology to verify damage, occupancy and ownership, when traditional methods of inspection are not responsive in providing assistance in a timely manner.[52] In addition, some have suggested that an advisory council be constituted by state, local officials and first responders, to ensure that necessary actions are implemented with regard to emergency planning and preparedness.[53] Information management systems that would allow responders to track and share information more openly and more efficiently could be standardized.[54] As noted by one observer, "the fallout from the storm prompted soul-searching, transformation and reform. Many things have been gained in the years since, but only after so much was lost."[55]

[50] Bill Bytheway. (2007, March 15). *The Evacuation of Older People: The Case of Hurricane Katrina*. Available at http://understandingkatrina.ssrc.org/Bytheway/ (accessed on March 25, 2013); and Joseph Scanlon. (2006, June 11). *Two Cities, Two Evacuations: Some Thoughts on Moving People Out*. Available at http://understandingkatrina.ssrc.org/Scanlon/ (accessed on April 5, 2013).

[51] Ben Depoorter. (2006). Horizontal Political Externalities: The Supply and Demand of Disaster Management. *Duke Law Journal*. 56(3), 101, at passim; Marla Nelson et al. (2007). Planning, Plans, and People: Professional Expertise, Local Knowledge, and Governmental Action in Post-Hurricane Katrina New Orleans. The University of New Orleans. *Cityscape: A Journal of Policy Development and Research*. 9(3), 23, 35–37.

[52] U.S. Senate Committee on Homeland Security and Government Affairs. (2006). *Hurricane Katrina: A National Still Unprepared*. Washington, DC: U.S. Government Printing Office, p. 620. Retrieved from www.gpoaccess.gov/serialset/creports/katrinanation.html.

[53] Sheila R. Zedlewski. (2006, February). *Building a Better Safety Net for the New New Orleans*. Washington, DC: The Urban Institute. Available at www.urban.org/afterkatrina/ (accessed on April 7, 2013).

[54] Marshal L. Vanderford et al. (2007). Emergency Communication Challenges in Response to Hurricane Katrina: Lessons from the Centers for Disease Control and Prevention. *Journal of Applied Communication Research*. 35(1), 9.

[55] Solnit (2015), *supra* note 46.

Public–Private Partnerships: A Myanmar Village and Second Muse

Finally, in the area of public–private partnerships, helpful insights can be drawn by examining the response of a village community in Myanmar following Cyclone Nargis and the work of SecondMuse in grassroots crowd-designed open-data platforms for disaster response. These community decision-making approaches emphasizing partnership, collaboration, sharing of resources, efficiency and local access to and creation of knowledge resulted in positive examples of harnessing the "power of mass collaboration" in the case of SecondMuse and timely, unified, efficient and rapid recovery in the case of a village in Myanmar.

In the case of Myanmar's cyclone disaster, community cohesion and consultation were essential to successful recovery program implementation.[56] This was demonstrated by a small community where preexisting capacity for consultation enabled careful planning and systematic and coordinated follow up with only modest targeted loans.[57] The story of the Myanmar village reflects an example of how community-based partnerships building on existing structures of collaboration led to the saving of many lives and a rapid and efficient recovery process. The local assembly organized "themselves to provide food and water for all people specially children and the elderly. They beg[a]n to assess the damage in properties and the number of people affected and lives lost."[58]

Due in large part to the strong community-based consultation skills developed through regular community meetings and an emphasis on unity that existed prior to the cyclone, the community has now largely recovered.

Alongside the example of the village in Myanmar, a growing number of public–private partnerships including those involved in the development of crowd source technology for humanitarian relief have emerged in recent years. The growing use of crowd source technology such as crowd mapping and resource tracking being universally accessible, collaboratively designed, subject to ongoing improvement and responsive to on-the-ground needs reflects in many respects the emerging UN governance mechanisms developed to support the creation of such technology.[59] These tools can harness

[56] Aceh Community Assistance Research Project (2007), *supra* note 14.

[57] See Chapter 9.

[58] Interview, Respondent Village June 15, 2013 regarding activities of the local Baha'i community.

[59] For complete discussion, see S. Ali. (2014). *Crowd Sourced Governance in a Post-disaster Context. International and Comparative Law Quarterly*, Cambridge University Press.

the power of mass collaboration to quickly aggregate, gather, translate, geolocate, publish and distribute information about urgent needs, using cloud-, crowd- and SMS-based technologies.[60]

The experience of SecondMuse in facilitating collaborative innovation and assisting individuals and organizations to access inspiration using collaboration processes supported by technology and social media has led to insights into how such partnerships can advance understanding and communication.[61]

Supporting a growing culture of global reflection and learning are among the key contributions of SecondMuse and its partners. For example, in a project called *Understanding Risk* coordinated with the World Bank to engage thousands of technical experts and practitioners from more than 130 countries around the world in sharing their experiences in preparing for and responding to natural disasters, the collaborative online global community served as a forum to enable practitioners from diverse backgrounds and across disciplines to share ideas and to spur the development and use of new innovations and technologies in the field of disaster risk.[62]

It is clear that there is a shifting emphasis toward greater collaboration with the private sector in developing technology for humanitarian efforts. This trend reflects insights from new governance literature as discussed in Chapter 1 on the role of expanded participation and partnership on the part of governments and non-state actors in solving public problems; a learning-focused orientation; and the role of the state as a convener, catalyst and coordinator. For instance, according to UNCTAD, in the realm of disaster response and development "much of the required investment will come from the private sector. Experience shows that the private sector has been the most innovative player and the major driving force behind e-business and ICT development."[63] Therefore, an approach that merges public action with private-sector initiative in a mutually supportive manner will contribute to a more effective response.[64]

[60] UN Foundation. (2011). *Disaster Relief 2.0*. Available at www.unfoundation.org/assets/pdf/disaster-relief-20-report.pdf (accessed on March 19, 2014).

[61] SecondMuse. (2012). *What Are We Up To*. Available at www.secondmuse.com/ (accessed March 19, 2014).

[62] Ibid., p. 44.

[63] UNCTAD. (2004). *Partnership for Development: Information and Knowledge for Development*, pp. 6–7. Available at unctad.org/en/docs/td394_en.pdf (accessed on March 19, 2014).

[64] Ibid.

Policy Recommendations for Improving the Quality of Local–Global Coordination in Relief Efforts: Survey Findings

In addition to the findings of these studies exploring the dynamics of local response to natural disasters, survey respondents provided insights into the dynamics, challenges and lessons learned from the perspective of those engaged in the work of post-disaster relief.[65]

Given the challenges in localized disaster response, practitioners at the international, state and local levels had a number of suggestions for improving the overall quality of local–global coordination in humanitarian relief efforts. These suggestions fell in the categories of local capacity building and training, logistical support at the local level, improvement in networking and coordination, initiating planning at the community level, accountability and information sharing and greater attention to cultural sensitivity and language.

Local Training and Capacity Building

The need for greater capacity building in coordination, planning and disaster preparedness and risk reduction at the local level was highlighted by at least eight survey respondents. One respondent noted that "capacity building programs [should focus on assisting] local [communities] to be able to collaborate with international organizations."[66] This would include training in "strategic decision making" to enable "more involvement in strategic [planning]."[67] Elaborating further, one respondent suggested that relief organizations:

> "1)... require... participation beyond the six-week mark of a disaster. 2) focus more on cash for work, and make sure local agencies are well-trained in delivery of such activities. 3) Work with local agencies to build their capacity in ... complaints management. 4) Convince the biggest players that they must treat concerns of implementing agencies who remain after the end of disaster response as significant and use them to inform responses."[68]

Other recommendations focused on decentralized training and developing local resources. One respondent suggested that the "focus [should

[65] For additional discussion, see S. Ali. (2015). Toward Peer Presence in Post-disaster Governance: An Empirical Study. *Hastings Journal of International and Comparative Law.* 38 (Summer), 243–274.

[66] Disaster Aid Survey Respondent, November 04, 2013 9:32 p.m.

[67] Disaster Aid Survey Respondent, October 28, 2013 8:17 p.m.

[68] Disaster Aid Survey Respondent, December 05, 2013 8:15 p.m.

be] on leadership [with]in [the] country."[69] Efforts should be made to "promote HR from around the world and not just the global north."[70] In addition, the focus should be on "systemic decentralized decision making for response."[71] Another suggested the need for ongoing training "throughout the country ...[of] possible facilitators such as schoolteachers or community leaders [in] disaster preparedness and action plan[ning]."[72] Highlighting the significance of local capacity building, one relief worker noted, "local capacity building for disaster risk reduction is critical for effective disaster response."[73]

Greater Logistical Support and Information Sharing at the Local Level

In addition to training and capacity building, several respondents highlighted the need for enhanced logistical support and improvement in access to necessary supplies at the local level. In particular, "stock and medicine and food" as well as "supporting volunteers"[74] were regarded as key needs. Using locally sourced goods "based on the real needs of people on the ground using locally [placed] human and material resources"[75] should "be among the factors to be given high priority."[76] One aid worker noted the need for "reform of funding channels [and] more reliable and long-term support [rather than an] outdated ... project [based approach]" and "increase[d] meaningful participation of target groups."[77]

Several respondents believed that disaster response could be improved by "more attention to data [collection]"[78] and "improved data sharing."[79] Such improvements would enhance "accountability and transparency"[80] by having a "more open and [transparent]... coordination"[81] process. Accountability, some aid workers suggested, could be enhanced by the use of "accountability benchmarks"[82] such as "HAP / Sphere / People in

69 Disaster Aid Survey Respondent, December 02, 2013 3:02 p.m.
70 Ibid.
71 Ibid.
72 Disaster Aid Survey Respondent, January 13, 2014 6:15 p.m.
73 Disaster Aid Survey Respondent, November 12, 2013 2:32 p.m.
74 Disaster Aid Survey Respondent, January 13, 2014 6:07 p.m.
75 Disaster Aid Survey Respondent, December 06, 2013 7:51 p.m.
76 Disaster Aid Survey Respondent, December 05, 2013 8:26 p.m.
77 Disaster Aid Survey Respondent, October 28, 2013 6:40 p.m.
78 Disaster Aid Survey Respondent, May 10, 2013 4:13 a.m.
79 Disaster Aid Survey Respondent, May 01, 2013 4:38 a.m.
80 Disaster Aid Survey Respondent, January 13, 2014 5:43 p.m.
81 Disaster Aid Survey Respondent, January 13, 2014 4:25 p.m.
82 Disaster Aid Survey Respondent, January 13, 2014 3:42 p.m.

Aid."[83] Likewise, training in such aid benchmarks (including "Sphere, INEE MS, ALNAP, HAP People in Aid, etc.) and codes of conduct"[84] would improve "evidence based planning and implementation."[85]

Improvements in Networking and Coordination

Most respondents had specific suggestions for improving networking and coordination among various actors in disaster relief. One noted a need for "a more integrated but decentralized approach" in which "beneficiary involvement should be central" and "community based organizations must share a consultative platform with international NGO's and institutions engaged in relief."[86] This is especially challenging in situations where "humanitarian aid is needed most" and "the local / national infrastructure is missing or is not functioning ... The challenge is to offer and deliver humanitarian aid but within the limits of [a] country's sovereignty."[87] However, reflecting a top-down approach to the concept of "participation" as consisting of "incorporating" local leaders into preexisting "organizational discussion and decision-making,"[88] without engaging such members in the design of such organizations, indicates that a gap still exists in achieving genuine participation in access to and generation of knowledge.

One respondent noted a need for organizations to "collaborate and work more together, than separate" and to "be more efficient and prevent too many NGO's [from being] in one place while other [areas] are not receiving help."[89] In this respect, "hybrid networking"[90] including "vertical and horizontal coordination and information sharing"[91] can be explored. It was also recommended that coordination processes be simplified by using "technology to reduce cost"[92] and "be made mandatory at all levels, most importantly at the headquarter levels."[93]

[83] Disaster Aid Survey Respondent, January 13, 2014 3:42 p.m.
[84] Disaster Aid Survey Respondent, October 29, 2013 6:56 p.m.
[85] Ibid.
[86] Disaster Aid Survey Respondent, January 13, 2014 4:18 p.m.
[87] Disaster Aid Survey Respondent, April 27, 2013 5:23 a.m.
[88] Ibid.
[89] Disaster Aid Survey Respondent, January 13, 2014 5:00 p.m.
[90] Disaster Aid Survey Respondent, January 13, 2014 5:58 p.m.
[91] Disaster Aid Survey Respondent, January 13, 2014 5:05 p.m.
[92] Disaster Aid Survey Respondent, January 13, 2014 4:18 p.m.
[93] Disaster Aid Survey Respondent, May 04, 2013 8:12 p.m.

Information sharing and centralization through "one coordination node"[94] and "standardization in assessment formats" was suggested.[95] Other respondents similarly noted the need for "improved coordination,"[96] particularly in "effective planning and implementation"[97] and "monitoring and evaluation."[98] One noted, "I think one of the essential points is that a good discussion happens and a clear understanding [of] who is able to do what,"[99] including agreement on relief "procedures."[100] Careful "select[ion] of local partners"[101] was also highlighted, along with the need to "establ[ish] a formal space and voice for the local [community] in response programming and management."[102] Some suggested that the local government might be in a "good position to host a platform to facilitate coordination in humanitarian relief efforts"[103] given the need for "a steering committee to coordinate all relief efforts."[104]

Some progress has been observed in relief coordination over the years. One respondent noted that "over the years I have been seeing massive improvement in response to disasters, more and more are [international] organizations (the UN mainly) with global forward operative bases located in key geographical areas [enabling] response [with]in hours."[105]

Initiating Planning at the Community Level

Perhaps the largest number of respondents had suggestions centering on improving local collaboration in post-disaster response efforts and "end[ing] client-patron relationships"[106] between international organizations and local actors and "involving partners at the beginning of planning."[107] One respondent noted that a "key element of [her organization's] success is 'being a local deeply rooted organization.'"[108] Similarly,

94 Disaster Aid Survey Respondent, December 16, 2013 10:04 p.m.
95 Ibid.
96 Disaster Aid Survey Respondent, December 02, 2013 3:21 a.m.
97 Ibid.
98 Ibid.
99 Disaster Aid Survey Respondent, October 30, 2013 7:42 p.m.
100 Disaster Aid Survey Respondent, November 20, 2013 11:59 p.m.
101 Disaster Aid Survey Respondent, October 28, 2013 6:42 p.m.
102 Disaster Aid Survey Respondent, October 28, 2013 10:59 a.m.
103 Disaster Aid Survey Respondent, May 17, 2013 12:50 a.m.
104 Disaster Aid Survey Respondent, June 15, 2013 10:23 a.m.
105 Disaster Aid Survey Respondent, April 26, 2013 11:14 p.m.
106 Disaster Aid Survey Respondent, October 28, 2013 11:39 a.m.
107 Disaster Aid Survey Respondent, May 07, 2013 7:21 p.m.
108 Disaster Aid Survey Respondent, November 05, 2013 4:44 a.m.

an aid worker put it succinctly: "the people/communities effected must lead the way. Paternalism is ineffective and unacceptable."[109] Another respondent noted "always start with the local community first and maintain ongoing open communication as much as possible, while maintaining a system of accountability."[110] Such community-focused planning arises out of a sense of "respect for local staff involve[d] in community priority setting."[111]

Specific suggestion on how to facilitate increased local collaboration centered on creative use of technology, mandating participation in cluster meetings and giving funding leverage to local actors. For example, one aid worker suggested "local involvement should be mandated by the UN for all activities ... Those at [the] global level should be held accountable for involvement at [the] local level."[112] One respondent suggested "replac[ing] bureaucratic information flows and decision making for a distributed knowledge / crowd sourced system focusing on ensuring access and usability."[113] Another emphasized developing accountability mechanisms such that affected communities become "the stakeholders for their own development – [they should] set their own priorities (beyond health and safety); allow locally affected people a mechanism to hold aid agencies accountable [for] providing or not providing the required aid."[114] Putting this into practice, one respondent suggested that it is important to "ensure there is a reason for international organizations to engage in coordination by providing the local organization with more leverage over the international organizations."[115] Encouraging community "participation in cluster meetings"[116] was also suggested as a way of increasing local input.

The objective of locally based planning is that through such partnership, rather than "simply providing relief and then leaving ... the local [community] should be able to sustain [the programs] by themselves."[117] One respondent noted that state and civil society actors should be "in the driver's seat, taking the example of development cooperation."[118]

[109] Disaster Aid Survey Respondent, April 25, 2013 9:25 p.m.
[110] Disaster Aid Survey Respondent, January 13, 2014 5:51 p.m.
[111] Disaster Aid Survey Respondent, May 01, 2013 8:44 p.m.
[112] Disaster Aid Survey Respondent, May 01, 2013 4:44 a.m.
[113] Disaster Aid Survey Respondent, January 13, 2014 5:36 p.m.
[114] Disaster Aid Survey Respondent, January 13, 2014 4:52 p.m.
[115] Disaster Aid Survey Respondent, October 30, 2013 9:15 p.m.
[116] Disaster Aid Survey Respondent, October 28, 2013 9:27 p.m.
[117] Disaster Aid Survey Respondent, January 13, 2014 3:37 p.m.
[118] Disaster Aid Survey Respondent, October 28, 2013 7:13 p.m.

Locally based planning also helps to ensure avoiding "the duplication of resources and programs" by "using local resources [and] local traditional knowledge."[119] It also serves to provide greater integration between long- and short-term planning, as one aid worker noted:

> we need to rethink and rework our current practice so that it becomes driven by locals. We also need to move beyond the artificial distinction between "relief" and "development." That smart, dedicated, well-intentioned, experienced people continue to insist on this divide indicates that we, as a field, have gone seriously off the rails.[120]

At the same time, the notion that those affected by disasters are merely "recipients" of "whatever is done in their communities"[121] rather than partners in redevelopment, again reflects the gap that exists between existing practices and genuine participation.

Perhaps more critical than disaster response is disaster preparedness at the local level. One respondent noted, "it is always good for international agencies to develop strong contingency plans with local organizations, particularly in areas vulnerable to disaster events. Whilst designing these plans it is important that local organizations have full ownership of these plans so that at the onset of an emergency event they are able to respond in an effective manner on an equal footing."[122]

While the majority of respondents agreed that locally based planning was critical, one respondent noted that in some cases, depending on the governance situation on the ground, if "local administration is hampered,"[123] then "international technical assistance [may]" provide additional support.[124] Another observed that "each case has to be dealt with in relation to loca[l] context … Challenges are always there as there are no identical situations. Studies, guidelines, protocols, policies are fine … but they need to be universal enough to guide the application process in each particular context, there is no universal solution for humanitarian challenges."[125] Furthermore, determining who represents the "local voice" must be considered carefully, as one aid worker noted:

> A trained local elite in some settings could be better connected to global thinking and pre-conceptions than to local communities and therefore are

[119] Disaster Aid Survey Respondent, November 29, 2013 4:51 p.m.
[120] Disaster Aid Survey Respondent, May 08, 2013 11:01 p.m.
[121] Ibid.
[122] Disaster Aid Survey Respondent, November 25, 2013 11:23 p.m.
[123] Disaster Aid Survey Respondent, November 18, 2013 3:07 a.m.
[124] Ibid.
[125] Disaster Aid Survey Respondent, November 17, 2013 7:40 p.m.

not ideal for representing "local." Mechanisms need to be in place to avoid that this elite becomes a barrier for participation of the true "local."[126]

Attitudinal Frameworks: Cultural Sensitivity, Humility and a Learning Framework

The final set of suggestions can be grouped into what might be described as attitudinal frameworks for disaster response. These attitudes focused on a service orientation, humility and a learning approach to disaster response.

With regard to a service orientation, one aid worker suggested: "just be sincere [and] ... perform optimally in the best possible way."[127] With regard to cultural and language sensitivity, one aid worker noted that there is a need to "pay attention to context and culture (eg use of language), [and] consideration of [the] fact that one size does not fit all."[128] Another suggested the need for "more investment in real time translation services. Clusters [need] to make more effort to link to pre-existing networks. Invest and support national networks before [a] disaster, not just in the response phase."[129]

Finally, an attitude of learning was regarded as critical. In practice, this would mean "regular exchange of lesson learn[ed] and insight[s] gain[ed] among the humanitarian partners ... [and] engage local partner[s] and local communit[ies] with their traditional response skills and knowledge."[130]

Conclusion

A number of challenges continue to hamper effective global–local collaboration in disaster response. These include perceptions of those affected by disasters as "recipients" rather than partners in response and a top-down notion of participation as consisting convincing local communities to come on board with preexisting response programs. Case studies demonstrate that among the keys to overcoming these challenges is the long-term development of local capacity to access and generate local knowledge through consultation, multi-stakeholder decision making where cohesion

[126] Disaster Aid Survey Respondent, May 01, 2013 4:40 a.m.
[127] Disaster Aid Survey Respondent, January 13, 2014 5:26 p.m.
[128] Disaster Aid Survey Respondent, December 06, 2013 7:58 p.m.
[129] Disaster Aid Survey Respondent, October 28, 2013 11:24 a.m.
[130] Disaster Aid Survey Respondent, December 05, 2013 4:13 p.m.

is fostered. In particular, it has been observed that "project mechanisms that bring about peaceful conflict resolution can have positive spillover effects: they frequently lead to stronger intergroup relations, participation, and problem solving in the community."[131] The survey findings suggest that progress is being made in designing response efforts that give greater leverage to local participants in designing, implementing, procuring and monitoring relief efforts.

The principal finding of the empirical study of this book that there is a statistically significant correlation between the level of engagement with a local community and perceived effectiveness of response. Notwithstanding the randomness of disasters and "multiplicity of players [which] makes comprehensive analysis difficult,"[132] the policy suggestions included here call on policy makers to reflect on "who is the community" affected by displacement.[133] While disasters "humble the human effort to bring order to the world,"[134] continued efforts to research,[135] learn from and understand how to advance our response to natural disasters will support the ongoing development of community capacity to participate in "the generation"[136] of knowledge and the ability "to act upon such knowledge."[137] International, state, regional, private-sector and community actors all have an important role to play in advancing our understanding of how such networks can effectively collaborate at the local level to achieve a global, decentralized yet coordinated process of post-disaster humanitarian assistance.

[131] Patrick Barron and Rachael Diprose. (2011). *Contesting Development: Participatory Projects and Local Conflict Dynamics in Indonesia*. Yale University Press.

[132] T. E. Drabek and D. A. McEntire. (2002). Emergent Phenomena and Mulitorganizational Coordination in Disasters: Lessons from the Research Literature. *International Journal of Emergencies and Disasters* [online], 20 (2), 197–224. Available at http://ijmed.org/articles/574/download/ (accessed October 29, 2012).

[133] S. Sterrett and J. Reich. (2007). Prayer and Social Welfare: Race and Service after Hurricane Katrina. In H. Potter (Ed.), *Racing the Storm*. Lanham: Lexington Books, pp. 135–156.

[134] David D. Caron and Charles Leben. (2001). *The International Aspects of Natural and Industrial Catastrophes*. The Hague Academy of International Law: Martinus Nijhoff Publishers, pp. 3–4.

[135] See, for example, Herman B. Leonard. (2009). *Managing Crises: Responses to Large-Scale Emergencies* (coeditor and coauthor with Arnold M. Howitt) Washington, DC: CQ Press.

[136] Universal House of Justice. (2010). Ridvan Message 2010 (letter). Available at: http://universalhouseofjustice.bahai.org/ridvan-messages/20100421_001.

[137] Ibid., pp. 8–9.

SELECT BIBLIOGRAPHY

Abraham, D. S. (2011, March 16). How bad communication is undermining Japan's crisis response. *The Atlantic*. Retrieved from www.theatlantic.com/international/archive/2011/03/how-bad-communication-is-undermining-japans-crisis-response/72573/.

Aceh Community Assistance Research Project. (2007). *The Acehnese Gampong Three Years On: Assessing Local Capacity and Reconstruction Assistance in Post-tsunami Aceh*. Report of the Aceh Community Assistance Research Project (ACARP) December 2007.

Acemoglu, D. and Robinson, J. (2012). *Why Nations Fail*. New York: Crown.

Active Learning Network for Accountability and Performance in Humanitarian Action. (2007). Synthesis report: expanded summary – joint evaluation of the international response to the Indian Ocean Tsunami. *Tsunami Evaluation Coalition*. Retrieved from www.alnap.org/ourwork/tec.aspx.

ActionAid. (2011, October 27). Thailand floods – ActionAid's response. Retrieved from www.actionaid.org.uk/103061/thailand_floods___actionaids_response.html.

Agua Consult Ltd. Prepared for the European Commission's Directorate General for Humanitarian Aid, 30 May 2012, available at http://ec.europa.eu/echo/files/evaluation/2012/Participation_Final-Rep.pdf.

Ahdieh, Robert B. (2005). The Role of Groups in Norm Transformation: A Dramatic Sketch, in Three Parts. *Chicago Journal of International Law*, Vol. 6, 231.

(2007). From Federalism to Intersystemic Governance: The Changing Nature of Modern Jurisdiction. *Emory Law Journal*, Vol. 57, No. 1, 1–30.

Aldrich, Daniel P. and Crook, Kevin. (2008, September 1). Strong Civil Society as a Double-Edged Sword: Siting Trailers in Post-Katrina New Orleans. *Political Research Quarterly*, Vol. 61(3), 379–389. Retrieved from http://ssrn.com/abstract=960497.

Alexander, David. (2006). Globalization of Disaster: Trends, Problems and Dilemmas. *Journal of International Affairs*, Vol. 59(2), 1.

Alexander, Lisa T. (2009). Stakeholder Participation in New Governance: Lessons From Chicago's Public Housing Reform Experiment. *Georgetown Journal on Poverty Law & Policy*, Vol. 16, 117.

(2010). Reflections on Success and Failure in New Governance and the Role of the Lawyer. *Wisconsin Law Review Symposium Afterword*, 737–748.

Ali, Shahla F. (2010, March). Measuring Success in Devolved Collaboration. *Journal of Land Use & Environmental Law*, Vol. 26, 181–206. Retrieved from http://ssrn.com/abstract=1569339.

Ali, S. and Kabau, T. (2014). Self Governance by Humanitarian Non-State Actors in Health and Nutrition Relief. *Depaul Journal of Health Law*, 16.2, 141–164.

Allen, Troy D. (2007). Katrina: Race, Class, and Poverty: Reflections and Analysis. *Journal of Black Studies*, Vol. 37(4), 466.

Andrew, Wear. (2012). Collaborative Approaches to Regional Governance – Lessons from Victoria. *Australian Journal of Public Administration*, Vol. 71(4), 469.

Ansell, Chris. and Gash, Alison. (2007). Collaborative Governance in Theory and Practice. *Journal of Public Administration Research and Theory*. Vol 18(4), 543.

ANSI Homeland Security Standards Panel (HSSP). (2007, May 5). Lessons learned from Hurricane Katrina and the role for standards and conformity assessment programs. ANSI Publication. Retrieved from http://publicaa.ansi.org/sites/apdl/Documents/Standards Activities/Homeland Security Standards Panel/ANSI-HSSP Katrina Workshop Report.pdf.

AON Benfield. (2011). *Thailand Floods Event Recap Report*. Chicago: Impact Forecasting LLC.

Arroyo, Susan, Rodriguez, Martha and Prex, Ricardo. (2009). *Information Management and Communication in Emergencies and Disasters Manual for Disaster Response Teams*. Washington, DC: Pan American Health Organization.

Asian Development Bank. (2011, November 21). News release: ADB gives emergency support to Thailand after worst floods in over 50 years. Retrieved from http://th.one.un.org/presscentre/documents/Thailand_EmergencyAssistanceforFlooding_NR.pdf.

Association for Aid and Relief Japan (AAR). (2011, June 10). Three months since the Great East Earthquake: activity report. Retrieved from http://reliefweb.int/report/japan/three-months-great-east-japan-earthquake-activity-report.

Association of State and Territorial Health Officials (US), et al. (2006). States of preparedness: health agency progress 2006. Retrieved from www.tisp.org/index.cfm?pk=download&id=10980&pid=10261.

Association of State and Territorial Health Officials. (2008). Before the swarm: guidelines for the emergency management of mosquito-borne disease outbreaks. Retrieved from www.cdc.gov/ncidod/dvbid/westnile/resources/BeforetheSwarm.pdf.

Audet, François. (2011). What Future Role for Local Organizations? A Reflection on the Need for Humanitarian Capacity-Building. *International Review of the Red Cross*, Vol. 93(884), 1151.

Australian Red Cross. (2009). Five years on. Retrieved from www.redcross.org.au/asia-quake-and-tsunamis-disaster.aspx.

Austrian Development Cooperation. (2009). International humanitarian aid policy document. Retrieved from www.entwicklung.at/uploads/media/PD_International_humanitarian_aid_03.pdf.

Axelrod, Robert M. (1984). *The Evolution of Cooperation*. New York: Basic Books.

Ayuda a Haiti. (2010, March 18). Movimientos sociales haitianos denuncian su exclusión total en conferencia de donantes. Retrieved from http://plataforma-ayuda-haiti.blogspot.hk/2010/06/movimientos-sociales-haitianos.html (in Spanish).

Bakewell, Oliver. (2000). Uncovering Local Perspectives on Humanitarian Assistance and Its Outcomes. *Disasters*, Vol. 24(2), 103.

Banipal, Kulwinder. (2006). Strategic Approach to Disaster Management: Lessons Learned from Hurricane Katrina. *Disaster Prevention and Management*, Vol. 15(3), 484.

BAPPENAS. (2005). *Indonesia: Preliminary Damage and Loss Assessment: The December 26, 2004 Natural Disaster*. BAPPENAS and the International Donor Community.

Barber, Rebecca. (2009). Facilitating Humanitarian Assistance in International Humanitarian and Human Rights Law. *International Review of the Red Cross*, Vol. 91 (874), 371.

Barredo, Jose. (2007). Major Flood Disasters in Europe: 1950–2005. *Nat Hazards*. Vol. 42, 125.

Barron, Patrick and Diprose, Rachael. (2011). *Contesting Development: Participatory Projects and Local Conflict Dynamics in Indonesia*, New Haven, CT: Yale University Press.

Bass, Stephan, Ramasamy, Selvaraju, de Pryck, Jennie Dey and Battista, Federica. (2008) Disaster risk management systems analysis – a guide book. Rome: *Food and Agriculture Organization of the United Nations*. Retrieved from ftp://ftp.fao.org/docrep/fao/011/i0304e/i0304e.pdf.

BBC. (2011, October 22). Thailand floods: Crisis 'to last four to six weeks'. Retrieved from www.bbc.co.uk/news/world-asia-pacific-15413818.

Bea, Keith (coordinator). (2007, March 6). Federal emergency management policy changes after hurricane katrina: a summary of statutory provisions. Congressional Research Service. Retrieved from www.fas.org/sgp/crs/homesec/RL33729.pdf.

Bellah, Robert N., Madsen, Richard, Sullivan, William M., Swidler, A., Tipton, Steven M. (1985). *Habits of the Heart: Individualism and Collectivism in American Life*. New York: Harper and Row.

Bellavita, Christopher. (2005, August). Changing Homeland Security: An Opportunity for Competence. *Homeland Security Affairs*, Vol. 1(2), 63. Retrieved from www.hsaj.org/?article=1.2.5.

Bellerive, Jean Max. (2010, March). Haiti earthquake PDNA: assessment of damage, losses, general and sectoral needs. Annex to Government of the Republic of Haiti (2011, March), *The Action Plan for National Recovery and Development of Haiti*. Government of Haiti. Retrieved from www.kirkensnodhjelp.no/contentassets/ee77fa84ec654fb2a01ac3ea8f72bd98/haiti_action_eng.pdf.

Bernard, Vincent. (2011). Editorial: The Future of Humanitarian Action. *International Review of the Red Cross*, Vol. 93(884), 891.

Berry, A.W. (2012, March 22). 7 breakdowns in Haiti's rebuilding efforts: Haitians losing patience with camp life and poor governance as fundamental problems remain. Retrieved from www.globalpost.com/dispatches/globalpost-blogs/rights/haiti-rebuilding-7-breakdowns.

Beyrer, Chris, Suwanvanichkij, Voravit, Mullany, Luke C., Richards, Adam K., Franck, Nicole, Samuels, Aaron and Lee, Thomas J. (2006). Responding to AIDS, Tuberculosis, Malaria, and Emerging Infectious Diseases in Burma: Dilemmas of Policy and Practice. *PLOS Medicine*, Vol. 3(10), 1733.

Bhattacharjee, Abhijit and Lossio, Roberta. (2011, January). Evaluation of OCHA response to the Haiti earthquake – Final report. Retrieved from https://ochanet.unocha.org/p/Documents/Evaluation of OCHA Response to the Haiti Earthquake.pdf.

Biberson, Philippe and Jean, François. (1999). The Challenges of Globalization of International Relief and Development. *Nonprofit and Voluntary Sector Quarterly*, Vol. 28, 104.

Binder, Andrea and Grunewald, Francois. (2010). IASC cluster approach evaluation, 2nd phase country study, April 2010 – Haiti. Global Public Policy Institute. Retrieved from www.gppi.net/fileadmin/gppi/GPPi-URD_Cluster_II_Evaluation_HAITI_e.pdf.

Binder, Andrea, Grunewald, Francois and Georges, Yvio. (2010, August 31). Inter-agency real-time evaluation in Haiti: 3 months after the earthquake – Final report. Global Public Policy Institute. Retrieved from www.alnap.org/pool/files/haiti-ia-rte-1-final-report-en.pdf.

Blake, Eric S. Landsea, Christopher W., and Gibney, Ethan J. (2011). The deadliest, costliest and most intense United States tropical cyclones from 1851 to 2010 (and other frequently requested hurricane facts), National Climatic Data Center, National Hurricane Center. National Oceanic and Atmospheric Administration. Retrieved from www.nhc.noaa.gov/pdf/nws-nhc-6.pdf.

Blazeby, Leonard and Fisher, David. (2010). Promoting International Humanitarian Law and International Disaster Response Laws, Rules and Principles within the Commonwealth. *Commonwealth Law Bulletin*, Vol. 36(4), 709.

Brennan, Richard J. and Nandy, Robin. (2001). Complex Humanitarian Emergencies: A Major Global Health Challenge. *Emergency Medicine*, Vol. 13, 147.

Brezina, Timothy. (2008). What Went Wrong in New Orleans? An Examination of the Welfare Dependency Explanation. *Social Problems*, Vol. 55(1), 23.

Brooks, Nick. and Adger, W. Neil. (2003). *Country level risk measures of climate-related natural disasters and implications for adaption to climate change.* Tyndall Centre Working Paper No. 26. Tyndall Centre for Climate Change Research and Centre for Social and Economic Research on the Global Environment. Retrieved from www.researchgate.net/publication/228647518_Country_level_risk_measures_of_climate-related_natural_disasters_and_implications_for_adaptation_to_climate_change/file/9fcfd50ac160b4645e.pdf.

Burby, Raymond J. (2006). Decisions for Hazardous Areas Hurricane Katrina and the Paradoxes of Government Disaster Policy: Bringing About Wise Governmental. *Annals of the American Academy of Political and Social Science*, Vol. 604, 171.

Burns, Peter and Thomas, Matthew O. (2006, March). The Failure of the Nonregime: How Katrina Exposed New Orleans as a Regimeless City. *Urban Affairs Review*, Vol. 41, 517.

Butt, Simon, Nasu, Hitoshi and Nottage, Luke. (2014). *Asia-Pacific Disaster Management - Comparative and Socio-Legal Perspectives*. Heidelberg: Springer.

Bytheway, Bill. (2007, March 15). The evacuation of older people: the case of Hurricane Katrina. *Understanding Katrina: Perspectives from the Social Sciences.* Retrieved from http://understandingkatrina.ssrc.org/Bytheway/.

Campbell, Yolonda. (2011). New Governance in Action: Community Health Centers and the Public Health Service Act. *Saint Louis University Journal of Health Law and Policy*, Vol. 4, 397.

Campeau, L. (2007, May). Aceh and Nias, Indonesia: Results Achieved Using Community Reconstruction Following the Tsunami Disaster in December 2004. *Sourcebook on Emerging Good Practice.* 2nd edn. Retrieved from www.mfdr.org/sourcebook/2ndEdition/5-4Indonesia-Aceh&Nias.pdf.

Caplan, Bryan. (2013, November 13). Why Nations Fail: A Contrarian Take. EconLog, available at: http://econlog.econlib.org/archives/2013/11/why_nations_fai.html

Caron, David, D., Jelly, Michael J. and Telesetsky, Anastasia. (2014 August). *The International Law of Disaster Relief.* Cambridge: Cambridge University Press.

Caron, David D. and Leben, Charles. (2001). *The International Aspects of Natural and Industrial Catastrophes.* Hague: The Hague Academy of International Law: Martinus Nijhoff Publishers, p. 3–4.

Carafano, J. J. (2011). *The Great Eastern Japan Earthquake: Assessing Disaster Response and Lessons for the United States.* Washington, DC: The Heritage Foundation.

Carlson, Sabina and Lambert, Nona. (2010). The Virtual Field: Remote Crisis Mapping of the Haitian Earthquake. *The Fletcher Journal of Human Security*, Vol. XXV, 87.

Carpenter, Guy. (2012, October 28). Thailand flood 2011: executive summary. *CaptialIdeas*. Retrieved from www.gccapitalideas.com/2012/10/28/thailand-flood-2011-executive-summary/.

Carwile, William. (2005, August). Unified Command and the State-Federal Response to Hurricane Katrina in Mississippi. *Homeland Security Affairs*, Vol. 1(2), 73. Retrieved from www.hsaj.org/?article=1.2.6.

CBC News. (2013, March 13). Japan gives Canada $1M for tsunami debris cleanup. Retrieved from: www.cbc.ca/news/canada/british-columbia/story/2013/03/13/bc-tsunami-debris-clean-up-japan-money.html.

CDAC Network. (n.d.). *CDAC Haiti, What We Do*. Communicating with disaster affected communities. Retrieved from www.cdacnetwork.org/public/about/cdac-haiti.

Centers for Disease Control and Prevention. (2012). Identifying vulnerable older adults and legal options for increasing their protection during all-hazards emergencies: a cross-sector guide for states and communities. US Department of Health and Human Services. Retrieved from www.cdc.gov/phpr/documents/aging.pdf.

Center for Economic and Policy Issues (CEPR). (2010, March 17). Haitian government must not be bypassed in relief and reconstruction efforts. Retrieved from www.cepr.net/index.php/blogs/relief-and-reconstruction-watch/haitian-government-must-not-be-bypassed-in-relief-and-reconstruction-efforts.

Center for Economic and Policy Issues (CEPR). (2010, March 19). Haitian NGOs decry total exclusion from donors' conferences on Haitian reconstruction. Retrieved from www.cepr.net/index.php/blogs/relief-and-reconstruction-watch/qhaitian-ngos-decry-total-exclusion-from-donors-conferences-on-haitian-reconstructionq.

Chaiken, Miriam S., Deconinck, Hedwig and Degefie, Tedbabe. (2006). The Promise of a Community-Based Approach to Managing Severe Malnutrition: A Case Study from Ethiopia. *Food and Nutrition Bulletin*, Vol. 27(2), 95.

Charlotin, Manolia. (2010, March 11). Connecting with a voice from Haiti's grassroots. *Boston Haitian Reporter*. Retrieved from www.bostonhaitian.com/columns/2010/connecting-voice-haitis-grassroots.

Chen, Lincoln C., Evans, Tim G. and Cash, Richard A. (1999). Health as a Global Public Good. In Inge Kaul, Isabelle Grunberg and Marc A. Stern (Eds.), *Global Public Goods: International Cooperation in the 21st Century* (pp. 284–305). New York: Oxford University Press.

Chimni, B. S. (2000). Globalization, Humanitarianism and the Erosion of Refugee Protection. *Journal of Refugee Studies*, Vol. 13(3), 243.

Chinkin, Christine. (1998). The Role of Non-Governmental Organizations in Standard Setting, Monitoring and Implementation of Human Rights. In Joseph J. Norton, Mads Andenas and Mary Footer (Eds.), *The Changing World of International Law in the Twenty-First Century: A Tribute to the Late Kenneth R. Simmonds* (pp.45–66) The Hague: Kluwer Law International.

Church World Service (CWS). (2011, April 21). 'Still humanitarian gaps in Japan relief,' says Church World Service. Retrieved from: http://reliefweb.int/report/japan/'still-humanitarian-gaps-japan-relief'-says-church-world-service.

Church World Service Asia/Pacific. (2011, December 2). Thailand foods: situation report & emergency appeal. Retrieved from www.cwsasiapacific.org/wp-content/uploads/2012/01/2011.12.02-CWS-ACT-Thai-Flood-Sit-Rep.web_.pdf.

Clermont, Clarine, Sanderson, David, Sharma, Anusha and Spraos, Helen, et al. (2011, March). Urban disasters – lessons from Haiti: study of member agencies' responses to the earthquake in Port au Prince, Haiti, January 2010. *Report for the Disasters Emergency Committee (DEC)*. Retrieved from www.dec.org.uk/sites/default/files/files/Evaluations/Haiti/DEC-Haiti-urban-study.pdf.

Coca-Cola. (2011, November 21). The Coca-Cola system donates more than 2 million USD for flood victims in thailand. Retrieved from www.coca-colacompany.com/press-center/company-articles/the-coca-cola-system-donates-more-than-2-million-usd-for-flood-victims-in-thailand.

Cocking, Jane and Bastable Andy. (2010, October). Water, Sanitation and Public Health Reflections on Oxfam's Experience. *Humanitarian Exchange Magazine*, Vol. 48, 20.

COGJ-DM, Cabinet Office, Government of Japan: Disaster Management. (2011). Disaster management in Japan. Retrieved from www.bousai.go.jp/1info/pdf/saigaipanf_e.pdf.

Cohen, Amy J. (2008). Negotiation, Meet New Governance: Interests, Skills, and Selves. *Law & Soc. Inquiry*, Vol. 33, 503.

Cohen, Rick. (2012, December 5). Clinton: NGOs (Nonprofits) uniquely useful in networks. Nonprofit Quarterly. Retrieved from www.nonprofitquarterly.org/philanthropy/21455-clinton-ngos-nonprofits-uniquely-useful-in-networks.html.

Cohen, Roberta. (2006, January 12). *Measuring Indonesia's Response to the Tsunami at Workshop on "One Year after the Tsunami: Public Perceptions and Policy."* Washington, DC : Woodrow Wilson Center.

Coicaud, Jean-Marc and Heiskanen, Veijo. (2001). *The Legitimacy of International Organizations*. Tokyo; New York: United Nations University Press.

Colby-Bottel, SherriLynn. (2005, November). Doing anthropology in New Orleans, before and after Katrina. *Anthropology News*. American Anthropological Association. Retrieved from www.aaanet.org/press/an/1105/Colby_Bottel.htm.

Coles, Kimberley. (2007). *Democratic Designs: International Intervention and Electoral Practices in Postwar Bosnia-Herzegovina*. Ann Arbor: University of Michigan Press.

Coleman, Les. (2006). Frequency of Man-made Disasters in the 20th Century. *Journal of Contingencies and Crisis Management*. Vol.14(1), 3.

Collier, Paul. (2010, March 3). The Crisis in Haiti Shows We Need a New Approach to NGOs: A Hybrid Agency Run by Government and Donors Could Better Direct Aid. *The Independent*, 1-2. Retrieved from www.independent.co.uk/voices/commentators/paul-collier-the-crisis-in-haiti-shows-we-need-a-new-approach-to-ngos-1917822.html.

Comfort, Louise K. (2006, March). Cities at Risk: Hurricane Katrina and the Drowning of New Orleans. *Urban Affairs Review*, Vol. 41, 501.

Committee on Economic, Social and Cultural Rights. (1999, April 26–May 14). Substantive Issues Arising in the Implementation of the International Covenant on Economic, Social and Cultural Rights: General Comment 12; the Right to Adequate Food. E/C.12/1999/5 (Geneva).

Congleton, Roger D. (2006). The Story of Katrina: New Orleans and the Political Economy of Catastrophe. *Public Choice*, Vol. 127(1). Retrieved from http://rdc1.net/forthcoming/KATRINA3.pdf.

Constable, Mark. (2008). Disaster Mythology: Looting in New Orleans. *Disaster Prevention and Management*, Vol. 17(4), 519.

Cottle, Simon and Nolan, David. (2007). Global Humanitarianism and the Changing Aid-Media Field. *Journalism Studies*, Vol. 8(6), 862.

Crawford, Kate. (2010, October). Coordination and the Tenure Puzzle in Haiti. *Humanitarian Exchange Magazine*, Vol. 48, 7.

Credit Suisse. (2012, February 13). Thailand's post-flood recovery: turning the tide. Retrieved from https://doc.research-and-analytics.csfb.com/docView?language=ENG&format=PDF&document_id=804818550&source_id=em&serialid=%2FuPFdB3n5KRuP7HWRGJetxYWrNJETP4p9yMKQXENObY%3D.

CRS Report for Congress. (2006, November 15). Federal emergency management policy changes after Hurricane Katrina: a summary of statutory provisions. Congressional Research Service. Retrieved from www.fas.org/sgp/crs/homesec/RL33729.pdf.

Cutter, Susan L. (2006, June 11). The geography of social vulnerability: race, class and catastrophe. *Understanding Katrina: Perspectives from the Social Sciences*. Retrieved from http://understandingkatrina.ssrc.org/Cutter/.

Da Silva, Jo. (2010). Lessons from Aceh: key considerations in post-disaster reconstruction. Practical Action Publishing. Retrieved from www.alnap.org/pool/files/lessonsfromaceh.pdf.

Daniell and Vervaeck. (2011). CATDAT Yearly Review of Damaing Earthquakes in 2011, available at: http://earthquake-report.com/2012/01/09/catdat-damaging-earthquakes-database-2011-annual-review/.

Daniels, George L. and Loggins, Ginger Miller. (2007). Conceptualizing Continuous Coverage: A Strategic Model for Wall-to-Wall Local Television Weather Broadcasts. *Journal of Applied Communication Research*, Vol. 35(1), 48.

Davidson, Adam and Kenney, Caitlin. (2010, June 11). How foreign aid hurts Haitian farmers. Retrieved from www.npr.org/blogs/money/2010/06/10/127750586/how-foreign-aid-is-hurting-haitian-farmers.

Davis, Lucy. (2012, January 10). Haiti progress report January–December 2011, 13. Retrieved from www.oxfam.org/en/policy/haiti-progress-report.

Davis, Lynn E., et al. (2007). Hurricane katrina: lessons for army planning and operations. RAND corporation: Santa Monica, CA. Retrieved from www.rand.org/pubs/monographs/2007/RAND_MG603.pdf.

Dechaine, D. Robert. (2002). Rhetoric of Global Community Humanitarian Space and the Social Imaginary: Médecins Sans Frontières/Doctors Without Borders and the Rhetoric of Global Community. *Journal of Communication Inquiry*, Vol. 26, 354.

Denawa, M. (2005). Behind the accounts of the Great Kanto earthquake of 1923. Retrieved from http://library.brown.edu/cds/kanto/denewa.html.

Dennis King. (2010). The Haiti earthquake: breaking new ground in the humanitarian information landscape. *Humanitarian Exchange Magazine*. Retrieved from https://hiu.state.gov/Products/Haiti_EarthquakeHumanitarianInformation_2010Jul_HIU.pdf.

Depoorter, Ben. (2006). Horizontal Political Externalities: The Supply and Demand of Disaster Management. *Duke Law Journal*, Vol. 56(3), 101.

Dercon, B. and Kusumawijaya, M. (2007). Two years of settlement recovery in Aceh and Nias: what should the planners have earned? Paper submitted to the 43rd ISOCARP Congress, Antwerp, Belgium.

Diamond, Jared. (2012, July 06). What Makes Countries Rich or Poor? *New York Review of Books*.

Direct Relief International. (2005). 2004 Indian Ocean Earthquake and Tsunami. Retrieved from www.directrelief.org/emergency/2004-indian-ocean-earthquake-tsunami.

Disaster Justice. (2012). The Geography of Human Capability. *Duke Environmental Law and Policy Forum*, Vol. 23, 23;

Disaster Prevention and Mitigation Act B.E. 2550 [A.D. 2007]. Retrieved from http://photo-journ.com/wp-content/uploads/2011/11/Disaster-Prevention-and-Mitigation-Act.pdf.

Dodo, A., Xu, N., Davidson, R.A. and Nozick, L.K. (2005). Optimizing Regional Earthquake Mitigation Investment Strategies. *Earthquake Spectra*, Vol. 21(2), 305.

Donahue, Amy and Tuohy, Robert. (2006, July). Lessons We Don't Learn: A Study of the Lessons of Disasters, Why We Repeat Them, and How We Can Learn Them. *Homeland Security Affairs*, Vol. 2(2), 39. Retrieved from www.hsaj.org/?article=2.2.4.

Donahue, John. (2004, March). On collaborative governance. *Corporate Social Responsibility Initiative – Working Paper No.2.* Retrieved from www.hks.harvard.edu/m-rcbg/CSRI/publications/workingpaper_2_donahue.pdf.

(2013, June). *Collaborative Governance Private Roles for Public Goals in Turbulent Times*. Princeton: Princeton University Press.

Dorf, Michael C. and Sabel, Charles E. (1998). A Constitution of Democratic Experimentalism. *Columbia Law Review*, Vol. 98, 267.

Douyon, Frantz and Holly, Daniel. (2004). *Haïti de l'indépendance à la dépendance*. Paris: Editions L'Harmattan.

Drabek, Thomas E. and McEntire, D.A. (2002). Emergent Phenomena and Mulitorganizational Coordination in Disasters: Lessons from the Research Literature. *International Journal of Emergencies and Disasters*, Vol. 20(2), 197. Retrieved from http://ijmed.org/articles/574/download/.

Dreier, Peter. (2006, March). Katrina and Power in America. *Urban Affairs Review*, Vol. 41, 528.

Drolshammer, Jens and Pfeifer, Michael. (2001). *The Internationalization of the Practice of Law*. The Hague: Kluwer Law International.

Duffield, Mark. (2001). Governing the Borderlands: Decoding the Power of Aid. *Disasters*, Vol. 25(4), 308.

Duffield, Mark, Macrae, Joanna and Curtis, Devon. (2001). Politics and Humanitarian Aid. *Disasters*, Vol. 25(4), 269.

Duplat, Patrick and Parry, Emilie. (2012, March 2). Haiti: from the ground up. *Refugees International Field Report*. Retrieved from www.refugeesinternational.org/policy/field-report/haiti-ground.

Easterly, William. (2006). *The White Man's Burden: Why the West's Effort to Aid the Rest Have Done so Much Ill and So Little Good*. New York: The Penguin Press.

(2012, March 24). The Roots of Hardship: Despite Massive Amounts of Aid, Poor Countries Tend to Stay Poor. Maybe Their Institutions Are the Problem. *Wall Street Journal*, available at: wsj.com/articles/SB10001424052702304724404577293714016708378

Edgington, D. (2010). *Reconstructing Kobe: the geography of crisis and opportunity*. Vancouver, BC: UBC Press.

Efendi, Johari. (2013, June). Civic engagement and collaborative governance in post-conflict societies Case study, Ambon, Indonesia. *Digital dissertation consortium*. Retrieved from https://scholarsbank.uoregon.edu/xmlui/bitstream/handle/1794/13274/Efendi_oregon_0171N_10705.pdf?sequence=1.

Egeland, Jan. (2005). Towards a Stronger Humanitarian Response System. *Forced Migration Review*, Vol. 24 (IDP Supplement), 4. Retrieved from www.fmreview.org/FMRpdfs/FMR24/IDP%20Supplement/01.pdf.

Eikenberry, Angela M., Arroyave, Verónica and Cooper, Tracy. (2007). Administrative Failure and the International NGO Response to Hurricane Katrina. *Public Administration Review*, Vol. 67, 160.

ECB, Emergency Capacity Building, *The Good Enough Guide*, www.ecbproject.org/the-good-enough-guide/the-good-enough-guid (accessed on May 13, 2013).

Europa. (n.d.). Communication from the Commission to the Council and the European Parliament Humanitarian Food Assistance. Retrieved from http://eur-lex.europa.eu/LexUriServ/LexUriServ.do?uri=CELEX:52010DC0126:EN:NOT.

(2010, May 28). Humanitarian food assistance. Retrieved from http://europa.eu/legislation_summaries/humanitarian_aid/ah0005_en.htm.

European Commission. (n.d.). The union's humanitarian aid: fit for purpose? Stakeholder Consultation Document. Retrieved from http://ec.europa.eu/echo/files/policies/consultations/20121210_Fit-for-purpose.pdf.

Evans, Brad and Reid, Julian. (2014). *Resilient Life: The Art of Living Dangerously*. Cambridge: Polity Press (Wiley)

Evrard, Luc. (2011, January). Haiti: sortir de la dépendance humanitaire. *Revue Humanitaire*. Retrieved from www.medecinsdumonde.org/index.php/Publications/Livres/Recit-Haiti-sortir-de-la-dependance-humanitaire.

Evrard, Luc and Salignon, Pierre. (n.d.). Haiti cannot wait! Humanitarian Practice Network, Blog: The Humanitarian Space. Retrieved from www.odihpn.org/index.php?option=com_k2&view=item&layout=item&id=3128.

Farber, Daniel. (2007). Disaster Law and Inequality. *Law and Inequality*, Vol. 25, 297

Farber, Daniel and Faure, Michael. (2010). *Disaster Law*. Cheltenham: Edward Elgar Pubishing.

Farber, Daniel A, Chen, Jim, Verchicken, Robert and Sun, Lisa. (2009). *Disaster Law and Policy* (2nd edn). Philadelphia: *Wolters Kluwer Law & Business and Aspen Publication*

Farber, Daniel, Introduction: Legal Scholarship, the Disaster Cycle, and the Fukushima Accident. *Duke Environmental Law & Policy Forum*, Vol. 23, 1.

Farmer, Paul. (2010, July 27). Focus on Haiti. Partners in Health: The Road to Recovery. *Testimony to the Congressional Black Caucus* (blog) Retrieved from www.pih.org/blog/focus-on-haiti-the-road-to-recovery-a-six-month-review.

Federal Emergency Management Agency (FEMA). (n.d.). A Guide to the Disaster Declaration Process. Retrieved from www.fema.gov/pdf/rrr/dec_proc.pdf.

Federal Emergency Management Agency (FEMA). (2011). National Disaster Recovery Framework Strengthening Disaster Recovery for the Nation. Retrieved from www.fema.gov/pdf/recoveryframework/ndrf.pdf.

Federal Emergency Management Agency (FEMA). (2013, May). Information Sheet National Response Framework. Retrieved from www.fema.gov/library/viewRecord.do?id=7373.

Federal Emergency Management Agency (FEMA). (2013, May). Overview of the National Planning Frameworks. Retrieved from www.fema.gov/library/viewRecord.do?id=7361.

Federal Financial Institutions Examination Council. (2006, June 15). Lessons Learned From Hurricane Katrina: Preparing Your Institution for a Catastrophic Event. Retrieved from www.ffiec.gov/pdf/katrina_lessons.pdf.

Feinman, Gary M. and Fisher, Christopher T. (2005, November). The dangers of ignoring the evidence: hurricanes, hazards and survival. *Anthropology News*. American Anthropological Association. Retrieved from www.aaanet.org/press/an/1105/Feinman_Fisher.htm.

Feldman, Eric A. (2013). Fukushima: Catastrophe, Compensation, and Justice in Japan. *DePaul Law Review*, Vol. 62, p. 335.

Ferris, Elizabeth and Ferro-Ribeiro, Sara. (2012, March). Protecting People in Cities: The Disturbing Case of Haiti, *Disasters*. Vol. 36, 43. Retrieved from www.brookings.edu/research/articles/2012/03/protection-haiti-ferris.

Flatt, Victor B. and Stys, Jeffrey J. (2013). Long Term Recovery in Disaster Response and the Role of Non-Profits. In Susan Sterett (Ed.), *Disaster and Sociolegal Studies*. New Orleans, LA: Onati Socio-Legal Series, Quid Pro Books.

Financial Tracking Services (FTS). (2011). Japan 2011: Total Humanitarian Funding, List of all Humanitarian Pledges, Commitments and Contributions in 2011. Retrieved from http://fts.unocha.org/reports/daily/ocha_R10c_C105_Y2011_asof___1303211530.pdf.

Fisher, David. (2009). The International Federation of Red Cross and Red Crescent Societies and the IDRL Guidelines. *Commonwealth Law Bulletin*, Vol. 35(4), 743.

Food Assistance Convention (adopted April 25, 2012, entry into force January 1, 2013). Available at: www.foodassistanceconvention.org/convention/FoodAssistance.pdf (accessed on May 11, 2013).

Food Assistance Convention. (n.d.). About FAC. Retrieved from www.foodassistanceconvention.org/en/about_fac/about.aspx.

Forgette, Richard, Dettrey, Bryan, Van Boening, Mark and Swanson, David A. (2009). Before, Now, and After: Assessing Hurricane Katrina Relief. *Population Research and Policy Review*, Vol. 28(1), 31.

Fox, Fiona. (2001). New Humanitarianism: Does It Provide a Moral Banner for the 21st Century?. *Disasters*, Vol. 25(4), 275.

Freeman, Jody. (1997). Collaborative Governance in the Administrative State. *UCLA Law Review*, Vol. 45, 1.

Frenda, Steven J., Knowles, Eric D., Saletan, William, and Loftus, Elizabeth F. (2013). False Memories of Fabricated Political Events. Legal Studies Research Paper Series No. 2013–87. *Journal of Experimental Social Psychology*, Vol. 49, 280.

Friedman, Lawrence M. (1969). Legal Culture and Social Development. *Law and Society Review*, Vol. 4, 29.

Fussell, Elizabeth. (2006, June 11). Leaving New Orleans: Social Stratification, Networks, and Hurricane Evacuation. *Understanding Katrina: Perspectives from the Social Sciences*. Retrieved from http://understandingkatrina.ssrc.org/Fussell/.

G20 Disaster Risk Management Report. (2012). *Improving the Assessment of Disaster Risks to Strengthen Financial Resilience: A Special Joint G20 Publication by the Government of Mexico and the World Bank*. Washington, DC: International Bank for Reconstruction and Development.

Galbraith, John and Menshikov, Stanislav. (1988). *Capitalism, Communism, and Coexistence: From the Bitter Past to a Better Prospect.* Boston: Houghton Mifflin.

Gasseer, Naeema Al, Dresden, Elissa, Keeney, Gwen Brumbaugh and Warren, Nicole. (2004). Status of Women and Infants in Complex Humanitarian Emergencies. *Journal of Midwifery and Women's Health*, Vol. 49(4), 7.

Geography Association (GA). (2011). Japan Tsunami – March 2011. Retrieved on from: www.geography.org.uk/resources/japantsunami.

Geology.com. (2005). 2004 Indonesia Tsunami Maps. Retrieved from http://geology.com/articles/tsunami-map.shtml.

Gilman, Nils. (2006, June 11). What Katrina teaches about the meaning of racism. *Understanding Katrina: Perspectives from the Social Sciences.* Retrieved from http://understandingkatrina.ssrc.org/Gilman/.

Goldman, Lynn and Coussens, Christine (rapporteurs). (2007). Environmental public health impacts of disasters: Hurricane Katrina. The National Academies Press: Washington, DC. Retrieved from www.nap.edu/catalog/11840.html.

Good Humanitarian Donorship, 'Principles and Good Practice of Humanitarian Donorship' (endorsed in Stockholm, June 17, 2003) paragraph 7. Available at: www.goodhumanitariandonorship.org/gns/principles-good-practice-ghd/overview.aspx (accessed on May 19, 2014).

Google Crisis Response. (2012, March 7). 3/11: Google crisis response began. Retrieved from www.google.org/crisisresponse/kiroku311/chapter_01.html.

(2012, July 20). Difficulties of communication in immediate post disaster Japan: Twitter's role as the greatest communication tool in the Great East Japan Earthquake. Retrieved from www.google.org/crisisresponse/kiroku311/chapter_18.html.

Gottlieb, David J. (2006). Katrina Consequences: What has the Government Learned? *Loyola Law Review*, Vol. 52, 1113.

Gould, Charles. (2009). The Right to Housing Recovery After Natural Disasters. *Harvard Human Rights Journal.* Vol.22(1), 169.

Gould, Dick. (2005, November). Identifying Victims after a Disaster. *Anthropology News.* American Anthropological Association. Retrieved from www.aaanet.org/press/an/1105/Gould.htm.

Government of Canada-Office of Critical Infrastructure Protection and Emergency Preparedness (GC-OCIPEP). (2001). *Seismic Hazard, Building Codes, and Mitigation Options for Canadian Buildings.* Ottawa: University of Ottawa.

Graham, Stephen. (2006, June 11). Cities Under Siege: Katrina and the Politics of Metropolitan America. *Understanding Katrina: Perspectives from the Social Sciences.* Retrieved from http://understandingkatrina.ssrc.org/Graham/.

Green, Stuart P. (2007). Looting, Law, and Lawlessness. *Tulane Law Review*, Vol. 81, Hurricane Katrina Symposium. Retrieved from http://papers.ssrn.com/sol3/papers.cfm?abstract_id=917440.

Greenberger, Michael. (2005, October). The role of federal government in response to catastrophic health emergencies: lessons learned from Hurricane

Katrina. University of Maryland School of Law, Legal Studies Research Paper, No 2005–52. Retrieved from http://papers.ssrn.com/sol3/papers.cfm?abstract_id=824184.

Greenstein, Robert. (2005, October 20). Meeting the basic needs of Hurricane Katrina victims: recommendations to federal, policymakers. Center on Budget and Policy Priorities. Retrieved from www.cbpp.org/files/9-9-05pov.pdf.

Greet, Neil. (2008). ADF Experience on Humanitarian Operations: A New Idea? *Security Challenges*, Vol. 4(2), 45.

Griffin, Stephen M. (2006, March). Stop federalism before it kills again: reflections on Hurricane Katrina. Public Law and Legal Theory Research Paper Series, Research Paper No. 06-04, Tulane University School of Law. Retrieved from http://ssrn.com/abstract= 894470.

Guha-Sapir, Debby, Vos, Femke, Below, Regina and Ponserre, Sylvain, (2011). Annual Disaster Statistical Review 2010 – The number and trends. Brussels: Centre for Research on the Epidemiology of Disasters (CRED) and Université catholique de Louvain. Retrieved from http://crmi-undp.org/documents/documentos/98.pdf.

Guttry, Andrea, Gestri, Marco and Venturini, Gabriella. (2012). *International Disaster Response Law*. Hague, Netherlands: T.M.C. Asser Press.

Haiti Equality Collective. (2010). Ensuring Haitian women's participation and leadership in all stages of national relief and reconstruction – A coalition gender shadow report of the 2010 Haiti PDNA. *The Haiti Gender Shadow Report*. Retrieved from www.genderaction.org/publications/2010/gsr.pdf.

Hallegatte, Stephane and Przyluski, Valentin. (2010, December). The economics of natural disasters concepts and methods, Sustainable Development Network. The World Bank. Retrieved from www-wds.worldbank.org/external/default/WDSContentServer/IW3P/IB/2010/12/21/000158349_20101221155640/Rendered/PDF/WPS5507.pdf.

Hanson, Jon and Hanson, Kathleen. (2006). The Blame Frame: Justifying (Racial) Injustice in America. Harvard Public Law Working Paper, No. 08-47. *Harvard Civil Rights-Civil Liberties Law Review*, Vol. 41, 413.

Happel, Ellie. (2012, March 1). 'Returning to Zero': forced evictions in Haiti's displaced persons camps. Canada Haiti Action Network. Retrieved from http://canadahaitiaction.ca/content/returning-zero-forced-evictions-haitis-displaced-persons-camps and http://rabble.ca/blogs/bloggers/roger-annis/2012/02/%E2%80%98returning-zero-forced-evictions-haitis-displaced-persons-camps.

Harmer, Adele and Cotterrell, Lin. (2005, September 20). Diversity in Donorship: The Changing Landscape of Official Humanitarian Aid. *Humanitarian Policy Group Research Report*. Retrieved from http://dspace.cigilibrary.org/jspui/bitstream/123456789/22633/1/Diversity%20in%20Donorship%20The%20changing%20landscape%20of%20official%20humanitarian%20aid%20fe1.pdf?1.

Haver, Katherine and Rencoret, Nicole. (2011, February). Haiti earthquake response: mapping and analysis of gaps and duplications in evaluations. Retrieved from www.alnap.org/resource/6063.aspx.

Heath, J. Benton. (2011). Disasters, Relief, and Neglect: The Duty to Accept Humanitarian Assistance and the Work of the International Law Commission. *International Law and Politics*, Vol. 43, 419.

(2012, October 21). Accountability in the United Nations Humanitarian System: the Consequences of Institutional Choice in Disaster Response. Paper presented at ASIL 2012 Midyear Meeting (2012, October 20–21). Retrieved from www.asil.org/midyearmeeting2012/pdfs/papers/Heath-Humanitarian-ASIL%20final-2012-1.pdf.

Heikkila, T. and Gerlak, A. K. (2013). Building a Conceptual Approach to Collective Learning: Lessons for Public Policy Scholars. *Policy Studies Journal*, 41: 484–512. doi: 10.1111/psj.12026

Heintze, Hans-Joachim and Zwitter, Andrej. ed. (2011). *International Law and Humanitarian Assistance: A Crosscut Through Legal Issues Pertaining to Humanitarianism*. New York: Springer.

Henderson, David. (2013, April 04). Acemoglu and Robinson on the Wealth of Nations. EconLog, available at: http://econlog.econlib.org/archives/2013/04/acemoglu_and_ro_1.html

Herz, Ansel. (2010, March 30). Haiti: looking more and more like a war zone. Inter Press Service News Agency (IPS). Retrieved from www.ipsnews.net/2010/03/haiti-looking-more-and-more-like-a-war-zone/.

Higgins, Rosalyn. (1986). The Attitude of Western States towards Legal Aspects of the Use of Force. In A. Cassese (Ed.), *The Current Legal Regulation of the Use of Force*. Dordrecht: Martinus Nijhoff Publishers.

Hilgartner, Stephen. (2007). Overflow and Containment in the Aftermath of Disaster. *Social Studies of Science*, Vol. 37(1), 153.

Hoen, Herman Willem. (2001). *Good Governance in Central and Eastern Europe: The Puzzle of Capitalism by Design*. Cheltenham: Edward Elgar Publication.

Hoffmann, Sharona. (2008–2009). Preparing for Disaster: Protecting the Most Vulnerable in Emergencies. *U.C. Davis Law Review*. Vol. 42, 1491.

Holmes, John. (2010, October). Learning the Lessons of Haiti. *Humanitarian Exchange Magazine*, Vol. 48, 1.

Hooks, Jonathan and Miller, Trisha. (2006–2007). Continuing Storm: How Disaster Recovery Excludes Those Most in Need. *California Western Law Review*, Vol. 43, 21; Robert Verchick. (2012–2013).

Horwitz, Steven. (2008, March). Making hurricane response more effective: lessons from the private sector and the coast guard during katrina. *Mercatus Policy Series*. Global Prosperity Initiative. Retrieved from www.mercatus.org/globalprosperity.

Humanitarian Accountability Project (HAP) & International Organisation for Migration (IOM). (2010). *2010 Camp Committee Assessment: A Tool for*

Deciding How to Work with Camp Committees. Port-au-Prince: Humanitarian Accountability Project.

IBM Corporation. (2005). *2005 Tsunami Relief Efforts WHO conference Panel 2.17*. Retrieved from www.who.int/hac/events/tsunamiconf/presentations/2_17_private_sector_brent_ppt.pdf.

Ichimura, H. (2012). The current state and challenges: temporary radio broadcasting stations for the Great East Japan Earthquake Disaster. *Regional Society and Communication Media in Japan, No. 154*. Institute of Economic and Political Studies, Kansai University. Retrieved from www.kansai-u.ac.jp/Keiseiken/books/sousho154.htm.

Iglesias, Gabrielle. (n.d.). Lessons on resilience from the 2011 Central Thailand floods. Retrieved from www.asiapacificadapt.net/adaptationforum2012/sites/default/files/Gabrielle%20Iglesias_Panel6B_Iglesias.pdf.

Imase, M. (2012). Lessons learnt from "Information flow" during the Great East Japan Earthquake and local participation: the case of outlying islands Urato in Shiogama City. (2012, Dec). Civic Action Clearinghouse. Retrieved from http://sicnpo.jp/saigai110311/imase-urado2012.pdf.

Innocent, Darlye Elise. (2010). Untying the hands to tie the feet: a qualitative look at the vulnerabilities of post-earthquake Haiti and the transformative process necessary for national refoundation. (PhD Dissertation). Arizona State University.

Inomata, Tadanori. (2012). *Financing for Humanitarian Operations in the United Nations System* (United Nations, Geneva: JIU/REP/2012/11, 133 www.unjiu.org/en/reports-notes/JIU%20Products/JIU_REP_2012_11_English.pdf accessed April 23, 2014.

Institute of Energy Economics(IEEJ). (2012). Coal trends: trends in coal supply, demand and prices as seen from statistics. Retrieved from http://eneken.ieej.or.jp/data/4583.pdf.

Inter-Agency Standing Committee (IASC). (2006, November 24). *Guidance Note on Using the Cluster Approach to Strengthen Humanitarian Response*, 2, 2.

Inter-agency Standing Committee (IASC). (2010, July 5). Response to the humanitarian crisis in Haiti – following the 12 January 2010 earthquake, achievements, challenges and lessons to be learned. Tranblemanntè 2010 nan peyi Ayiti. Retrieved from www.humanitarianinfo.org/IASC/pageloader.aspx?page=content-news-newsdetails&newsid=143.

IASC Task Team. (2007, May). *Operational Guidance on Designating Sector/Cluster Leads in Major New Emergencies*, 2, Geneva.

International Commission on Intervention and State Sovereignty. (2001, December). The responsibility to protect. Retrieved from http://idl-bnc.idrc.ca/dspace/bitstream/10625/18432/6/116998.pdf.

International Committee of the Red Cross. (1998). International solidarity and the globalization of responsibility in meeting today's humanitarian challenges. Address by Mr. Cornelio Sommaruga, President of the International Committee of the Red Cross, at the Opening Meeting of UNHCR 49th

Executive Committee. Retrieved from www.icrc.org/eng/resources/documents/misc/57jpef.htm.

International Federation of Red Cross and Red Crescent Societies (IFRC). (n.d.). IDRL Guidelines. Retrieved from www.ifrc.org/en/what-we-do/idrl/idrl-guidelines/.

(n.d.). The International Federation of Red Cross and Red Crescent Societies (IFRC). Retrieved from www.ifrc.org/en/who-we-are/the-movement/ifrc/.

International Organisation for Migration (IOM). (n.d.). IOM Fact Sheet: Haiti Earthquake Displacement and Shelter Strategy. Retrieved from www.iom.int/jahia/webdav/shared/shared/mainsite/published_docs/brochures_and_info_sheets/IOMFactSheet.pdf.

(2012, March). Overview of IOM's flood relief efforts during the Thai flood crisis 2011/12. Retrieved from www.iom.int/jahia/webdav/shared/shared/mainsite/activities/countries/docs/thailand/Overview-IOM-Flood-Response-Thailand-March-2012.pdf.

International Recovery Platform (IRP). (2008). Great Hanshin-Awaji Earthqauke, 1985. Retrieved from www.recoveryplatform.org/assets/file/irp_casestudies/irp-cs-8-jpn.pdf.

Irons, Larry. (2005, August). Hurricane Katrina as a Predictable Surprise. *Homeland Security Affairs*, Vol. 1(2), 89. Retrieved from www.hsaj.org/?article=1.2.7.

Ives, Kim. (n.d.). Haiti reconstruction: factories, not fields. North American Congress on Latin America (nacla). Retrieved from https://nacla.org/node/6547.

Izzo, Nitrato Valerio. (2013). Law, State and the Politics of Catastrophes: A Critical Perspective on Epiphanies of Injustice and the Need for Protection. In Susan Sterett (Ed.), *Disaster and Sociolegal Studies*. New Orleans, LA: Onati Socio-Legal Series, Quid Pro Books.

Jakobsen, Peter Viggo. (2002). The Transformation of United Nations Peace Operations in the 1990s: Adding Globalization to the Conventional `End of the Cold War Explanation. *Cooperation and Conflict*, Vol. 37, 267.

James, C. D. and Cameron, C. (2002). The 1923 Tokyo Earthquake and Fire. National Information Service for Earthquake Engineering. Retrieved from http://nisee.berkeley.edu/kanto/tokyo1923.pdf.

Japan Times. (2011). Tohoku joins Tepco in rationing power. Retrieved from www.japantimes.co.jp/news/2011/03/16/news/tohoku-joins-tepco-in-rationing-power/#.

Jiang, Shibo. (2013). International Disaster Response Law and Policy in China: Evolution, Problem and Resolution. *Chinese Journal of International Law*. Vol. 12(3), 455.

Joint Commission Resources Inc., et al. (2005). Standing together: an emergency planning guide for America's communities. Retrieved from www.jointcommission.org/assets/1/18/planning_guide.pdf.

Joint Statement by the Council and the Representatives of the Governments of the Member States meeting within the Council, European Parliament and the

European Commission, "The European Consensus on Humanitarian Aid" Official Journal of the European Union, C 25/1 (2008, January 30) paragraph 4.

Julmy, Stephanie. (2011, February). Coordinating the Earthquake Response: Lessons from Leogane, Western Haiti. *Humanitarian Exchange Magazine*, Vol. 49, 26. Retrieved from www.odihpn.org/humanitarian-exchange-magazine/issue-49/coordinating-the-earthquake-response-lessons-from-leogane-western-haiti.

Kabau, Tom and Ali, Shahla(2015). A Human Rights Based Approach to the Regulation of Humanitarian Relief: The Emerging Obligation to Incorporate Local Participation, *Brooklyn Journal of International Law.*, Vol. 40(3), 791.

Kagan, Robert A.. (2003). *Adversarial Legalism and American Government: The American Way of Life*. Cambridge: Harvard University Press.

Kapur, G. Bobby and Smith, Jeffrey. (2011). *Emergency Public Health: Preparedness and Response*. Sudbury: Jones & Bartlett.

Karkkainen, Bradley C. (2004). Reply: "New Governance" in Legal Thought and in the World: Some Splitting as Antidote to Overzealous Lumping. *Minn. L. Rev.*, Vol. 89, 471.

Karlberg, Michael. (2004). *Beyond the Culture of Contest: From Adversarialism to Mutualism in an Age of Interdependence*. Oxford: George Ronald Publishers Ltd.

Kaufman, Sarah Beth. (2006, June 11). The criminalization of New Orleanians in Katrina's wake. *Understanding Katrina: Perspectives from the Social Sciences*. Retrieved from http://understandingkatrina.ssrc.org/Kaufman/.

Keck, Margaret and Sikkink, Kathryn. (1998). *Activists Beyond Borders: Transnational Advocacy Networks in International Politics*. New York: Cornell University Press.

Kennedy, Kerry. (2010, July 26). Haiti relief is not charity: a rights-based approach to aid. Inter Press Service (IPS). Retrieved from www.ipsnews.net/2010/07/haiti-relief-is-not-charity-a-rights-based-approach-to-aid/.

Keohane, Robert O. and Nye, Joseph S. Jr. (2000). Globalization: What's New? What's Not? (And So What?). *Foreign Policy*, Vol. 118, 104.

Keohane, Robert O., Ostrom, Elinor and Harvard University Center for International Affairs. (1995). *Local Commons and Global Interdependence: Heterogeneity and Cooperation in Two Domains*. London: Thousand Oaks; CA: Sage Publications.

Kettl, Donald F. (2006). Is the Worst Yet to Come? *Annals of the American Academy of Political and Social Science*, Vol. 604, 273.

King, Dennis. (2010, October). The Haiti Earthquake: Breaking New Ground in the Humanitarian Information Landscape. *Humanitarian Exchange Magazine*, Vol. 48, 23.

King, Joyce E. and Robertson, Clyde C. (2007). A Teaching and Learning Methodology for Healing the Wounds of Distance, Displacement, and Loss Caused by Hurricane Katrina. *Journal of Black Studies*, Vol. 37(4), 469.

Klarreich, Kathie and Polman, Linda. (2012, November 12). The NGO Republic of Haiti: The International Humanitarian Effort to Help the Devastated Country Has Left Out Its People. *The Nation*. 11, 12.

Knabb, Richard D., Rhome, Jamie R., and Brown, Daniel P. (2005, December). Tropical cyclone report Hurricane Katrina, August 23–30, 2005. National Hurricane Center. Retrieved from www.nhc.noaa.gov/pdf/TCR-AL122005_Katrina.pdf.

Koontanakulvong, Sucharit. (n.d.). Thailand floods 2011: causes and future management system. Retrieved from http://management.kochi-tech.ac.jp/ssms_papers/sms12-4498_7c90ae72211effcb8ee119e2a1eddeba.pdf.

Krause, Monika. (2006, June 11). New Orleans: the public sphere of the disaster. *Understanding Katrina: Perspectives from the Social Sciences*. Retrieved from http://understandingkatrina.ssrc.org/Krause/.

Kumar, C. Raj. and Srivastava, D.K. (2006). *Tsunami and Disaster Management: Law and Governance*. Hong Kong: Sweet and Maxwell Asia

Kysar, Douglas A. and McGarity, Thomas Owen. (2006). Did NEPA drown New Orleans? The leeves, the blame game, and the hazards of hindsight. Cornell Legal Studies Research Paper No. 06-024. Retrieved from http://ssrn.com/abstact=928869.

Lakoff, Andrew. (2006, June 10). From disaster to catastrophe: the limits of preparedness. *Understanding Katrina: Perspectives from the Social Sciences*. Retrieved from http://understandingkatrina.ssrc.org/Lakoff/.

Landesman, Linda Young. (2001) *Public Health Management of Disasters: The Practice Guide*. Washington, DC: American Public Health Association.

Laursen, Heather. (2011). Non-profit disaster relief discourse of the American Red Cross in Hurricane Katrina and Haiti. (Master thesis). Ottawa, Canada: Carleton University.

Leeder, Jessica. (2010, May 8). Fake encampments spring up in Haiti. *The Globe & Mail*. Retrieved from www.theglobeandmail.com/news/world/fake-encampments-spring-up-in-haiti/article1320052/.

Lehmkuhl, D. (2008) Control Modes in the Age of Transnational Governance. *Law & Policy*, Vol. 30 (No.3), 336. Available at: http://onlinelibrary.wiley.com/doi/10.1111/j.1467-9930.2008.00281.x/abstract

Lehr, Amy. (2010). Old and New Governance Approaches to Conflict Minerals: All are Better than One. *Harvard International Law Journal*, Vol. 58, 148.

Leonard, Herman B. and Howitt, Arnold M. (2009). *Managing Crises: Responses to Large-Scale Emergencies*, Washington DC: CQ Press.

Lepard, Brian D. (2003). *Rethinking Humanitarian Intervention: A Fresh Legal Approach Based on Fundamental Ethical Principles in International Law and World Religions*. University Park, PA: Pennsylvania State University Press.

Levs, J. (2012, April 11). Tsunami scare tests new life-saving procedures. *CNN*. Retrieved from http://edition.cnn.com/2012/04/11/world/asia/indonesia-earthquake-differences/index.html.

Lindsay, Reed. (2010, March 29). Haiti's Excluded. *The Nation*, Vol. 290, 18.

Lobel, Orly. (2004(a)). Setting the Agenda for New Governance Research. *Minnesota Law Review*, Vol. 89, 498, 505.

(2004(b)). The Renew Deal: The Fall of Regulation and the Rise of Governance. *Minnesota Law Review* 89, 342.

(2012, November). New governance as regulatory governance. University of San Diego Legal Studies Research Paper Series, Research Paper No. 12–101.

Longford, Sarah. (1999). OCHA One Year On: Is Humanitarian Coordination any Better?. *Humanitarian Exchange Magazine*, Vol 13, 10. Retrieved from www.odihpn.org/humanitarian-exchange-magazine/issue-13/ocha-one-year-on-is-humanitarian-coordination-any-better.

Lukes, Steven. (2006, June 11). Questions about power: lessons from the Louisiana Hurricane. *Understanding Katrina: Perspectives from the Social Sciences*. Retrieved from http://understandingkatrina.ssrc.org/Lukes/.

Lynch, Colum. (2010, February 17). Top U.N. aid official critiques Haiti aid efforts in confidential email, Turtle Bay/Foreign Policy. Retrieved from http://turtlebay.foreignpolicy.com/posts/2010/02/17/top_un_aid_official_critiques_haiti_aid_efforts_in_confidential_email.

Connolly, M. A. (2005). Communicable disease control in emergencies: a field manual. WHO. Retrieved from www.who.int/infectious-disease-news/IDdocs/whocds200527/ISBN_9241546166.pdf.

MADRE, et al. *Gender-based violence against Haitian women and girls in internal displacement camps: submission to the United Nations Universal Periodic Review, Republic of Haiti*. (2001, October). ¶ 20, 12th Session, Working Group on the Universal Periodic Review, Hum. Rts. Council, Oct. 3–14, 2011. Retrieved from http://ijdh.org/wordpress/wp-content/uploads/2011/03/UPR-GBV-Final-4-4-2011.pdf.

MacKinnon, I. (2008, August 15). Indonesia: Aceh villagers face homelessness again – in name of tsunami aid from US government. *The Guardian*. Retrieved from www.guardian.co.uk/world/2008/aug/15/tsunami2004.naturaldisasters.

Malik, O. (2011). In Japan, many undersea cables are damaged. *Gigaom*. Retrieved from http://gigaom.com/2011/03/14/in-japan-many-under-sea-cables-are-damaged/.

Manalu, Norma Susanti. (2005, April 14). Oral statement to UN commission on Human Rights at International Non-government Organization Forum on Indonesian Development, Geneva.

Marulanda, L., and Rizal, S. (2006). *Tsunami Evaluation Coalition: The International Community's Funding of the Tsunami Emergency and Relief – Local Response Study*. Tsunami Evaluation Coalition (TEC).

McDougal, Myres S., Reisman, Michael W. and Willard, Andrew R. (1988). The World Community: A Planetary Social Process. *Faculty Scholarship Series*, Paper 753.

McGuire, Michael and Schneck, Debra. (2010). What If Hurricane Katrina Hit in 2020? The Need for Strategic Management of Disasters. *Public Administration Review*, Vol. December 2010, Special Issue, S201. Retrieved from www.indiana.edu/~spea/research/focus_newsletter/mcguire_katrina.pdf.

McKillop, Heather. (2005, December). The aftermath of Katrina. *Anthropology News*. American Anthropological Association. Retrieved from www.aaanet.org/press/an/1205/AN2005Dec_mckillop.pdf.

MDF – JRF Secretariat. (2012, October). *Lessons Learned from Post-Disaster Reconstruction in Indonesia*. World Bank Group.

Medecins Sans Frontieres. (2006, July 20). Indonesia: quick local response to tsunami. Retrieved from www.msf.org.hk/index.php?option=com_content&view=article&id=365:indonesia-quick-local-response-to-tsunami&lang=en.

Menkel-Meadow, Carrie. Scaling Up Deliberative Democracy as Dispute Resolution in Health Care Reform: A Work in Progress. *Law and Contemporary Problems*, Vol. 74(3), 1–30.

Metz, Manfred. (2010, October). Emergency food assistance in Haiti: lessons learned from a post-earthquake GTZ operation in Leogane. *Humanitarian Exchange Magazine*, Vol. 48, 25.

Meyer, Johon. (2002). Globalization, National Culture, and the Future of the World Polity. *Hong Kong Journal of Sociology* Vol. 3, 1.

Miller, DeMond Shondell. (2007). Book Review: Come Hell or High Water: Hurricane Katrina and the Color of Disaster. *Journal of Black Studies*, Vol. 37(4), 568.

Miller, Ruth. (2009). *Law in Crisis – The Ecstatic Subject of Natural Disaster*. Stanford, California: Stanford University Press.

Ministry of Finance, Royal Thai Government and The World Bank. (2012, January 18). Thailand flooding 2554 rapid assessment for resilient recovery and reconstruction planning. Retrieved from www.undp.org/content/dam/thailand/docs/UNDP_RRR_THFloods.pdf.

Ministry of Foreign Affairs. (2011). Humanitarian aid policy of Japan. Retrieved from www.mofa.go.jp/policy/emergency/pdfs/aid_policy_japan.pdf.

Ministry of Foreign Affairs (MOFA). (2011). The guideline on policy promotion for the revitalization of Japan. Retrieved from www.mofa.go.jp/announce/jfpu/2011/5/0520_2_1.html.

Moe, Tun Lin. (2010). Cleanup after Katrina: An Analysis on Policy, Process, Priorities, Problems, and Politics. *Disaster Prevention and Management*, Vol. 19(3), 314.

Molotch, Harvey. (2006, June 11). Death on the roof: race and bureaucratic failure. *Understanding Katrina: Perspectives from the Social Sciences*. Retrieved from http://understandingkatrina.ssrc.org/Molotch/.

Moore, Sally F. (1973). Law and Social Change: The Semi-Autonomous Social Field as an Appropriate Subject of Study. *Law and Society Review*, Vol. 7, 719.

Moynihan, Donald P. (2007). From forest fires to Hurricane Katrina: case studies of incident command systems. IBM Center for the Business of Government. Retrieved from www.businessofgovernment.org/report/forest-fires-hurricane-katrina-case-studies-incident-command-systems.

(2009). The response to Hurricane Katrina. International Risk Governance Council: Geneva. Retrieved from http://irgc.org/wp-content/uploads/2012/04/Hurricane_Katrina_full_case_study_web.pdf.

Müller-Schwarze, Nina. (2005, December). TV images of the Katrina disaster. *Anthropology News*. American Anthropological Association. Retrieved from www.aaanet.org/press/an/1205/AN2005Dec_mullerschwarze.pdf.

Multidisciplinary Center for Earthquake Engineering Research (MCEER). (2013). The Great Tohoku, Japan Earthquake & Tsunami: facts, engineering, news and maps. Retrieved from http://mceer.buffalo.edu/infoservice/disasters/Honshu-Japan-Earthquake-Tsunami-2011.asp#3.

National Institute for Research Advancement (NIRA). (2011, September). Indexes for recovery and reconstruction following the Great East Japan Earthquake. Retrieved from www.nira.or.jp/pdf/1102english_report.pdf.

National Oceanic and Atmospheric Administration (NOAA). (2012). March 11, 2011 Japan Earthquake and Tsunami. National Geophysical Data Centre (NGDC). Retrieved from www.ngdc.noaa.gov/hazard/tsunami/pdf/2011_0311.pdf.

National Weather Service, National Hurricane Centre. (2012). Hurricane Katrina 2005. *Hurricanes in History*. Retrieved from www.nhc.noaa.gov/outreach/history/#katrina.

Nautilus Institute for Security and Sustainability (NISS). (2011). After the deluge: short and medium-term impacts of reactor damage caused by the Japan earthquake and tsunami. Retrieved from www.jpri.org/publications/friends/SRJapanReactors.pdf.

Nazarov, E. (2011). Emergency response management in Japan: final research report. Asian Disaster Reduction Centre. Retrieved from www.adrc.asia/aboutus/vrdata/finalreport/2011A_AZE_Emin_FRR.pdf.

Nejaime, Douglas. (2009). When New Governance Fails. *Ohio State Law Journal*, Vol. 70(2), 323–399.

Nelson, Marla, et al. (2007). Planning, Plans, and People: Professional Expertise, Local Knowledge, and Governmental Action in Post-Hurricane Katrina New Orleans. The University of New Orleans. *Cityscape: A Journal of Policy Development and Research*, Vol. 9(3), 23.

New Zealand Earthquake Commission. (2012). The value of lifeline seismic risk mitigation in Christ church. Earthquake Commission. Retrieved from http://static.squarespace.com/static/5006875e24ac21f35d8de8d2/t/51623b92e4b01df404d6819d/1365392274854/Assessing%20the%20Value%20of%20Lifeline%20Engineering%20in%20Christchurch%20-%20Tony%20F.pdf.

Nigg, Joanne M., et al. (2006). Housing Hurricane Katrina and the Flooding of New Orleans: Emergent Issues in Sheltering and Temporary Housing. *Annals of the American Academy of Political and Social Science*, Vol. 604, 113.

Noveck, B. S. (2011). The Single Point of Failure. In S. Van der Hof and M. Groothuis (Eds.), *Innovating Government* (The Hague: Asserr Press), pp. 77–99.

Nuclear Accident Independent Investigation Commission (NAIIC). (2012). The official report of the Fukushima Nuclear Accident Independent Investigation Commission. The National Diet of Japan. Retrieved from www.nirs.org/fukushima/naiic_report.pdf.

OCHA. (2011, February). *Evaluations Synthesis Report*, 5 OCHA Occasional Policy Briefing Series, 16. https://ochanet.unocha.org/p/Documents/OCHA%20Evaluations%20Synthesis%20Report%202010-latest.pdf (accessed on May 10, 2013).

OCHA. (2011, July 31). OCHA's Management Response Plan (MRP) to Internally-mandated Evaluation of OCHA Response to the Haiti Earthquake, available at https://ochanet.unocha.org/p/Documents/Haiti_Internal_Evaluation_31JUL2011.pdf (accessed on May 5, 2013).

O'Connor, Maura R. (2011, January 7). Does International Aid Keep Haiti Poor?. *Slate*. Retrieved from www.slate.com/articles/news_and_politics/dispatches/features/2011/does_international_aid_keep_haiti_poor/the_un_cluster_system_is_as_bad_as_it_sounds.html.

O'Donnell, Max R., Bacos, Dimitri and Bennish, Michael L. (2002). Nutritional Response to the 1998 Bangladesh Flood Disaster: Sphere Minimum Standards in Disaster Response. *Disasters*, Vol. 26(3), 229.

O'Hagan, Paul, Love, Katy and Rouse, Angela. (2010, October). An independent joint evaluation of the Haiti Earthquake Humanitarian Response. *CARE, Save the Children and the Emergency Capacity Building Project*. Retrieved from www.alnap.org/pool/files/1192.pdf.

O'Neill, William. (2010, January 14). Haiti: can catastrophe spur progress?. Social Science Research Council. Retrieved from www.ssrc.org/features/view/haiti-can-catastrophe-spur-progress/.

Office for the Coordination of Humanitarian Affairs, 'OCHA on Message: Humanitarian Principles' Retrieved from https://ochanet.unocha.org/p/Documents/OOMhumanitarianprinciples_eng_June12.pdf.

Office for the Coordination of Humanitarian Affairs and World Health Organisation. (2002, July – October). Annex 6 – Information Sheet BAKORNAS of *Assessment on Emergency Preparedness in Disaster Situations: Integrated Approach on Nationwide Preparedness Capacities and Capabilities within the Republic of Indonesia*. Retrieved from www.who.int/disasters/repo/8449_Attachements/Annex6-InformationSheetBAKORNAS.doc.

Office of the United Nations High Commissioner for Refugees. (2000). *Handbook for Emergencies*. 2nd edn. Retrieved from www.disaster-info.net/watermitigation/i/publications/Handbook/index_en.HTML.

Ogasawa, Haruno. (2000). *Living with Natural Disasters: Narratives of the Great Kanto and the Great Hanshin Earthquakes*. Evanston: Bell and Howell Information and Learning Company.

Okazaki, K. (n.d.) International activities for Earthquake Disaster Management. National Graduate Institute for Policy Studies. Retrieved from www.ipred-iisee.org/Kickoff/pdf/Prof.%20Kenji%20Okazaki.pdf.

Oliver-Smith, Anthony. (2006, June 11). *Understanding Katrina: Perspectives from the Social Sciences*. Retrieved from http://understandingkatrina.ssrc.org/Oliver-Smith/.

O'Malley, Pat. (2013). Uncertain Governance and Resilient Subjects in the Risk Society. In Susan Sterett (Ed.), *Disaster and Sociolegal Studies*. New Orleans, LA: Onati Socio-Legal Series, Quid Pro Books.

Ooms, Gorik and Hammonds, Rachel. (2008). Correcting Globalisation in Health:Transnational Entitlements versus the Ethical Imperative of Reducing Aid-Dependency. *Public Health Ethics*, 1(2), 154–170.

Ophiyandri, T. Amaratunga, D. and Pathirage, C. (2010). Community based post disaster housing reconstruction: Indonesian perspective. CIB 2010 World Congress, 10–13 May 2010, Salford Quays, United Kingdom.

Oxfam. (2012, January 10). *Haiti Progress Report: January-December 2011*. Retrieved from www.oxfam.org/en/policy/haiti-progress-report.pdf.

Page, Stephen. (2010). Integrative Leadership for Collaborative Governance: Civic Engagement in Seattle. *The Leadership Quarterly*, Vol.21(2), 246.

Patrick, Jonathan. (2001, June). Haiti earthquake response: emerging evaluation lessons. Evaluation Insights, Vol. 1, 2. Retrieved from www.oecd.org/countries/haiti/50313700.pdf.

People First Impact Method. (P-FIM). (2010). People first impact method 2010. Retrieved from www.p-fim.org/.

Perrow, Charles. (2005, August). Using Organizations: The Case of FEMA. *Homeland Security Affairs*, Vol. 1(2). Retrieved from www.hsaj.org/?article=1.2.4.

(2006, June 11). Using Organizations: the Case of FEMA. *Understanding Katrina: Perspectives from the Social Sciences*. Retrieved from http://understandingkatrina.ssrc.org/Perrow/.

Perry, Marcia. (2007). Natural Disaster Management Planning: A Study of Logistics Managers Responding to the Tsunami. *International Journal of Physical Distribution and Logistics Management*, Vol. 37(5), 409.

Picou, J. Steven, et al. (2007). Finding and Framing Katrina: the Social Construction of Disaster. In D. L., Brunsma, et al. (Eds.), *The Sociology of Katrina: Perspectives on a Modern Catastrophe*. Plymouth, UK: Rowman & Littlefield Publishers. Retrieved from http://understandingkatrina.ssrc.org/Dynes_Rodriguez/.

Pierre, John K. and Stephenson, Gail S. (2008). After Katrina: A Critical Look At FEMA's Failure to Provide Housing for Victims of Natural Disasters. *Louisiana*

Law Review, Vol. 68(2), 443. Retrieved from http://digitalcommons.law.lsu.edu/lalrev/vol68/iss2/6.

Pierre-Louis, Francois. (2011). Earthquakes, Nongovernmental Organizations, and Governance in Haiti. *Journal of Black Studies*, Vol. 42(2), 186.

Pisit Leeahtam and Cynn Treesraptanagul. (2012, April 12). After the floods: Thailand's long road to recovery. *East Asia Forum*. Retrieved from www.eastasiaforum.org/2012/04/12/after-the-floods-thailand-s-long-road-to-recovery/.

Pouligny, Béatrice. (2009). Supporting local ownership in humanitarian action. *Humanitarian Policy Paper Series* 6–7. Retrieved from www.gppi.net/fileadmin/gppi/GPPiPPR_local_ownership_2009.pdf.

Procopio, Claire H. and Procopio, Steven T. (2007). Do You Know What It Means to Miss New Orleans? Internet Communication, Geographic Community, and Social Capital in Crisis. *Journal of Applied Communication Research*, Vol. 35(1), 67.

Progressio. (2010, April 12). Three months on: Haiti must not miss opportunity to build "just and inclusive society". Press Release. Retrieved from www.progressio.org.uk/blog/news/three-months-haiti-must-not-miss-opportunity-build-%E2%80%9Cjust-and-inclusive%E2%80%9D-society.

Purdy, Jill. (2012). A Framework for Assessing Power in Collaborative Governance Processes. *Public Administration Review*, Vol.72(3), 409.

Quadir, Regina. (2012, February 14). The Great Flood of 2011, Thailand: A Firsthand Account. *Centers for Disease Control and Prevention*. Retrieved from http://blogs.cdc.gov/publichealthmatters/2012/02/the-great-flood-of-2011-thailand-a-firsthand-account-3/.

Quarantelli, Enrico. (2006, June 11). Catastrophes are different from disasters: some implications for crisis planning and managing drawn from Katrina. *Understanding Katrina: Perspectives from the Social Sciences*. Retrieved from http://understandingkatrina.ssrc.org/Quarantelli/.

Quenette, Andrea M. and Littlefield, Robert S. (2007). Crisis Leadership and Hurricane Katrina: The Portrayal of Authority by the Media in Natural Disasters. *Journal of Applied Communication Research*, Vol. 35(1), 26.

Quinn, Sandra Crouse. (2006). Hurricane Katrina: A Social and Public Health Disaster. *American Journal of Public Health*, Vol. 96(2), 204.

Ramachandran, Vijaya and Walz, Julie. Haiti: where has all the money gone? CGD Policy Paper 004. Centre for Global Development: Washington, D.C. Retrieved from www.cgdev.org/content/publications/detail/1426185.

Rapp, Geoffrey Christopher. (2006). Gouging: Terrorist Attacks, Hurricanes, and the Legal and Economic Aspects of Post-Disaster Price Regulation. *Kentucky Law Journal*, Vol. 94, 535.

Ratanavong, Nokeo. (2012, February 20–22). *Thailand floods damage and loss assessment: lessons learned*. Retrieved from www.itu.int/ITU-D/asp/CMS/Events/2012/emergencyworkshop/Nokeo_Ratanavong.pdf.

Reconstruction Agency (RA). (2013). Current status and path toward reconstruction. Retrieved from www.reconstruction.go.jp/english/130328_CurrentStatus_PathToward_FINAL.pdf.

Reed, Pamela Denise. (2007). From the Freedmen's Bureau to FEMA: A Post-Katrina Historical, Journalistic, and Literary Analysis. *Journal of Black Studies*, Vol. 37(4), 555.

Rhee, Robert J. (2006). Catastrophic Risk and Governance after Hurricane Katrina: A Postscript to Terrorism Risk in a Post-9/11 Economy. *Arizona State Law Journal*, Vol. 38, 581.

Rheuben, Joel. (2014) Government Liability For Regulatory Failure In The Fukushima Disaster: A Common Law Comparison. *Pacific Rim Law & Policy Journal*, Vol. 23, 113.

Rivera, Jason David and Miller, DeMond Shondell. (2007). Continually Neglected: Situating Natural Disasters in the African American Experience. *Journal of Black Studies*, Vol. 37(4), 502.

Rooyen, Michael van and Leaning, Jennifer. (2005). After the Tsunami-Facing the Public Health Challenges. *New England Journal of Medicine*, Vol. 352(5), 435.

Rosenbloom, David and Gong, Ting. (2013, June). Coproducing "Clean" Collaborative Governance. *Public Performance & Management Review*, Vol.36(4), 544.

Roughneen, S. (2011, October 10). Inside the Thailand flood zone. *The Diplomat*. Retrieved from http://thediplomat.com/2011/10/10/inside-the-thailand-flood-zone/.

Sachs, Jeffrey. (2012, September/October issue). Government, Geography, and Growth: The True Drivers of Economic Development. *Foreign Affairs*.

Salamon, Lester M. (2001). The New Governance and the Tools of Public Action: An Introduction. *Fordham Urban Law Journal*, Vol. 28, 1611.

Sandle, Mark. (2006). *Communism*. Oxon: Routledge.

Sarooshi, Dan. (2005). *International Organizations and their Exercise of Sovereign Powers*. Oxford: Oxford University Press.

Sassen, S. (2008). Neither Global nor National: Novel Assemblages of Territory, Authority and Rights. *Ethics & Global Politics Vol. 1(No. 1–2)*, Järfälla, Sweden: Co-Action Publishing.

(2006). *Territory, Authority, Rights from Medieval to Global Assemblages*. New Jersey: Princeton University Press.

Satterthwaite, Margaret L. (2011, May 6). Indicators in Crisis: Rights-Based Humanitarian Indicators in Post-Earthquake Haiti. *N.Y.U. Journal of International Law and Politics*, Vol. 43,. NYU School of Law, Public Law Research Paper No. 11–26, Retrieved from http://ssrn.com/abstract=1833530.

Save the Children (STC). (2012a). Fukushima families. Retrieved from http://reliefweb.int/sites/reliefweb.int/files/resources/PDF_111.pdf.

Save the Children (STC). (2012b). Japan one year on: save the Children's response & recovery program. Retrieved from http://reliefweb.int/sites/reliefweb.int/files/resources/PDF_112.pdf.

Scanlon, Joseph. (2006, June 11). Two cities, two evacuations: some thoughts on moving people out. *Understanding Katrina: Perspectives from the Social Sciences*. Retrieved from http://understandingkatrina.ssrc.org/Scanlon/.

Scheper, E. (2006). *Impact of the Tsunami Response on Local and National Capacities*. London: Tsunami Evaluation Coalition.

Schooner, Steven L. and Yukins, Christopher R. (2005). Emerging policy and practice issues. The George Washington University Law School, Public Law and Legal Theory Working Paper No. 193, 2005. Retrieved from http://ssrn.com/abstract=887355.

Schuller, Mark. (2010, October 4). Unstable foundations: impact of NGOs on human rights for Port-au Prince's internally displaced people. Retrieved from http://ijdh.org/wordpress/wp-content/uploads/2010/10/Report-unstable-foundations-final-2.pdf.

Scobbie, Ian., Pfaff, D. and Shukri, M. (2004). The Responsibility of States and Individuals. In *The International Criminal Court and Enlarging the Scope of International Humanitarian Law*. ICRC: Damascus.

Scott, C. (2001). Analysing Regulatory Space: Fragmented Resources and Institutional Design. *Public Law (Summer)*, 329.

SEEDS. (2011a). The 2011 Great Eastern Japan Earthquake. Situation Report No.17. Retrieved from http://reliefweb.int/sites/reliefweb.int/files/resources/Full_Report_1703.pdf.

(2011b). Who's doing what – emergency response by Japanese NGOs. Retrieved from http://reliefweb.int/report/japan/japan-eqtsunami-whos-doing-what-emergency-response-japanese-ngos.

Selznick, Philip. (1992). *The Moral Commonwealth: Social Theory and the Promise of Community*. Berkeley: University of California Press.

Sharkey, Patrick. (2007). Survival and Death in New Orleans: An Empirical Look at the Human Impact of Katrina. *Journal of Black Studies*, Vol. 37(4), 482.

Shore, Justin. (2010, March 20). Haitian NGOs Call for Inclusion on Reconstruction Plans. *The Human Rights Brief*, Vol. 17(3) 2. Center for Human Rights and Humanitarian Law. Retrieved from http://hrbrief.org/2010/03/haitian-ngos-call-for-inclusion-on-reconstruction-plans/.

Shrum, Wesley. (2007). Hurricane Stories, from Within. *Social Studies of Science*, Vol. 37(1), 97.

Sims, Benjamin. (2007a). The Day After the Hurricane': Infrastructure, Order, and the New Orleans Police Department's Response to Hurricane Katrina. *Social Studies of Science*, Vol. 37(1), 111.

(2007b). Things Fall Apart: Disaster, Infrastructure, and Risk. *Social Studies of Science*, Vol. 37(1), 93.

Simma, Bruno and Paulus, Andreas L. (1998). The 'International Community': Facing the Challenge of Globalization. *European Journal of International Law*, Vol. 9, 266.

Sipayung, B. A. (2007, July). Local versus international response: call for humility. In *Enhancing Southern capacity: rhetoric and reality* (Forced Migration Review No. 28), 9.

Slaughter, Anne.-Marie. (2004). *A New World Order*. Princeton: Princeton University Press.

Smith, Neil. (2006, June 11). There's no such thing as a natural disaster. *Understanding Katrina: Perspectives from the Social Sciences*. Retrieved from http://understandingkatrina.ssrc.org/Smith/.

Snyder, Mark. (2012, April 5). IOM's direct participation in forced evictions raises many questions. Canada Haiti Action Network. Retrieved from http://canadahaitiaction.ca/content/returning-zero-forced-evictions-haitis-displaced-persons-camps.

Solomon, Jason M. (2008). Law and Governance in the 21st Century Regulatory State. *Texas Law Review*, Vol. 86, 819–856.

(2010). New governance, preemptive self-regulation, and the blurring of boundaries in regulatory theory and practice. *Wisconsin Law Review*. 2010(2), 591–598.

Sondorp, Egbert, Tania, Kaiser and Zwi, Anthony. (2001). Beyond Emergency Care: Challenges to Health Planning in Complex Emergencies. *Tropical Medicine and International Health*, Vol. 6(12), 965.

Sontag, Deborah. (2012, August 15). Years after Haiti quake, safe housing is a dream for many. *The New York Times*. Retrieved from www.nytimes.com/2012/08/16/world/americas/years-after-haiti-quake-safe-housing-is-dream-for-multitudes.html?pagewanted=all.

Sparks, Dan. (2011, November 8). Thailand's worst floods in 50 years: international response and preparing for future disasters. Retrieved from www.globalhumanitarianassistance.org/thailands-worst-floods-in-50-years-international-response-and-preparing-for-future-disasters-3271.html.

Spence, Patric R., Lachlan, Kenneth A. and Griffin, Donyale R. (2007). Crisis Communication, Race, and Natural Disasters. *Journal of Black Studies*, Vol. 37(4), 539.

Sphere Project. (2004). The sphere project: humanitarian charter and minimum standards in disaster response: 2004 Edition. Oxfam. Retrieved from http://ocw.jhsph.edu/courses/refugeehealthcare/PDFs/SphereProjectHandbook.pdf.

Sphere Project. (2011). Humanitarian Charter and Minimum Standards in Humanitarian Response (3rd edn), Bourton on Dunsmore, Rugby, UK: Practical Action Publishing, Schumacher Centre for Technology and Development, 6.

Stanley J, Czerwinski. (2010). *Disaster Recovery: Experiences from Past Disasters Offer Insights for Effective Collaboration after Catastrophic Events*. Collingdale, PA: DIANE Publishing. Retrieved from www.gao.gov/new.items/d09811.pdf.

Steets, Julia, Grunewald, Francois, Binder, Andrea, de Geoffroy Veronique, Kauffmann, Domitille, Kruger, Susanna, Meier, Claudia and Sokpoh, Bonaventure. (2010, April). Cluster approach evaluation 2 synthesis report. IASC Cluster Approach Evaluation, 2nd Phase April 2010. Retrieved from www.gppi.net/fileadmin/gppi/GPPi-URD_Cluster_II_Evaluation_SYNTHESIS_REPORT_e.pdf.

Steinberg, Florian and Smid, P. (2010). *Rebuilding Lives and Homes in Aceh and Nias, Indonesia*. Asian Development Bank.

Steinberg, Laura, Santella, Nicholas and Zoli, Corri. (2011, February). Baton Rouge Post-Katrina: The Role of Critical Infrastructure Modeling in Promoting Resilience. *Homeland Security Affairs*, Vol. 7. Retrieved from www.hsaj.org/?article=7.1.7.

Stoddard, Abby, Harmer, Adele, Haver Katherine, Salomons, Dirk and Victoria Wheeler. (2007, November). Cluster Approach Evaluation. OCHA Evaluation and Studies Section (ESS). Retrieved from www.odi.org.uk/resources/download/3820.pdf.

Sterett, Susan. (2013). *Disaster and Sociolegal Studies*. New Orleans, LA: Onati Socio-Legal Series, Quid Pro Books.

Sterrett, S. and Reich, J. (2007). Prayer and Social Welfare: Race and Service after Hurricane Katrina. In H. Potter (Ed.), *Racing the Storm*. Lanham: Lexington Books.

Sturm. (2006). Gender Equity Regimes and the Architecture of Learning. In Grdinne de Bfirca and Joanne Scott. (Eds.), *Law and New Governance in the EU and the US*. Oxford; Portland, OR: Hart Publishing.

Suganuma, K. (2006). Recent Trends in Earthquake Disaster Management in Japan. *Quarterly Review*, Vol. 19, 91. Retrieved from www.houseoffoust.com/edano/Scribble_Japan_Earthquake/pdfs%5CSTTqr1907.pdf.

Susanna M. Hoffman. (2005, November). Katrina and Rita: A disaster anthropologist's thoughts. *Anthropology News*. American Anthropological Association. Retrieved from www.aaanet.org/press/an/1105/Hoffman.htm.

Susskind, L., et al. (1999). The Consensus Building Handbook. Thousand Oaks, CA: Sage Publications.

Suy, Eric. (2002). New Players in International Relations. In Gerard Kreijen, Marcel Brus, Jorri Duursma, Elisabeth de Vos and John Dugard (Eds.), *State, Sovereignty, and International Governance*. Oxford: Oxford University Press.

Sylves, Richard T. (2006). President Bush and Hurricane Katrina: A Presidential Leadership Study. *Annals of the American Academy of Political and Social Science*, Vol. 604, 26.

Takeda, Margaret B. and Helms, Marilyn M. (2006). Bureaucracy, Meet Catastrophe: Analysis of Hurricane Katrina Relief Efforts and Their Implications for Emergency Response Governance. *International Journal of Public Sector Management*, Vol. 19(4), 397.

Tan-Mullins, May, Rigg, Jonathan, Law, Lisa and Grundy-Warr, Carl. (2007). Re-Mapping the Politics of Aid: The Changing Structures and Networks of

Humanitarian Assistance in Post-Tsunami Thailand. *Progress in Development Studies*, Vol. 7, 327.

Teff, Melanie and Parry, Emilie. (2010, October 6). Haiti: still trapped in the emergency phase. *Field Report*, Refugees International. Retrieved from www.refugeesinternational.org/policy/field-report/haiti-still-trapped-emergency-phase.

Telford, J., Cosgrave, J. and Houghton, R. (2006). *Joint Evaluation of the International Response to the Indian Ocean Tsunami: Synthesis Report*. Tsunami Evaluation Coalition.

Termpittayapaisith, Arkhom. (2012, March 17). Thailand's management policy after Flood 2011. Retrieved from www.tni.ac.th/web/upload/files/pdf/advert/Talk3_ThaPolicy%20after%20flood%202011%20DG.pdf.

Thai Meteorological Department and World Meteorological Organization. (2012). Report: workshop on the development of a national strategy for integrated flood management for Thailand. Retrieved from www.apfm.info/pdf/Reports/THAILAND_IFM_REPORT_MARCH_2012.pdf.

The Associated Press (AP). (2010, January 27). Haiti government gets 1 cent of USAid dollar: another 33 cents is going to the US military for security and search efforts. Retrieved from www.nbcnews.com/id/35103622/.

The Austrian Foreign Ministry. (2011). Austrian embassy in Bangkok helps flood victims in Thailand. Retrieved from www.bmeia.gv.at/en/foreign-ministry/news/press-releases/2011/austrian-embassy-in-bangkok-helps-flood-victims-in-thailand.html.

The LAMP for Haiti Foundation, The Drexel Haiti Justice Project at The Earle Mack School of Law, Bureau des Avocats Internationaux, Institute for Justice & Democracy in Haiti & Lawyers' Earthquake Response Network. (2010). *Neglect in the Encampments: Haiti's second-wave Humanitarian Disaster*. Retrieved from http://ijdh.org/archives/10671.

The Nation Thailand. (2011, October 13). Private sector's supports. Retrieved from: www.nationmultimedia.com/business/Private-sectors-supports-30167574.html.

Tierney, Kathleen, et al. (2006). Metaphors Matter: Disaster Myths, Media Frames, and Their Consequences in Hurricane Katrina. *Annals of the American Academy of Political and Social Science*, Vol. 604, 57.

Trubek, David M. and Mosher, James S. (2003). New Governance, Employment Policy, and the European Social Model. In Jonathan Zeitlin and David M. Trubek (Eds.), *Governing Work and Welfare in a New Economy: European and American Experiments*. New York: Oxford University Press.

Twining, William. (2000). *Globalization and Legal Theory, Law in Context*. London: Butterworths.

(2005). Have Concepts, Will Travel: Analytical Jurisprudence in a Global Context. *International Journal of Law in Context*. Vol. 1(1), 5.

UN News Centre. (2012, May 3). Interview with Nigel Fisher, UN resident and humanitarian coordinator for Haiti. Retrieved from www.un.org/apps/news/newsmakers.asp?NewsID=50.

UN Office for the Coordination of Humanitarian Affairs (OCHA). (2011). Japan: Earthquake & Tsunami. Situation Report No.1. Retrieved from http://reliefweb.int/sites/reliefweb.int/files/resources/60C5286F730C9B6449257851004A922B-Full_Report.pdf.

UN Women. (2012, January 3). Leadership in communities: Thai women preparing for natural disaster. Retrieved from www.unwomen.org/2012/01/leadership-in-communities-thai-women-preparing-for-natural-disasters/.

UNESCO Bangkok. (2011, November 22). UN lends full support for Thailand flood response. Retrieved from www.unescobkk.org/news/article/un-lends-full-support-for-thailand-flood-response/.

UNEP. (2012). Managing post-disaster debris: the Japan experience. Retrieved from www.unep.org/pdf/UNEP_Japan_post-tsunami_debris.pdf.

UNICEF. (2011, November 10). Press Release: UNICEF provides 300,000 water, sanitation, hygiene items for flood victims. Retrieved from www.unicef.org/media/media_60473.html.

United Nations. (n.d.). Humanitarian and disaster relief assistance. United Nations Global Issues. Retrieved from www.un.org/en/globalissues/humanitarian/.

United Nations Country Team in Thailand. (2011, November 18). Press release: UN lends full support for Thailand flood response. Retrieved from www.un.or.th/presscentre/documents/111118UNCTPressReleaseonflooding.pdf.

United Nations General Assembly. (1991, December 19). Strengthening of the coordination of humanitarian emergency assistance of the United Nations. G.A. Res. 46/182, Annex, 34, 36, U.N. Doc. A/RES/46/182.

United Nations and the Inter-Agency Standing Committee. (2008). Civil-Military Guidelines and Reference for Complex Emergencies, 19. Available at: https://docs.unocha.org/sites/dms/Documents/ENGLISH%20VERSION%20Guidelines%20for%20Complex%20Emergencies.pdf (accessed on May 5, 2014).

United Nations Office for Disaster Risk Reduction. (2005, January 22). World Conference on Disaster Reduction (Hyogo Declaration). UN Doc A/CONF.206/6 paragraph 4.

United Nations Office for Disaster Risk Reduction. (n.d.). UNISDR in the UN System. Retrieved from www.unisdr.org/who-we-are/unisdr-in-un.

(n.d.). Who we are. Retrieved from www.unisdr.org/who-we-are.

United Nations Office for the Coordination of Humanitarian Affairs (OCHA). (n.d.). Coordination. Retrieved from www.unocha.org/what-we-do/coordination/overview.

United Nations Office for the Coordination of Humanitarian Affairs (OCHA). (n.d.). History of OCHA. Retrieved from www.unocha.org/about-us/who-we-are/history.

United Nations Office for the Coordination of Humanitarian Affairs (OCHA). (n.d.). Leadership. Retrieved from www.unocha.org/what-we-do/coordination/leadership/overview.

United Nations Office for the Coordination of Humanitarian Affairs (OCHA). (n.d.). Who we are. www.unocha.org/about-us/who-we-are.

United Nations Office for the Coordination of Humanitarian Affairs (OCHA). (2011, February). Evaluations synthesis report, 2010. OCHA Occasional Policy Briefing Series – No.5. Retrieved from https://ochanet.unocha.org/p/Documents/OCHA%20Evaluations%20Synthesis%20Report%202010-latest.pdf.

United Nations Office for the Coordination of Humanitarian Affairs (OCHA). (2011, July 31). OCHA's management response plan (MRP) to internally-mandated evaluation of OCHA response to the Haiti earthquake. Retrieved from https://ochanet.unocha.org/p/Documents/Haiti_Internal_Evaluation_31JUL2011.pdf.

United Nations Office for the Coordination of Humanitarian Affairs (OCHA). (2012). Coordination to save lives, history and emerging challenges. Policy and Studies Series 2012. Retrieved from https://ochanet.unocha.org/p/Documents/Coordination%20to%20Save%20Lives%20History%20and%20Emerging%20Challenges.pdf.

United States Executive Office of The President, et al. (2006). The federal response to Hurricane Katrina: lessons learned. Government Printing Office. Retrieved from http://library.stmarytx.edu/acadlib/edocs/katrinawh.pdf.

University of Haiti and Tulane University's Disaster Resilience Leadership Academy. (2011 January). Haiti humanitarian aid evaluation structured analysis summary report. Retrieved from www.drlatulane.org/groups/haiti-humanitarian-aid-evaluation.

UNOPS. (2011). Rebuilding Haiti, one year on. Retrieved from www.unops.org/SiteCollectionDocuments/rebuilding_haiti_unops_EN_web.pdf.

US Congress House of Representatives Committee On Energy And Commerce Subcommittee On Health Select Committee On Homeland Security Subcommittee On Emergency. (2003, March 27). *Furthering public health security: Project Bioshield: Joint hearing before the Subcommittee on Health of the Committee on Energy and Commerce, and the Subcommittee on Emergency Preparedness and Response of the Select Committee on Homeland Security, House of Representatives, One Hundred Eighth Congress, first session*. Retrieved from www.gpo.gov/fdsys/pkg/CHRG-108hhrg87480/pdf/CHRG-108hhrg87480.pdf.

US Congress House of Representatives Select Committee On Homeland Security Subcommittee On Emergency Preparedness And Response. (2003, September 24). *Disease surveillance systems: hearing of the Subcommittee on Emergency Preparedness and Response of the Select Committee on Homeland*

Security, House of Representatives, One Hundred Eighth Congress, first session. The US Government Printing Office. Retrieved from www.gpo.gov/fdsys/pkg/CHRG-108hhrg20168/pdf/CHRG-108hhrg20168.pdf.

US Congress Select Bipartisan Committee. (2006). A Failure of initiative: final report of the select bipartisan committee to investigate the preparation for and response to Hurricane Katrina. U.S Government Printing Office: Washington, DC. Retrieved from www.gpoaccess.gov/serialset/creports/katrina.html.

(2006). A Failure of initiative: supplemental report and document annex. US Government Printing Office: Washington, DC. Retrieved from www.gpoaccess.gov/serialset/creports/katrinasupp.html.

US Department of Health and Human Services, Office of Inspector General. (2006). Nursing home emergency preparedness and response during recent hurricanes. US Government Printing Office: Washington, DC. Retrieved from www.oig.hhs.gov/oei/reports/oei-06-06-00020.pdf.

US Department of Homeland Security. (2004). *National response plan.* Washington, DC. Retrieved from http://fas.org/irp/agency/dhs/nrp.pdf.

US Department of Homeland Security, Federal Emergency Management Agency. (2012). Crisis response and disaster resilience 2030: forging strategic action in an age of uncertainty. Washington, DC.

US Department of Homeland Security, Office of Inspector General. (2006). A performance review of FEMA's disaster management activities in response to Hurricane Katrina. US Government Printing Office: Washington, DC. Retrieved from www.dhs.gov/xoig/assets/mgmtrpts/OIG_06-32_Mar06.pdf.

US Government Accountability Office. (2005). Hurricane Katrina: providing oversight of the nation's preparedness, response, and recovery activities. Retrieved from www.gao.gov/new.items/d051053t.pdf.

(2005). Hurricanes Katrina and Rita: provision of charitable assistance. Retrieved from www.gao.gov/new.items/d06297t.pdf.

(2006). Coast guard: observations on the preparation, response, and recovery missions related to Hurricane Katrina. Retrieved from www.gao.gov/new.items/d06903.pdf.

(2006). Disaster preparedness: preliminary observations on the evacuation of hospitals and nursing homes due to hurricanes. Retrieved from www.gao.gov/new.items/d06443r.pdf.

(2006). Disaster preparedness: preliminary observations on the evacuation of vulnerable populations due to hurricanes and other disasters. Retrieved from www.gao.gov/new.items/d06790t.pdf.

(2006). Expedited assistance for victims of Hurricanes Katrina and Rita: FEMA's control weaknesses exposed the government to significant fraud and abuse. Retrieved from www.gao.gov/new.items/d06655.pdf.

US Government Accountability Office. (2006). Hurricane Katrina: better plans and exercises needed to guide the military's response to catastrophic natural disasters. Retrieved from www.gao.gov/new.items/d06643.pdf.

US Government Accountability Office. (2006). Hurricane Katrina: GAO's preliminary observations regarding preparedness, response, and recovery. Retrieved from www.gao.gov/new.items/d06442t.pdf.

(2006). Hurricanes Katrina and Rita: coordination between FEMA and the Red Cross should be improved for the 2006 hurricane season. Retrieved from www.gao.gov/new.items/d06712.pdf.

(2006). Statement by comptroller general David M. Walker on GAO's preliminary observations regarding preparedness and response to hurricanes Katrina and Rita. Retrieved from www.gao.gov/new.items/d06365r.pdf.

(2007). Observations on DHS and FEMA efforts to prepare for and respond to major and catastrophic disasters and address related recommendations and legislation. Retrieved from www.gao.gov/new.items/d07835t.pdf.

US Government Printing Office. (2006) Pandemic and all-hazards preparedness act. *Pubic Law 109–417*. Retrieved from www.gpo.gov/fdsys/pkg/PLAW-109publ417/pdf/PLAW-109publ417.pdf.

US Senate Committee on Homeland Security and Government Affairs. (2006). Hurricane Katrina: a nation still unprepared. US Government Printing Office: Washington, DC. Retrieved from www.gpoaccess.gov/serialset/creports/katrinanation.html.

USAID. (2005, January). *Tsunami relief and reconstruction*. Retrieved from http://indonesia.usaid.gov/en/USAID/Activity/340/Tsunami_Relief_and_Reconstruction.

Van der Heijden, Jerome. (2013). Looking forwards and sideways: trajectories of new governance theory. Amsterdam Law School Legal Studies, Research Paper No. 2013-04.

Vanderford, Marsha L., Nastoff, Teresa, Telfer, Jana L. and Bonzo, Sandra E. (2007). Emergency Communication Challenges in Response to Hurricane Katrina: Lessons from the Centers for Disease Control and Prevention. *Journal of Applied Communication Research*, Vol. 35(1), 9.

Verchick, Robert R. M. (2006, November 8). Risk, fairness, and the geography of disaster. Issues in legal scholarship, Issue 10, Loyola New Orleans Law Research Paper. Retrieved from http://ssrn.com/abstract=2214079.

Verdirame, Guglielmo. (2001). Testing the Effectiveness of International Norms: UN Humanitarian Assistance and Sexual Apartheid in Afghanistan. *Human Rights Quarterly*, Vol. 23(3), 733.

Vigdor, Jacob L. (2007, April). The Katrina effect: was there a bright side to the evacuation of greater New Orleans?. Working Paper 13022, National Bureau of Economic Research. Retrieved from www.nber.org/papers/w13022.

Vigdor, Jacob. (2008). The Economic Aftermath of Hurricane Katrina. *Journal of Economic Perspectives*, Vol. 22(4), 135. Retrieved from www.aeaweb.org/articles.php?doi=10.1257/jep.22.4.135.

Warren, Dorian T., et al. (2006, June 11). Katrina's Political Roots and Divisions: Race, Class, and Federalism in American Politics. *Understanding Katrina: Perspectives from the Social Sciences* (website) Retrieved from http://understandingkatrina.ssrc.org/FrymerStrolovitchWarren/.

Wall Street Journal (WSJ). (2013, June 19). Japan nuclear plant is found to have more tainted water. Retrieved from http://online.wsj.com/article/SB10001424127887323566804578554503732384118.html.

Waugh, William L. (2006). Shelter from the Storm: Repairing the National Emergency Management System after Hurricane Katrina. *Annals of the American Academy of Political and Social Science*, Vol. 604, 288.

(2006). The Political Costs of Failure in the Katrina and Rita Disasters. *Annals of the American Academy of Political and Social Science*, Vol. 604, 10.

Waymer, Damion and Heath, Robert L. (2007). Emergent Agents: The Forgotten Publics in Crisis Communication and Issues Management Research. *Journal of Applied Communication Research*, Vol. 35(1), 88.

Weeks, Elizabeth A. (2006). Lessons From Katrina: Response, Recovery and the Public Health Infrastructure. *DePaul Journal of Health Care Law*, Vol. 10(2), 251.

Wear, Andrew. (2012). Collaborative Approaches to Regional Governance – Lessons from Victoria. *Australian Journal of Public Administration*, Vol.71(4), 469.

Weiser, Philip J., et al. (2006, May 15). Toward a next generation architecture for public safety communications. University of Colorado Law Legal Studies Research Paper. Retrieved from http://papers.ssrn.com/sol3/papers.cfm?abstract_id=903151.

Wenger, Kaimipono David. (2012). Toyota jurisprudence in a Prius-recall world? – refining new governance discourse to avoid unintended acceleration. (Incomplete and Unpublished). Fourth Annual J. Reuben Clark Law Society Faculty Section Conference. Washington, DC: J. Reuben Clark Law Society.

Wetmore, Jameson M. (2007). Distributing Risks and Responsibilities: Flood Hazard Mitigation in New Orleans. *Social Studies of Science*, Vol. 37(1), 119.

WFP Thailand. (2011). *Provision of logistics support to the government of Thailand's response to floods in 28 districts.*

White, Ismail K., Philpot, Tasha S., Wylie, Kristin and McGowen, Ernest,. (2007). Feeling the Pain of My People: Hurricane Katrina, Racial Inequality, and the Psyche of Black America. *Journal of Black Studies*, Vol. 37(4), 523.

White House. (2006). The federal response to Hurricane Katrina: lessons learned. Retrieved from http://georgewbush-whitehouse.archives.gov/reports/katrina-lessons-learned/.

Whitehead, Judy. (2005, December). The neoliberal state in disaster management. *Anthropology News*. American Anthropological Association. Retrieved from www.aaanet.org/press/an/1205/AN2005Dec_whitehead.pdf.

Williams, R. H. (2005). Response to the 2004 Tsunami: an international perspective. In *Raising the Bar*. Global Public Policy Institute.

Williams, Rhodri C. (2011, December). *From shelter to housing: security of tenure and integration in protracted displacement settings*. Norwegian Refugee Council. Retrieved from www.nrc.no/?did=9642916.

Winston, Pamela, et al. (2006). Federalism after Hurricane Katrina: how can social programs respond to a major disaster. The Urban Institute. Retrieved from www.urban.org/UploadedPDF/311344_after_katrina.pdf.

World Bank Group. (n.d.). *The World Bank at Aceh, Indonesia: a model for community- driven development.*

(2005, February). *World Bank response to the Tsunami disaster.*

(2005, April). *Update on the World Bank response to the Tsunami disaster.*

(2009, December). *Five years after the Tsunami: continuing the commitment to reconstruction.*

(2011, December 13). The World Bank supports Thailand's post-floods recovery effort. Retrieved from www.worldbank.org/en/news/feature/2011/12/13/world-bank-supports-thailands-post-floods-recovery-effort.

(2012a). *Thai flood 2011: rapid assessment for resilient recovery and reconstruction planning*. Retrieved from www.gfdrr.org/sites/gfdrr.org/files/publication/Thai_Flood_2011_2.pdf.

(2012b). *Thai flood: overview on rapid assessment for resilient recovery and reconstruction planning*. Retrieved from www-wds.worldbank.org/external/default/WDSContentServer/WDSP/IB/2012/06/12/000356161_20120612014615/Rendered/PDF/698220WP0v10P106011020120Box370022B.pdf.

World Health Organization. (2005). *Malaria control in complex emergencies: an inter-agency field handbook*. Retrieved from http://whqlibdoc.who.int/publications/2005/924159389X_eng.pdf.

(2007) The cluster approach. Retrieved from www.who.int/hac/techguidance/tools/manuals/who_field_handbook/annex_7/en/index.html.

World Nuclear Association (WNA). (2013). Fukushima accident 2011. Retrieved from www.world-nuclear.org/info/Safety-and-Security/Safety-of-Plants/Fukushima-Accident-2011/#.

Yang-ho, Hong. (2001). Humanitarian Aid Toward North Korea: A Global Peace-Building Process. *East Asian Review*, Vol. 13(4), 21.

Yoon, Suthichai. (2011, October 20). Community-based approach needed for next big flood. Retrieved from www.nationmultimedia.com/opinion/Community-based-approach-needed-for-next-big-flood-30168060.html.

Yoshitsugu, Y. (2011). Roles of social media at the time of major disasters observed in the Great East Japan Earthquake: twitter as an example. *NHK Broadcast media research and analysis July 2011*. Retrieved from www.nhk.or.jp/bunken/summary/research/report/2011_07/20110702.pdf.

Young, Helen. (1999). Public Nutrition in Emergencies: An Overview of Debates, Dilemmas and Decision-making. *Disasters*, Vol. 23(4), 277.

Young, Iris. (2006). Katrina: Too Much Blame, Not Enough Responsibility. *Dissent*, Vol. 53(1), 41.

Yun S., Harold. (2015) Fukushima and New Zealand v. France Nuclear Tests: Can Japan be Brought to the International Court of Justice for Damages Caused by the Fukushima Plants? *Minnesota Journal of International Law*, 24 387.

Zaré, M. and Afrouz, S.G. (2012). Crisis Management of Tohoku; Japan Earthquake and Tsunami, 11 March 2011. *Iran Journal of Public Health*, Vol. 41(6), 12.

Zedlewski, Sheila R. (2006 February). Building a better safety net for the new New Orleans. The Urban Institute. Retrieved from www.urban.org/afterkatrina/.

Zuckerman, Stephen and Coughlin, Teresa. (2006, February). Initial health policy responses to hurricane Katrina and possible next steps. The Urban Institute. Retrieved from www.urban.org/afterkatrina/.

Zumbansen, Peer C. (2008). Transnational Law. In Jan Smits (Ed.), *Elgar Encyclopedia of Comparative Law*, (1st ed., Cheltenham: Edward Elgar., 2006)

Zumbansen, P. (2013). *Law and Legal Pluralism: Hybridity in Transnational Governance*. In P. Jurčys, P.F. Kjaer and R. Yatsunamim (Eds.), *Regulatory Hybridization in the Transnational Sphere* (pp.49–70) Leiden, Boston: Martinus Nijhoff Publishers.

(2011). Defining the space of transnational law: legal theory, global governance and legal pluralism. *Osgoode CLPE Research Paper 21/2011 Vo.7 No.05*. Available at SSRN: http://ssrn.com/abstract=1934044.

INDEX

For EU product safety concerns, contact us at Calle de José Abascal, 56–1°, 28003 Madrid, Spain or eugpsr@cambridge.org.

www.ingramcontent.com/pod-product-compliance
Lightning Source LLC
LaVergne TN
LVHW011528200926
848484LV00001B/184

* 9 7 8 1 1 0 7 1 0 6 3 9 0 *